W9-AUI-010

DATE DUE

11-05 M South			

nc 38-293

Dorling DK Kindersley

LONDON, NEW YORK, SYDNEY, DELHI,
PARIS, MUNICH, and JOHANNESBURG

Project Editors Lucy Hurst, Mary Atkinson, Francesca Baines
Art Editors Richard Czapnik, Sharon Grant, Venice Shone
Senior Editors John C. Miles, Scarlett O'Hara
Senior Art Editors Dorian Spencer Davies, Vicky Wharton,
C. David Gillingwater, Peter Radcliffe
Managing Editors Anne Kramer, Susan Malyan
Senior Managing Editor Linda Martin
Senior Managing Art Editor Julia Harris
US Editors Gary Werner and Margaret Parrish
Consultants Peter Goodwin *Keeper of HMS* Victory,
Christopher Gravett *Assistant curator of armour,
the Royal Armouries, H.M. Tower of London,* Gabrielle Murphy
DTP Designers Almudena Diaz, Andrew O'Brien, Karen Nettlefield
Production Josie Alabaster, Louise Barratt, Ruth Cobb, Lisa Moss,
Marguerite Fenn, Charlotte Traill, Jayne Wood

First American Edition, 2001

01 02 03 04 05 10 9 8 7 6 5 4 3 2 1

Published in the United States by DK Publishing, Inc.
95 Madison Avenue, New York, New York 10016

A CIP catalog record for this book is available from
the Library of Congress.

ISBN 0-7894-7964-8

Reproduced by Dot Gradations Ltd., Essex, England
Printed and bound by Artes Graphicas, Spain
D.L. TO: 694-2001

See our complete catalog at

www.dk.com

COOLEST
CROSS-SECTIONS
EVER

FIRE

FIRE
CONTROL UNIT

COOLEST
CROSS-SECTIONS
EVER

ILLUSTRATED BY
STEPHEN BIESTY

WRITTEN BY
RICHARD PLATT

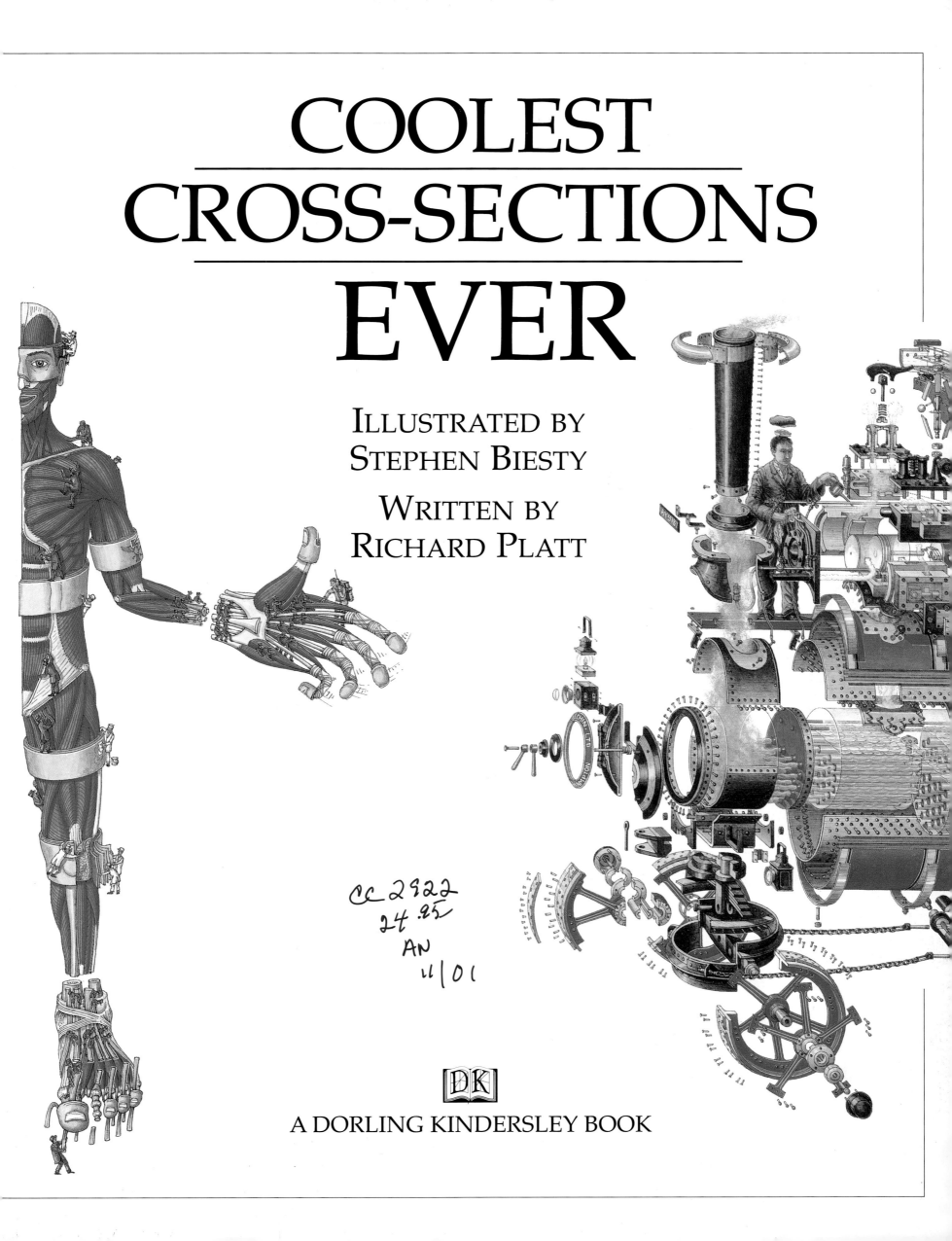

CC 2922
24.95
AN
11/01

DK

A DORLING KINDERSLEY BOOK

CONTENTS

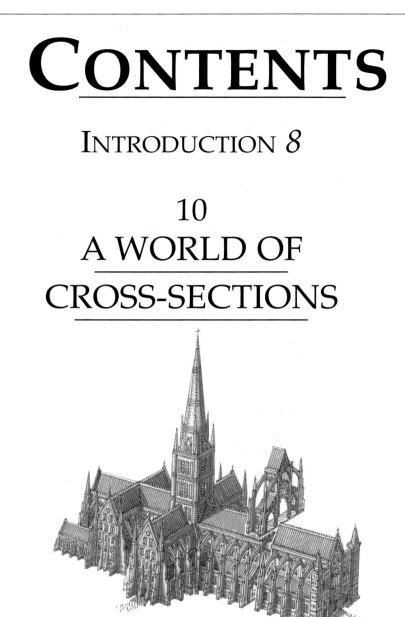

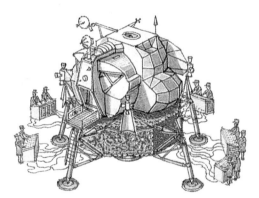

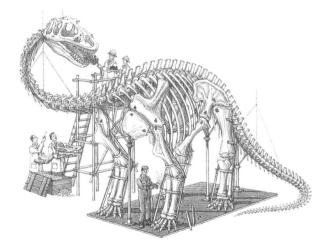

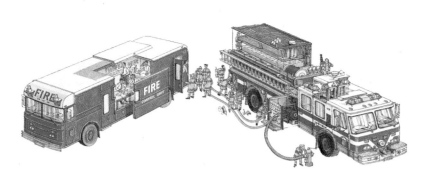

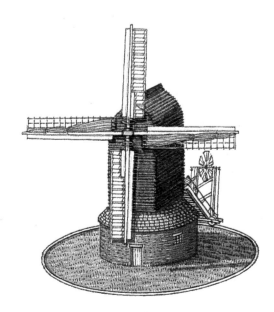

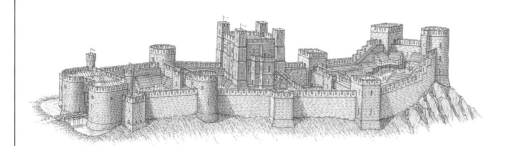

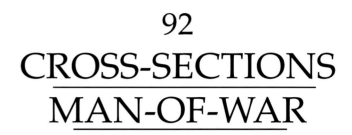

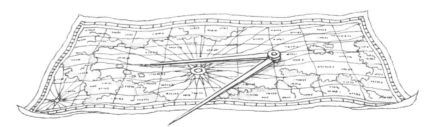

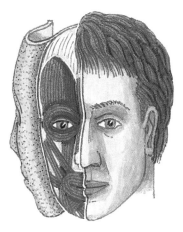
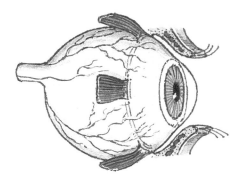
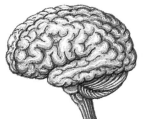
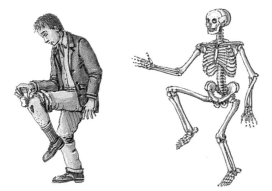
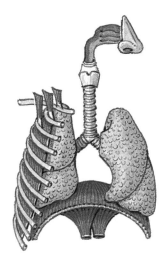

INTRODUCTION

"I couldn't believe that in medieval times the test for a good beer was to pour some onto a bench and sit on it for an hour! If you stuck to the bench the beer was good!"

"**Y**EARS AGO, WHEN DORLING KINDERSLEY first asked me to do a cross-section drawing I was very excited. I had always loved the wonderful cross-section illustrations by Lesley Ashwell Wood that used to appear in a 1960's comic for boys, called the *Eagle*. The illustrations in the *Eagle* cut objects in two to show their insides. One task that Dorling Kindersley set me was to take New York's famous Empire State Building and slice through it not once, but several times. In this way I could reveal even more of the detail and workings inside it without losing the sense of the whole building.

This was just the kind of challenge I wanted! As a boy, I had loved drawing busy scenes of big battles or castles teeming with people. Perhaps I am still a child at heart, but it is always the details of a story that I want to know – what did people eat in medieval times? Where did the crew of an 18th-century warship sleep? Where are the toilets on a space station? These are the kind of facts that help me to imagine what life might have been like at other moments in history, and to realize what kind of problems face architects and engineers past and present.

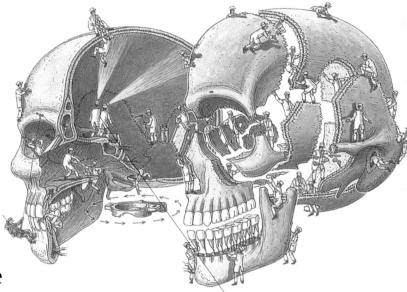

"I loved the idea of the skull being like a vast cave, waiting to be explored."

"I was told by a curator at the Black Country Museum (UK) that while working with heavy machinery, the best way to keep your lunch free of dirt and grime was to keep it under your hat."

The films I loved as a boy – the Hollywood epics like *Spartacus*, *The Vikings*, and *Ben-Hur* – were also full of people and detail. With casts of (quite literally) thousands, these films created fantastic pictures of the past. When I am doing an illustration, I think of those great films. Although I want my pictures to show how things work, or the layers that make up a machine, a building, or a landscape; I also want to hold a magnifying glass to the detail and bring to life the characters lurking in the background.

"Richard Platt read about a horrible parasite called an eyelash mite, and I couldn't resist sneaking one into my picture of the human eye."

"The rations of an 18th-century sailor turned my stomach – especially the maggots in the biscuits!"

I have been very lucky that the author of all my books, Richard Platt, shares my enthusiasm for revealing this sometimes gruesome side of life. Richard's research – and in particular his pursuit of weird and wonderful facts – has been invaluable, and without him the books would not have been the same.

Over 16,000 hours of work have gone into this volume – each main illustration takes about 150 hours, which works out to about three weeks. But the bigger the illustration the longer it takes, and the most labor-intensive was the *Saturn V* rocket, which took 453 hours, or nine weeks! Looking at all the illustrations together here, I think it has been time well spent. I hope that you do, too."

"I felt faint just reading the accounts of early surgeons – how things have changed! But I was also struck by the bravery of people back then."

A WORLD OF CROSS-SECTIONS

EXTRAORDINARY VIEWS of machines, buildings, and landscapes show you the world as you've never seen it before. Look through the layers of the spectacular Grand Canyon, see what lies behind the doors of the compartments of the space station, or discover how a Formula 1 race car is put together by seeing it taken apart!

OUR INCREDIBLE WORLD

"HELLO! I'M CHESTER THE TESTER. Stephen Biesty has asked me to help him find out how all kinds of fascinating things are made. Some are everyday objects such as a newspaper, others are amazing creations, like a rocket that can take humans to the Moon. Checking everything thoroughly is serious work – do you have any idea how much testing needs to be done in a chocolate factory? But my assistant, Hector the inspector, is going to help – so look out for us at work."

"Chester, would you mind testing my sandwiches. I'm not sure which ones are peanut butter and jelly!"

Skyscraper

"Now, let's see how fast this monster can move."

Model dinosaur

"Whoa – careful! These swords are really sharp."

Armor

Race car

"This string seems strong enough to me."

Nuclear power station

Plywood

Newspaper

Brick

"Have you seen my mummy?"

"The gunpowder testing is very noisy so I'm wearing my earplugs."

Gunpowder

"Incredible! The cannon still works after all these years."

Steam locomotive

"I wonder what happens here?"

Gas

"I don't get to travel like this very often!"

Drinking water

Underground railroad tunnel

"This beats the crush inside."

"Mission control, we have Chester on board. He's going to help us test conditions on the Moon to see if it can support extra-terrestrial life."

Saturn V rocket

Bridge

Boeing 777

Compact disc player

"Excuse me, cabin crew! Someone's taken a bite out of my lunch."
"Then I'm sure you'll enjoy it, sir! Chester's tested it, and he told me it was delicious."

"They assured me these wings worked – I just hope they're right. Ready, set, goooo..."

Wooden house

Soap

Pipe organ

"If only they'd install an electric organ, then I wouldn't have to test all these pipes."

Cathedral

False teeth

"I've got some extra sticky candy for testing these out."

"It's a great day for kite flying."

Photocopy

"This copier seems to have a screw loose!"

"Here we go Stephen, the plans for your next drawing."

Paper

Nail

Doughnut

Wig

Coin

Diamond ring

Plastic bottle

Chocolate bar

"Just doing a little last minute quality control testing. The last doughnut was delicious, but maybe I should check another just to be sure."

"I've heard of traveling by subway, but this is ridiculous!"

Matches

Milk

"No, no, the battery cable connects to that part, and that wire plugs into the horn . . . or is it the other way around?"

Car

Aluminum foil

"I need to change that bulb."

"Ppphhrrp! Wow, that's the last time I eat baked beans."

Athletic shoe

13

STEAM TRACTION ENGINE

HISSING, STEAMING, CLANKING, AND SHAKING THE ground, steam traction engines are like mechanical dinosaurs. Almost extinct, they were once the most modern form of power. Steam traction engines first appeared around 1860. At first they drove stationary farm machinery, such as threshers that separated kernels of grain from their husks. Later engines pulled plows or heavy road wagons, and turned fairground rides. For a while, steam represented a bright, labor-saving future. But the reign of the steam traction engine was a short one. By the beginning of the last century electric motors and internal combustion engines had begun to take over many of its tasks. Before long the puffing monsters were making their last journeys – to the junkyard or a museum.

On the belt
The engine could drive machinery, such as a threshing machine or a power saw, if a leather drive belt was looped around the flywheel. Often a steam traction engine would be used for threshing in fall and winter, and as a power saw at other times of the year.

Forced water
Since the boiler is under steam pressure, water must be fed in forcibly with an injector. When the engine was running well, the injector could often be heard "singing" quietly like a whistling kettle as it let jets of water into the boiler.

Smoke box door lock

Steering
All steam traction engines were self-propelled, but early models required a horse for steering. Harnessed between the shafts of the engine, the nags did not have to work hard.

Creating steam
Heat to boil the steam comes from burning coal in the firebox. The stoker continually feeds the fire to keep up a good supply of hot gases. Hot gases from the firebox flow through tubes inside the boiler, making them so hot they boil the water, creating steam. The gases then flow from the boiler tubes into the smoke box. From here, waste heat and sparks are blown out through the chimney.

What the steam does
Steam from the boiler flows up around the cylinder into the valve chest. A sliding valve lets steam shoot through the valve chest into the cylinder, pushing the piston forward. The valve then slides back to let steam in on the other side of the piston to push it backward. As the piston slides backward and forward, it pulls on the connecting rod and forces the crankshaft around. The turning of the crankshaft drives the flywheel.

Spud pan and chain
Steering was never easy on a steam traction engine. It relied on a hefty chain attached to a large drum between the front wheels, called the spud pan. When the driver turned the steering wheel, the steering bar pulled on chains to turn the wheels.

Governor
The "governor" was a device which regulated the engine speed. It was a valve opened and closed by two spinning metal ball weights. When the weights spun too fast, centrifugal force moved them outward, lifting the valve to let off steam and slow down the engine.

Safety valve

Cylinder casing containing piston

Regulator chest

Whistle

Piston

Sliding valve

Connecting rod

Registration plate

Chimney barrel

Blower valve (blows steam up the chimney)

Exhaust pipe

Smoke box

Valve chest

Smoke box door

Suspension springs

Water injector

Steel boiler

Steering chain

Boiler tubes heat water

Steering bar

Worm gear

Water jacket
Too much heat could make the boiler blow up. So, apart from the open grate at the bottom, the firebox was entirely encased in a jacket of water.

14

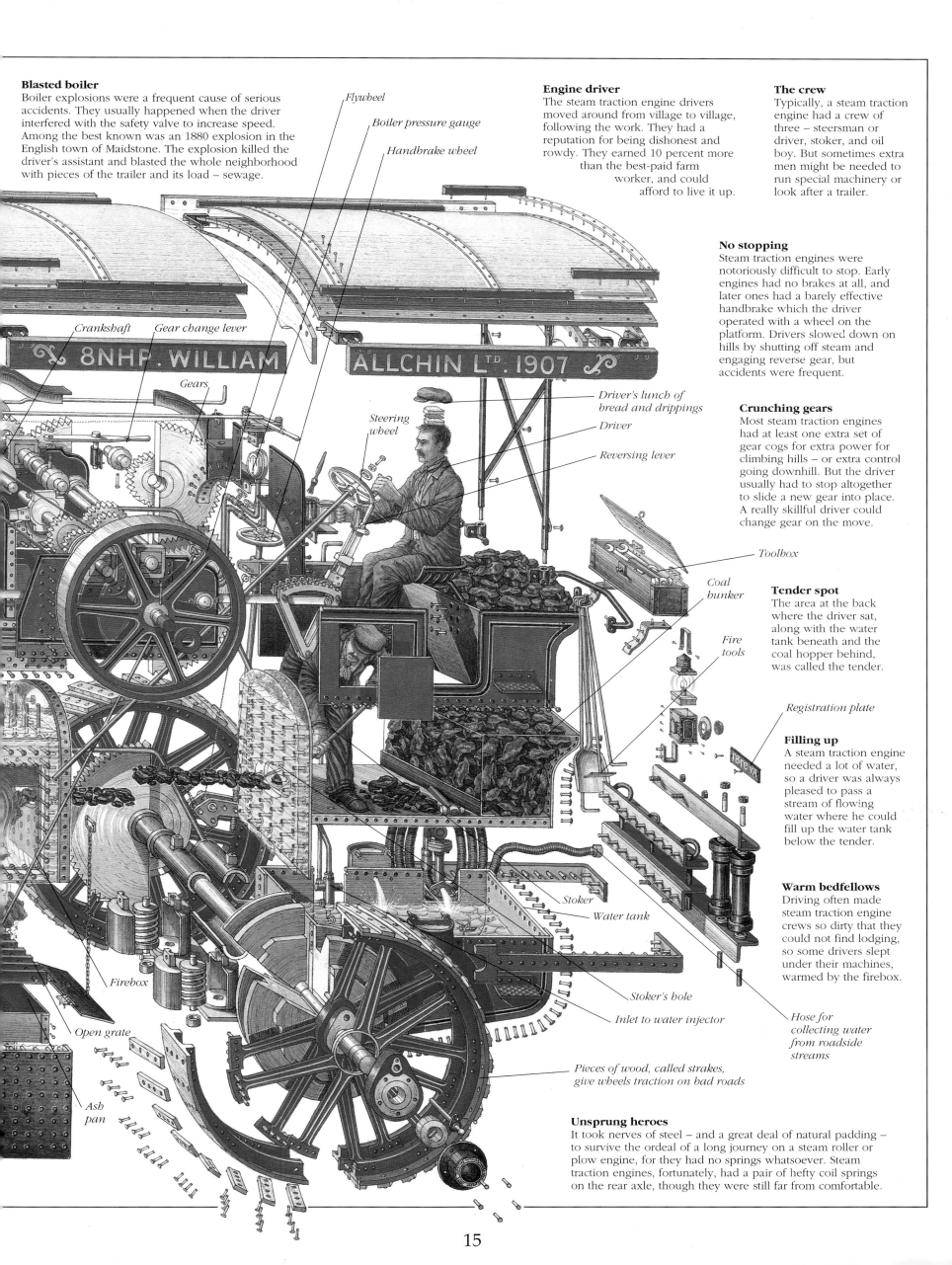

Blasted boiler
Boiler explosions were a frequent cause of serious accidents. They usually happened when the driver interfered with the safety valve to increase speed. Among the best known was an 1880 explosion in the English town of Maidstone. The explosion killed the driver's assistant and blasted the whole neighborhood with pieces of the trailer and its load – sewage.

Flywheel

Boiler pressure gauge

Handbrake wheel

Engine driver
The steam traction engine drivers moved around from village to village, following the work. They had a reputation for being dishonest and rowdy. They earned 10 percent more than the best-paid farm worker, and could afford to live it up.

The crew
Typically, a steam traction engine had a crew of three – steersman or driver, stoker, and oil boy. But sometimes extra men might be needed to run special machinery or look after a trailer.

No stopping
Steam traction engines were notoriously difficult to stop. Early engines had no brakes at all, and later ones had a barely effective handbrake which the driver operated with a wheel on the platform. Drivers slowed down on hills by shutting off steam and engaging reverse gear, but accidents were frequent.

Crankshaft   *Gear change lever*

8NHP. WILLIAM   **ALLCHIN L**^{TD}. **1907**

Gears

Steering wheel

Driver's lunch of bread and drippings

Driver

Reversing lever

Crunching gears
Most steam traction engines had at least one extra set of gear cogs for extra power for climbing hills – or extra control going downhill. But the driver usually had to stop altogether to slide a new gear into place. A really skillful driver could change gear on the move.

Toolbox

Coal bunker

Fire tools

Tender spot
The area at the back where the driver sat, along with the water tank beneath and the coal hopper behind, was called the tender.

Registration plate

Filling up
A steam traction engine needed a lot of water, so a driver was always pleased to pass a stream of flowing water where he could fill up the water tank below the tender.

Stoker

Water tank

Warm bedfellows
Driving often made steam traction engine crews so dirty that they could not find lodging, so some drivers slept under their machines, warmed by the firebox.

Firebox

Stoker's hole

Inlet to water injector

Open grate

Hose for collecting water from roadside streams

Ash pan

Pieces of wood, called strakes, give wheels traction on bad roads

Unsprung heroes
It took nerves of steel – and a great deal of natural padding – to survive the ordeal of a long journey on a steam roller or plow engine, for they had no springs whatsoever. Steam traction engines, fortunately, had a pair of hefty coil springs on the rear axle, though they were still far from comfortable.

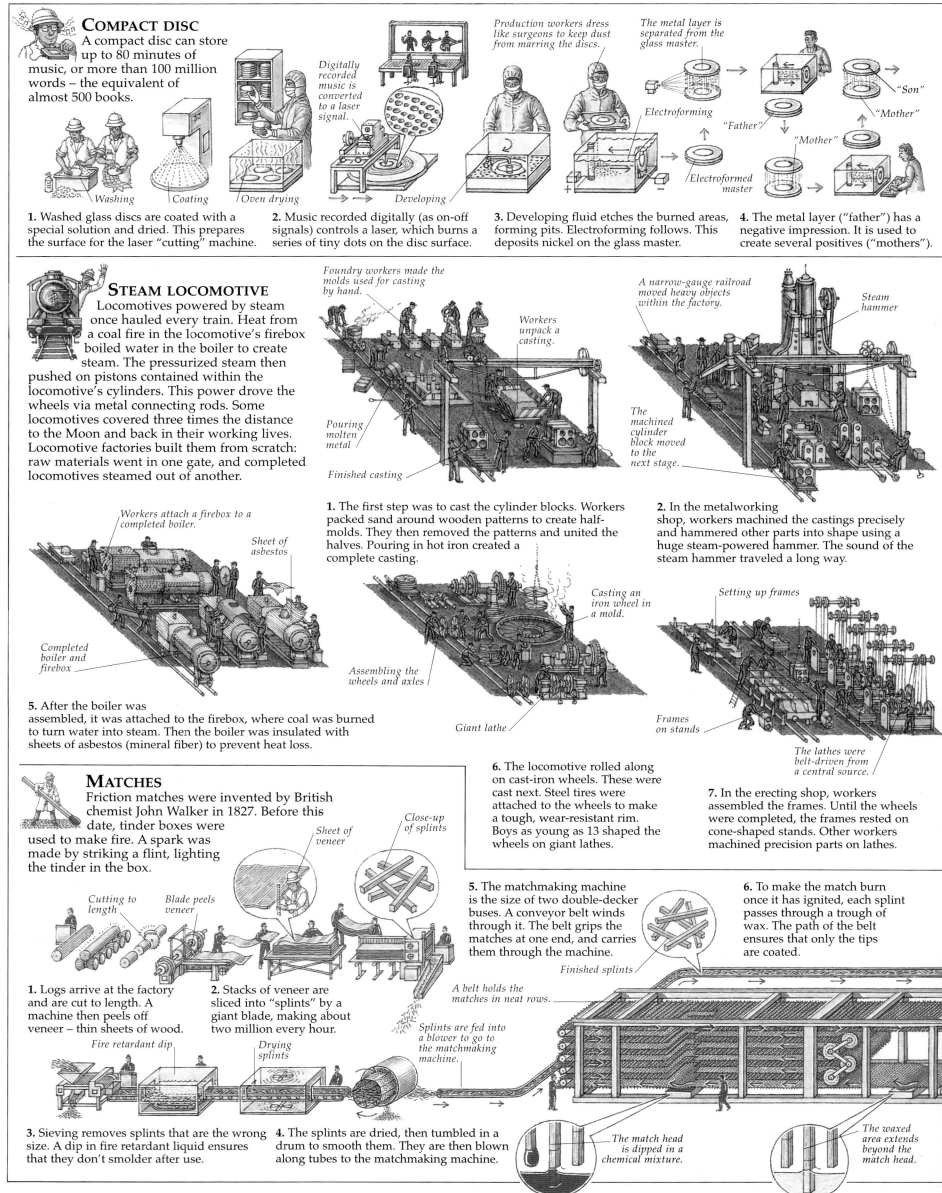

COMPACT DISC

A compact disc can store up to 80 minutes of music, or more than 100 million words – the equivalent of almost 500 books.

Washing *Coating* *Oven drying*

Digitally recorded music is converted to a laser signal.

Developing

Production workers dress like surgeons to keep dust from marring the discs.

The metal layer is separated from the glass master.

Electroforming

Electroformed master

"Father" *"Mother"* *"Son"* *"Mother"*

1. Washed glass discs are coated with a special solution and dried. This prepares the surface for the laser "cutting" machine.

2. Music recorded digitally (as on-off signals) controls a laser, which burns a series of tiny dots on the disc surface.

3. Developing fluid etches the burned areas, forming pits. Electroforming follows. This deposits nickel on the glass master.

4. The metal layer ("father") has a negative impression. It is used to create several positives ("mothers").

STEAM LOCOMOTIVE

Locomotives powered by steam once hauled every train. Heat from a coal fire in the locomotive's firebox boiled water in the boiler to create steam. The pressurized steam then pushed on pistons contained within the locomotive's cylinders. This power drove the wheels via metal connecting rods. Some locomotives covered three times the distance to the Moon and back in their working lives. Locomotive factories built them from scratch: raw materials went in one gate, and completed locomotives steamed out of another.

Foundry workers made the molds used for casting by hand.

Workers unpack a casting.

Pouring molten metal

Finished casting

A narrow-gauge railroad moved heavy objects within the factory.

Steam hammer

The machined cylinder block moved to the next stage.

Workers attach a firebox to a completed boiler.

Sheet of asbestos

Completed boiler and firebox

5. After the boiler was assembled, it was attached to the firebox, where coal was burned to turn water into steam. Then the boiler was insulated with sheets of asbestos (mineral fiber) to prevent heat loss.

1. The first step was to cast the cylinder blocks. Workers packed sand around wooden patterns to create half-molds. They then removed the patterns and united the halves. Pouring in hot iron created a complete casting.

Casting an iron wheel in a mold.

Assembling the wheels and axles

Giant lathe

2. In the metalworking shop, workers machined the castings precisely and hammered other parts into shape using a huge steam-powered hammer. The sound of the steam hammer traveled a long way.

Setting up frames

Frames on stands

The lathes were belt-driven from a central source.

6. The locomotive rolled along on cast-iron wheels. These were cast next. Steel tires were attached to the wheels to make a tough, wear-resistant rim. Boys as young as 13 shaped the wheels on giant lathes.

7. In the erecting shop, workers assembled the frames. Until the wheels were completed, the frames rested on cone-shaped stands. Other workers machined precision parts on lathes.

MATCHES

Friction matches were invented by British chemist John Walker in 1827. Before this date, tinder boxes were used to make fire. A spark was made by striking a flint, lighting the tinder in the box.

Sheet of veneer

Close-up of splints

Cutting to length *Blade peels veneer*

1. Logs arrive at the factory and are cut to length. A machine then peels off veneer – thin sheets of wood.

2. Stacks of veneer are sliced into "splints" by a giant blade, making about two million every hour.

5. The matchmaking machine is the size of two double-decker buses. A conveyor belt winds through it. The belt grips the matches at one end, and carries them through the machine.

6. To make the match burn once it has ignited, each splint passes through a trough of wax. The path of the belt ensures that only the tips are coated.

Finished splints

A belt holds the matches in neat rows.

Splints are fed into a blower to go to the matchmaking machine.

Fire retardant dip

Drying splints

3. Sieving removes splints that are the wrong size. A dip in fire retardant liquid ensures that they don't smolder after use.

4. The splints are dried, then tumbled in a drum to smooth them. They are then blown along tubes to the matchmaking machine.

The match head is dipped in a chemical mixture.

The waxed area extends beyond the match head.

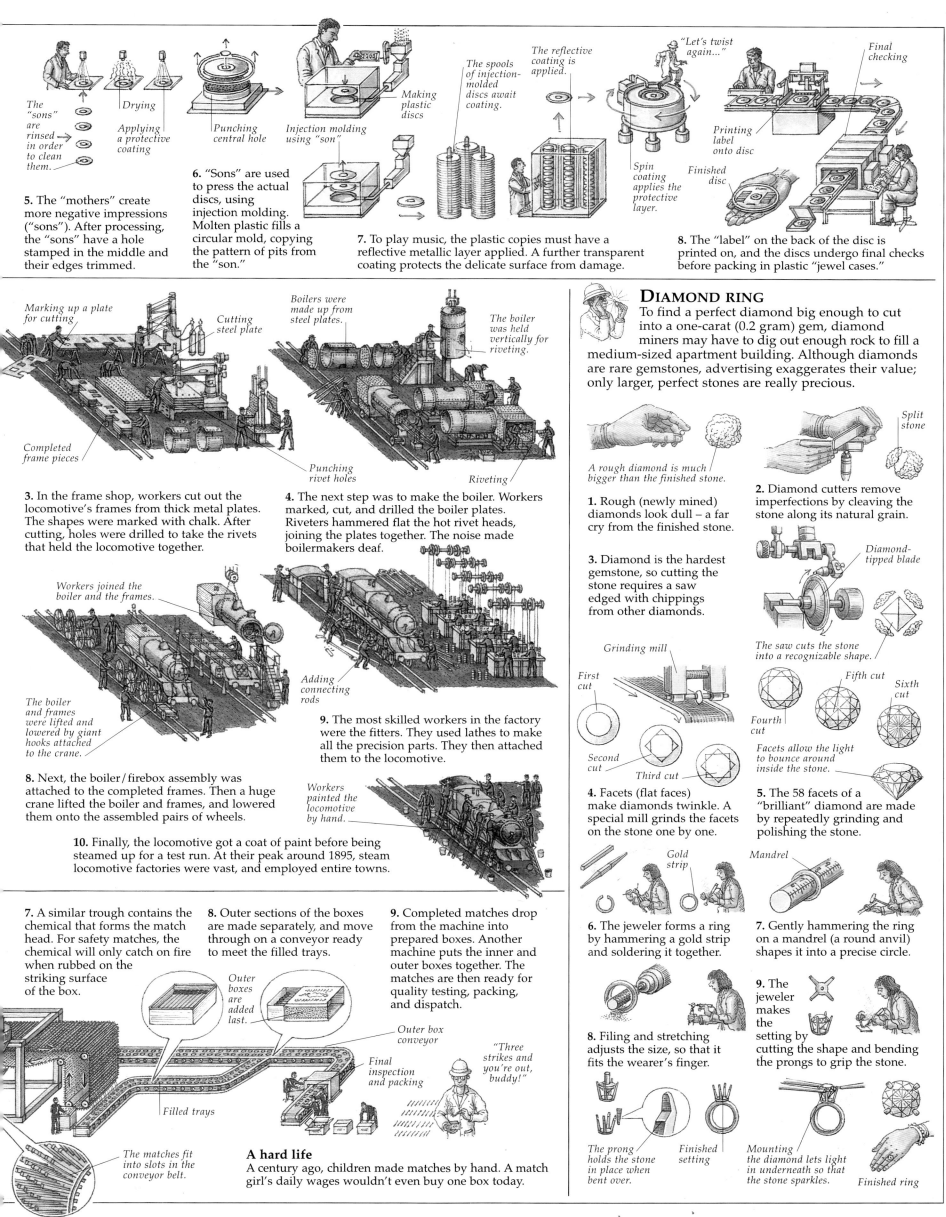

The "sons" are rinsed in order to clean them.

Drying

Applying a protective coating

Punching central hole

Making plastic discs

Injection molding using "son"

The spools of injection-molded discs await coating.

The reflective coating is applied.

"Let's twist again..."

Final checking

Spin coating applies the protective layer.

Printing label onto disc

Finished disc

5. The "mothers" create more negative impressions ("sons"). After processing, the "sons" have a hole stamped in the middle and their edges trimmed.

6. "Sons" are used to press the actual discs, using injection molding. Molten plastic fills a circular mold, copying the pattern of pits from the "son."

7. To play music, the plastic copies must have a reflective metallic layer applied. A further transparent coating protects the delicate surface from damage.

8. The "label" on the back of the disc is printed on, and the discs undergo final checks before packing in plastic "jewel cases."

Marking up a plate for cutting

Cutting steel plate

Boilers were made up from steel plates.

The boiler was held vertically for riveting.

Completed frame pieces

Punching rivet holes

Riveting

3. In the frame shop, workers cut out the locomotive's frames from thick metal plates. The shapes were marked with chalk. After cutting, holes were drilled to take the rivets that held the locomotive together.

4. The next step was to make the boiler. Workers marked, cut, and drilled the boiler plates. Riveters hammered flat the hot rivet heads, joining the plates together. The noise made boilermakers deaf.

Workers joined the boiler and the frames.

The boiler and frames were lifted and lowered by giant hooks attached to the crane.

Adding connecting rods

8. Next, the boiler/firebox assembly was attached to the completed frames. Then a huge crane lifted the boiler and frames, and lowered them onto the assembled pairs of wheels.

9. The most skilled workers in the factory were the fitters. They used lathes to make all the precision parts. They then attached them to the locomotive.

Workers painted the locomotive by hand.

10. Finally, the locomotive got a coat of paint before being steamed up for a test run. At their peak around 1895, steam locomotive factories were vast, and employed entire towns.

---

7. A similar trough contains the chemical that forms the match head. For safety matches, the chemical will only catch on fire when rubbed on the striking surface of the box.

8. Outer sections of the boxes are made separately, and move through on a conveyor ready to meet the filled trays.

9. Completed matches drop from the machine into prepared boxes. Another machine puts the inner and outer boxes together. The matches are then ready for quality testing, packing, and dispatch.

Outer boxes are added last.

Outer box conveyor

Filled trays

Final inspection and packing

"Three strikes and you're out, buddy!"

The matches fit into slots in the conveyor belt.

A hard life
A century ago, children made matches by hand. A match girl's daily wages wouldn't even buy one box today.

DIAMOND RING

To find a perfect diamond big enough to cut into a one-carat (0.2 gram) gem, diamond miners may have to dig out enough rock to fill a medium-sized apartment building. Although diamonds are rare gemstones, advertising exaggerates their value; only larger, perfect stones are really precious.

A rough diamond is much bigger than the finished stone.

Split stone

1. Rough (newly mined) diamonds look dull – a far cry from the finished stone.

2. Diamond cutters remove imperfections by cleaving the stone along its natural grain.

Diamond-tipped blade

3. Diamond is the hardest gemstone, so cutting the stone requires a saw edged with chippings from other diamonds.

The saw cuts the stone into a recognizable shape.

Grinding mill

First cut

Second cut

Third cut

Fourth cut

Fifth cut

Sixth cut

Facets allow the light to bounce around inside the stone.

4. Facets (flat faces) make diamonds twinkle. A special mill grinds the facets on the stone one by one.

5. The 58 facets of a "brilliant" diamond are made by repeatedly grinding and polishing the stone.

Gold strip

Mandrel

6. The jeweler forms a ring by hammering a gold strip and soldering it together.

7. Gently hammering the ring on a mandrel (a round anvil) shapes it into a precise circle.

8. Filing and stretching adjusts the size, so that it fits the wearer's finger.

9. The jeweler makes the setting by cutting the shape and bending the prongs to grip the stone.

The prong holds the stone in place when bent over.

Finished setting

Mounting the diamond lets light in underneath so that the stone sparkles.

Finished ring

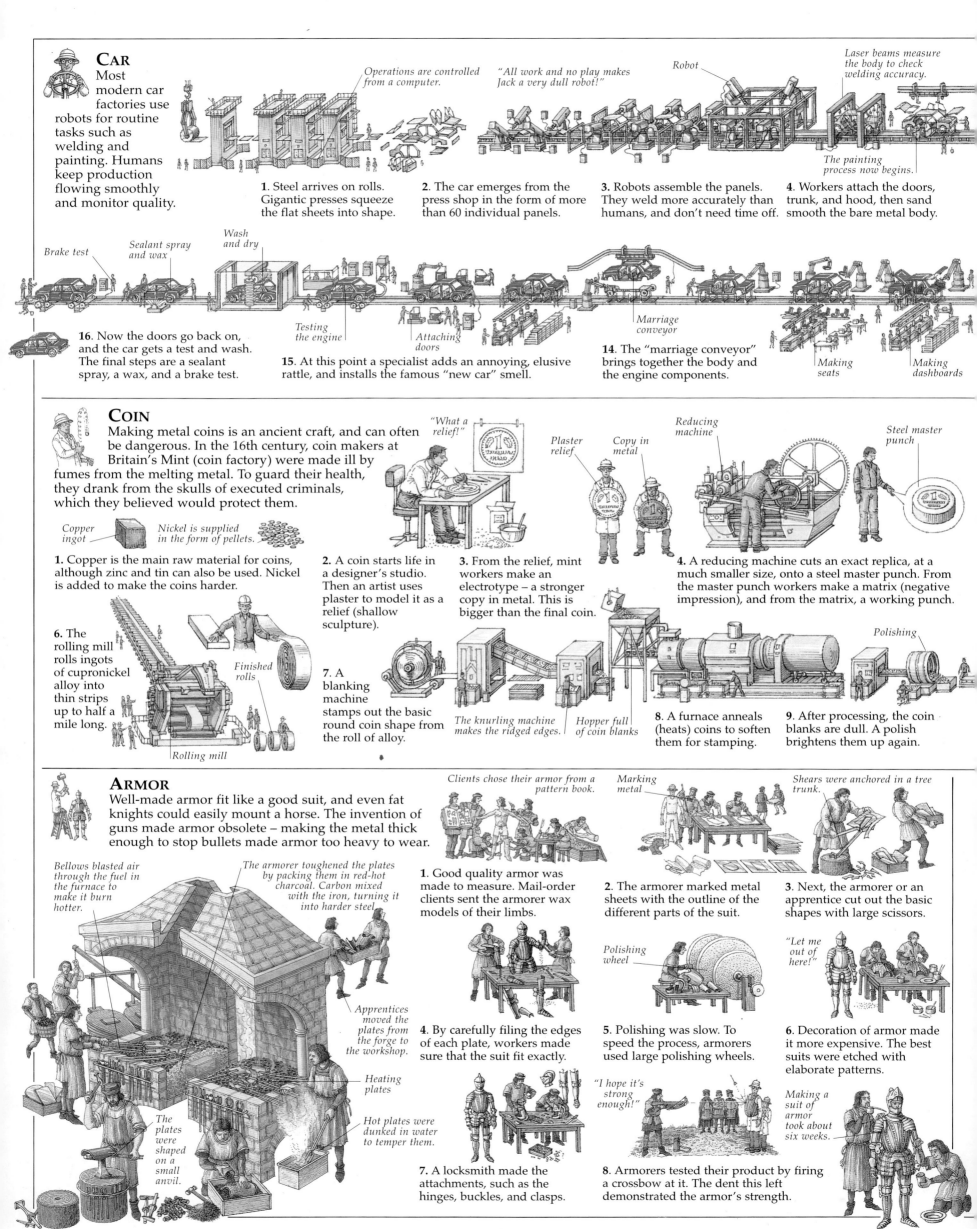

CAR

Most modern car factories use robots for routine tasks such as welding and painting. Humans keep production flowing smoothly and monitor quality.

Operations are controlled from a computer.

"All work and no play makes Jack a very dull robot!"

Robot

Laser beams measure the body to check welding accuracy.

The painting process now begins.

1. Steel arrives on rolls. Gigantic presses squeeze the flat sheets into shape.

2. The car emerges from the press shop in the form of more than 60 individual panels.

3. Robots assemble the panels. They weld more accurately than humans, and don't need time off.

4. Workers attach the doors, trunk, and hood, then sand smooth the bare metal body.

Brake test   *Sealant spray and wax*   *Wash and dry*   *Testing the engine*   *Attaching doors*   *Marriage conveyor*   *Making seats*   *Making dashboards*

16. Now the doors go back on, and the car gets a test and wash. The final steps are a sealant spray, a wax, and a brake test.

15. At this point a specialist adds an annoying, elusive rattle, and installs the famous "new car" smell.

14. The "marriage conveyor" brings together the body and the engine components.

COIN

Making metal coins is an ancient craft, and can often be dangerous. In the 16th century, coin makers at Britain's Mint (coin factory) were made ill by fumes from the melting metal. To guard their health, they drank from the skulls of executed criminals, which they believed would protect them.

"What a relief!"   *Plaster relief*   *Copy in metal*   *Reducing machine*   *Steel master punch*

Copper ingot   *Nickel is supplied in the form of pellets.*

1. Copper is the main raw material for coins, although zinc and tin can also be used. Nickel is added to make the coins harder.

6. The rolling mill rolls ingots of cupronickel alloy into thin strips up to half a mile long.

Finished rolls   *Rolling mill*

2. A coin starts life in a designer's studio. Then an artist uses plaster to model it as a relief (shallow sculpture).

3. From the relief, mint workers make an electrotype – a stronger copy in metal. This is bigger than the final coin.

7. A blanking machine stamps out the basic round coin shape from the roll of alloy.

The knurling machine makes the ridged edges.   *Hopper full of coin blanks*

4. A reducing machine cuts an exact replica, at a much smaller size, onto a steel master punch. From the master punch workers make a matrix (negative impression), and from the matrix, a working punch.

Polishing

8. A furnace anneals (heats) coins to soften them for stamping.

9. After processing, the coin blanks are dull. A polish brightens them up again.

ARMOR

Well-made armor fit like a good suit, and even fat knights could easily mount a horse. The invention of guns made armor obsolete – making the metal thick enough to stop bullets made armor too heavy to wear.

Clients chose their armor from a pattern book.   *Marking metal*   *Shears were anchored in a tree trunk.*

Bellows blasted air through the fuel in the furnace to make it burn hotter.

The armorer toughened the plates by packing them in red-hot charcoal. Carbon mixed with the iron, turning it into harder steel.

Apprentices moved the plates from the forge to the workshop.

Heating plates

The plates were shaped on a small anvil.

Hot plates were dunked in water to temper them.

1. Good quality armor was made to measure. Mail-order clients sent the armorer wax models of their limbs.

2. The armorer marked metal sheets with the outline of the different parts of the suit.

3. Next, the armorer or an apprentice cut out the basic shapes with large scissors.

Polishing wheel

"Let me out of here!"

4. By carefully filing the edges of each plate, workers made sure that the suit fit exactly.

5. Polishing was slow. To speed the process, armorers used large polishing wheels.

6. Decoration of armor made it more expensive. The best suits were etched with elaborate patterns.

"I hope it's strong enough!"

Making a suit of armor took about six weeks.

7. A locksmith made the attachments, such as the hinges, buckles, and clasps.

8. Armorers tested their product by firing a crossbow at it. The dent this left demonstrated the armor's strength.

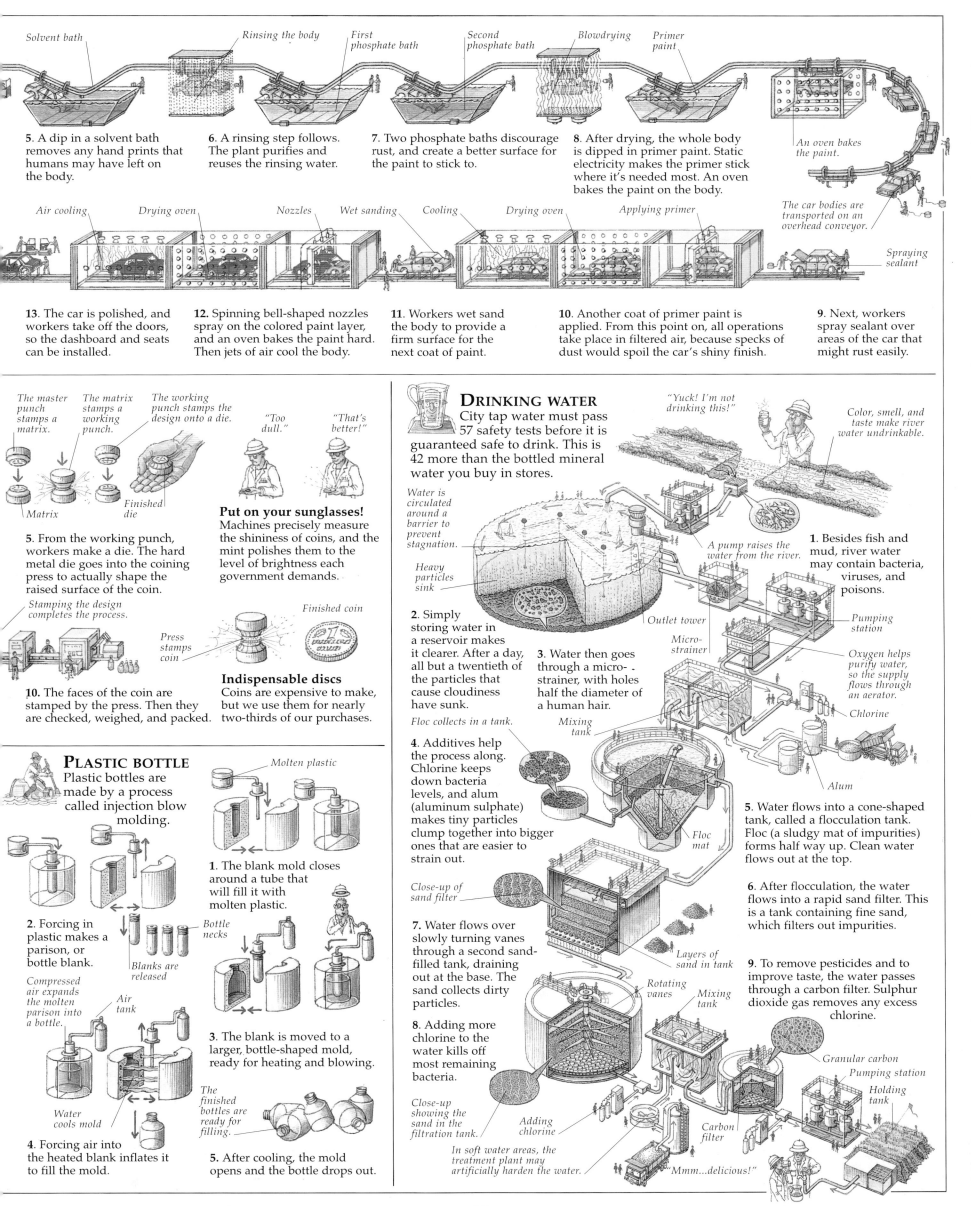

5. A dip in a solvent bath removes any hand prints that humans may have left on the body.

Solvent bath

Rinsing the body

6. A rinsing step follows. The plant purifies and reuses the rinsing water.

First phosphate bath

7. Two phosphate baths discourage rust, and create a better surface for the paint to stick to.

Second phosphate bath

Blowdrying

8. After drying, the whole body is dipped in primer paint. Static electricity makes the primer stick where it's needed most. An oven bakes the paint on the body.

Primer paint

An oven bakes the paint.

The car bodies are transported on an overhead conveyor.

Air cooling

Drying oven

Nozzles

Wet sanding

Cooling

Drying oven

Applying primer

Spraying sealant

13. The car is polished, and workers take off the doors, so the dashboard and seats can be installed.

12. Spinning bell-shaped nozzles spray on the colored paint layer, and an oven bakes the paint hard. Then jets of air cool the body.

11. Workers wet sand the body to provide a firm surface for the next coat of paint.

10. Another coat of primer paint is applied. From this point on, all operations take place in filtered air, because specks of dust would spoil the car's shiny finish.

9. Next, workers spray sealant over areas of the car that might rust easily.

The master punch stamps a matrix.

The matrix stamps a working punch.

The working punch stamps the design onto a die.

"Too dull."

"That's better!"

Matrix

Finished die

5. From the working punch, workers make a die. The hard metal die goes into the coining press to actually shape the raised surface of the coin.

Put on your sunglasses! Machines precisely measure the shininess of coins, and the mint polishes them to the level of brightness each government demands.

Stamping the design completes the process.

Press stamps coin

Finished coin

10. The faces of the coin are stamped by the press. Then they are checked, weighed, and packed.

Indispensable discs Coins are expensive to make, but we use them for nearly two-thirds of our purchases.

PLASTIC BOTTLE

Plastic bottles are made by a process called injection blow molding.

Molten plastic

2. Forcing in plastic makes a parison, or bottle blank.

Compressed air expands the molten parison into a bottle.

Air tank

Blanks are released

Bottle necks

1. The blank mold closes around a tube that will fill it with molten plastic.

3. The blank is moved to a larger, bottle-shaped mold, ready for heating and blowing.

Water cools mold

The finished bottles are ready for filling.

4. Forcing air into the heated blank inflates it to fill the mold.

5. After cooling, the mold opens and the bottle drops out.

DRINKING WATER

City tap water must pass 57 safety tests before it is guaranteed safe to drink. This is 42 more than the bottled mineral water you buy in stores.

"Yuck! I'm not drinking this!"

Color, smell, and taste make river water undrinkable.

Water is circulated around a barrier to prevent stagnation.

Heavy particles sink

A pump raises the water from the river.

1. Besides fish and mud, river water may contain bacteria, viruses, and poisons.

2. Simply storing water in a reservoir makes it clearer. After a day, all but a twentieth of the particles that cause cloudiness have sunk.

Outlet tower

Micro-strainer

Pumping station

3. Water then goes through a micro-strainer, with holes half the diameter of a human hair.

Oxygen helps purify water, so the supply flows through an aerator.

Floc collects in a tank.

Mixing tank

Chlorine

4. Additives help the process along. Chlorine keeps down bacteria levels, and alum (aluminum sulphate) makes tiny particles clump together into bigger ones that are easier to strain out.

Floc mat

Alum

5. Water flows into a cone-shaped tank, called a flocculation tank. Floc (a sludgy mat of impurities) forms half way up. Clean water flows out at the top.

Close-up of sand filter

7. Water flows over slowly turning vanes through a second sand-filled tank, draining out at the base. The sand collects dirty particles.

6. After flocculation, the water flows into a rapid sand filter. This is a tank containing fine sand, which filters out impurities.

Layers of sand in tank

8. Adding more chlorine to the water kills off most remaining bacteria.

Rotating vanes

Mixing tank

9. To remove pesticides and to improve taste, the water passes through a carbon filter. Sulphur dioxide gas removes any excess chlorine.

Close-up showing the sand in the filtration tank.

Adding chlorine

Carbon filter

Granular carbon

Pumping station

Holding tank

In soft water areas, the treatment plant may artificially harden the water.

"Mmm...delicious!"

RACE CAR

COMPARING A FORMULA 1 RACE CAR TO A
family sedan is like comparing an outfit from a shopping mall chain store to a gown from a top fashion designer. Every aspect of a race car is custom made. The cockpit fits around the driver's body like a tight pair of jeans, so drivers have to watch their weight just like a supermodel. The first Formula 1 race of the year is in many ways like a fashion show. Everyone stares at the new cars, examining every detail and watching how the design affects each car's performance on the track.

THE DESIGN
Designers aim to make the body light but strong. Its shape helps the car grip the track.

Working from the drawings, a team of modelmakers sculpt the body shape in miniature.

Tracing the contours of the model with a three-dimensional digitizing arm copies its shape into a computer.

THE BODY OF THE CAR
The shape of a car's body has a huge effect on speed, so designers determine this first. Engineers must then find room for all the car's other components – such as the engine and suspension – in the tiny body. To give all cars an equal chance, strict rules govern every construction detail.

1. One of the biggest dangers to drivers is a fuel fire. A quarter of the car's weight when the race starts is highly flammable fuel, and drivers sit in front of the tank. Shock-absorbing panels protect it, and a puncture-resistant bladder stops fuel from leaking in a crash.

2. On a passenger car, the suspension smooths the ride. On a race car, it must stop the car from bouncing up, as this reduces the wheel's grip on the track. Bump-detecting sensors feed information to a central computer that operates the hydraulic jacks controlling the height of each wheel. The basic layout of the suspension is easy to modify at the track by adjusting the car's computer.

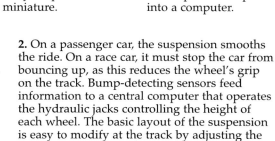

Fuel tank

Bolts made of titanium metal are stronger than steel, but weigh a third less.

Rollover loop

Rear shock absorbers

The gearbox is part of the transmission system that carries power from the engine to the wheels.

Clutch

Transverse gear box

Position of rear axle

Gear stick

Accelerator

Clutch

Break

THE ENGINE
In the 1950s, race car constructors used engines "borrowed" from other vehicles, including fire engines! Today, all racing engines are specially built for high power and low weight. Honda engines from the 1980s took this approach to an extreme. Mixing fuel with compressed air, their engines generated 20 times as much power as a passenger car engine of the same size.

Clutch plate

Camshaft

Crankshaft

Water radiator

Oil radiator

Housing for engine management systems

1. The engine uses less than a third of all the fuel it burns to move the car around the track. More is wasted in noise and heat from the exhaust.

2. Race teams change engines as often as most people change their underwear. After each race, mechanics dismantle the car, remove the engine and ship it back to the manufacturers. The engine may be reused the following season, but it is often replaced by a newer, faster model.

Computer monitoring
Sensors all over the car monitor its performance, and an on-board computer stores the information. Technicians collect the information during a pit stop, or the car broadcasts a short burst of data by radio.

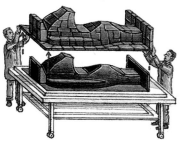

BUILDING THE BODY
A computer-controlled milling machine cuts molds for the body from flat panels.

Stacking up the panels and putting them together creates the final form for the mold. These are smoothed by hand.

Fabricators first paint over release agents and wax to prevent sticking, and then coat the form with epoxy resin.

Next the form is carefully covered with about 10 layers of carbon fiber sheeting. This is the mold.

To strengthen the body, it is "cured" in an oven at 250° F (120° C) – just hot enough to cook dessert.

On the computer, engineers can plan how the body will fit together with other components. The computer model will also guide cutters that make molds for the full-sized car.

To simulate a race, a huge fan blows air across the model in a wind tunnel, and a conveyor belt turns the wheels. Sensors measure drag, down-force, and vibration. These tests help predict how the car will behave on the track.

While the fan is switched off, engineers run into the tunnel and change tiny details of the car. They have to hurry, because wind tunnel time is very expensive.

Modifications that improve the flow of air over the model will make the full-sized car go faster.

THE "CLOTHES" OF THE CAR

The flaps, spoilers, and tires are like the race car's clothes. Engineers decide on the basic outfit at the design stage. But many of these parts are easy to remove. The pit crew exchanges them to make small adjustments to the car's performance. The spoilers work like an upside-down aircraft wing. The faster the car goes, the more it is pressed to the ground, improving the grip of the tires.

Spoilers (wings) at the front and back create a downward force that is greater than the car's weight.

THE FINISHING TOUCHES

Finishing touches include a shiny paint finish and advertising for sponsors – companies that give money to racing teams in exchange for publicity. The more money a sponsor provides, the larger and more prominent their logo appears on the car. The technicians must position the company logos carefully to keep all the sponsors happy.

Six-point harness

The seat is not padded and the driver feels every bump.

THE DRIVER

Drivers wear fireproof clothes made of multiple layers of high-temperature-resistant nylon. If there's a fire, the suit keeps out the flames for half a minute. An emergency canister supplies compressed air to the helmet, preventing drivers from suffocating or breathing in poisonous fumes. The eye-slit of the fireproof fibreglass-reinforced helmet is narrow to protect against flying debris.

Epaulettes are reinforced so the driver can be dragged from a burning wreck.

"Even his underwear is flame resistant!"

Brake pads

The housings for the brakes are designed to channel air across the discs to cool them. As drivers brake, the carbon-fiber discs glow red hot. They work best at 660-930° F (350-500° C).

The nose is designed to crumple and absorb shock on impact.

The chassis of the car is made up of two layers of carbon fiber, with either an aluminum honeycomb structure or a flame-resistant material called "Nomex" in the middle.

Race teams use many different tires, changing them for different circuits and different weather.

Spoiler

Technicians monitor data on the car's performance.

PIT STOP

During a race, cars call in at the pits (small workshops) for refueling, new tires, data download, and other maintenance. A team of up to 50 mechanics and technicians work at dizzying speed to get the car back into the race as quickly as possible. With three mechanics on each wheel, changing all four tires takes 10 seconds or less.

Rear left wheel mechanics

Refuelers

Front left wheel mechanics

Most cars are made from five moldings or fewer. During assembly, technicians add aluminum bulkheads to strengthen the cockpit.

"Right, let's try it again with you in the driver's seat."

Before a new car can race, it must pass stringent safety tests and survive simulated side and front impacts.

Rear quick-lift jack operator

Front quick-lift jack operator

Rear right wheel mechanics

Front right wheel mechanics

Chief mechanic with the lollipop for signalling to the driver

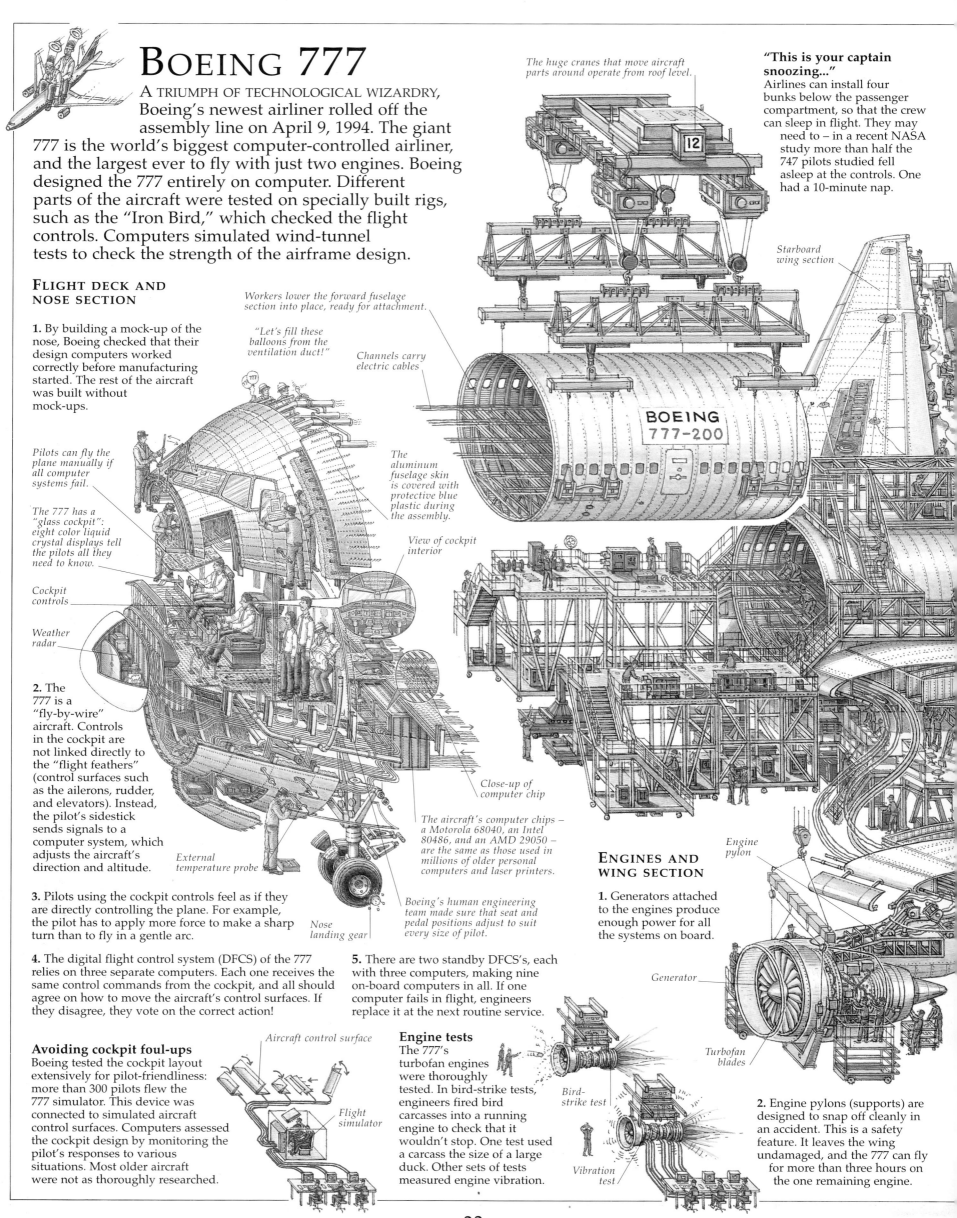

BOEING 777

A TRIUMPH OF TECHNOLOGICAL WIZARDRY, Boeing's newest airliner rolled off the assembly line on April 9, 1994. The giant 777 is the world's biggest computer-controlled airliner, and the largest ever to fly with just two engines. Boeing designed the 777 entirely on computer. Different parts of the aircraft were tested on specially built rigs, such as the "Iron Bird," which checked the flight controls. Computers simulated wind-tunnel tests to check the strength of the airframe design.

FLIGHT DECK AND NOSE SECTION

1. By building a mock-up of the nose, Boeing checked that their design computers worked correctly before manufacturing started. The rest of the aircraft was built without mock-ups.

2. The 777 is a "fly-by-wire" aircraft. Controls in the cockpit are not linked directly to the "flight feathers" (control surfaces such as the ailerons, rudder, and elevators). Instead, the pilot's sidestick sends signals to a computer system, which adjusts the aircraft's direction and altitude.

3. Pilots using the cockpit controls feel as if they are directly controlling the plane. For example, the pilot has to apply more force to make a sharp turn than to fly in a gentle arc.

4. The digital flight control system (DFCS) of the 777 relies on three separate computers. Each one receives the same control commands from the cockpit, and all should agree on how to move the aircraft's control surfaces. If they disagree, they vote on the correct action!

5. There are two standby DFCS's, each with three computers, making nine on-board computers in all. If one computer fails in flight, engineers replace it at the next routine service.

Avoiding cockpit foul-ups
Boeing tested the cockpit layout extensively for pilot-friendliness: more than 300 pilots flew the 777 simulator. This device was connected to simulated aircraft control surfaces. Computers assessed the cockpit design by monitoring the pilot's responses to various situations. Most older aircraft were not as thoroughly researched.

Engine tests
The 777's turbofan engines were thoroughly tested. In bird-strike tests, engineers fired bird carcasses into a running engine to check that it wouldn't stop. One test used a carcass the size of a large duck. Other sets of tests measured engine vibration.

ENGINES AND WING SECTION

1. Generators attached to the engines produce enough power for all the systems on board.

2. Engine pylons (supports) are designed to snap off cleanly in an accident. This is a safety feature. It leaves the wing undamaged, and the 777 can fly for more than three hours on the one remaining engine.

"This is your captain snoozing..."
Airlines can install four bunks below the passenger compartment, so that the crew can sleep in flight. They may need to – in a recent NASA study more than half the 747 pilots studied fell asleep at the controls. One had a 10-minute nap.

The huge cranes that move aircraft parts around operate from roof level.

Starboard wing section

Workers lower the forward fuselage section into place, ready for attachment.

"Let's fill these balloons from the ventilation duct!"

Channels carry electric cables

Pilots can fly the plane manually if all computer systems fail.

The 777 has a "glass cockpit": eight color liquid crystal displays tell the pilots all they need to know.

Cockpit controls

Weather radar

The aluminum fuselage skin is covered with protective blue plastic during the assembly.

View of cockpit interior

Close-up of computer chip

The aircraft's computer chips – a Motorola 68040, an Intel 80486, and an AMD 29050 – are the same as those used in millions of older personal computers and laser printers.

External temperature probe

Nose landing gear

Boeing's human engineering team made sure that seat and pedal positions adjust to suit every size of pilot.

Aircraft control surface

Flight simulator

Bird-strike test

Vibration test

Engine pylon

Generator

Turbofan blades

FUSELAGE AND PASSENGER COMPARTMENT

1. Once the fuselage sections are joined, workers install heating, air conditioning, and electrical equipment. Special seat rails allow the seating arrangement to be changed easily: it takes just three hours to replace seats with an extra lavatory. On a 747 this takes two days.

2. Temperatures at cruising altitude are as low as -67° F (-55° C), so workers pack fireproof insulation panels between the inner and outer layers of the 777 fuselage.

The cabin layout can be tailored to an airline's individual requirements.

Pack them in!
The circular shape of the cabin allows airlines to pack in economy class seats 10 abreast. Business class passengers sit eight abreast, and first class passengers sit six abreast.

3. As the passenger cabin takes shape, workers install the in-flight entertainment system. Every passenger can listen to their choice of CD-quality music, and the system alone is as complex as a whole aircraft was five years ago. Some airlines may allow passengers to play in a virtual casino, betting on a roulette wheel to try to win back the price of their ticket.

4. The overhead luggage lockers are easy to install and remove. Airlines can move the lockers around without disturbing the ducting above.

5. Moisture condensing on the aircraft's cold skin gives designers headaches, because it causes corrosion, and can drip onto passengers' heads. Boeing solved the problem simply by tying sponges to the roof struts.

Plastic fantastic
Nearly one-tenth of the aircraft is made of advanced composites, like the carbon-fiber-reinforced plastic used in some tennis rackets. Most of the composites are used in the tail – the rudder is the largest all-composite part. The saving in weight allows a 777 to carry an extra 13 passengers and their luggage.

6. The APU (auxiliary power unit) at the rear of the aircraft powers electrical systems when the main engines are switched off.

7. The designers of the 777 paid special attention to the lavatories. Slam-proof seats make the journey more peaceful for passengers sitting nearby.

8. "Liquid leakage" from the lavatories was a serious source of corrosion on earlier aircraft. Since the lavatories can be repositioned easily on the 777, the designers incorporated flooring containing special alloy metals to compensate for passengers with a poor aim.

9. The spray-painting team coat the exterior of the aircraft with paint to a depth of exactly 75 thousandths of a millimeter. A thinner layer would not provide enough protection; too much paint adds to the aircraft's weight and fuel bill.

10. The 777 burns one-third less fuel than a 747, but still requires four road tankers to fill its tanks. Passengers could get to their destination using half as much fuel if – instead of flying in a 777 – they drove there by car.

But do they flap?
The 777's wings were also designed on computer. They were subjected to extensive simulator testing before designers attached them to the fuselage.

3. The 777's wings are so huge that there is room to park 42 cars on them. The long wings make the airliner difficult to park in airport bays designed for smaller aircraft.

4. Computer-controlled machines attach the rivets that hold many parts of the aircraft together. In 10 seconds, the machine drills, reams, and countersinks the hole, inserts and tightens the rivet, and shaves and smooths down the rivet head.

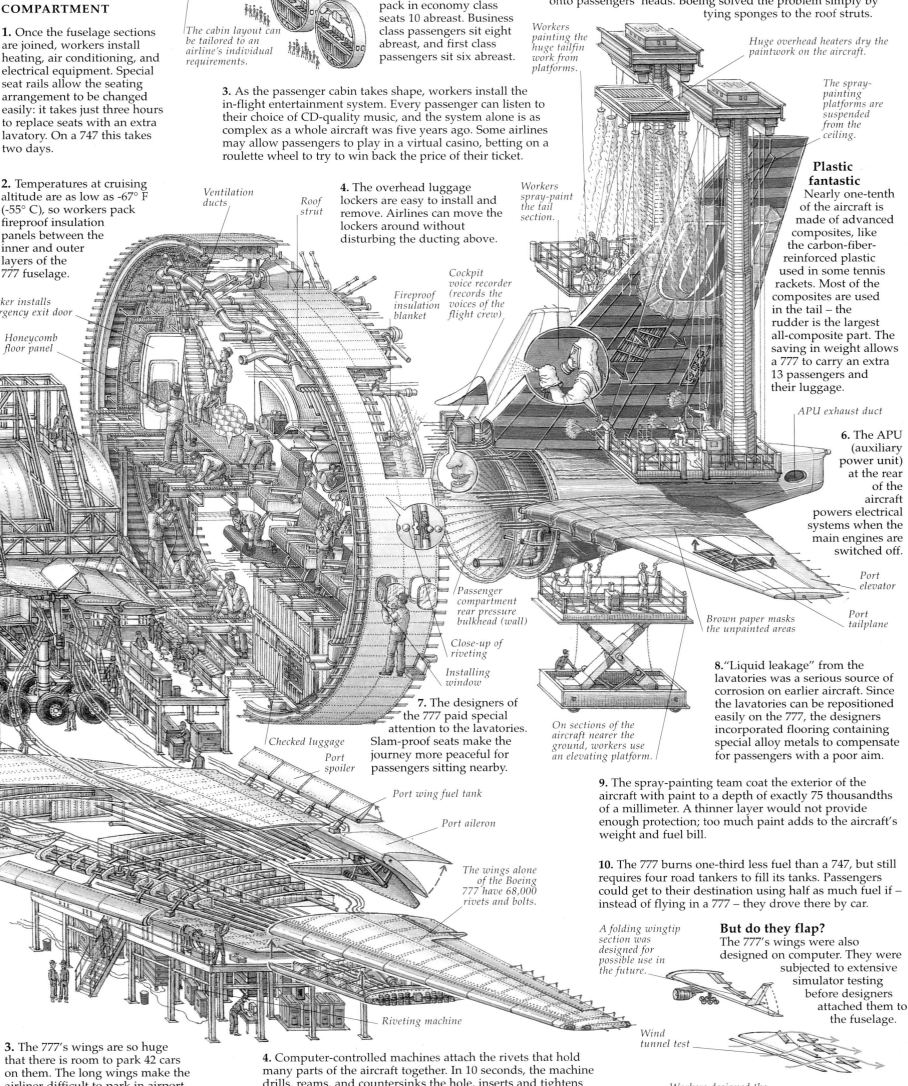

Ventilation ducts

Roof strut

Worker installs emergency exit door

Honeycomb floor panel

Workers painting the huge tailfin work from platforms.

Huge overhead heaters dry the paintwork on the aircraft.

The spray-painting platforms are suspended from the ceiling.

Workers spray-paint the tail section.

Cockpit voice recorder (records the voices of the flight crew)

Fireproof insulation blanket

APU exhaust duct

Passenger compartment rear pressure bulkhead (wall)

Close-up of riveting

Installing window

Checked luggage

Port spoiler

Port wing fuel tank

Port aileron

Port elevator

Port tailplane

Brown paper masks the unpainted areas

On sections of the aircraft nearer the ground, workers use an elevating platform.

The wings alone of the Boeing 777 have 68,000 rivets and bolts.

A folding wingtip section was designed for possible use in the future.

Wind tunnel test

Riveting machine

Workers designed the wings on computers.

AIRPORT

IF FLYING WAS AS CHAOTIC AS DRIVING, AIR TRAVEL would soon end. The sky would be black with tiny aircraft. Mid-air collisions would be so common that newspapers wouldn't report them. At popular destinations planes would wait for the lights to change, revving their engines and honking. Then they would race to see who was first down the runway. Of course, it wouldn't work. Flying is just too complex for each of us to own a plane. So at the airport we give up the privacy of our cars. We trust our luggage to a stranger and share the journey with others. Perhaps if we did the same on the roads our world would be a safer, more peaceful, and more pleasant place.

Air traffic control
The job of air traffic control is to route aircraft safely to their destination. To do this, controllers must make sure aircraft never come too close in flight, or when taking off and landing.

Keeping the skies safe
The approach control facility monitors aircraft beyond the circle handled by the visual control room.

Lights out
Aircraft monitored by the approach control facility are tracked on radar screens. Older screens are dim, so staff work in a darkened room.

Nice view
Aircraft within 5 miles (8 km) of the airport are under the control of staff in the visual control room.

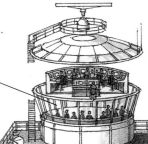

Visual control

AIR TRAFFIC CONTROL

Approach control facility

Computer center

A souvenir perhaps?
If you thought the business of airports was transportation, you'd be wrong. Commercial operations, including gift shops, bars, and restaurants bring in up to 60 percent of an airport's income.

Check in
International flights generally have computerized check-in. However, the procedure is simpler for domestic flights, and a manual system is quicker than a computer.

TERMINAL UPPER FLOOR (DEPARTURES)
GREEN FLOW

Bags of space
On average, every 10 passengers on international flights have 13 pieces of checked luggage.

Search me
X-rays and searches stop would-be hijackers from carrying on guns. However, there is no quick way to screen all checked bags for bombs.

Multi-story parking lot

Elevator to parking levels

PARKING LOT AND ROAD ACCESS

Underground access road

Counting cars
Airport parking lots have to be vast. Los Angeles airport has nearly 19,000 spaces, and if all the cars left at once, they'd form a line nearly 60 miles (100 km) long.

Distant gates
Big airports sprawl over huge areas, so "people movers" are needed for passengers transferring between flights. At Dallas-Fort Worth airport the most distant gates are 4.5 miles (7 km) apart.

Parking bill or phone number?
As anybody who has driven to an airport knows, the parking lot is a great moneymaker. It provides up to a sixth of the airport's profits.

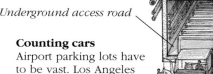

Underground railroad train

Passenger check-in

Not so rapid access
Rapid transport systems linking national airports to the city are popular with passengers: half of the passengers to London's Gatwick airport take the train.

Baggage claim carousel

Customs inspection area

Take the train
The belts carrying luggage are like a miniature rail complex within the terminal: Frankfurt airport has 25 miles (40 km) of track.

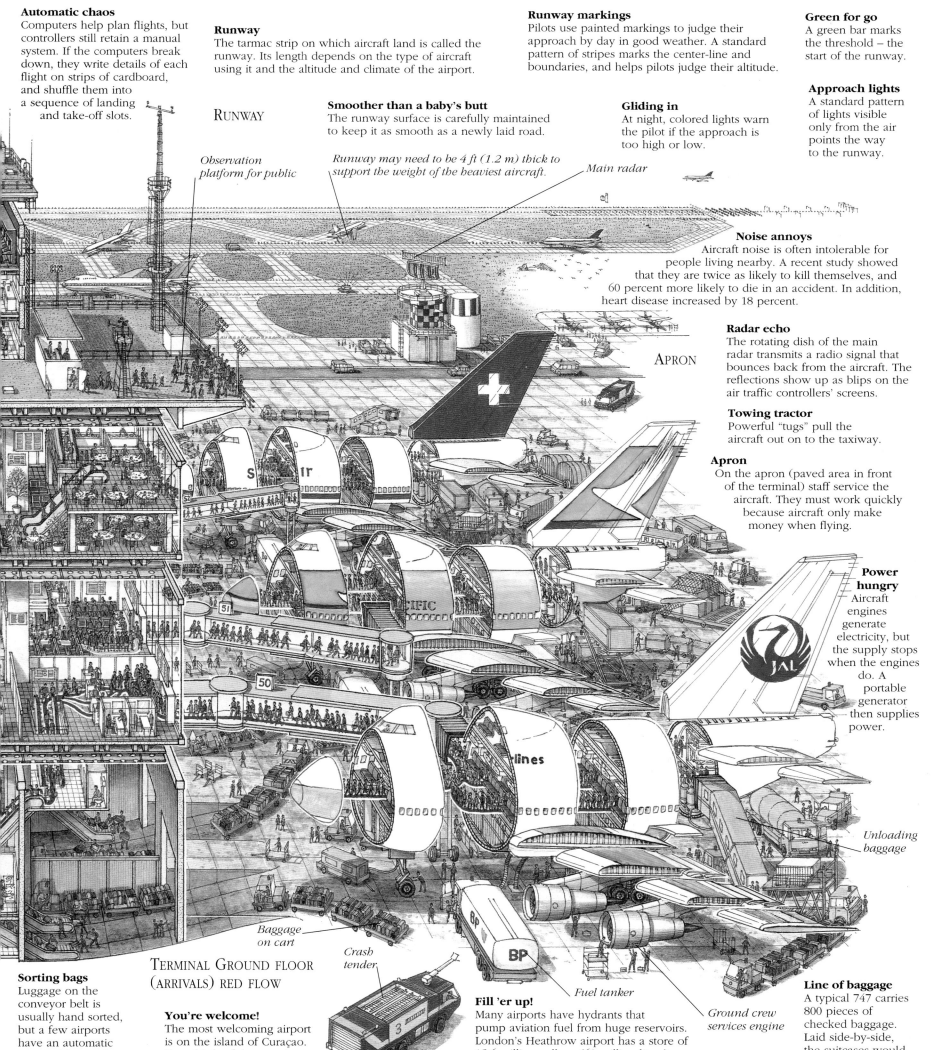

Automatic chaos
Computers help plan flights, but controllers still retain a manual system. If the computers break down, they write details of each flight on strips of cardboard, and shuffle them into a sequence of landing and take-off slots.

Runway
The tarmac strip on which aircraft land is called the runway. Its length depends on the type of aircraft using it and the altitude and climate of the airport.

Runway

Observation platform for public

Smoother than a baby's butt
The runway surface is carefully maintained to keep it as smooth as a newly laid road.

Runway may need to be 4 ft (1.2 m) thick to support the weight of the heaviest aircraft.

Main radar

Runway markings
Pilots use painted markings to judge their approach by day in good weather. A standard pattern of stripes marks the center-line and boundaries, and helps pilots judge their altitude.

Gliding in
At night, colored lights warn the pilot if the approach is too high or low.

Green for go
A green bar marks the threshold – the start of the runway.

Approach lights
A standard pattern of lights visible only from the air points the way to the runway.

Noise annoys
Aircraft noise is often intolerable for people living nearby. A recent study showed that they are twice as likely to kill themselves, and 60 percent more likely to die in an accident. In addition, heart disease increased by 18 percent.

Apron

Radar echo
The rotating dish of the main radar transmits a radio signal that bounces back from the aircraft. The reflections show up as blips on the air traffic controllers' screens.

Towing tractor
Powerful "tugs" pull the aircraft out on to the taxiway.

Apron
On the apron (paved area in front of the terminal) staff service the aircraft. They must work quickly because aircraft only make money when flying.

Power hungry
Aircraft engines generate electricity, but the supply stops when the engines do. A portable generator then supplies power.

Unloading baggage

Sorting bags
Luggage on the conveyor belt is usually hand sorted, but a few airports have an automatic system. This reads flight numbers from bar codes on tags. The system pushes the bags off the main belt into "branch lines" that lead to the right aircraft.

You're welcome!
The most welcoming airport is on the island of Curaçao. Two-thirds of the people visiting the airport go there to welcome friends or family, or to say "farewell." In Paris, however, only about one visitor in 15 is a greeter or a sender.

Terminal Ground floor (Arrivals) red flow

Baggage on cart

Crash tender

Smelly rescue
Firefighters are ready for everything. One major European airport is near a sewage treatment plant, and rescue teams are equipped with an inflatable boat and hovercraft, in case a plane overshoots the runway and lands in a sludge pond.

Fill 'er up!
Many airports have hydrants that pump aviation fuel from huge reservoirs. London's Heathrow airport has a store of 15.6 million gallons (60 million liters).

Fuel tanker

Ground crew services engine

Line of baggage
A typical 747 carries 800 pieces of checked baggage. Laid side-by-side, the suitcases would stretch six times the length of the aircraft.

Get moving!
Baggage from an arriving 747 can be waiting on the carousels within 12 minutes, but some airlines take three times as long.

SATURN V

WHEN THE AMERICAN SPACE PROGRAM FINALLY achieved a Moon landing on July 20, 1969, the Apollo 11 spacecraft was launched by a powerful rocket called Saturn V. The most powerful rocket ever, Saturn V was used to launch all the Apollo spacecraft on lunar missions. The rocket alone stood 363 feet (110 meters) high and had three stages, each of which fell away when it ran out of fuel. To follow what happened as Saturn V took off, start at the the first stage at the bottom right of the page.

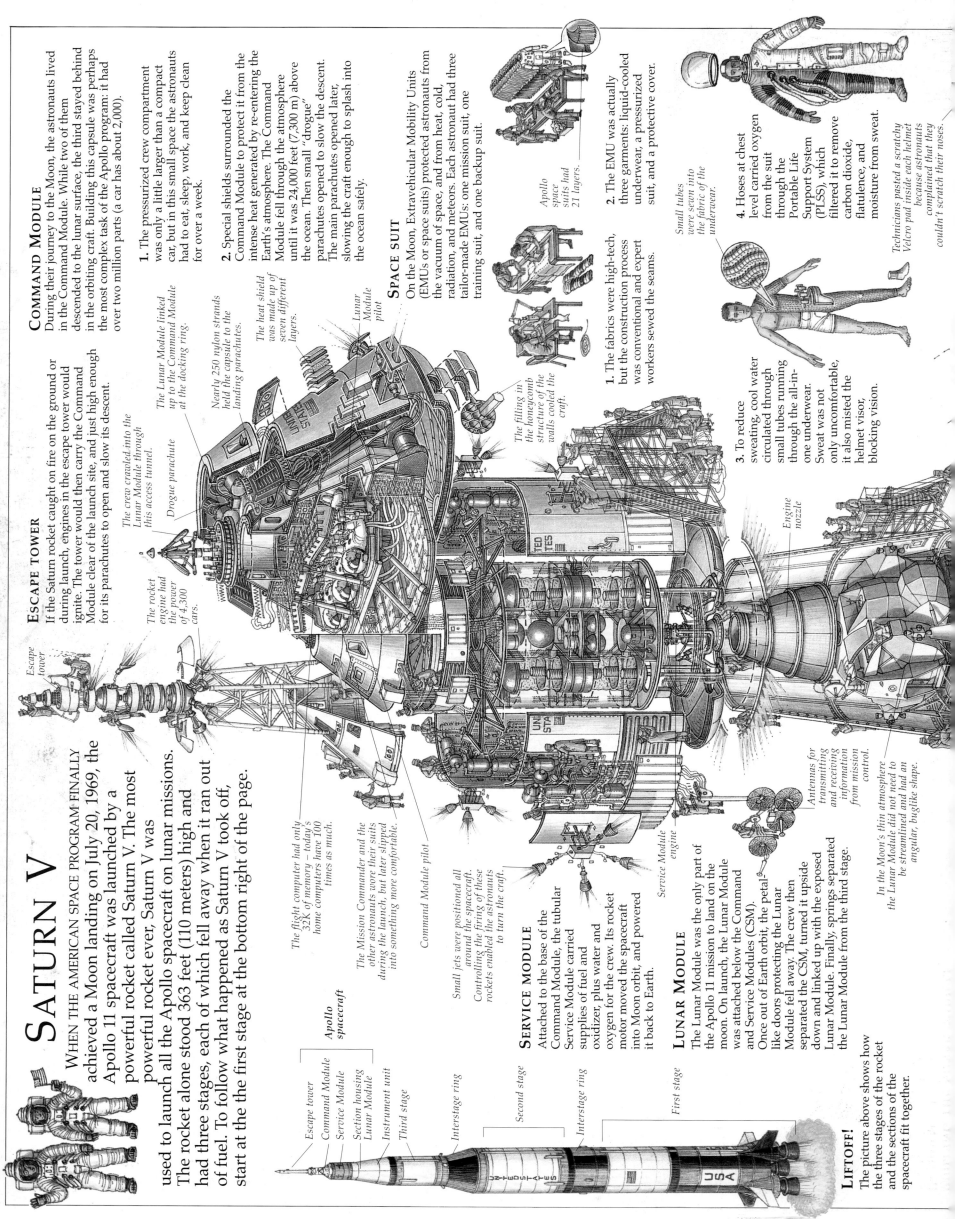

COMMAND MODULE

During their journey to the Moon, the astronauts lived in the Command Module. While two of them descended to the lunar surface, the third stayed behind in the orbiting craft. Building this capsule was perhaps the most complex task of the Apollo program: it had over two million parts (a car has about 2,000).

1. The pressurized crew compartment was only a little larger than a compact car, but in this small space the astronauts had to eat, sleep, work, and keep clean for over a week.

2. Special shields surrounded the Command Module to protect it from the intense heat generated by re-entering the Earth's atmosphere. The Command Module fell through the atmosphere until it was 24,000 feet (7,300 m) above the ocean. Then small "drogue" parachutes opened to slow the descent. The main parachutes opened later, slowing the craft enough to splash into the ocean safely.

SPACE SUIT

On the Moon, Extravehicular Mobility Units (EMUs or space suits) protected astronauts from the vacuum of space, and from heat, cold, radiation, and meteors. Each astronaut had three tailor-made EMUs: one mission suit, one training suit, and one backup suit.

1. The fabrics were high-tech, but the construction process was conventional and expert workers sewed the seams.

2. The EMU was actually three garments: liquid-cooled underwear, a pressurized suit, and a protective cover.

3. To reduce sweating, cool water circulated through small tubes running through the all-in-one underwear. Sweat was not only uncomfortable, it also misted the helmet visor, blocking vision.

4. Hoses at chest level carried oxygen from the suit through the Portable Life Support System (PLSS), which filtered it to remove carbon dioxide, flatulence, and moisture from sweat.

Apollo space suits had 21 layers.

Small tubes were sewn into the fabric of the underwear.

Technicians pasted a scratchy Velcro pad inside each helmet because astronauts complained that they couldn't scratch their noses.

ESCAPE TOWER

If the Saturn rocket caught on fire on the ground or during launch, engines in the escape tower would ignite. The tower would then carry the Command Module clear of the launch site, and just high enough for its parachutes to open and slow its descent.

Escape tower

The crew crawled into the Lunar Module through this access tunnel.

The Lunar Module linked up to the Command Module at the docking ring.

Nearly 250 nylon strands held the capsule to the landing parachutes.

The heat shield was made up of seven different layers.

Lunar Module pilot

Drogue parachute

The rocket engine had the power of 4,300 cars.

The filling in the honeycomb structure of the walls cooled the craft.

Engine nozzle

SERVICE MODULE

Attached to the base of the Command Module, the tubular Service Module carried supplies of fuel and oxidizer, plus water and oxygen for the crew. Its rocket motor moved the spacecraft into Moon orbit, and powered it back to Earth.

The flight computer had only 32K of memory – today's home computers have 100 times as much.

The Mission Commander and the other astronauts wore their suits during the launch, but later slipped into something more comfortable.

Small jets were positioned all around the spacecraft. Controlling the firing of these rockets enabled the astronauts to turn the craft.

Command Module pilot

Service Module engine

Antennas for transmitting and receiving information from mission control.

LUNAR MODULE

The Lunar Module was the only part of the Apollo 11 mission to land on the moon. On launch, the Lunar Module was attached below the Command and Service Modules (CSM). Once out of Earth orbit, the petal-like doors protecting the Lunar Module fell away. The crew then separated the CSM, turned it upside down and linked up with the exposed Lunar Module. Finally, springs separated the Lunar Module from the third stage.

In the Moon's thin atmosphere the Lunar Module did not need to be streamlined and had an angular, buglike shape.

Apollo spacecraft:

- Escape tower
- Command Module
- Service Module
- Section housing Lunar Module
- Instrument unit
- Third stage
- Interstage ring
- Second stage
- Interstage ring
- First stage

LIFTOFF!

The picture above shows how the three stages of the rocket and the sections of the spacecraft fit together.

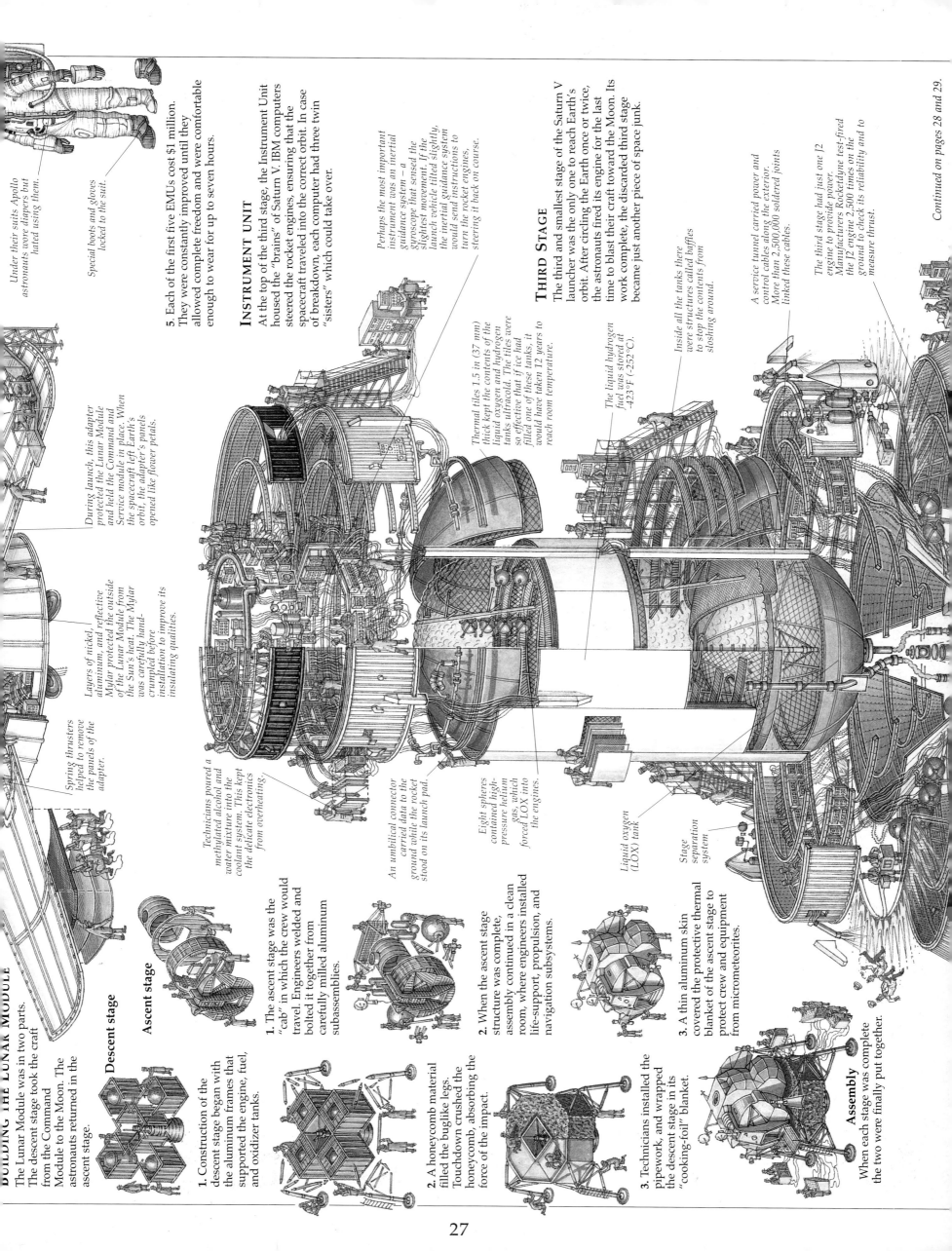

Under their suits Apollo astronauts wore diapers but hated using them.

Special boots and gloves locked to the suit.

5. Each of the first five EMUs cost $1 million. They were constantly improved until they allowed complete freedom and were comfortable enough to wear for up to seven hours.

INSTRUMENT UNIT

At the top of the third stage, the Instrument Unit housed the "brains" of Saturn V. IBM computers steered the rocket engines, ensuring that the spacecraft traveled into the correct orbit. In case of breakdown, each computer had three twin "sisters" which could take over.

Perhaps the most important instrument was an inertial guidance system – a gyroscope that sensed the slightest movement. If the launch vehicle tilted slightly, the inertial guidance system would send instructions to turn the rocket engines, steering it back on course.

THIRD STAGE

The third and smallest stage of the Saturn V launcher was the only one to reach Earth's orbit. After circling the Earth once or twice, the astronauts fired its engine for the last time to blast their craft toward the Moon. Its work complete, the discarded third stage became just another piece of space junk.

The third stage had just one J2 engine to provide power. Manufacturers Rocketdyne test-fired the J2 engine 2,500 times on the ground to check its reliability and to measure thrust.

Continued on pages 28 and 29.

A service tunnel carried power and control cables along the exterior. More than 2,500,000 soldered joints linked these cables.

Inside all the tanks there were structures called baffles to stop the contents from sloshing around.

The liquid hydrogen fuel was stored at -423°F (-252°C).

Thermal tiles 1.5 in (37 mm) thick kept the contents of the liquid oxygen and hydrogen tanks ultracold. The tiles were so effective that if ice had filled one of these tanks, it would have taken 12 years to reach room temperature.

An umbilical connector carried data to the rocket while it stood on its launch pad.

Eight spheres contained high-pressure helium gas, which forced LOX into the engines.

Liquid oxygen (LOX) tank

Stage separation system

BUILDING THE LUNAR MODULE

The Lunar Module was in two parts. The descent stage took the craft from the Command Module to the Moon. The astronauts returned in the ascent stage.

During launch, this adapter protected the Lunar Module and held the Command and Service module in place. When the spacecraft left Earth's orbit, the adapter's panels opened like flower petals.

Layers of nickel, aluminum, and reflective Mylar protected the outside of the Lunar Module from the Sun's heat. The Mylar was carefully hand-crumpled before installation to improve its insulating qualities.

Spring thrusters helped to remove the panels of the adapter.

Technicians poured a methylated alcohol and water mixture into the coolant system. This kept the delicate electronics from overheating.

Descent stage

Ascent stage

1. Construction of the descent stage began with the aluminum frames that supported the engine, fuel, and oxidizer tanks.

1. The ascent stage was the "cab" in which the crew would travel. Engineers welded and bolted it together from carefully milled aluminum subassemblies.

2. A honeycomb material filled the buglike legs. Touchdown crushed the honeycomb, absorbing the force of the impact.

2. When the ascent stage structure was complete, assembly continued in a clean room, where engineers installed life-support, propulsion, and navigation subsystems.

3. Technicians installed the pipework, and wrapped the descent stage in its "cooking-foil" blanket.

3. A thin aluminum skin covered the protective thermal blanket of the ascent stage to protect crew and equipment from micrometeorites.

Assembly

When each stage was complete the two were finally put together.

Continued from pages 26 and 27.

LUNAR ROVER

To enable astronauts to explore a greater area of the Moon's surface, three missions carried an electric buggy called the Lunar Roving Vehicle (LRV). Its appearance and expense caused some American politicians to question "how three golf carts could cost $40 million?"

The third stage had just one J2 engine to provide power. Manufacturers Rocketdyne test-fired the J2 engine 2,500 times on the ground to check its reliability and to measure thrust.

Tiny auxiliary propulsion rockets fine-tuned the spacecraft's position in Earth's orbit.

Workers assembling the tank aligned its rings using sophisticated measuring devices and old-fashioned plumb lines.

1. The LRV's three-piece chassis had to be light, yet strong enough to transport two astronauts, their equipment, and rock samples.

Navigation device

2. A navigation device pointed the direction and distance to the Lunar Module. Such complex equipment raised the cost.

Retrorockets helped separate the rocket's stages when the third stage engine fired.

The wheels had outer rubber treads.

Wire wheels provided a firm grip on the thick dust of the Moon's surface.

3. Manufacturers Boeing made special "tires" using mesh-covered piano wire.

Workers test the folding mechanism.

4. The Rover folded into a box the size of a refrigerator to stow away in the Lunar Module. To unfold and assemble it astronauts simply pulled a cord.

SECOND STAGE

When fuel ran out in the first stage, explosives detached it, and the five second-stage engines ignited. They lifted the Saturn V launcher and its payload – the Apollo spacecraft – to an altitude of 114 miles (184 km).

A "honeycomb" structure, similar to the shape of wax cells in a beehive, made the walls of Saturn V extremely strong. Chester wasn't too sure what to expect, but wore his bee suit, just in case.

1. The fuel and oxidizer in the second-stage tanks weighed as much as three blue whales, yet the tanks had no supporting structure inside. They were built like an egg; in proportion to their diameter, the immensely strong walls were as thin as an eggshell.

2. The huge pipe that refueled the second stage pumped 138 gallons (630 liters) a second – fast enough to fill the fuel tank of a car in just a tenth of a second.

J2 rocket engines burned liquid hydrogen and liquid oxygen.

Interstage ring

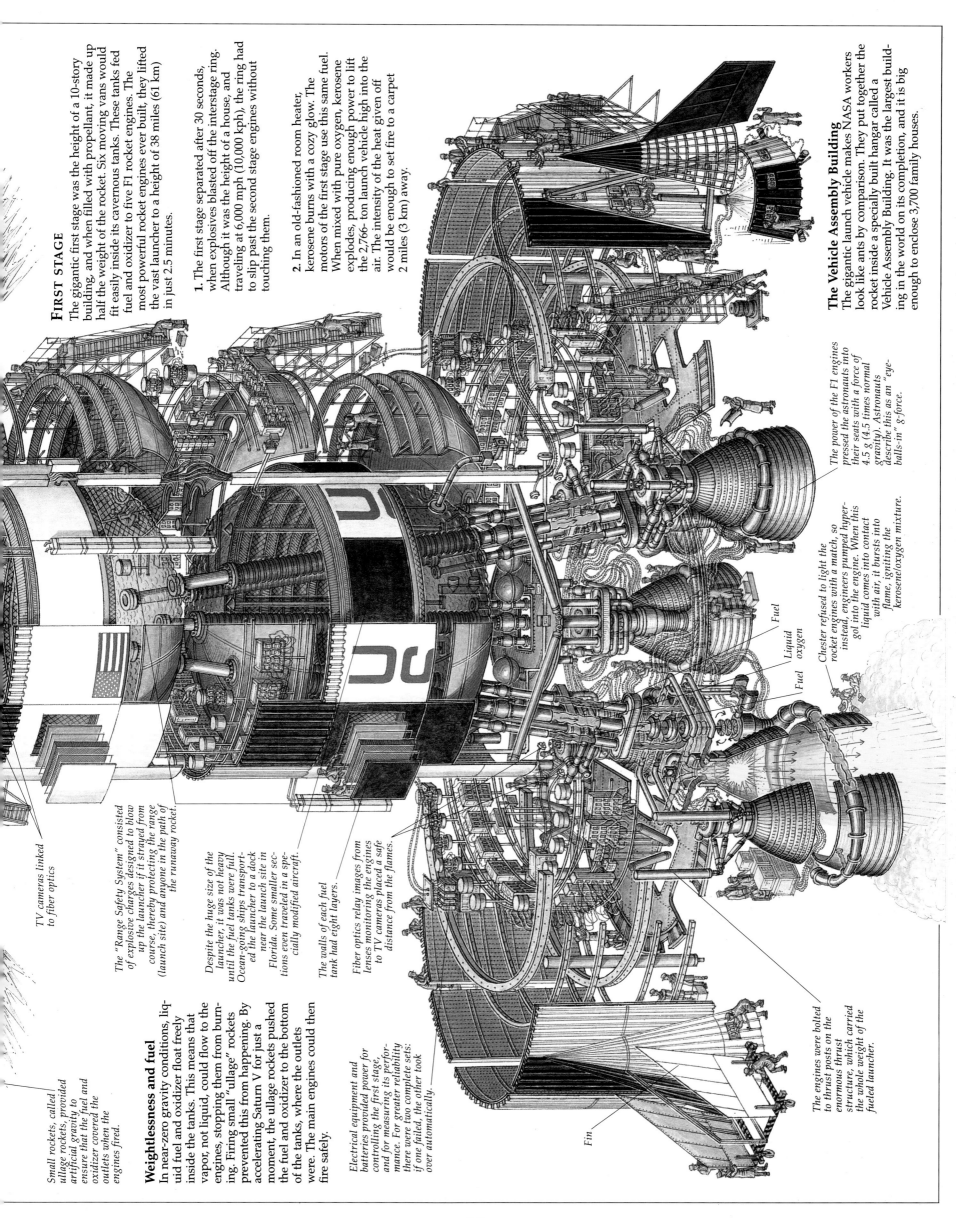

FIRST STAGE

The gigantic first stage was the height of a 10-story building, and when filled with propellant, it made up half the weight of the rocket. Six moving vans would fit easily inside its cavernous tanks. These tanks fed fuel and oxidizer to five F1 rocket engines. The most powerful rocket engines ever built, they lifted the vast launcher to a height of 38 miles (61 km) in just 2.5 minutes.

1. The first stage separated after 30 seconds, when explosives blasted off the interstage ring. Although it was the height of a house, and traveling at 6,000 mph (10,000 kph), the ring had to slip past the second stage engines without touching them.

2. In an old-fashioned room heater, kerosene burns with a cozy glow. The motors of the first stage use this same fuel. When mixed with pure oxygen, kerosene explodes, producing enough power to lift the 2,766- ton launch vehicle high into the air. The intensity of the heat given off would be enough to set fire to a carpet 2 miles (3 km) away.

The Vehicle Assembly Building
The gigantic launch vehicle makes NASA workers look like ants by comparison. They put together the whole rocket inside a specially built hangar called a Vehicle Assembly Building. It was the largest building in the world on its completion, and it is big enough to enclose 3,700 family houses.

The power of the F1 engines pressed the astronauts into their seats with a force of 4.5 g (4.5 times normal gravity). Astronauts describe this as an "eye-balls-in" g-force.

Chester refused to light the rocket engines with a match, so instead, engineers pumped hypergol into the engine. When this liquid comes into contact with air, it bursts into flame, igniting the kerosene/oxygen mixture.

Fuel

Liquid oxygen

Fuel

Small rockets, called ullage rockets, provided artificial gravity to ensure that the fuel and oxidizer covered the outlets when the engines fired.

Weightlessness and fuel
In near-zero gravity conditions, liquid fuel and oxidizer float freely inside the tanks. This means that vapor, not liquid, could flow to the engines, stopping them from burning. Firing small "ullage" rockets prevented this from happening. By accelerating Saturn V for just a moment, the ullage rockets pushed the fuel and oxidizer to the bottom of the tanks, where the outlets were. The main engines could then fire safely.

Electrical equipment and batteries provided power for controlling the first stage, and for measuring its performance. For greater reliability there were two complete sets: if one failed, the other took over automatically.

Fiber optics relay images from lenses monitoring the engines to TV cameras placed a safe distance from the flames.

The walls of each fuel tank had eight layers.

Despite the huge size of the launcher, it was not heavy until the fuel tanks were full. Ocean-going ships transported the launcher to a dock near the launch site in Florida. Some smaller sections even traveled in a specially modified aircraft.

The "Range Safety System" consisted of explosive charges designed to blow up the launcher if it strayed from course, thereby protecting the range (launch site) and anyone in the path of the runaway rocket.

TV cameras linked to fiber optics

The engines were bolted to thrust posts on the enormous thrust structure, which carried the whole weight of the fueled launcher.

Fin

SPACE STATION

Satellite capture
One of the main uses of the space station is the repair of damaged satellites. The crew uses the remote manipulator arm to capture the satellite, or to transfer it from the *Teleoperator* robot that collects the satellite from a distant orbit.

WHICH WAY IS UP? HERE ON EARTH, THE ANSWER IS EASY. BUT TO AN ASTRONAUT on board a space station, it's a silly question. "Standing up" or "putting down a book" don't mean very much when everything is weightless. We get a sense of up and down from gravity. Scientists on the space station call this weightlessness "microgravity." They plan to use it to make ultrapure crystals, or exotic alloys (mixtures) of metals. Microgravity can be a problem, though. Walking is hard when there's no gravity to press your feet against the "floor" and keep the coffee in the cup. American and Russian astronauts have found solutions to these problems and in December 1998 they began assembling a vast International Space Station 250 miles (400 km) above the Earth. When complete, it may look something like this.

Remote manipulator arm

Teleoperator robot

Spaceplane
To travel between the space station and Earth, European crews use a spaceplane. Like the space shuttle, this rides into space on top of a rocket, and then flies back like a plane.

Bags of trash are collected to be carried back to Earth

CREW AND SUPPLIES SHUTTLE – USA

Cockpit controls

Forward reaction-control jets

Landing gear

Air purification
Lithium hydroxide cartridges purify the air in the cabins. Condensing the moisture from the astronauts' breath provides them with drinking water.

HEALTHCARE/HOSPITAL MODULE – RUSSIA

Solar concentrators

Solar concentrators
Solar concentrators focus sunlight on water-filled tubes. The boiling water spins turbines that power generators.

Solar array

Radiators disperse heat from inside space station

Space junk
Solar arrays convert sunlight into valuable electricity. Their size makes them vulnerable to damage by orbiting debris left by earlier space missions. The station orbits at 5 miles (8 km) a second, and at this speed space junk just half the size of a pea does as much damage as a bowling ball traveling at 60 miles (100 km) an hour on Earth. There are more than 70,000 pieces of space junk this size in orbit.

Soyuz descent module

SCIENTIFIC MODULE – RUSSIA

Soyuz orbital module

Entering station at Russian end

TV camera monitors exterior

Remote manipulator arm
Astronauts can use the remote manipulator arm to move themselves toward objects away from the station.

Spektr satellite for geophysical studies

Cosmonaut on EVA mission

Docking port

Large airlock for EVA

Which way is up?
To give astronauts a sense of standing upright, each module has a "floor," two "walls," and a "ceiling." Lights are always in the ceiling, and frequently-needed supplies and controls are in the walls.

Docking maneuver
Cosmonauts are experts at docking maneuvers: they have been using the technique to supply and re-crew their space stations since the 1960s. There are up to six ports where modules can dock.

Hatch

MAINTENANCE MODULE

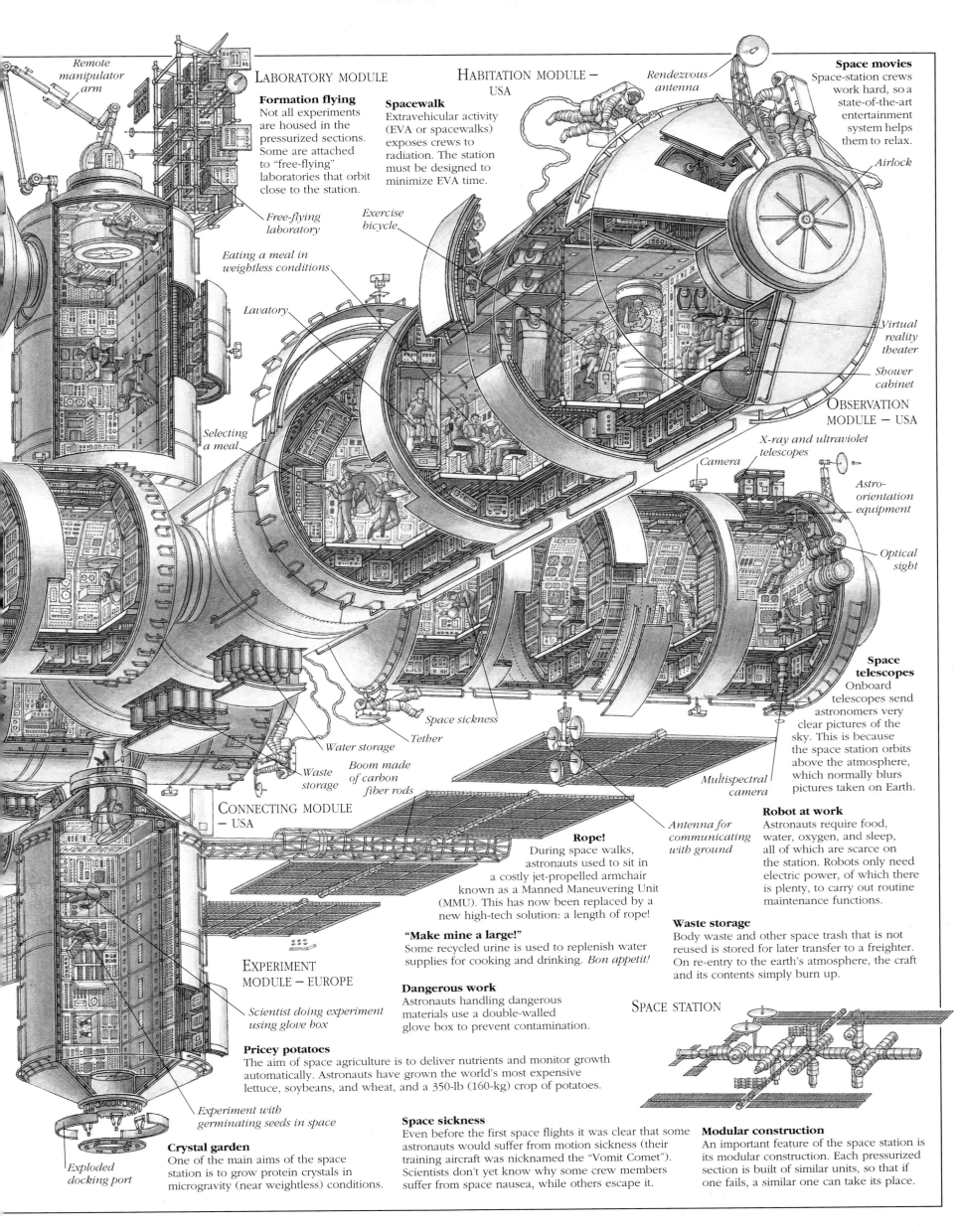

Remote manipulator arm

LABORATORY MODULE

Formation flying
Not all experiments are housed in the pressurized sections. Some are attached to "free-flying" laboratories that orbit close to the station.

Free-flying laboratory

Eating a meal in weightless conditions

Lavatory

Selecting a meal

HABITATION MODULE – USA

Spacewalk
Extravehicular activity (EVA or spacewalks) exposes crews to radiation. The station must be designed to minimize EVA time.

Exercise bicycle

Rendezvous antenna

Space movies
Space-station crews work hard, so a state-of-the-art entertainment system helps them to relax.

Airlock

Virtual reality theater

Shower cabinet

OBSERVATION MODULE – USA

X-ray and ultraviolet telescopes

Camera

Astro-orientation equipment

Optical sight

Space sickness

Tether

Water storage

Waste storage

Boom made of carbon fiber rods

CONNECTING MODULE – USA

Multispectral camera

Space telescopes
Onboard telescopes send astronomers very clear pictures of the sky. This is because the space station orbits above the atmosphere, which normally blurs pictures taken on Earth.

Antenna for communicating with ground

Rope!
During space walks, astronauts used to sit in a costly jet-propelled armchair known as a Manned Maneuvering Unit (MMU). This has now been replaced by a new high-tech solution: a length of rope!

"Make mine a large!"
Some recycled urine is used to replenish water supplies for cooking and drinking. *Bon appetit!*

Dangerous work
Astronauts handling dangerous materials use a double-walled glove box to prevent contamination.

Robot at work
Astronauts require food, water, oxygen, and sleep, all of which are scarce on the station. Robots only need electric power, of which there is plenty, to carry out routine maintenance functions.

Waste storage
Body waste and other space trash that is not reused is stored for later transfer to a freighter. On re-entry to the earth's atmosphere, the craft and its contents simply burn up.

SPACE STATION

EXPERIMENT MODULE – EUROPE

Scientist doing experiment using glove box

Pricey potatoes
The aim of space agriculture is to deliver nutrients and monitor growth automatically. Astronauts have grown the world's most expensive lettuce, soybeans, and wheat, and a 350-lb (160-kg) crop of potatoes.

Experiment with germinating seeds in space

Crystal garden
One of the main aims of the space station is to grow protein crystals in microgravity (near weightless) conditions.

Exploded docking port

Space sickness
Even before the first space flights it was clear that some astronauts would suffer from motion sickness (their training aircraft was nicknamed the "Vomit Comet"). Scientists don't yet know why some crew members suffer from space nausea, while others escape it.

Modular construction
An important feature of the space station is its modular construction. Each pressurized section is built of similar units, so that if one fails, a similar one can take its place.

CITY CROSS-SECTION

TIME MACHINES REALLY DO EXIST. ARCHAEOLOGISTS – SCIENTISTS WHO study how our ancestors lived – use them to travel back into the past. They call their time machines "shovels." With the aid of shovels, trowels, and even soft brushes, archaeologists carefully remove layer after layer of soil. Digging deeper and deeper, they travel back in time, for they know that, at any one spot, the objects close to the surface are more recent; those buried deepest are the oldest. As archaeologists sift through what remains of past peoples, they piece together pictures of vanished ages. Far below the city streets lies solid rock. Now paleontologists take over the journey. They study fossils – stone casts of the animals and plants from the past. From fossils they can judge what life was like before humans arrived. The oldest rocks of all contain no fossils. Formed billions of years ago, before life began, they are a reminder that our Earth was once a ball of dust spinning in cold black space.

TODAY

Under the sidewalk
Beneath pedestrians' feet run the arteries of the city. Natural gas and water flow along pipes, and electric cables supply power. Sewers take waste away from buildings, and communications cables ferry data and telephone calls.

Dangerous digging
Workers on any city building site have to thread their way carefully through the maze of underground pipes and cable, but they have another hazard to contend with in some parts of the world: unexploded bombs.

Aerial bombing
World War II (1939–45) was the first war in which aerial bombardment played a major part. Bombs killed few citizens, but destroyed many houses: for each death in London, England, 35 people became homeless.

WAR

High-rise buildings
Skyscrapers give the modern city a gap-toothed horizon. Two innovations made them possible. In 1854 American Elisha Otis (1811–1861) created the first safe elevators; they eliminated exhausting climbs for top-floor employees of even the highest building. Cheap steel-making was the other breakthrough. Instead of using thick walls to support upper storys, a steel skeleton carried the weight.

Multistory parking garage
Early multistory parking garages spared the driver the hassle of driving up and down winding ramps: instead an elevator carried the vehicle to its space.

Winding ramp

Subway system
Because of traffic congestion, most major capital cities have created subway networks. London's Underground, built in 1863, is the oldest and the biggest, with 255 miles (411 km) of track underground and on the surface.

Traffic circle

Homeless people sheltering in cardboard boxes

Subway train in tunnel

Missed!
World War II bombs were "gravity bombs": They just fell to the ground when the bomber released them. Bombing was a hit-and-miss affair, and more than 90 percent missed the target.

Bomb damage

Bomb

Factories
Europe's population grew rapidly in the 18th century, and towns grew especially fast. People moved to cities to find work as machine operators in the new factories.

Fire engine

Bomb crater

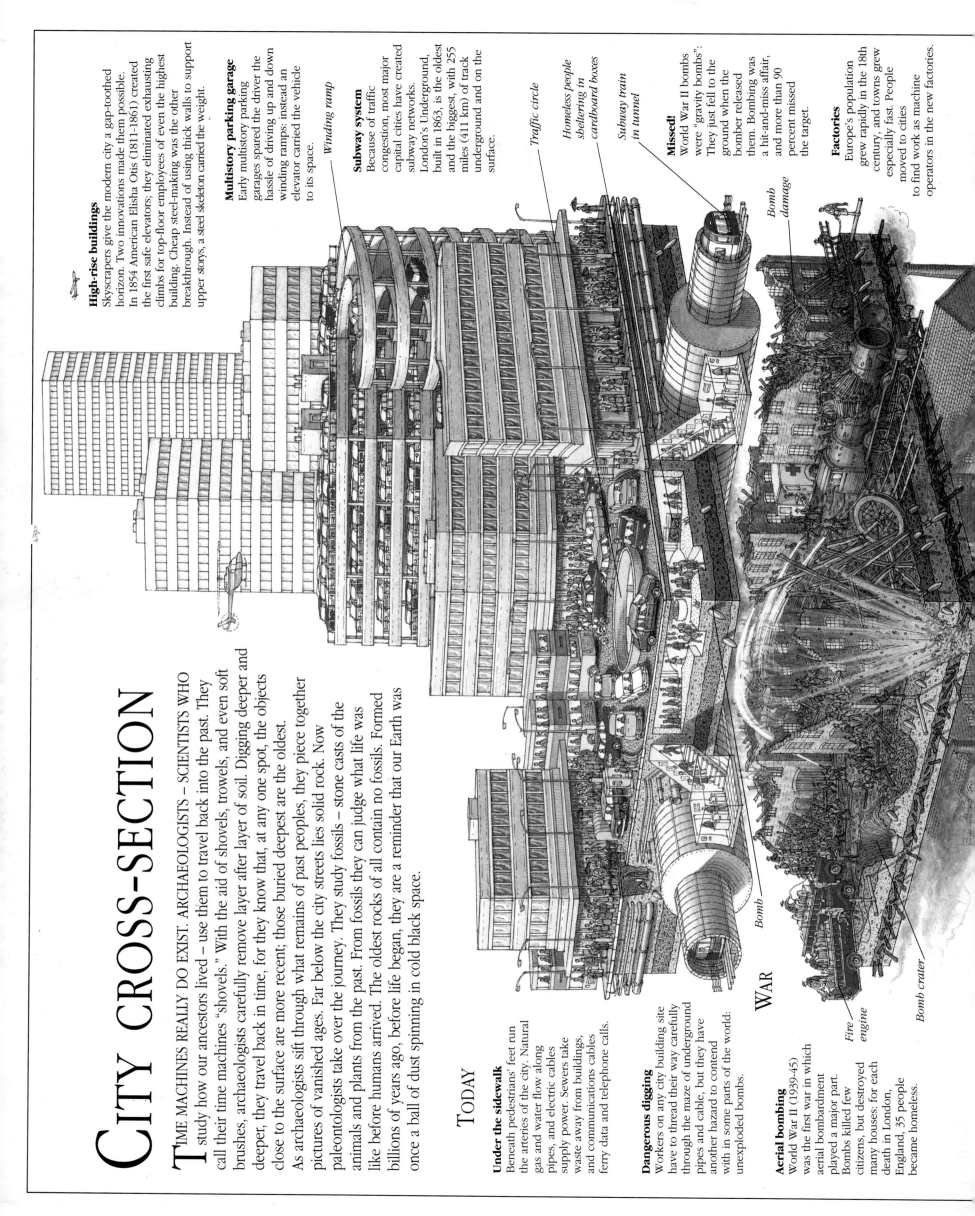

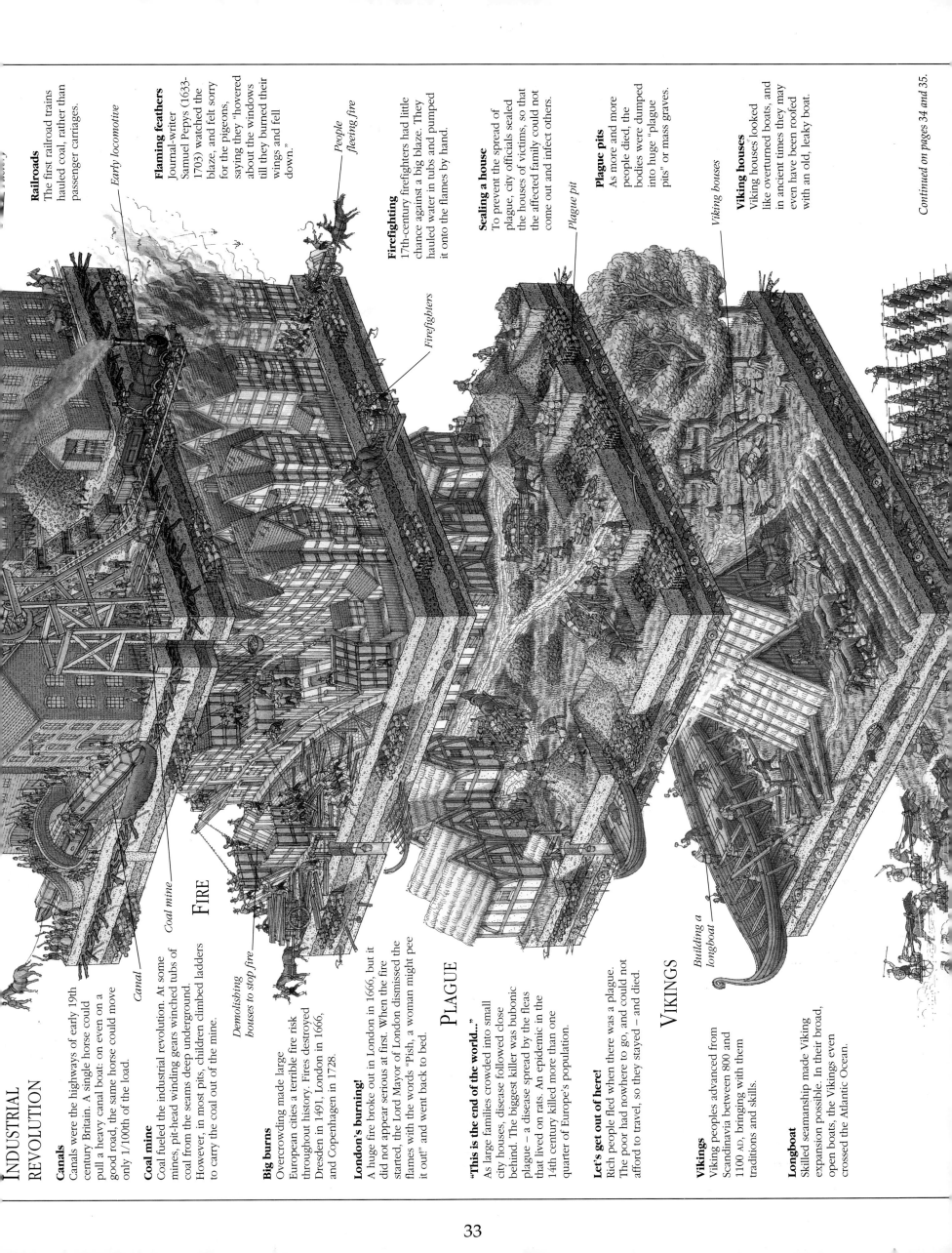

INDUSTRIAL REVOLUTION

Canals
Canals were the highways of early 19th century Britain. A single horse could pull a heavy canal boat: on even on a good road, the same horse could move only 1/100th of the load.

Coal mine
Coal fueled the industrial revolution. At some mines, pit-head winding gears winched tubs of coal from the seams deep underground. However, in most pits, children climbed ladders to carry the coal out of the mine.

Big burns
Overcrowding made large European cities a terrible fire risk throughout history. Fires destroyed Dresden in 1491, London in 1666, and Copenhagen in 1728.

London's burning!
A huge fire broke out in London in 1666, but it did not appear serious at first. When the fire started, the Lord Mayor of London dismissed the flames with the words "Pish, a woman might pee it out!" and went back to bed.

FIRE

"This is the end of the world..."
As large families crowded into small city houses, disease followed close behind. The biggest killer was bubonic plague – a disease spread by the fleas that lived on rats. An epidemic in the 14th century killed more than one quarter of Europe's population.

Let's get out of here!
Rich people fled when there was a plague. The poor had nowhere to go, and could not afford to travel, so they stayed – and died.

PLAGUE

Vikings
Viking peoples advanced from Scandinavia between 800 and 1100 AD, bringing with them traditions and skills.

Longboat
Skilled seamanship made Viking expansion possible. In their broad, open boats, the Vikings even crossed the Atlantic Ocean.

VIKINGS

Railroads
The first railroad trains hauled coal, rather than passenger carriages.

Early locomotive

Flaming feathers
Journal-writer Samuel Pepys (1633-1703) watched the blaze, and felt sorry for the pigeons, saying they "hovered about the windows till they burned their wings and fell down."

People fleeing fire

Firefighting
17th-century firefighters had little chance against a big blaze. They hauled water in tubs and pumped it onto the flames by hand.

Firefighters

Sealing a house
To prevent the spread of plague, city officials sealed the houses of victims, so that the affected family could not come out and infect others.

Plague pit

Plague pits
As more and more people died, the bodies were dumped into huge "plague pits" or mass graves.

Viking houses
Viking houses looked like overturned boats, and in ancient times they may even have been roofed with an old, leaky boat.

Viking houses

Canal

Coal mine

Demolishing houses to stop fire

Building a longboat

Continued on pages 34 and 35.

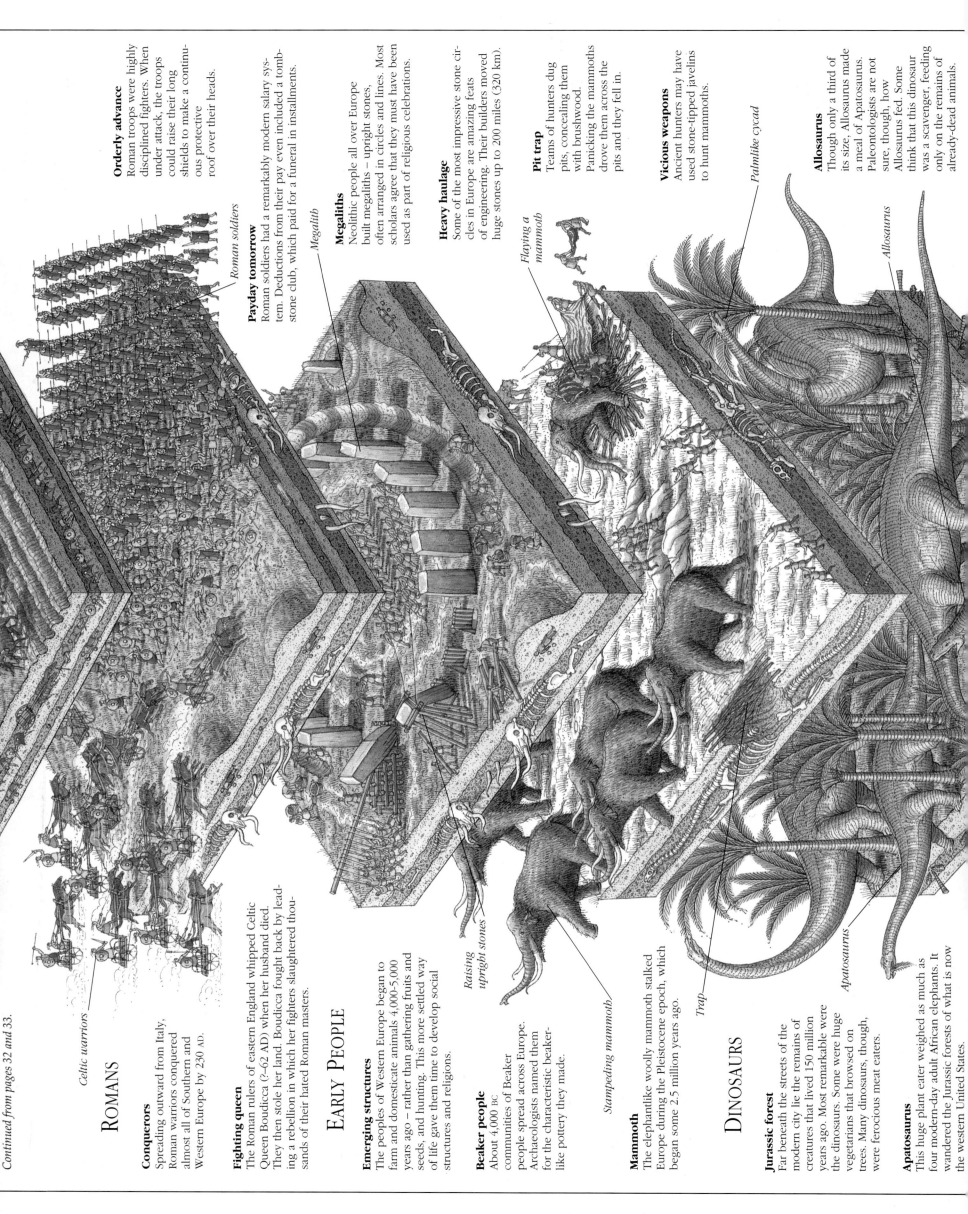

Continued from pages 32 and 33.

Celtic warriors

ROMANS

Conquerors

Spreading outward from Italy, Roman warriors conquered almost all of Southern and Western Europe by 230 AD.

Fighting queen

The Roman rulers of eastern England whipped Celtic Queen Boudicca (?–62 AD) when her husband died. They then stole her land. Boudicca fought back by leading a rebellion in which her fighters slaughtered thousands of their hated Roman masters.

EARLY PEOPLE

Emerging structures

The peoples of Western Europe began to farm and domesticate animals 4,000–5,000 years ago – rather than gathering fruits and seeds, and hunting. This more settled way of life gave them time to develop social structures and religions.

Raising upright stones

Beaker people

About 4,000 BC communities of Beaker people spread across Europe. Archaeologists named them for the characteristic beaker-like pottery they made.

Stampeding mammoth

Mammoth

The elephantlike woolly mammoth stalked Europe during the Pleistocene epoch, which began some 2.5 million years ago.

DINOSAURS

Jurassic forest

Far beneath the streets of the modern city lie the remains of creatures that lived 150 million years ago. Most remarkable were the dinosaurs. Some were huge vegetarians that browsed on trees. Many dinosaurs, though, were ferocious meat eaters.

Apatosaurus

This huge plant eater weighed as much as four modern-day adult African elephants. It wandered the Jurassic forests of what is now the western United States.

Orderly advance

Roman troops were highly disciplined fighters. When under attack, the troops could raise their long shields to make a continuous protective roof over their heads.

Roman soldiers

Payday tomorrow

Roman soldiers had a remarkably modern salary system. Deductions from their pay even included a tombstone club, which paid for a funeral in installments.

Megalith

Megaliths

Neolithic people all over Europe built megaliths – upright stones, often arranged in circles and lines. Most scholars agree that they must have been used as part of religious celebrations.

Heavy haulage

Some of the most impressive stone circles in Europe are amazing feats of engineering. Their builders moved huge stones up to 200 miles (320 km).

Flaying a mammoth

Pit trap

Teams of hunters dug pits, concealing them with brushwood. Panicking the mammoths drove them across the pits and they fell in.

Vicious weapons

Ancient hunters may have used stone-tipped javelins to hunt mammoths.

Palmlike cycad

Allosaurus

Though only a third of its size, Allosaurus made a meal of Apatosaurus. Paleontologists are not sure, though, how Allosaurus fed. Some think that this dinosaur was a scavenger, feeding only on the remains of already-dead animals.

Allosaurus

Apatosaurus

Trap

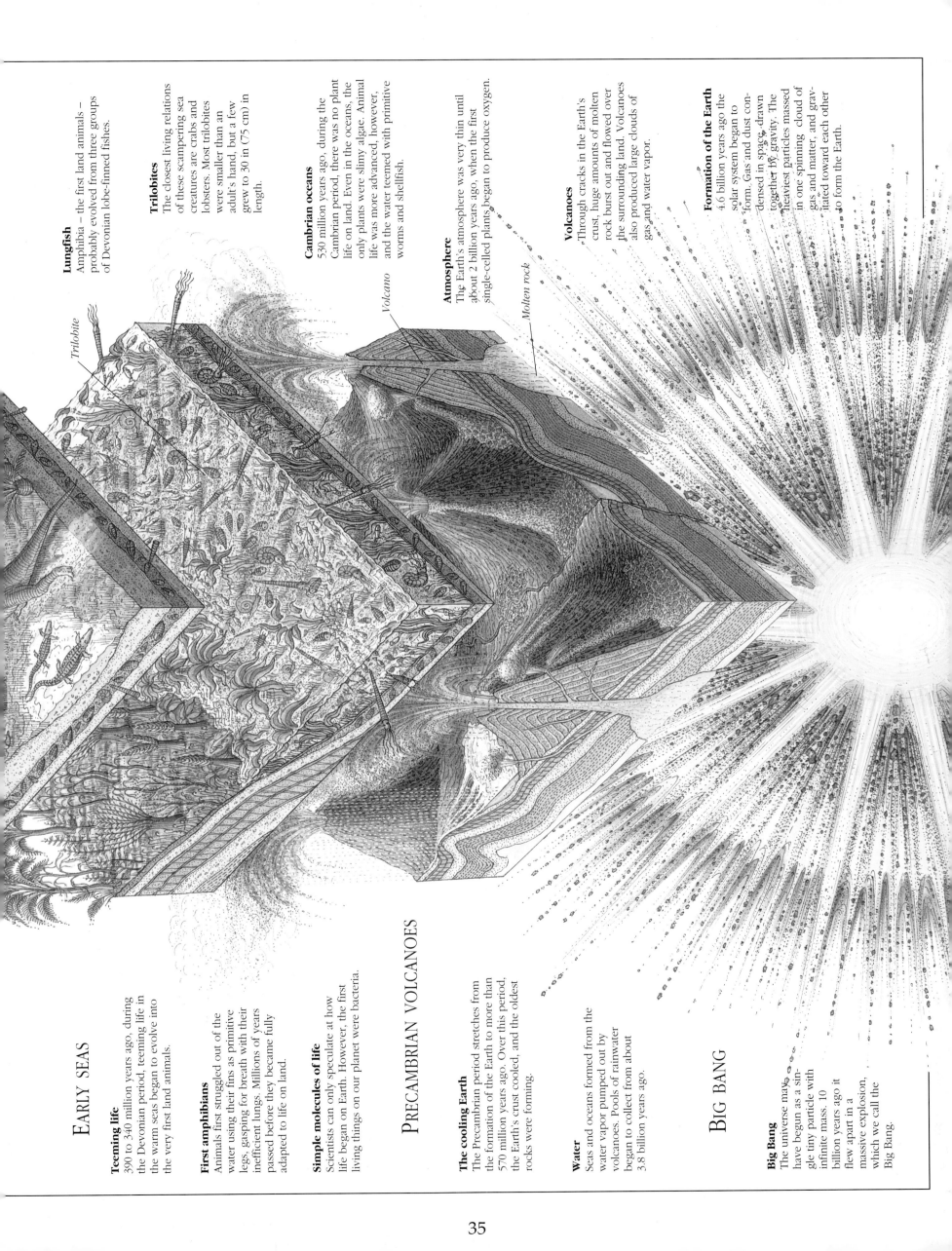

EARLY SEAS

Teeming life
390 to 340 million years ago, during the Devonian period, teeming life in the warm seas began to evolve into the very first land animals.

First amphibians
Animals first struggled out of the water using their fins as primitive legs, gasping for breath with their inefficient lungs. Millions of years passed before they became fully adapted to life on land.

Simple molecules of life
Scientists can only speculate at how life began on Earth. However, the first living things on our planet were bacteria.

PRECAMBRIAN VOLCANOES

The cooling Earth
The Precambrian period stretches from the formation of the Earth to more than 570 million years ago. Over this period, the Earth's crust cooled, and the oldest rocks were forming.

Water
Seas and oceans formed from the water vapor pumped out by volcanoes. Pools of rainwater began to collect from about 3.8 billion years ago.

BIG BANG

Big Bang
The universe may have begun as a single tiny particle with infinite mass. 10 billion years ago it flew apart in a massive explosion, which we call the Big Bang.

Lungfish
Amphibia – the first land animals – probably evolved from three groups of Devonian lobe-finned fishes.

Trilobites
The closest living relations of these scampering sea creatures are crabs and lobsters. Most trilobites were smaller than an adult's hand, but a few grew to 30 in (75 cm) in length.

Cambrian oceans
530 million years ago, during the Cambrian period, there was no plant life on land. Even in the oceans, the only plants were slimy algae. Animal life was more advanced, however, and the water teemed with primitive worms and shellfish.

Volcano

Atmosphere
The Earth's atmosphere was very thin until about 2 billion years ago, when the first single-celled plants began to produce oxygen.

Molten rock

Volcanoes
Through cracks in the Earth's crust, huge amounts of molten rock burst out and flowed over the surrounding land. Volcanoes also produced large clouds of gas and water vapor.

Formation of the Earth
4.6 billion years ago the solar system began to form. Gas and dust condensed in space, drawn together by gravity. The heaviest particles massed in one spinning cloud of gas and matter, and gravitated toward each other to form the Earth.

Trilobite

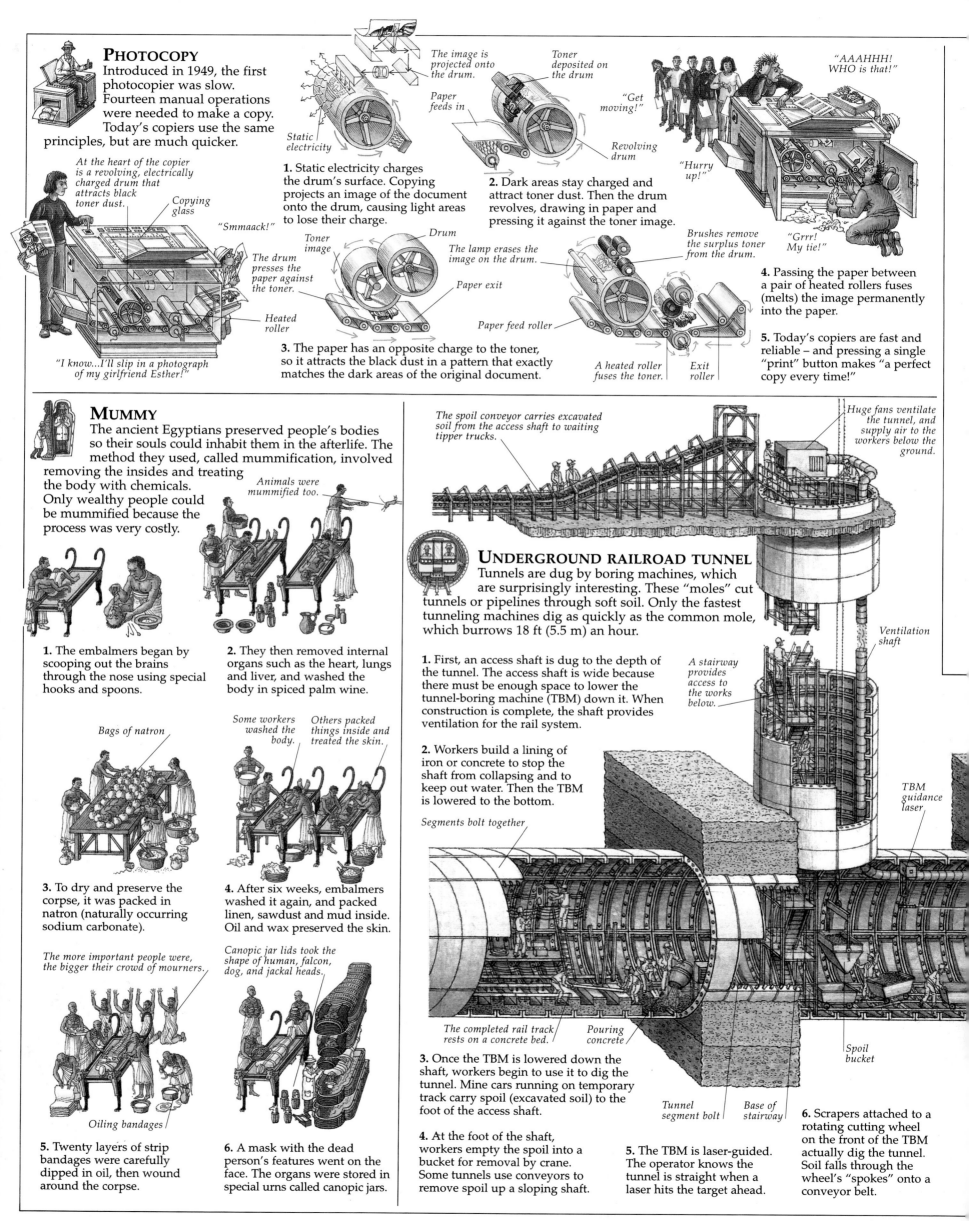

PHOTOCOPY

Introduced in 1949, the first photocopier was slow. Fourteen manual operations were needed to make a copy. Today's copiers use the same principles, but are much quicker.

At the heart of the copier is a revolving, electrically charged drum that attracts black toner dust.

Copying glass

"Smmaack!"

The drum presses the paper against the toner.

Toner image

Drum

Heated roller

"I know...I'll slip in a photograph of my girlfriend Esther!"

Static electricity

The image is projected onto the drum.

Paper feeds in

The lamp erases the image on the drum.

Paper exit

Paper feed roller

1. Static electricity charges the drum's surface. Copying projects an image of the document onto the drum, causing light areas to lose their charge.

3. The paper has an opposite charge to the toner, so it attracts the black dust in a pattern that exactly matches the dark areas of the original document.

Toner deposited on the drum

Revolving drum

"Get moving!"

"Hurry up!"

2. Dark areas stay charged and attract toner dust. Then the drum revolves, drawing in paper and pressing it against the toner image.

Brushes remove the surplus toner from the drum.

A heated roller fuses the toner.

Exit roller

"AAAHHH! WHO is that!"

"Grrr! My tie!"

4. Passing the paper between a pair of heated rollers fuses (melts) the image permanently into the paper.

5. Today's copiers are fast and reliable – and pressing a single "print" button makes "a perfect copy every time!"

MUMMY

The ancient Egyptians preserved people's bodies so their souls could inhabit them in the afterlife. The method they used, called mummification, involved removing the insides and treating the body with chemicals. Only wealthy people could be mummified because the process was very costly.

Animals were mummified too.

1. The embalmers began by scooping out the brains through the nose using special hooks and spoons.

2. They then removed internal organs such as the heart, lungs and liver, and washed the body in spiced palm wine.

Bags of natron

Some workers washed the body.

Others packed things inside and treated the skin.

3. To dry and preserve the corpse, it was packed in natron (naturally occurring sodium carbonate).

4. After six weeks, embalmers washed it again, and packed linen, sawdust and mud inside. Oil and wax preserved the skin.

The more important people were, the bigger their crowd of mourners.

Canopic jar lids took the shape of human, falcon, dog, and jackal heads.

Oiling bandages

5. Twenty layers of strip bandages were carefully dipped in oil, then wound around the corpse.

6. A mask with the dead person's features went on the face. The organs were stored in special urns called canopic jars.

UNDERGROUND RAILROAD TUNNEL

Tunnels are dug by boring machines, which are surprisingly interesting. These "moles" cut tunnels or pipelines through soft soil. Only the fastest tunneling machines dig as quickly as the common mole, which burrows 18 ft (5.5 m) an hour.

The spoil conveyor carries excavated soil from the access shaft to waiting tipper trucks.

Huge fans ventilate the tunnel, and supply air to the workers below the ground.

A stairway provides access to the works below.

Ventilation shaft

TBM guidance laser

Segments bolt together

The completed rail track rests on a concrete bed.

Pouring concrete

Tunnel segment bolt

Base of stairway

Spoil bucket

1. First, an access shaft is dug to the depth of the tunnel. The access shaft is wide because there must be enough space to lower the tunnel-boring machine (TBM) down it. When construction is complete, the shaft provides ventilation for the rail system.

2. Workers build a lining of iron or concrete to stop the shaft from collapsing and to keep out water. Then the TBM is lowered to the bottom.

3. Once the TBM is lowered down the shaft, workers begin to use it to dig the tunnel. Mine cars running on temporary track carry spoil (excavated soil) to the foot of the access shaft.

4. At the foot of the shaft, workers empty the spoil into a bucket for removal by crane. Some tunnels use conveyors to remove spoil up a sloping shaft.

5. The TBM is laser-guided. The operator knows the tunnel is straight when a laser hits the target ahead.

6. Scrapers attached to a rotating cutting wheel on the front of the TBM actually dig the tunnel. Soil falls through the wheel's "spokes" onto a conveyor belt.

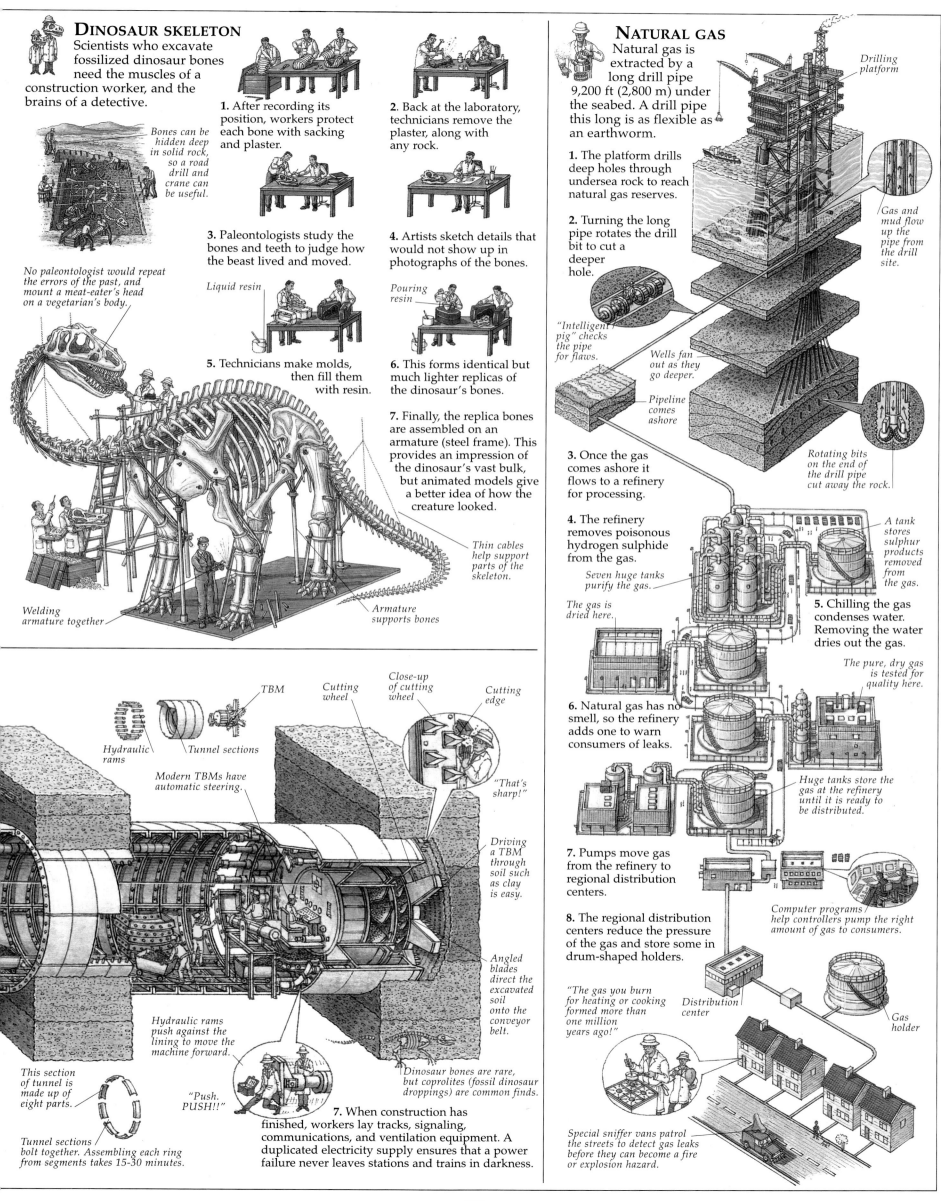

DINOSAUR SKELETON

Scientists who excavate fossilized dinosaur bones need the muscles of a construction worker, and the brains of a detective.

Bones can be hidden deep in solid rock, so a road drill and crane can be useful.

No paleontologist would repeat the errors of the past, and mount a meat-eater's head on a vegetarian's body.

1. After recording its position, workers protect each bone with sacking and plaster.

2. Back at the laboratory, technicians remove the plaster, along with any rock.

3. Paleontologists study the bones and teeth to judge how the beast lived and moved.

4. Artists sketch details that would not show up in photographs of the bones.

Liquid resin

Pouring resin

5. Technicians make molds, then fill them with resin.

6. This forms identical but much lighter replicas of the dinosaur's bones.

7. Finally, the replica bones are assembled on an armature (steel frame). This provides an impression of the dinosaur's vast bulk, but animated models give a better idea of how the creature looked.

Thin cables help support parts of the skeleton.

Welding armature together

Armature supports bones

NATURAL GAS

Natural gas is extracted by a long drill pipe 9,200 ft (2,800 m) under the seabed. A drill pipe this long is as flexible as an earthworm.

Drilling platform

1. The platform drills deep holes through undersea rock to reach natural gas reserves.

2. Turning the long pipe rotates the drill bit to cut a deeper hole.

Gas and mud flow up the pipe from the drill site.

"Intelligent pig" checks the pipe for flaws.

Wells fan out as they go deeper.

Pipeline comes ashore

Rotating bits on the end of the drill pipe cut away the rock.

3. Once the gas comes ashore it flows to a refinery for processing.

4. The refinery removes poisonous hydrogen sulphide from the gas.

Seven huge tanks purify the gas.

The gas is dried here.

A tank stores sulphur products removed from the gas.

5. Chilling the gas condenses water. Removing the water dries out the gas.

The pure, dry gas is tested for quality here.

6. Natural gas has no smell, so the refinery adds one to warn consumers of leaks.

Huge tanks store the gas at the refinery until it is ready to be distributed.

7. Pumps move gas from the refinery to regional distribution centers.

8. The regional distribution centers reduce the pressure of the gas and store some in drum-shaped holders.

Computer programs help controllers pump the right amount of gas to consumers.

"The gas you burn for heating or cooking formed more than one million years ago!"

Distribution center

Gas holder

Special sniffer vans patrol the streets to detect gas leaks before they can become a fire or explosion hazard.

TBM

Cutting wheel

Close-up of cutting wheel

Cutting edge

Hydraulic rams

Tunnel sections

Modern TBMs have automatic steering.

"That's sharp!"

Driving a TBM through soil such as clay is easy.

Hydraulic rams push against the lining to move the machine forward.

Angled blades direct the excavated soil onto the conveyor belt.

This section of tunnel is made up of eight parts.

Tunnel sections bolt together. Assembling each ring from segments takes 15-30 minutes.

"Push. PUSH!!"

Dinosaur bones are rare, but coprolites (fossil dinosaur droppings) are common finds.

7. When construction has finished, workers lay tracks, signaling, communications, and ventilation equipment. A duplicated electricity supply ensures that a power failure never leaves stations and trains in darkness.

Fire!

BURNING IN A CITY, FIRE IS LIKE A DANGEROUS MONSTER. You can often smell the hot-tempered beast before you see it. As a fire grows by consuming everything in its path you hear its voice, first crackling then roaring in your ears. For urban residents, the fire monster is an old enemy, and one that has never been far away.

Today we're learning how to control the monster and curb its appetite. At home, simple safety precautions such as inexpensive smoke detectors warn of danger. If flames take hold, an emergency call brings brave firefighters rushing to the blaze. Water from their hoses cools the flames, and creates steam that starves the fire of the air it needs to burn.

Aerial ladder

Don't panic
Recent research suggests that fire rarely causes panic. Though aware of the danger, people usually help each other escape. A stampede to safety happens only when victims believe the fire is about to cut off their escape route.

Anybody here?
Firefighters must search every room to check that there's nobody unconscious, asleep, or perhaps too old or ill to move.

Getting hoses
Elevator shafts in new buildings are fire protected, so firefighters use them to rush hoses to floors where they are needed.

Hydraulic platform

Hydraulic snorkel

Bad buttons
Some elevator buttons don't need pressing; the heat of your hand calls the elevator. In a fire, they're fatal – the heat calls the elevator to the burning floor.

Damp risers
In most nations, tall buildings must have damp risers – pipes that channel water to hydrants on each floor. Firefighters connect hoses directly to the damp riser.

Spreading smoke
An elevator shaft can channel choking smoke everywhere. Newer buildings now incorporate pressurizing fans that force air into the elevator shaft, keeping it free of smoke.

Helicopter rescues victims

Sprinkler

Chopper rescue
When the tallest buildings catch on fire, rescue by helicopter may be the only escape for those trapped on the upper floors.

Alarming facts
Fire alarms should alert everyone in the building to the danger. Nevertheless, experience shows that when there are no other signs of fire, some people don't recognize the alarm signal, or they just prefer to ignore it.

Aerial platform rescues people

In the dark
In a smoke-filled room, visibility is zero, and firefighters have to navigate by touch alone. As they search, they reel out a cord, so that they can retrace their steps to safety.

Sprinklers at work
By spraying a fire with water, automatic sprinklers can put out flames before they take hold. Room temperatures much higher than 140°F (60°C) fracture a soft metal strip or a tiny glass bulb on the sprinkler nozzle; water then sprays out, covering about 130 sq ft (12 sq m).

Smoke rises through ventilating shafts

Save my pianos!
Automatic sprinklers are not new. Henry S. Parmelee of Connecticut invented them in 1875 to protect his piano factory from fire. New England cotton mills made them a success – the fibers they processed made the mills a big fire risk, and without a sprinkler system, mill owners couldn't get fire insurance.

Fog nozzle sprays wide area

A long way down
The tallest turntable ladders reach floors up to 165 ft (50 m) above the ground.

Fireboat
When a dockside building bursts into flames, fire authorities can call on the city fireboat to help. It more often sprays water or foam on burning ships.

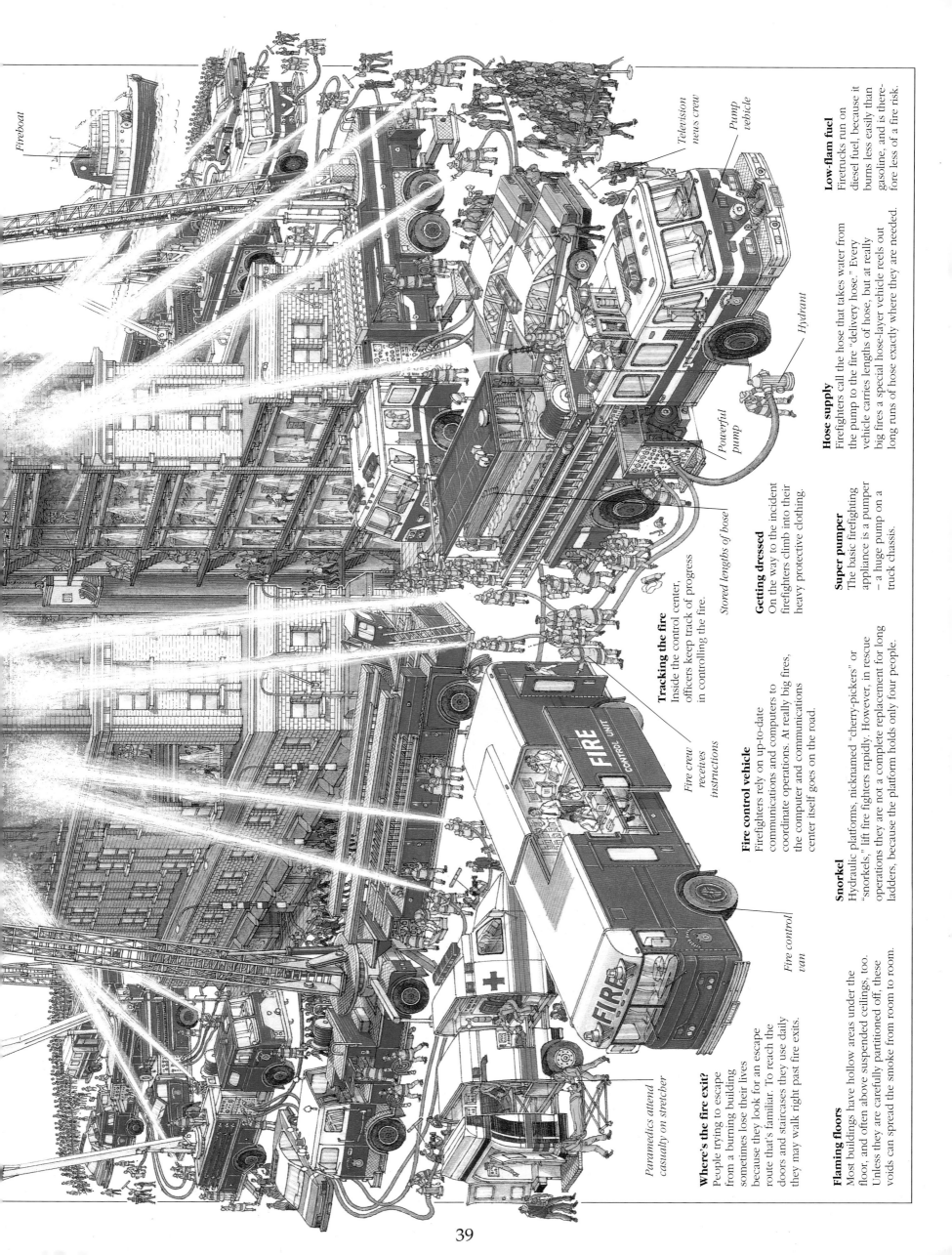

Fireboat

Television news crew

Pump vehicle

Low-flam fuel
Firetrucks run on diesel fuel, because it burns less easily than gasoline, and is therefore less of a fire risk.

Hydrant

Hose supply
Firefighters call the hose that takes water from the pump to the fire "delivery hose." Every vehicle carries lengths of hose, but at really big fires a special hose-layer vehicle reels out long runs of hose exactly where they are needed.

Powerful pump

Stored lengths of hose

Tracking the fire
Inside the control center, officers keep track of progress in controlling the fire.

Getting dressed
On the way to the incident firefighters climb into their heavy protective clothing.

Fire crew receives instructions

Fire control vehicle
Firefighters rely on up-to-date communications and computers to coordinate operations. At really big fires, the computer and communications center itself goes on the road.

Super pumper
The basic firefighting appliance is a pumper – a huge pump on a truck chassis.

Snorkel
Hydraulic platforms, nicknamed "cherry-pickers" or "snorkels," lift fire fighters rapidly. However, in rescue operations they are not a complete replacement for long ladders, because the platform holds only four people.

Fire control van

Paramedics attend casualty on stretcher

Where's the fire exit?
People trying to escape from a burning building sometimes lose their lives because they look for an escape route that's familiar. To reach the doors and staircases they use daily they may walk right past fire exits.

Flaming floors
Most buildings have hollow areas under the floor, and often above suspended ceilings, too. Unless they are carefully partitioned off, these voids can spread the smoke from room to room.

MOVIE STUDIO

IN THE WORLD OF MOVIES, NOTHING IS QUITE LIKE IT SEEMS. BUILDINGS that seem to tower on screen are just tiny models. The giant squid dragging a ship beneath the waves is a latex puppet. A space station turns out to be a large sheet of canvas. Making these illusions look convincing requires the skills of a huge team of people, including set designers, background painters, and model-makers. These specialists craft the film in a studio complex. Teams may work for months on tiny details of a set – only to see it flash by on the screen in a few seconds.

Studio city
The sound stages, where filming takes place, are like huge sheds. They are carefully soundproofed, so that the sensitive microphones don't pick up the noise from traffic and aircraft outside. Though this drawing shows filming taking place on three sets all at once, normally only one of them would be in use at any time.

The backroom boys (and girls)
The sound stage is vast and obvious, but it's only a small fraction of the whole. Clustered around the cavernous set there's a maze of small workshops. Inside them an army of technicians and support staff work. Without their support the production would sink.

Animatronics
Model-makers mold latex foam into elaborate monster masks and screen creatures, such as a small squid. Tiny motors hidden inside the rubber skin control movement of the limbs, and facial expressions.

Distant illusion
Carpenters build a quarter-scale replica of the Buddha statue. When it appears in the background it will look like the full-size statue four times farther away. Without such perspective tricks, the studio would need to be four times as big.

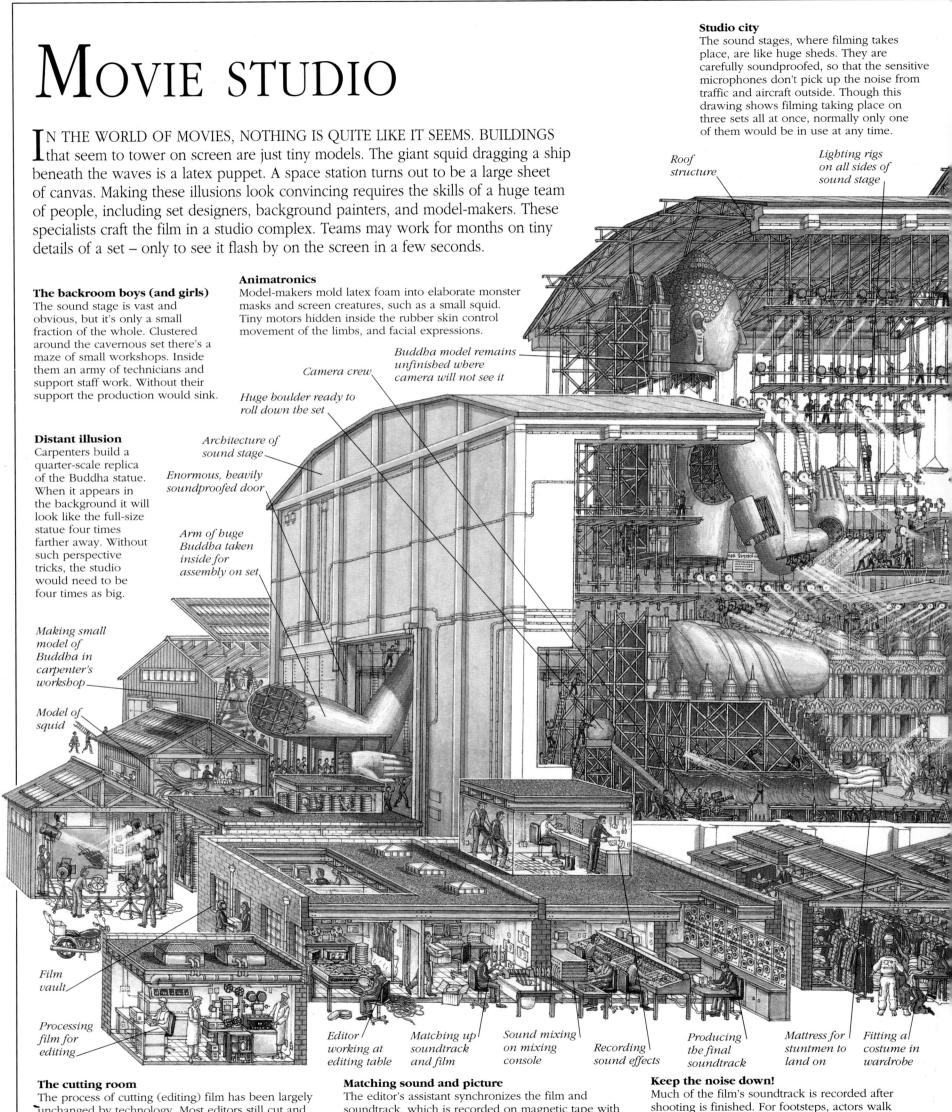

Roof structure

Lighting rigs on all sides of sound stage

Camera crew

Buddha model remains unfinished where camera will not see it

Huge boulder ready to roll down the set

Architecture of sound stage

Enormous, heavily soundproofed door

Arm of huge Buddha taken inside for assembly on set

Making small model of Buddha in carpenter's workshop

Model of squid

Film vault

Processing film for editing

Editor working at editing table

Matching up soundtrack and film

Sound mixing on mixing console

Recording sound effects

Producing the final soundtrack

Mattress for stuntmen to land on

Fitting a costume in wardrobe

The cutting room
The process of cutting (editing) film has been largely unchanged by technology. Most editors still cut and join a cutting print (positive copy) of film shot in the camera. This will be used as a guide for cutting the negative from which the final prints are made.

Matching sound and picture
The editor's assistant synchronizes the film and soundtrack, which is recorded on magnetic tape with sprocket-holes, just like film. The assistant checks that the "clap" sound at the start of each scene lines up with the film frame showing the clapboard closing.

Keep the noise down!
Much of the film's soundtrack is recorded after shooting is finished. For footsteps, actors walk around on simulated patches of "gravel path" or "fall leaves." The final sound of the film may consist of 30 or 40 tracks mixed together.

Big building
Sound stages can be vast. Pinewood Studios in England could hold over 570 double-decker buses.

Dry ice inside rocket for blast-off effect

Huge rocket model for Sci-fi film

Speedy sprayguns
Painted backdrops are often used because they are so cheap and quick to produce. Two painters might take just a few days to conjure up a background the size of a tennis court.

Studio city
The biggest studios are vast complexes of buildings sprawling over an area as large as some towns. Universal City in California is the biggest. Covering 0.6 sq miles (1.7 sq km), the studio has its own fire department, zoo, stables, and police department.

That sinking feeling
Stuntmen replace regular actors for dangerous sequences. Stunts are filmed from a distance and later edited carefully. Stuntmen stood in for women stars in the past, but laws have made this illegal in the United States. The studio can employ a stuntman in drag only when all available stuntwomen have refused the part.

Wet weekend
To simulate rivers, lakes, and oceans, set-builders create vast water-filled tanks. The largest tank ever built filled an old German airship hangar. Constructed in 1929, the 2,000-ft (600-m) long tank represented Russia's River Volga.

Rubber crustacean
Like the small squid in the model shop, this giant is a latex model. It's a kind of huge puppet, realistic only on the side that faces the cameras. This doesn't mean it's harmless: the rubber shark in *Jaws* (US 1975, producer William S. Gilmore Jr.) accidentally sank the ship carrying the cast and crew, sending the camera to the seabed.

Stirring up a storm
To simulate a hurricane, movie-makers attach an aircraft propeller to a powerful electric motor. Besides a convincing storm, the vast fan creates a lot of noise, and a realistic sound-track must be added later.

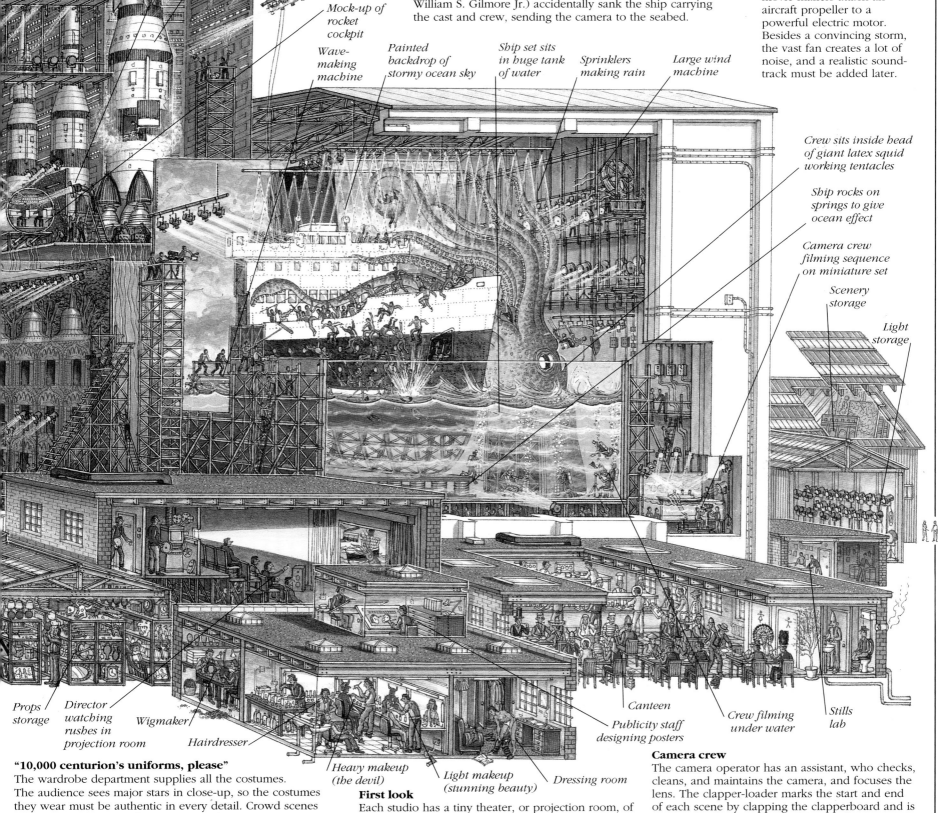

Mock-up of rocket cockpit

Wave-making machine

Painted backdrop of stormy ocean sky

Ship set sits in huge tank of water

Sprinklers making rain

Large wind machine

Crew sits inside head of giant latex squid working tentacles

Ship rocks on springs to give ocean effect

Camera crew filming sequence on miniature set

Scenery storage

Light storage

Props storage

Director watching rushes in projection room

Wigmaker

Hairdresser

Heavy makeup (the devil)

Light makeup (stunning beauty)

Dressing room

Canteen

Publicity staff designing posters

Crew filming under water

Stills lab

"10,000 centurion's uniforms, please"
The wardrobe department supplies all the costumes. The audience sees major stars in close-up, so the costumes they wear must be authentic in every detail. Crowd scenes require vast numbers of costumes: on the 1951 movie, *Quo Vadis*, the wardrobe department kept track of 29,000 outfits.

First look
Each studio has a tiny theater, or projection room, of its own. There the director views the "rushes" – quick prints of all the scenes shot the previous day.

Camera crew
The camera operator has an assistant, who checks, cleans, and maintains the camera, and focuses the lens. The clapper-loader marks the start and end of each scene by clapping the clapperboard and is responsible for loading the film. The key grip on the movie is responsible for moving the camera.

DAILY NEWSPAPER

"READ ALL ABOUT IT" SHOUTS THE NEWSPAPER seller. When earthquakes strike or wars break out, we want to read the news in our daily paper as soon as it happens, or preferably sooner! Filling newspapers with eyewitness reports and dramatic pictures is a challenge almost as demanding as predicting the future. To collect stories, journalists and photographers travel all over the world, often to dangerous places. The stories are then sent or taken to the newspaper offices, where a team processes the information to create pages on computer terminals. At a printing site, the pages are converted into negative film from which a printing plate is produced. Many newspapers worldwide are printed on a press like this one, where a large roll of paper, or web, is used in a continuous printing process. Now read on!

"My truth detector can spot a liar," says Chester.

NEWS GATHERING

Reporters and photographers travel the country to collect news. Only the larger papers can afford to send journalists abroad to report on international events.

Much foreign news comes from news agencies that employ journalists and photographers worldwide. The agency operates a telephone wire service to send a story to a newspaper.

Every day, departmental chiefs of a newspaper meet with the editor to discuss the day's news stories. Together they decide which stories and pictures to include in the following day's newspaper.

News happens 24 hours a day, and the night editor has to be ready to make changes right through the night – up until the moment when printing starts in the early hours of the morning.

In the newsroom, copy editors, picture editors, and designers lay out each page of the newspaper on computer terminals. Large screens show them how each page will look.

Sometimes journalists type their news stories straight onto laptop computers, and send, or "file," them directly with a newspaper by telephone line or by satellite phone.

Where possible, reporters return to the newspaper's offices to file their stories, and many journalists work there on background or information articles called features.

Many newspapers keep their selling price down by earning money from advertising. Sales staff sell space in the newspaper, taking down details by phone.

Satellite links allow journalists to send in stories from almost anywhere.

When a story arrives at a newspaper, it is routed to the correct desk by computer.

PLATEMAKING

For each page, four separate printing plates are made, one for each color (see below). Technicians first create a copy of the page on clear film in an image setter. This is passed to a processor that develops the film, creating a negative. In an exposure unit, the film is brought into contact with an aluminum plate coated with a special emulsion. Light shining through the film causes chemical changes in the emulsion. Areas struck by light become greasy so ink will stick to them.

Image setter

Processor

Exposure unit

A machine dries the finished plate

Printing plates are thin enough to wrap around cylinders inside the press.

PRINTING IN COLOR

The paper runs through four units of the press. These are almost identical – the only difference between them is that each prints a different color. The first unit prints the cyan (blue) parts of pictures; the second, the magenta (purple) areas; the third, the yellow areas; and the final unit at the top of the press prints the black areas and the black type. By varying the intensity of these four colors, it is possible to create every color of the rainbow.

THE PRINTING PRESS

When it reaches the printing press, the web runs through the four different color units. A printing plate is attached to one of the rollers in each unit, while other rollers transfer ink from a feed trough. Access points everywhere in the press allow technicians to reach inside for maintenance and adjustment.

The fourth set of rollers prints both sides with the final color of the process – black.

FOLDING AND CUTTING

After printing, the paper reaches the top of the press. It runs over rollers that direct the web back down again into the folder. The first blade slits the paper in two, then each half passes through a pair of forming rollers that fold it down the middle. Blades cut the paper and the collecting cylinder puts in more folds. The assembled newspaper drops into a paddle-wheel assembly, which then drops the whole thing onto a delivery belt.

Folding knife and collecting cylinder

Forming rollers

Clips attach the newspapers to an endless chain that carries the papers to packing points.

The third set of rollers prints both sides with the yellow portions of every color picture.

Blanket cylinder

Ink roller

Plate cylinder

Dampening rollers

Ink roller

Water spray bar

Ink feed

Ink trough

Ink pump

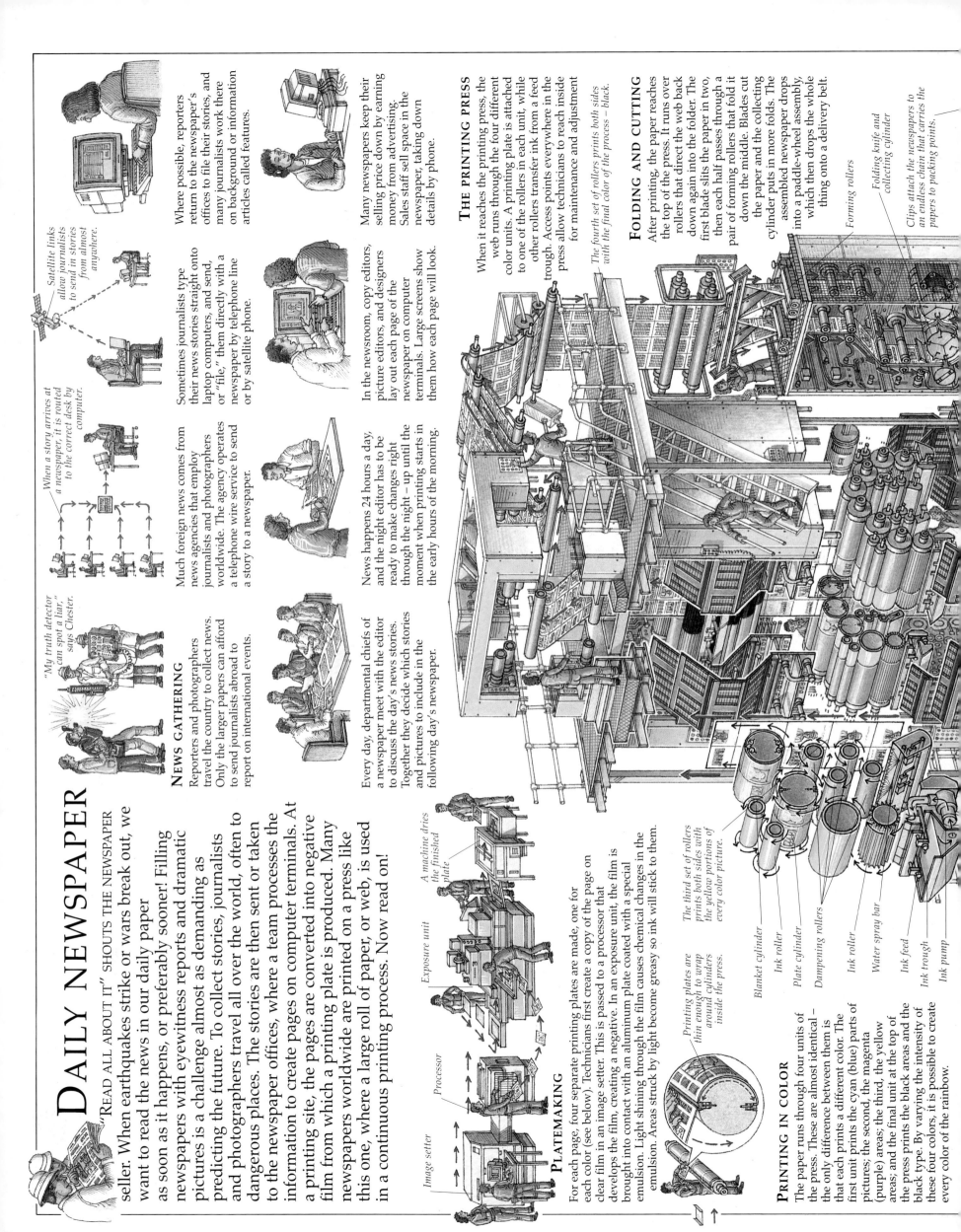

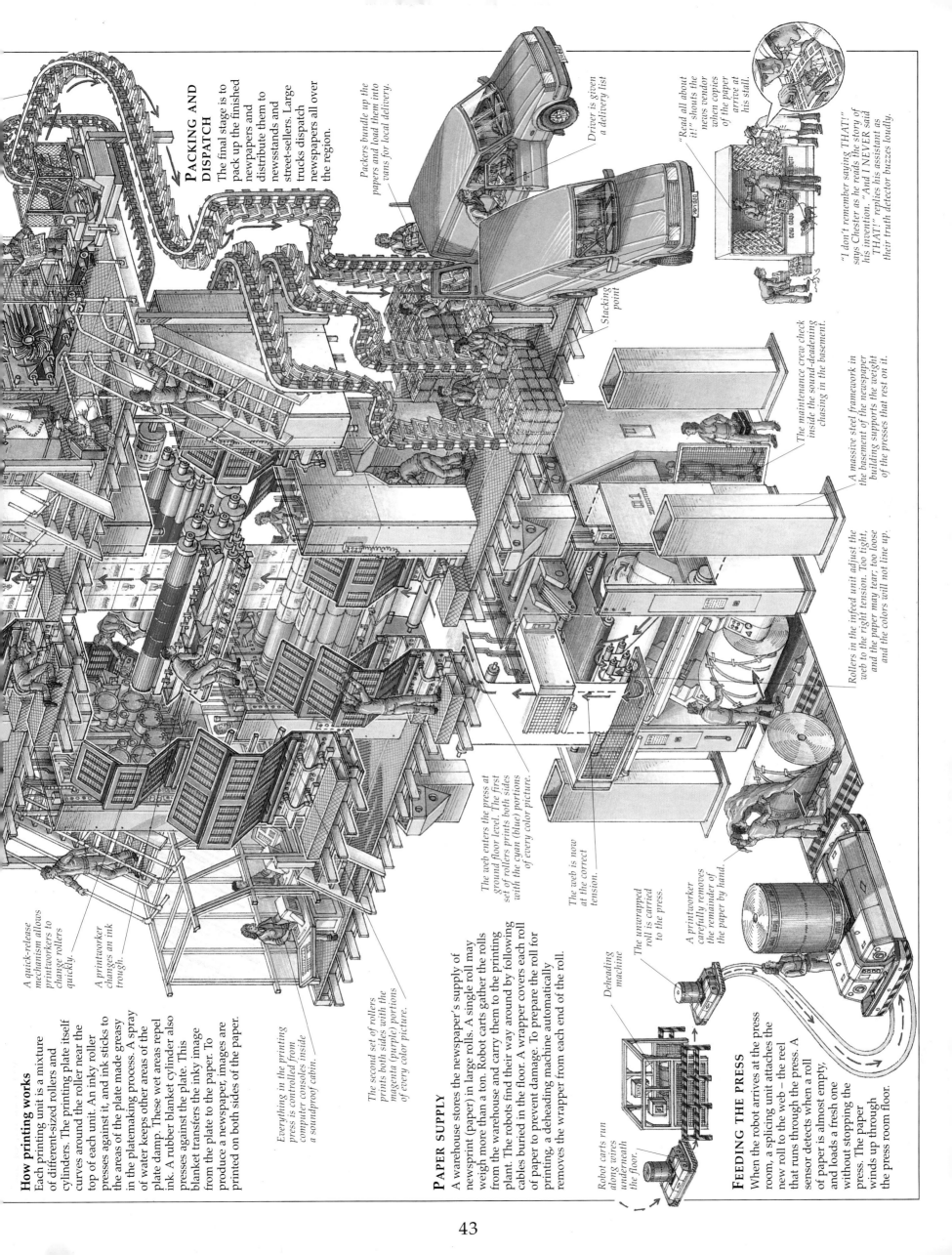

How printing works

Each printing unit is a mixture of different-sized rollers and cylinders. The printing plate itself curves around the roller near the top of each unit. An inky roller presses against it, and ink sticks to the areas of the plate made greasy in the platemaking process. A spray of water keeps other areas of the plate damp. These wet areas repel ink. A rubber blanket cylinder also presses against the plate. This blanket transfers the inky image from the plate to the paper. To produce a newspaper, images are printed on both sides of the paper.

A quick-release mechanism allows printworkers to change rollers quickly.

A printworker changes an ink trough.

Everything in the printing press is controlled from computer consoles inside a soundproof cabin.

The second set of rollers prints both sides with the magenta (purple) portions of every color picture.

PAPER SUPPLY

A warehouse stores the newspaper's supply of newsprint (paper) in large rolls. A single roll may weigh more than a ton. Robot carts gather the rolls from the warehouse and carry them to the printing plant. The robots find their way around by following cables buried in the floor. A wrapper covers each roll of paper to prevent damage. To prepare the roll for printing, a deheading machine automatically removes the wrapper from each end of the roll.

The web enters the press at ground floor level. The first set of rollers prints both sides with the cyan (blue) portions of every color picture.

The web is now at the correct tension.

Deheading machine

The unwrapped roll is carried to the press.

A printworker carefully removes the remainder of the paper by hand.

Robot carts run along wires underneath the floor.

FEEDING THE PRESS

When the robot arrives at the press room, a splicing unit attaches the new roll to the web – the reel that runs through the press. A sensor detects when a roll of paper is almost empty, and loads a fresh one without stopping the press. The paper winds up through the press room floor.

PACKING AND DISPATCH

The final stage is to pack up the finished newpapers and distribute them to newsstands and street-sellers. Large trucks dispatch newspapers all over the region.

Packers bundle up the papers and load them into vans for local delivery.

Driver is given a delivery list.

"Read all about it!" shouts the news vendor when copies of the paper arrive at his stall.

"I don't remember saying THAT!" says Chester as he reads the story of his invention. "And I NEVER said THAT!" replies his assistant as their truth detector buzzes loudly.

Stacking point

The maintenance crew check inside the sound-deadening framework in the basement.

A massive steel framework in the basement of the newspaper building supports the weight of the presses that rest on it.

Rollers in the infeed unit adjust the web to the right tension. Too tight, and the paper may tear; too loose and the colors will not line up.

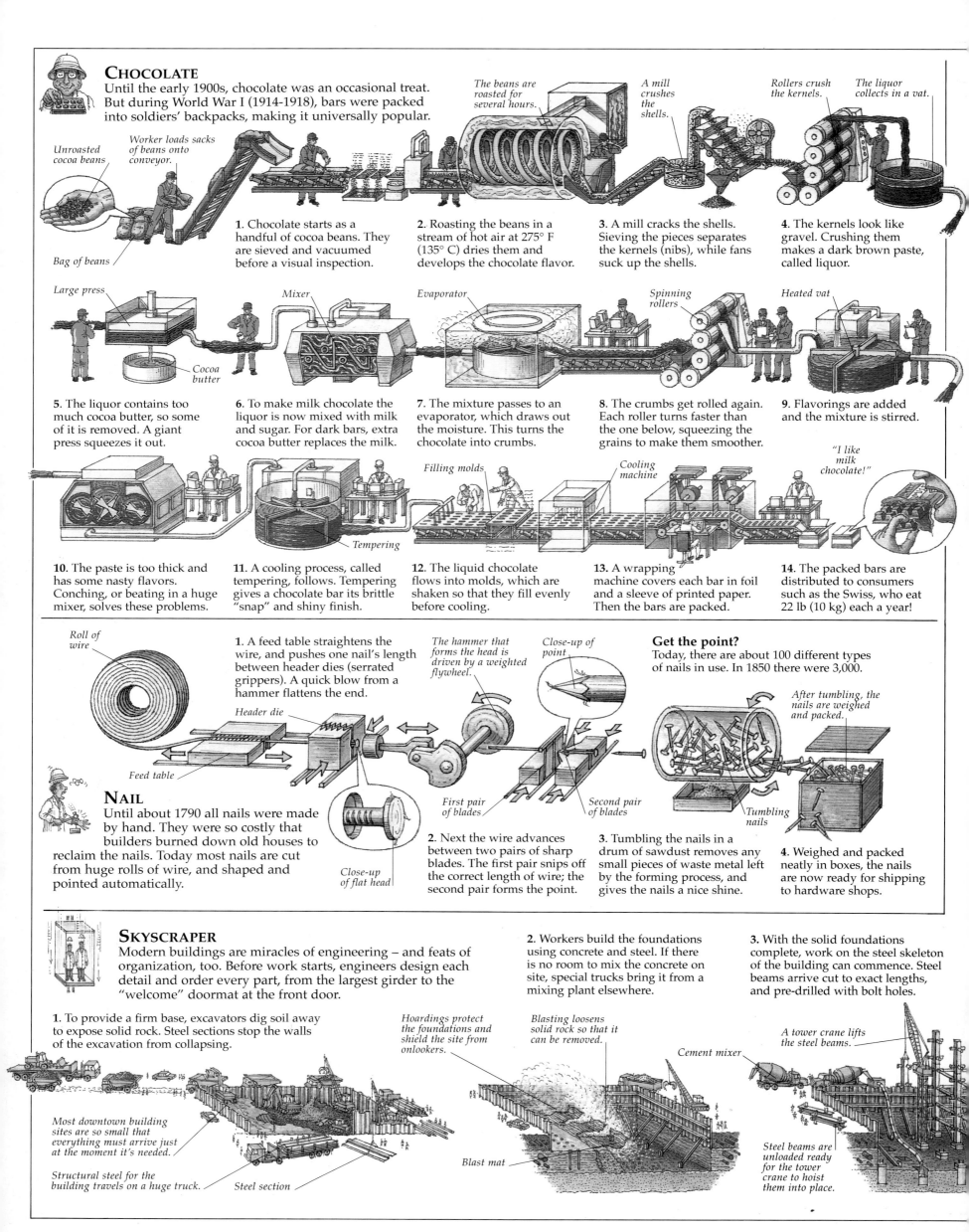

CHOCOLATE

Until the early 1900s, chocolate was an occasional treat. But during World War I (1914-1918), bars were packed into soldiers' backpacks, making it universally popular.

The beans are roasted for several hours.

A mill crushes the shells.

Rollers crush the kernels.

The liquor collects in a vat.

Unroasted cocoa beans

Worker loads sacks of beans onto conveyor.

Bag of beans

1. Chocolate starts as a handful of cocoa beans. They are sieved and vacuumed before a visual inspection.

2. Roasting the beans in a stream of hot air at 275° F (135° C) dries them and develops the chocolate flavor.

3. A mill cracks the shells. Sieving the pieces separates the kernels (nibs), while fans suck up the shells.

4. The kernels look like gravel. Crushing them makes a dark brown paste, called liquor.

Large press

Mixer

Evaporator

Spinning rollers

Heated vat

Cocoa butter

5. The liquor contains too much cocoa butter, so some of it is removed. A giant press squeezes it out.

6. To make milk chocolate the liquor is now mixed with milk and sugar. For dark bars, extra cocoa butter replaces the milk.

7. The mixture passes to an evaporator, which draws out the moisture. This turns the chocolate into crumbs.

8. The crumbs get rolled again. Each roller turns faster than the one below, squeezing the grains to make them smoother.

9. Flavorings are added and the mixture is stirred.

"I like milk chocolate!"

Filling molds

Cooling machine

Tempering

10. The paste is too thick and has some nasty flavors. Conching, or beating in a huge mixer, solves these problems.

11. A cooling process, called tempering, follows. Tempering gives a chocolate bar its brittle "snap" and shiny finish.

12. The liquid chocolate flows into molds, which are shaken so that they fill evenly before cooling.

13. A wrapping machine covers each bar in foil and a sleeve of printed paper. Then the bars are packed.

14. The packed bars are distributed to consumers such as the Swiss, who eat 22 lb (10 kg) each a year!

Roll of wire

1. A feed table straightens the wire, and pushes one nail's length between header dies (serrated grippers). A quick blow from a hammer flattens the end.

The hammer that forms the head is driven by a weighted flywheel.

Close-up of point

Get the point?
Today, there are about 100 different types of nails in use. In 1850 there were 3,000.

Header die

After tumbling, the nails are weighed and packed.

Feed table

Close-up of flat head

First pair of blades

Second pair of blades

Tumbling nails

NAIL

Until about 1790 all nails were made by hand. They were so costly that builders burned down old houses to reclaim the nails. Today most nails are cut from huge rolls of wire, and shaped and pointed automatically.

2. Next the wire advances between two pairs of sharp blades. The first pair snips off the correct length of wire; the second pair forms the point.

3. Tumbling the nails in a drum of sawdust removes any small pieces of waste metal left by the forming process, and gives the nails a nice shine.

4. Weighed and packed neatly in boxes, the nails are now ready for shipping to hardware shops.

SKYSCRAPER

Modern buildings are miracles of engineering – and feats of organization, too. Before work starts, engineers design each detail and order every part, from the largest girder to the "welcome" doormat at the front door.

2. Workers build the foundations using concrete and steel. If there is no room to mix the concrete on site, special trucks bring it from a mixing plant elsewhere.

3. With the solid foundations complete, work on the steel skeleton of the building can commence. Steel beams arrive cut to exact lengths, and pre-drilled with bolt holes.

1. To provide a firm base, excavators dig soil away to expose solid rock. Steel sections stop the walls of the excavation from collapsing.

Hoardings protect the foundations and shield the site from onlookers.

Blasting loosens solid rock so that it can be removed.

A tower crane lifts the steel beams.

Cement mixer

Most downtown building sites are so small that everything must arrive just at the moment it's needed.

Structural steel for the building travels on a huge truck.

Steel section

Blast mat

Steel beams are unloaded ready for the tower crane to hoist them into place.

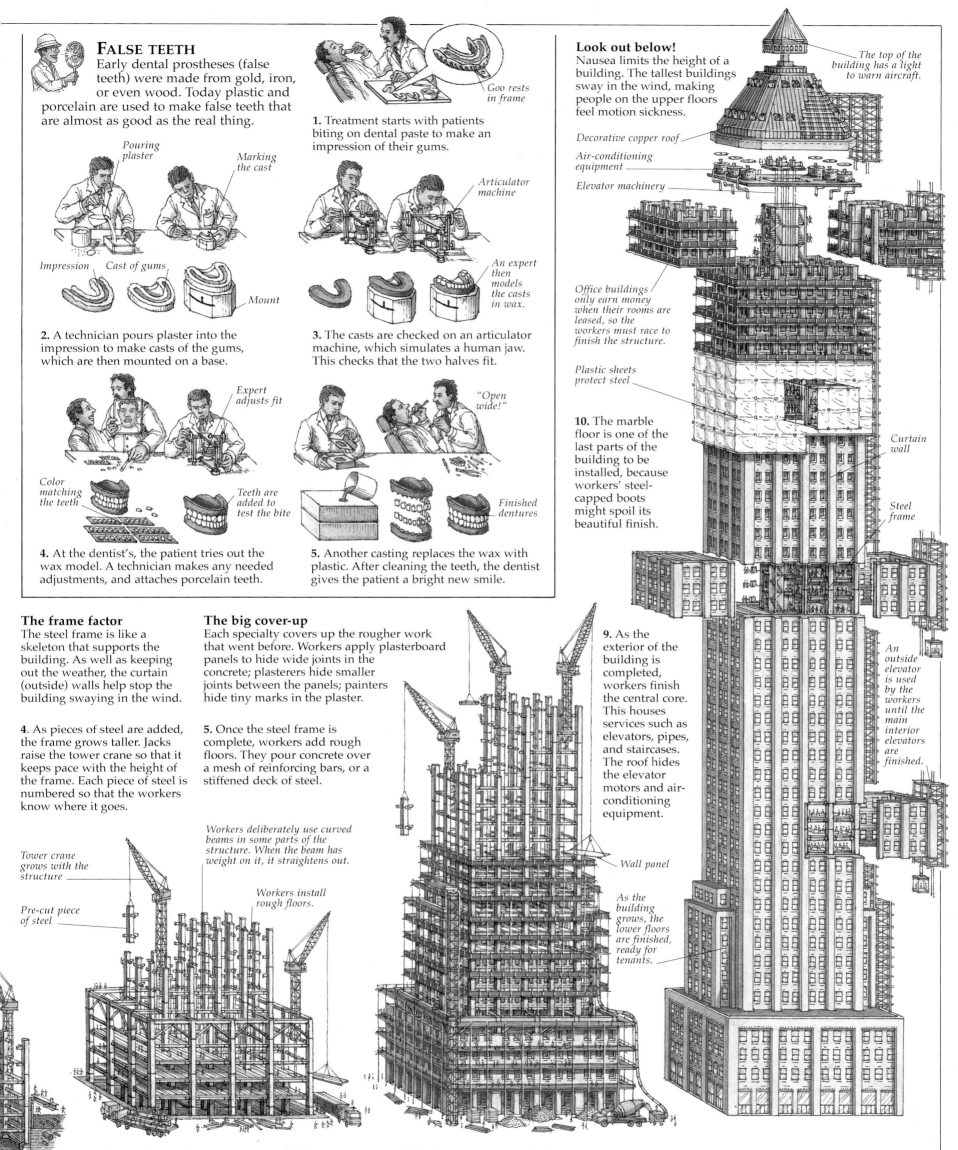

FALSE TEETH

Early dental prostheses (false teeth) were made from gold, iron, or even wood. Today plastic and porcelain are used to make false teeth that are almost as good as the real thing.

Goo rests in frame

1. Treatment starts with patients biting on dental paste to make an impression of their gums.

Pouring plaster

Marking the cast

Impression *Cast of gums*

Mount

2. A technician pours plaster into the impression to make casts of the gums, which are then mounted on a base.

Articulator machine

An expert then models the casts in wax.

3. The casts are checked on an articulator machine, which simulates a human jaw. This checks that the two halves fit.

Expert adjusts fit

Color matching the teeth

Teeth are added to test the bite

4. At the dentist's, the patient tries out the wax model. A technician makes any needed adjustments, and attaches porcelain teeth.

"Open wide!"

Finished dentures

5. Another casting replaces the wax with plastic. After cleaning the teeth, the dentist gives the patient a bright new smile.

The frame factor

The steel frame is like a skeleton that supports the building. As well as keeping out the weather, the curtain (outside) walls help stop the building swaying in the wind.

4. As pieces of steel are added, the frame grows taller. Jacks raise the tower crane so that it keeps pace with the height of the frame. Each piece of steel is numbered so that the workers know where it goes.

Tower crane grows with the structure

Pre-cut piece of steel

The big cover-up

Each specialty covers up the rougher work that went before. Workers apply plasterboard panels to hide wide joints in the concrete; plasterers hide smaller joints between the panels; painters hide tiny marks in the plaster.

5. Once the steel frame is complete, workers add rough floors. They pour concrete over a mesh of reinforcing bars, or a stiffened deck of steel.

Workers deliberately use curved beams in some parts of the structure. When the beam has weight on it, it straightens out.

Workers install rough floors.

6. The scaffolding helps workers reach the exterior. On the upper floors, scaffolding hangs from the building's steel frame.

7. To clad the building, cranes winch the insulated curtain wall panels into position, and workers standing inside the building set them in place.

Look out below!

Nausea limits the height of a building. The tallest buildings sway in the wind, making people on the upper floors feel motion sickness.

The top of the building has a light to warn aircraft.

Decorative copper roof

Air-conditioning equipment

Elevator machinery

Office buildings only earn money when their rooms are leased, so the workers must race to finish the structure.

Plastic sheets protect steel

10. The marble floor is one of the last parts of the building to be installed, because workers' steel-capped boots might spoil its beautiful finish.

Curtain wall

Steel frame

9. As the exterior of the building is completed, workers finish the central core. This houses services such as elevators, pipes, and staircases. The roof hides the elevator motors and air-conditioning equipment.

Wall panel

An outside elevator is used by the workers until the main interior elevators are finished.

As the building grows, the lower floors are finished, ready for tenants.

8. Once the frame, floors, and walls are in place, contractors can install the electrical, plumbing, and air-conditioning equipment, and fire sprinklers.

VENICE

IMAGINE A CITY ON THE SEA. HALF SINKING, HALF FLOATING, ITS ROOFS AND GLITTERING towers rise mysteriously from swirling mist. This magic place was Venice in the 17th century. Already 11 centuries old, the city had begun as a mudbank refuge from wars on Italy's mainland. Protected from attack by its shallow lagoon, Venice grew into a great world power. An exclusive club of noblemen led by the Doge (duke) ruled Venice ruthlessly. They became wealthy by controlling overland trade between Asia and Europe. The discovery of a sea route to Asia ended the monopoly in 1488; and despite the centuries of decline that followed, the city's fabulous beauty and legendary art treasures survived almost unchanged. The picture below shows the central section of the city.

Doge
The Doge of Venice (left) wore elaborate robes made of costly fabrics. He also wore a pointed golden cap called the *cornu*.

Canals
Instead of streets, Venice is criss-crossed by water-filled canals. The biggest, the Grand Canal, is wide and lined with marble palaces. Others are tiny, and one even goes right underneath a church!

Piazza
St. Mark's Piazza is a vast square, roughly the size of 45 tennis courts. It has always been the center of life in the city.

Help!
"Streets full of water, please advise" cabled Robert Benchley (1889-1945) when he saw the city's thoroughfares. His telegram was a joke, but every visitor must share a little of the American writer's surprise on first glimpsing the Venetian canals.

Campanile
The famous Campanile (bell tower) of St. Mark's dominates the skyline. Completed in the 12th century, the tower has been restored several times. In the 15th century criminals dangled in iron cages from the south side as punishment.

Campanile bells
The five bells of the Campanile all had different meanings. The largest, *Marangona*, rang at the start and end of the day's work. *Nona* sounded at noon; and the smallest, *Maleficio*, signalled an execution.

Venetian symbol
The winged lion was St. Mark's mascot. It appears on buildings all over Venice.

Campanile

Rialto bridge

Grand Canal

Though Venice is less than 3 miles (5 km) long, the city's 177 canals total 28 miles (45 km).

Piazza

Granary

Merchant ship brings grain

Granary
Large stocks of flour and grain in the warehouses (*Fontegheto della farina*) enabled the rulers of Venice to keep down bread prices and avoid food riots.

Mint
At the *Zecca* (Mint), workers struck the gold ducats that were the currency of Venice. The coin kept its constant size and purity for more than 500 years, but eventually became known as the *zecchino*. From this word we get the word "sequin."

Mint
Library

Books shelved
Venetians began planning a public library around 1360, but the building to house it was not completed until 1591.

Foundations
The buildings of Venice rest on piles: thousands of wooden posts hammered into lagoon bed clay.

Piles are made of Istrian pine: the wood gets harder as it ages.

Layout of buildings with canals between

Bridges
Walking across all the bridges in Venice would be a huge task. There are so many that even guide books lose count. The famous Rialto bridge, which spans the Grand Canal, was designed by the architect Antonio da Ponte (1512-1595).

Venice and visitors
Venice has always been a well-oiled tourist machine, finely tuned to separate visitors from their money as quickly as possible. Even in the 14th century, 500 years before the word "tourist" was first used, the city had inspectors to check travelers' hotels.

Lagoon
Venice sits in a lagoon which separates it from Italy's mainland. In many places the water is only waist deep, but dredged channels allow large ships to reach the shore and to travel out into the Adriatic Sea.

St. Mark's Basilica
Once the private chapel of the Doge's palace, the Basilica is named for St. Mark, one of Jesus Christ's 12 disciples (followers). The *Pala d'Oro* is the Basilica's greatest treasure. This great altar screen is crafted from gold and studded with precious stones. It took 500 years to complete.

St. Mark's

Doge's palace
In the palace the Doge and his family lived in legendary luxury: the wife of the 24th Doge was said to have bathed in morning dew collected by her servants.

Pala d'Oro

Prison cell

Council chamber

Chamber of the Great Council
The meeting room for Venice's governing body of aristocrats was huge. It had to be, because the Great Council had more than 1,200 members by 1311.

Bridge of Sighs

Terrible ten
After an attempt to overthrow the Doge in the 14th century, Venetians appointed a council of ten noblemen to make quick decisions. They had great power, and organized a secret service that extended to every possible corner of the known world.

Doge's palace

Unholy trinity
The most feared men in Venice were the three Inquisitors chosen from the Council of Ten. They dealt with matters of state security, and could order the death of almost anyone.

Gondola

Smaller city barge

Doge stands on prow (front) of barge

Piazzetta

Bucintoro

Gondolas
The rented rowboats of Venice, called gondolas, are like water taxis.

Dull hull
Wealthy families once richly decorated their private gondolas, but from 1562 these glitzy boats were outlawed.

Death in Venice
The Piazzetta in front of the Piazza was the site for the city's public executions. Between the two columns the executioner hanged prisoners, or cut their heads off. Bored with humdrum slaughter, he buried three traitors alive here in 1405, leaving only their legs visible.

Bucintoro
The Doge's barge, *Bucintoro*, was the grandest ship in the Venetian fleet. Once a year, the Doge sailed out into the lagoon on it for a ceremony that symbolized the city's control of the ocean.

Bridge of Sighs
This famous bridge links the Doge's Palace to the office of the Inquisitor. The name comes from the mournful sound that prisoners made as they crossed the canal, for they knew they faced execution or torture.

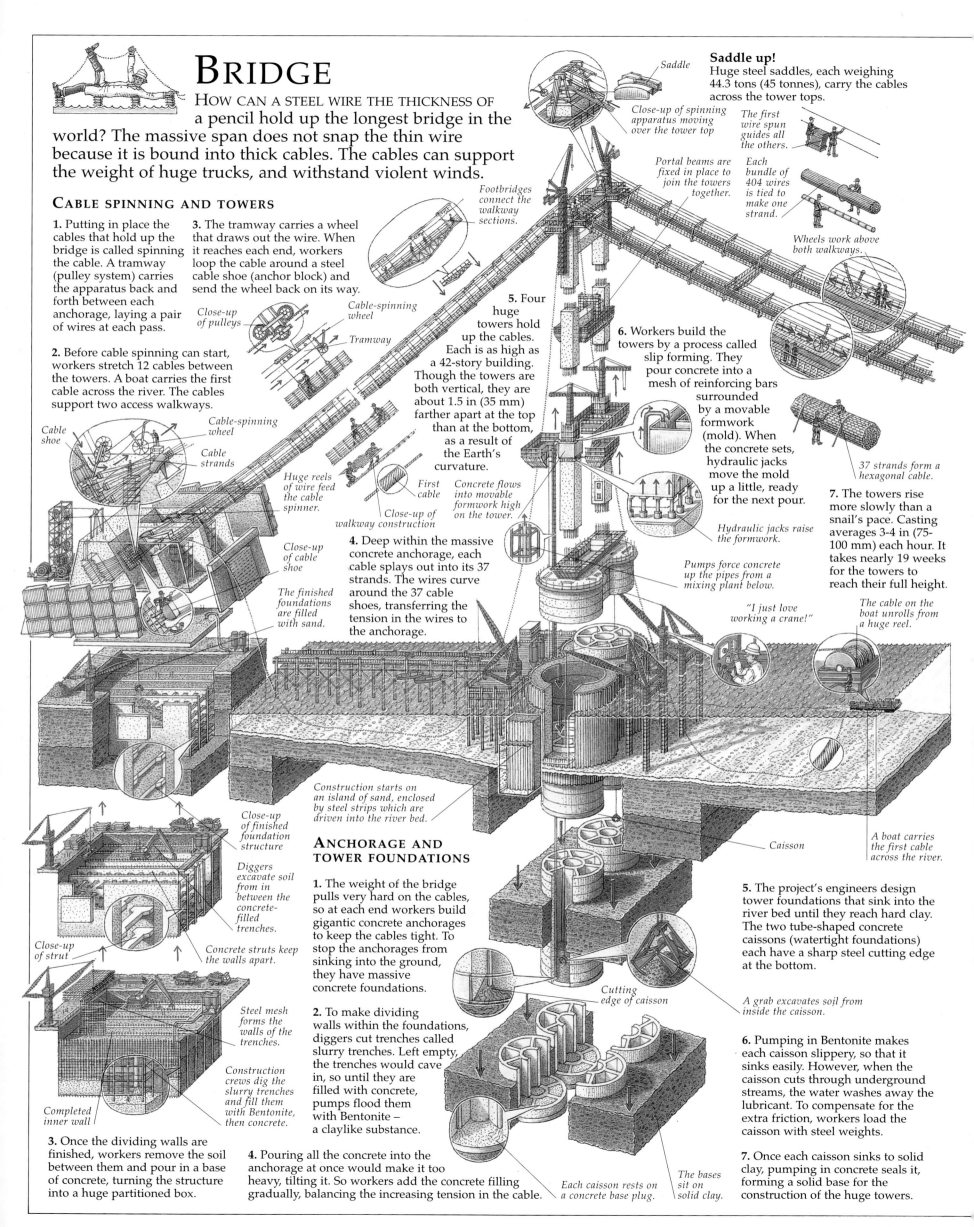

BRIDGE

HOW CAN A STEEL WIRE THE THICKNESS OF a pencil hold up the longest bridge in the world? The massive span does not snap the thin wire because it is bound into thick cables. The cables can support the weight of huge trucks, and withstand violent winds.

CABLE SPINNING AND TOWERS

1. Putting in place the cables that hold up the bridge is called spinning the cable. A tramway (pulley system) carries the apparatus back and forth between each anchorage, laying a pair of wires at each pass.

2. Before cable spinning can start, workers stretch 12 cables between the towers. A boat carries the first cable across the river. The cables support two access walkways.

3. The tramway carries a wheel that draws out the wire. When it reaches each end, workers loop the cable around a steel cable shoe (anchor block) and send the wheel back on its way.

Close-up of pulleys

Cable-spinning wheel

Tramway

Cable shoe

Cable-spinning wheel

Cable strands

Huge reels of wire feed the cable spinner.

Close-up of cable shoe

First cable

Close-up of walkway construction

The finished foundations are filled with sand.

Footbridges connect the walkway sections.

Saddle

Saddle up!
Huge steel saddles, each weighing 44.3 tons (45 tonnes), carry the cables across the tower tops.

Close-up of spinning apparatus moving over the tower top

The first wire spun guides all the others.

Portal beams are fixed in place to join the towers together.

Each bundle of 404 wires is tied to make one strand.

Wheels work above both walkways.

37 strands form a hexagonal cable.

5. Four huge towers hold up the cables. Each is as high as a 42-story building. Though the towers are both vertical, they are about 1.5 in (35 mm) farther apart at the top than at the bottom, as a result of the Earth's curvature.

Concrete flows into movable formwork high on the tower.

6. Workers build the towers by a process called slip forming. They pour concrete into a mesh of reinforcing bars surrounded by a movable formwork (mold). When the concrete sets, hydraulic jacks move the mold up a little, ready for the next pour.

Hydraulic jacks raise the formwork.

Pumps force concrete up the pipes from a mixing plant below.

7. The towers rise more slowly than a snail's pace. Casting averages 3-4 in (75-100 mm) each hour. It takes nearly 19 weeks for the towers to reach their full height.

"I just love working a crane!"

The cable on the boat unrolls from a huge reel.

4. Deep within the massive concrete anchorage, each cable splays out into its 37 strands. The wires curve around the 37 cable shoes, transferring the tension in the wires to the anchorage.

Close-up of finished foundation structure

Diggers excavate soil from in between the concrete-filled trenches.

Concrete struts keep the walls apart.

Close-up of strut

Steel mesh forms the walls of the trenches.

Construction crews dig the slurry trenches and fill them with Bentonite, then concrete.

Completed inner wall

Construction starts on an island of sand, enclosed by steel strips which are driven into the river bed.

ANCHORAGE AND TOWER FOUNDATIONS

1. The weight of the bridge pulls very hard on the cables, so at each end workers build gigantic concrete anchorages to keep the cables tight. To stop the anchorages from sinking into the ground, they have massive concrete foundations.

2. To make dividing walls within the foundations, diggers cut trenches called slurry trenches. Left empty, the trenches would cave in, so until they are filled with concrete, pumps flood them with Bentonite – a claylike substance.

3. Once the dividing walls are finished, workers remove the soil between them and pour in a base of concrete, turning the structure into a huge partitioned box.

4. Pouring all the concrete into the anchorage at once would make it too heavy, tilting it. So workers add the concrete filling gradually, balancing the increasing tension in the cable.

Caisson

A boat carries the first cable across the river.

Cutting edge of caisson

A grab excavates soil from inside the caisson.

5. The project's engineers design tower foundations that sink into the river bed until they reach hard clay. The two tube-shaped concrete caissons (watertight foundations) each have a sharp steel cutting edge at the bottom.

6. Pumping in Bentonite makes each caisson slippery, so that it sinks easily. However, when the caisson cuts through underground streams, the water washes away the lubricant. To compensate for the extra friction, workers load the caisson with steel weights.

Each caisson rests on a concrete base plug.

The bases sit on solid clay.

7. Once each caisson sinks to solid clay, pumping in concrete seals it, forming a solid base for the construction of the huge towers.

48

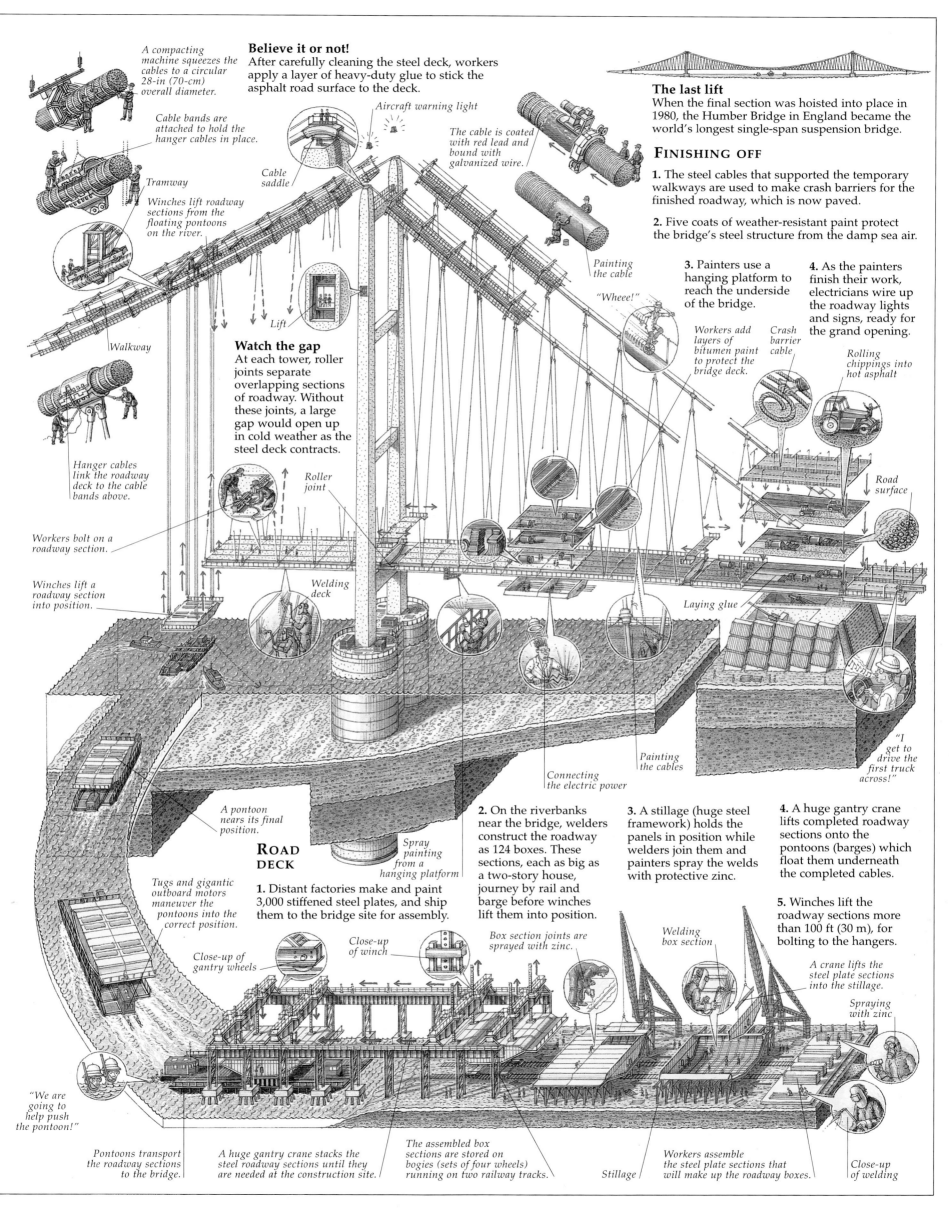

A compacting machine squeezes the cables to a circular 28-in (70-cm) overall diameter.

Cable bands are attached to hold the hanger cables in place.

Believe it or not!
After carefully cleaning the steel deck, workers apply a layer of heavy-duty glue to stick the asphalt road surface to the deck.

Aircraft warning light

The cable is coated with red lead and bound with galvanized wire.

The last lift
When the final section was hoisted into place in 1980, the Humber Bridge in England became the world's longest single-span suspension bridge.

Tramway

Cable saddle

FINISHING OFF

1. The steel cables that supported the temporary walkways are used to make crash barriers for the finished roadway, which is now paved.

Winches lift roadway sections from the floating pontoons on the river.

Painting the cable

2. Five coats of weather-resistant paint protect the bridge's steel structure from the damp sea air.

Lift

"Wheee!"

3. Painters use a hanging platform to reach the underside of the bridge.

4. As the painters finish their work, electricians wire up the roadway lights and signs, ready for the grand opening.

Walkway

Watch the gap
At each tower, roller joints separate overlapping sections of roadway. Without these joints, a large gap would open up in cold weather as the steel deck contracts.

Workers add layers of bitumen paint to protect the bridge deck.

Crash barrier cable

Rolling chippings into hot asphalt

Hanger cables link the roadway deck to the cable bands above.

Roller joint

Road surface

Workers bolt on a roadway section.

Welding deck

Laying glue

Winches lift a roadway section into position.

Painting the cables

Connecting the electric power

"I get to drive the first truck across!"

A pontoon nears its final position.

ROAD DECK

2. On the riverbanks near the bridge, welders construct the roadway as 124 boxes. These sections, each as big as a two-story house, journey by rail and barge before winches lift them into position.

3. A stillage (huge steel framework) holds the panels in position while welders join them and painters spray the welds with protective zinc.

4. A huge gantry crane lifts completed roadway sections onto the pontoons (barges) which float them underneath the completed cables.

Tugs and gigantic outboard motors maneuver the pontoons into the correct position.

1. Distant factories make and paint 3,000 stiffened steel plates, and ship them to the bridge site for assembly.

Spray painting from a hanging platform

5. Winches lift the roadway sections more than 100 ft (30 m), for bolting to the hangers.

Welding box section

Close-up of gantry wheels

Close-up of winch

Box section joints are sprayed with zinc.

A crane lifts the steel plate sections into the stillage.

Spraying with zinc

"We are going to help push the pontoon!"

Pontoons transport the roadway sections to the bridge.

A huge gantry crane stacks the steel roadway sections until they are needed at the construction site.

The assembled box sections are stored on bogies (sets of four wheels) running on two railway tracks.

Workers assemble the steel plate sections that will make up the roadway boxes.

Stillage

Close-up of welding

TOWER BRIDGE

LONDON, ENGLAND'S, LANDMARK BRIDGE LOOKS LIKE A TALLER twin of the city's famous Tower nearby. Yet for all the pinnacles and parapets, the castlelike masonry is only skin deep. Under its stone cladding the bridge has a skeleton of steel. Built at the end of the 19th century to relieve traffic congestion, Tower Bridge is a bascule bridge. When tall ships sail up London's Thames River, the two bascules, or leaves that carry the roadway, lift to allow ships to pass underneath.

Original paintwork
Painters covered the metalwork of the bridge with three coats of "bright chocolate" paint before opening day.

Royal opening
The bridge had a royal opening in 1894. Excited crowds gazed as the bridge opened. But not everything went according to plan. Amplified sound was still 20 years in the future, so the royal opening speeches were completely inaudible more than a few feet from the platform.

Chain links
Bridges that link the piers to the banks on either side are suspension bridges; so the supports for the roadway are called "chains," despite the fact that they are really girders.

Heavy see-saw!
The word *bascule* means "see-saw" in French. On Tower Bridge, lead and steel weights counterbalance the bascules. Each weighs 320 tons (325 tonnes) – as much as 40 African elephants.

Weighty wind
Each bascule, or leaf, weighs 1,200 tons (1,220 tonnes) and is 100 ft (30 m) long. On a still day, little force is needed to lift the bridge. Yet the bridge can still open against the strongest gale-force gusts, equivalent to lifting each leaf with 150 cars parked on it.

Tower of strength
The original specification for the bridge required that it would be capable of being armed with guns.

Spiral staircase access to roof space

Elevator winding gear

Gothic revival Scottish baronial architecture

Suspension chains

Interior steel framework

Heraldic achievement (crest)

Bascule

High level walkway

Bascule locking bolt

Elevator carries 25 passengers to high level walkway

Stairs to 2nd floor

Control cabin

Nighttime signal light

Levers to operate bridge

Anchor tie to north approach road

North approach road

Gas lamp

Anchor tie inside concrete block

Entrance to the Tower of London

Archway leading to "Dead Man's Hole"

Pier clad in Cornish granite

Gault brickwork in cement

Machinery chamber contains two lifting engines

Lead counterweight

Passageway to accumulator chamber

Plunger

Pig iron weights

Dead Man's Hole
An archway under the north approach road gave access to "Dead Man's Hole" – a temporary morgue for bodies fished out of the river close to the bridge.

Bridgemaster's perks
The bridge employed 80 people, 14 on watch at any one time, including a superintendent engineer and a bridgemaster, who had an official residence nearby.

Open wide
The bridge had to provide a very wide opening so that vast square-rigged sailing ships could pass through easily under wind power.

Built on mud
The bridge foundations stand not on bedrock, but on clay. To prevent the bridge from sinking, it rests on huge foundations. The engineers kept the weight down to less than the pressure of someone standing on your toe.

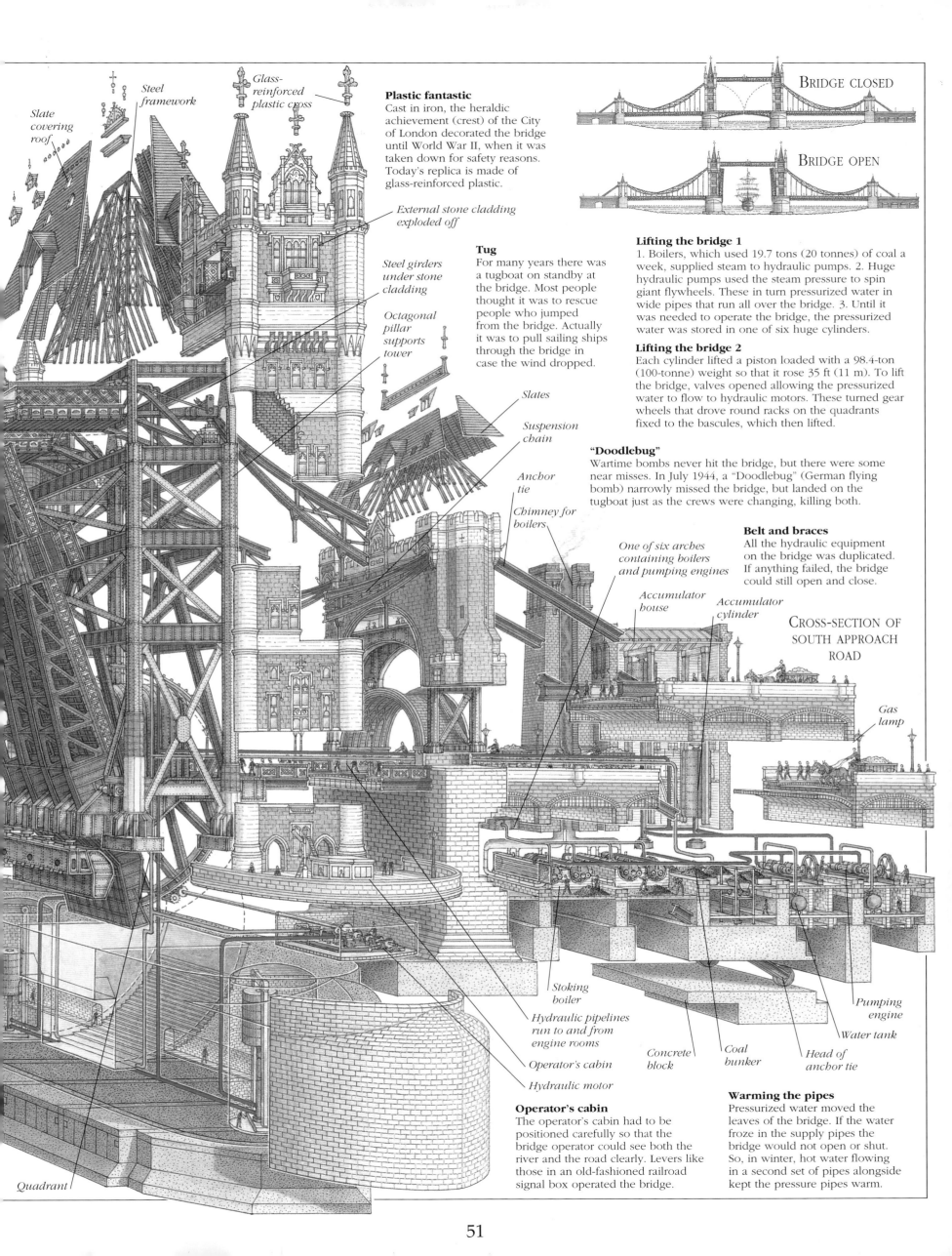

Slate covering roof

Steel framework

Glass-reinforced plastic cross

Plastic fantastic
Cast in iron, the heraldic achievement (crest) of the City of London decorated the bridge until World War II, when it was taken down for safety reasons. Today's replica is made of glass-reinforced plastic.

External stone cladding exploded off

Tug
For many years there was a tugboat on standby at the bridge. Most people thought it was to rescue people who jumped from the bridge. Actually it was to pull sailing ships through the bridge in case the wind dropped.

Steel girders under stone cladding

Octagonal pillar supports tower

Slates

Suspension chain

Anchor tie

Chimney for boilers

BRIDGE CLOSED

BRIDGE OPEN

Lifting the bridge 1
1. Boilers, which used 19.7 tons (20 tonnes) of coal a week, supplied steam to hydraulic pumps. 2. Huge hydraulic pumps used the steam pressure to spin giant flywheels. These in turn pressurized water in wide pipes that run all over the bridge. 3. Until it was needed to operate the bridge, the pressurized water was stored in one of six huge cylinders.

Lifting the bridge 2
Each cylinder lifted a piston loaded with a 98.4-ton (100-tonne) weight so that it rose 35 ft (11 m). To lift the bridge, valves opened allowing the pressurized water to flow to hydraulic motors. These turned gear wheels that drove round racks on the quadrants fixed to the bascules, which then lifted.

"Doodlebug"
Wartime bombs never hit the bridge, but there were some near misses. In July 1944, a "Doodlebug" (German flying bomb) narrowly missed the bridge, but landed on the tugboat just as the crews were changing, killing both.

Belt and braces
All the hydraulic equipment on the bridge was duplicated. If anything failed, the bridge could still open and close.

One of six arches containing boilers and pumping engines

Accumulator house

Accumulator cylinder

CROSS-SECTION OF SOUTH APPROACH ROAD

Gas lamp

Stoking boiler

Hydraulic pipelines run to and from engine rooms

Operator's cabin

Hydraulic motor

Concrete block

Coal bunker

Head of anchor tie

Pumping engine

Water tank

Quadrant

Operator's cabin
The operator's cabin had to be positioned carefully so that the bridge operator could see both the river and the road clearly. Levers like those in an old-fashioned railroad signal box operated the bridge.

Warming the pipes
Pressurized water moved the leaves of the bridge. If the water froze in the supply pipes the bridge would not open or shut. So, in winter, hot water flowing in a second set of pipes alongside kept the pressure pipes warm.

ANTARCTIC BASE

IN THE MOST ISOLATED PLACE ON EARTH THE SUN NEVER SETS IN SUMMER —
and winter is one long night. The climate is so hostile that no plant or animal can survive for long in the open. This place is the South Pole. It lies at the heart of Antarctica, a vast ice-covered continent. Antarctica was largely unexplored until 70 years ago. Today, scientists line up to work at this cold and remote polar base. Why? Because astronomers can peer at the stars for months on end, without daytime interrupting their work. Biologists gain a super-clean laboratory: Antarctic air is the purest on Earth. And even the ice cap itself is a remarkable archive. Locked in its layers of compressed snow is a 150,000-year-old record of the Earth's climate.

Polar night
Night begins in March with a twilight that lasts a month. "Morning" comes six months later. In the winter's sky, the stars circle continuously, without rising or setting as they do elsewhere on Earth.

Freewheeling
Tracked vehicles are the main form of transportation at the pole. Coastal bases also use huge wheeled trucks called Deltas, plus motorcycles and snowmobiles.

Delta vehicle

Tracked vehicle

Weather station

Snowmobile

Explorer's memorial
This drawing is based on the Amundsen-Scott South Pole Station. Roald Amundsen (1872-1928) planted the Norwegian flag at the pole on December 14, 1911. The expedition led by British explorer Robert Scott (1869-1912) reached the pole a month later, but Scott's team perished on the return journey.

Steel arches form tunnel

Fuel storage

Garage entrance

Underneath the arches
Steel arches provide much of the indoor space at the base. Their shape has been chosen so that the arches shed as much snow as possible.

The ozone hole
One of the most important jobs of the polar base is to monitor the Earth's ozone layer. Each year a hole in the ozone layer opens above Antarctica, and scientists at the base use their instruments to judge how much of a threat this poses.

Cooking area

Supplies storage

Ice on the move
The ice sheet on which the polar station rests is moving slowly. The base moves along with it.

Don't throw water
The low temperatures at the base freeze all water vapor, drying wood buildings until they are like kindling. Fire is thus always a hazard.

Roof arch rests on sides of ice trench

Dormitory area

ICE MOVEMENT

Ice moves 33 ft (10 m) per year – the length of three small cars.

Work in progress
Maintaining the base demands constant work. Many of the structures are nearing the end of their useful life, and the whole base will need to be replaced in a few years.

Ancient meteorites (rocks from space) lodged in rock layers beneath ice

Polar day
At the poles, day and night don't take turns as they do on the rest of the planet. In "daytime" – which lasts the whole summer – the sun never sets: instead it just circles in the sky.

Airdrop
Supplies for the South Pole base are ferried in by air. In summer aircraft can land on a prepared strip. Winter supplies are dropped by parachute.

Doomed dome
The most visible building at the base is the 65-ft (50-m) wide geodesic dome. However, the aluminum dome is gradually being covered by snow and ice, and this will eventually crush it.

Clear skies mean better views
Astronomers like using their telescopes at the pole because the sky is exceptionally clear. The biting frost freezes all the water vapor out of the atmosphere that normally blurs observations.

Eco-tourism
Sightseeing flights do little harm to the fragile polar environment, but the impact of the 4,000 tourists who visit each year is controversial. Their 8,000 stamping boots can damage coastal lichens that take decades to grow.

Supply drop

Radio antenna

Geodesic dome

Weather
Meteorologists at the pole collect weather data for scientific research, and for guidance to aircraft flying over Antarctica.

Coastal bases
Most of the bases on Antarctica are on the coast, far from the South Pole itself.

Rocky research
Close to the coast, summer thaw exposes the rock surface. Parts of Antarctica are "dry valleys" which are never snow-covered. The dark color of the exposed rock absorbs energy from the sun, warming the ground enough to evaporate any snow that falls.

Laboratory block

Dome interior

This ice cream's cold!
Cooks at the base have to learn some odd skills. Stored in the dome, ice cream sets solid and must be thawed in a microwave oven before it's soft enough to eat.

Danger: thick ice
An enormously thick sheet of ice covers Antarctica. Each layer of snow that falls on Antarctica compresses the snow below. The compressed snow, called firn, turns a bluish green color. Ice cores taken by scientists provide a record of the Earth's climate over thousands of years.

Moving Earth
Antarctica is almost earthquake-free, but there are more than 10 seismological (earthquake recording) stations on the ice cap. They log quakes originating elsewhere.

Weather balloon launch site

It's cold here!
Antarctica holds the record for the coldest weather anywhere on earth. In 1983 the temperature at the Russian *Vostok* base dropped to -128.6°F (-89.2°C). Mercury thermometers stop working at -40°F (-40°C), and even alcohol thermometers can freeze, so meteorologists have to use special thermometers.

The 300 club
The staff wintering over at the base make most of their own entertainment. Some join "The 300 Club" – a society which gets its name from the joining ceremony. Would-be members run from the sauna into the snow wearing only shoes, thus experiencing a temperature drop of 300 degrees Fahrenheit.

Windy too
The polar continent is also the world's windiest place. In some places wind speeds reach 200 mph (320 km/h), and rarely drop below 30 mph (48 km/h).

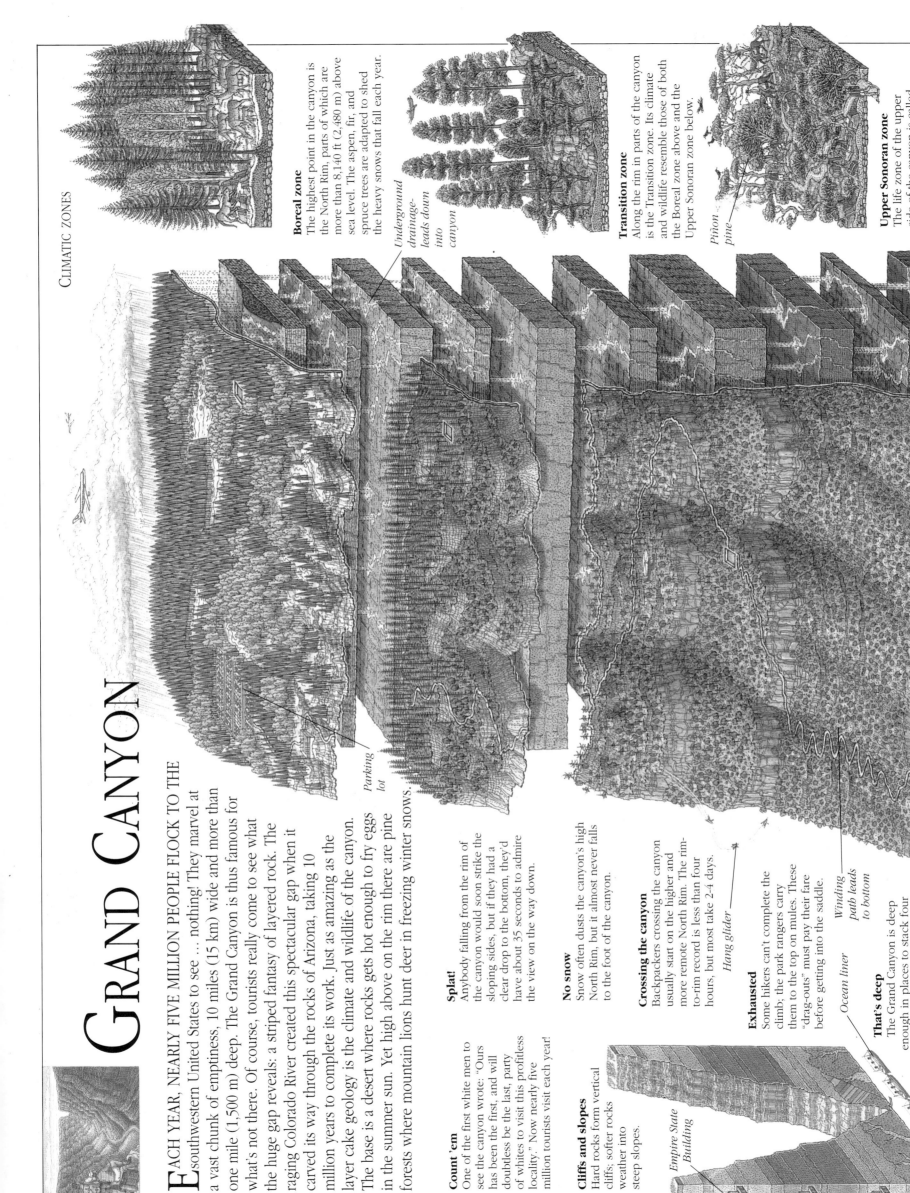

GRAND CANYON

E ACH YEAR, NEARLY FIVE MILLION PEOPLE FLOCK TO THE southwestern United States to see ... nothing! They marvel at a vast chunk of emptiness, 10 miles (15 km) wide and more than one mile (1,500 m) deep. The Grand Canyon is thus famous for what's not there. Of course, tourists really come to see what the huge gap reveals: a striped fantasy of layered rock. The raging Colorado River created this spectacular gap when it carved its way through the rocks of Arizona, taking 10 million years to complete its work. Just as amazing as the layer cake geology is the climate and wildlife of the canyon. The base is a desert where rocks gets hot enough to fry eggs in the summer sun. Yet high above on the rim there are pine forests where mountain lions hunt deer in freezing winter snows.

Boreal zone
The highest point in the canyon is the North Rim, parts of which are more than 8,140 ft (2,480 m) above sea level. The aspen, fir, and spruce trees are adapted to shed the heavy snows that fall each year.

Underground drainage-leads down into canyon

Transition zone
Along the rim in parts of the canyon is the Transition zone. Its climate and wildlife resemble those of both the Boreal zone above and the Upper Sonoran zone below.

Piñon pine

Upper Sonoran zone
The life zone of the upper side of the canyon is called the Upper Sonoran zone. At the top, juniper and piñon pine trees dominate.

Parking lot

Count 'em
One of the first white men to see the canyon wrote: "Ours has been the first, and will doubtless be the last, party of whites to visit this profitless locality." Now nearly five million tourists visit each year!

Cliffs and slopes
Hard rocks form vertical cliffs; softer rocks weather into steep slopes.

Splat!
Anybody falling from the rim of the canyon would soon strike the sloping sides, but if they had a clear drop to the bottom, they'd have about 35 seconds to admire the view on the way down.

No snow
Snow often dusts the canyon's high North Rim, but it almost never falls to the foot of the canyon.

Crossing the canyon
Backpackers crossing the canyon usually start on the higher and more remote North Rim. The rim-to-rim record is less than four hours, but most take 2–4 days.

Hang glider

Exhausted
Some hikers can't complete the climb; the park rangers carry them to the top on mules. These "drag-outs" must pay their fare before getting into the saddle.

Winding path leads to bottom

Ocean liner

That's deep
The Grand Canyon is deep enough in places to stack four Empire State Buildings, one on top of the other. Its maximum width at the base is equivalent to five ocean liners lined up bow-to-stern.

Empire State Building

54

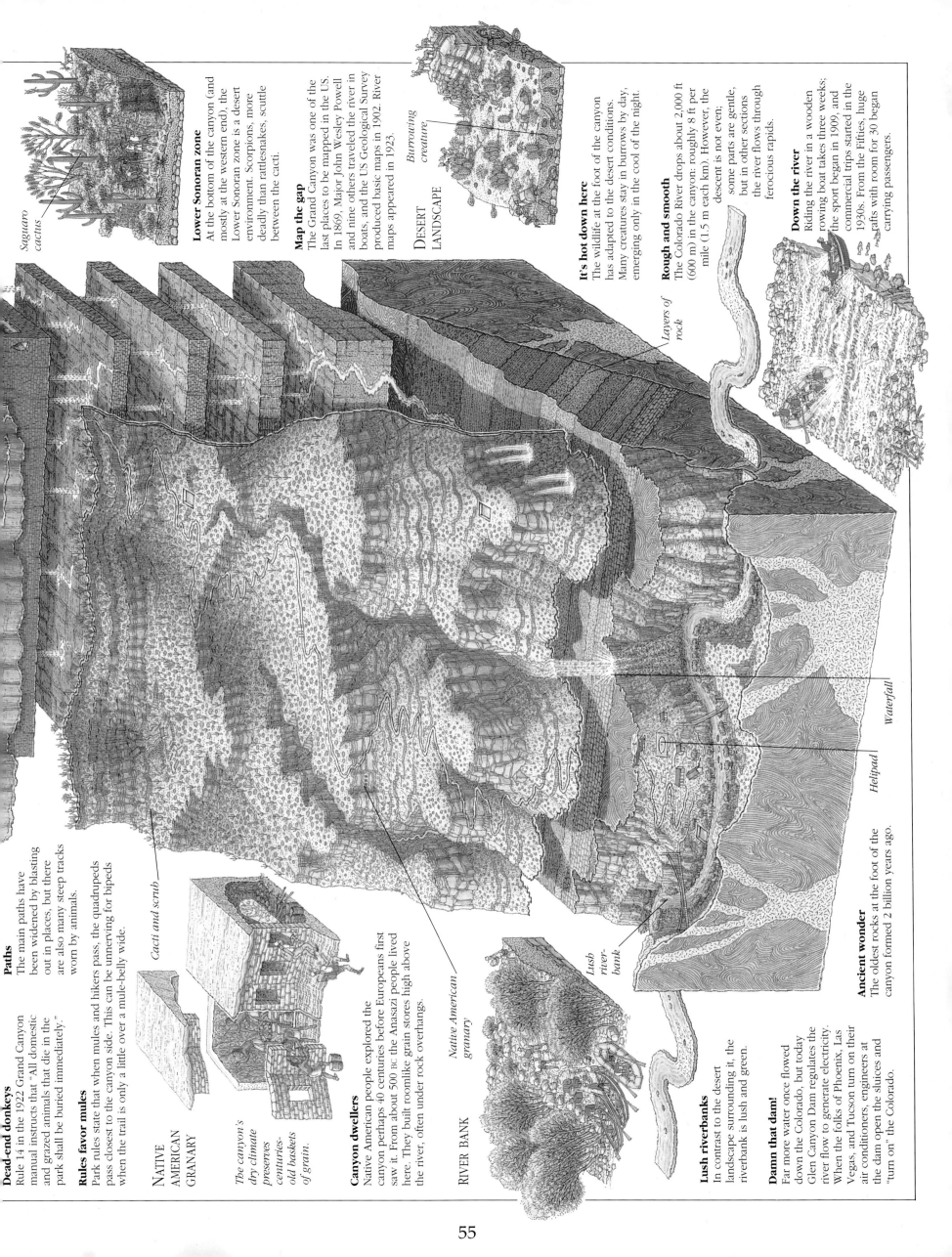

Dead-end donkeys

Rule 14 in the 1922 Grand Canyon manual instructs that "All domestic and grazed animals that die in the park shall be buried immediately.".

Rules favor mules

Park rules state that when mules and hikers pass, the quadrupeds pass closest to the canyon side. This can be unnerving for bipeds when the trail is only a little over a mule-belly wide.

Saguaro cactus

Lower Sonoran zone

At the bottom of the canyon (and mostly at the western end), the Lower Sonoran zone is a desert environment. Scorpions, more deadly than rattlesnakes, scuttle between the cacti.

Map the gap

The Grand Canyon was one of the last places to be mapped in the US. In 1869, Major John Wesley Powell and nine others traveled the river in boats, and the US Geological Survey produced basic maps in 1902. River maps appeared in 1923.

Burrowing creature

DESERT LANDSCAPE

It's hot down here

The wildlife at the foot of the canyon has adapted to the desert conditions. Many creatures stay in burrows by day, emerging only in the cool of the night.

Rough and smooth

The Colorado River drops about 2,000 ft (600 m) in the canyon: roughly 8 ft per mile (1.5 m each km). However, the descent is not even; some parts are gentle, but in other sections the river flows through ferocious rapids.

Layers of rock

Down the river

Riding the river in a wooden rowing boat takes three weeks; the sport began in 1909, and commercial trips started in the 1930s. From the Fifties, huge rafts with room for 30 began carrying passengers.

Cacti and scrub

NATIVE AMERICAN GRANARY

The canyon's dry climate preserves centuries-old baskets of grain.

Canyon dwellers

Native American people explored the canyon perhaps 40 centuries before Europeans first saw it. From about 500 BC the Anasazi people lived here. They built roomlike grain stores high above the river, often under rock overhangs.

Native American granary

Paths

The main paths have been widened by blasting out in places, but there are also many steep tracks worn by animals.

Lush riverbank

RIVER BANK

Lush riverbanks

In contrast to the desert landscape surrounding it, the riverbank is lush and green.

Damn that dam!

Far more water once flowed down the Colorado, but today Glen Canyon Dam regulates the river flow to generate electricity. When the folks of Phoenix, Las Vegas, and Tucson turn on their air conditioners, engineers at the dam open the sluices and "turn on" the Colorado.

Waterfall

Helipad

Ancient wonder

The oldest rocks at the foot of the canyon formed 2 billion years ago.

DESERT LIFE

MORE THAN A FIFTH of the Earth's lands are deserts – dry wastelands that seem empty of life. The driest is Chile's Atacama Desert. In its parched heart no rain fell for 400 years. Despite their appearance, though, deserts are not lifeless. Hardy plants and animals thrive by conserving scarce water in ingenious ways. And in some deserts wandering people follow the rare rains. These nomads don't spend all their time trudging through sand dunes in searing heat. Sandy deserts make up only one seventh of all desert lands. More often gravel, pebbles, or small stones cover the ground, and some deserts are like platforms of bare rock. Nor are deserts always hot: even the vast Sahara Desert in Africa is chilly at night, and cold deserts such as North America's Great Basin have freezing winter days.

The fennec fox's large ears shed heat and help it hear the lizards, rodents, and insects that it eats.

Burrowing animals
Foxes, scorpions, snakes, and other animals shelter in burrows or under rocks to escape the daytime heat. They come out at night to feed.

Desert rodents get all their moisture from dry seeds and never need to drink water.

To save water desert mammals produce highly concentrated urine.

Some desert plants have long roots to help them find water deep in the soil.

When it rains, water will suddenly sweep down this dried-up river bed, known as a wadi.

The water in this river has flowed from a distant rainy area. There is a thin strip of fertile soil on each side of the river, then the land changes abruptly back to desert.

Highland desert areas are often just bare rock, shaped by the wind. This type of desert is called hammada.

Water hole

The camel's hump contains fat which it can convert into water when water is scarce.

Camels can drink a bathtub full of water and then go for days without a drop. This makes them ideal for transporting goods across the desert.

Water travels along an aquifer

Sief dunes

Transverse dunes

Barchans

Beacons mark desert roads which often become covered by sand.

Four-wheel drive trucks are rapidly replacing camels . Trucks usually travel in convoys in case one breaks down.

Sand and rocks carried by the wind scoop out shallow depressions called "blowouts."

Arabian Desert
The Arabian Desert in the Middle East is both sandy and rocky. Other than patches of fertile land near oases and where the land has been artificially irrigated, most of the region is dry and barren. It is mainly uninhabited, except by the Bedouin, because of the lack of water for drinking and farming. In the rocky desert areas, rock is blasted by the hot, dry winds and worn away by freak flash floods.

Aquifer
Sometimes there is water in the ground deep under the desert. This water fell as rain over 8,000 years ago, when the climate in the region was wetter, and has collected in a soft layer of rock, called an aquifer (which means "carries water"). The aquifers supply water to wells.

Sandy desert
In the Arabian Desert, sandy desert areas are called *erg*. As the wind blows the sand around it forms dunes in a variety of shapes. Barchans are crescent-shaped dunes, while seif dunes are long ridges. Where there is a lot of sand and a strong wind blowing from one direction, "transverse" dunes form at right angles to the wind.

Desert clothes
The Bedouin wear clothes that protect them from the extreme heat and cold of the desert climate. Loose robes shield them from the Sun and let air flow around the body. Headcloths can also be wrapped around the face for protection in sandstorms.

Traditional water supplies

In many desert areas village wells get their water supplies from underground tunnels called *qanats*. The water flows from sources up to 25 miles (40 km) away. The tunnels stop water from evaporating, and their gentle slope makes pumping unnecessary. Traditionally they are dug using only hand tools, and building them is very hard work – a 3 mile (5 km) *qanat* takes seven years to build. Yet in Iran 40,000 *qanats* supply up to half of the country's water.

Desert plants

The date palm is a common desert plant. It grows along rivers, at oases, or anywhere where there is water. Dates provide a nutritious staple food for villagers and nomads, and they do not rot in the heat. If water is available for irrigation, farmers can grow all kinds of crops in the desert. In the Negev desert in Israel, they grow apricots, avocados, citrus fruits, and cereals.

Cities in the desert

Living in the desert is no longer just for the Bedouin. Now that large quantities of water can be pumped in, many cities have been built in desert regions. In the United States, the cities of Phoenix and Tucson have grown up in the middle of the Sonoran Desert. Most of Phoenix's water is pumped across the desert from the Colorado River.

Watering the modern way

If deep wells can supply enough water, farmers can use gigantic sprinkler systems to irrigate the desert soils. On flat land center-pivot sprinklers water huge, round fields as big as 80 soccer fields. The green rings are big enough to be seen clearly by astronauts aboard the orbiting space shuttle. In addition to water, the sprinklers spray the crops with fertilizer and pesticides. Automatic controls shut off the water supply when the soil is just wet enough.

The water is channeled to the crops.

This simple water wheel is turned by a cow. It drives a lower wheel with buckets on it that scoop water out of the river and empty it into an irrigation ditch.

This ancient device, called a shadoof, is used to raise water from a river onto the fields. Water from the bucket is poured into pipes or ditches which carry it between the rows of crops.

Crops that are watered by sprinkler systems grow in circles. These circles are planted with hardy cereal crops, such as wheat and millet.

Date plantation

The sprinkler arms rotate like the hands of a watch. The rings in the crops are left by the wheels on the sprinkler arm.

Wells sunken into the aquifer supply water to the village.

Fault

Oasis

Oasis

Water from an aquifer sometimes comes to the surface naturally through a fault in the rock layers. This forms an oasis. Palm trees and other plants grow there because of the water supply.

Pumping station

Harvesting water – or mining it?

Traditional methods of raising water from aquifers under the desert are very inefficient. With the aid of drilling equipment and powerful pumps, engineers can reach much deeper aquifers, and suck far more water out of them. These deep wells could last for ever, but only if the pumps *harvest* the aquifer – drawing water no faster than rain replenishes the supply. Pumping more quickly *mines* the aquifer, rapidly exhausting the supply, or drawing in salt water that poisons the well.

The tent is divided into separate areas for men and women. The men often entertain guests in their quarters, while the women cook, weave, and take care of the children.

Camels extract almost all the water from their dung, so the Bedouin can fuel their fires with it after just a few hours drying.

The Bedouin

The Bedouin are desert nomads. They live in tents that they can take with them from place to place. The tents are made of goat's hair cloth, supported by poles and tied to the ground with guy ropes. The word Bedouin means "people of the desert," but these desert people call themselves *Ahl-el-beit* – "people of the tent."

Smart housing

Traditional buildings in desert regions are shaped for comfort. Houses have small windows to keep the heat out; thick walls provide protection from the sun by day, but store its heat so they are warm in the cold desert nights.

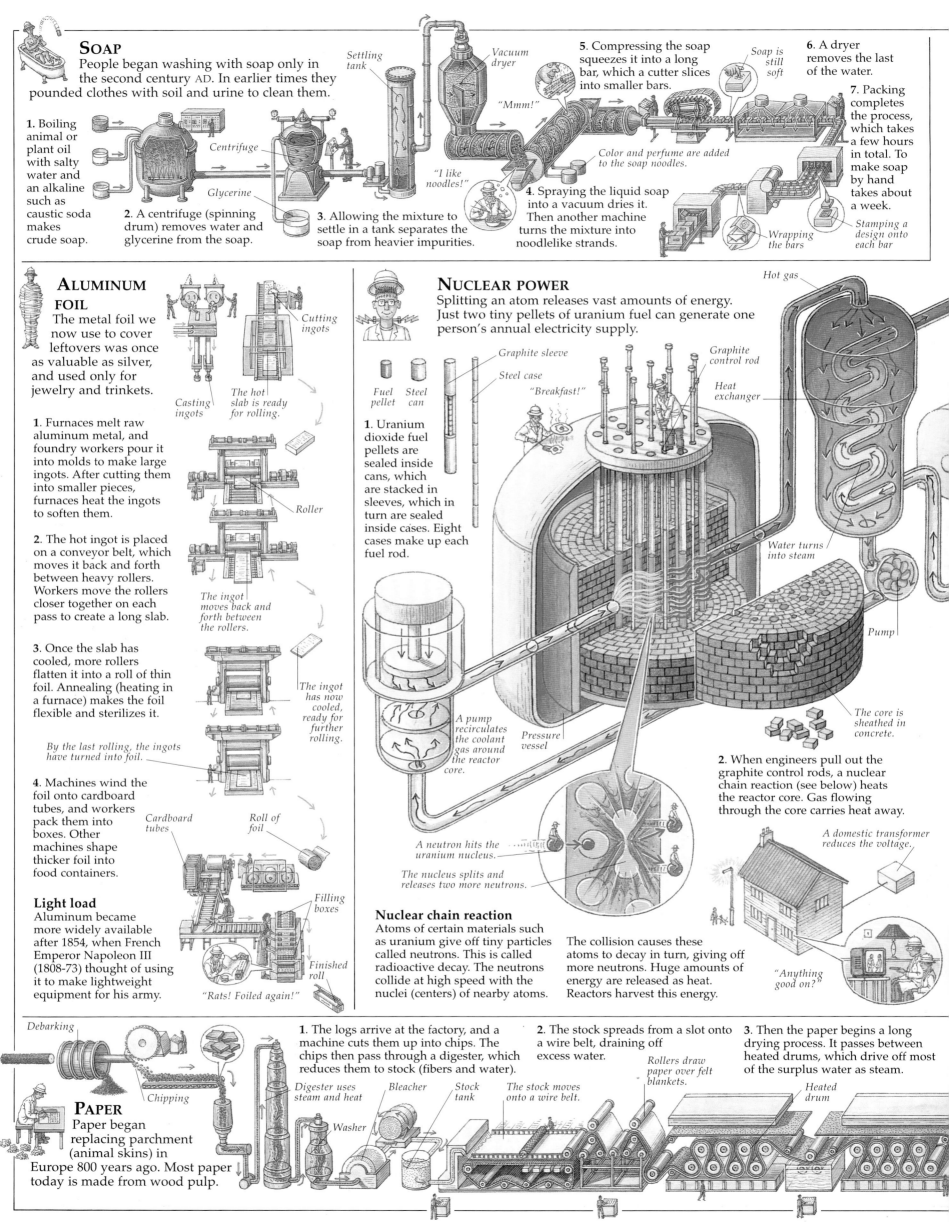

SOAP

People began washing with soap only in the second century AD. In earlier times they pounded clothes with soil and urine to clean them.

1. Boiling animal or plant oil with salty water and an alkaline such as caustic soda makes crude soap.

2. A centrifuge (spinning drum) removes water and glycerine from the soap.

3. Allowing the mixture to settle in a tank separates the soap from heavier impurities.

4. Spraying the liquid soap into a vacuum dries it. Then another machine turns the mixture into noodlelike strands.

5. Compressing the soap squeezes it into a long bar, which a cutter slices into smaller bars.

6. A dryer removes the last of the water.

7. Packing completes the process, which takes a few hours in total. To make soap by hand takes about a week.

Settling tank

Vacuum dryer

Centrifuge

Glycerine

"Mmm!"

"I like noodles!"

Color and perfume are added to the soap noodles.

Soap is still soft

Wrapping the bars

Stamping a design onto each bar

ALUMINUM FOIL

The metal foil we now use to cover leftovers was once as valuable as silver, and used only for jewelry and trinkets.

1. Furnaces melt raw aluminum metal, and foundry workers pour it into molds to make large ingots. After cutting them into smaller pieces, furnaces heat the ingots to soften them.

2. The hot ingot is placed on a conveyor belt, which moves it back and forth between heavy rollers. Workers move the rollers closer together on each pass to create a long slab.

3. Once the slab has cooled, more rollers flatten it into a roll of thin foil. Annealing (heating in a furnace) makes the foil flexible and sterilizes it.

4. Machines wind the foil onto cardboard tubes, and workers pack them into boxes. Other machines shape thicker foil into food containers.

Light load
Aluminum became more widely available after 1854, when French Emperor Napoleon III (1808-73) thought of using it to make lightweight equipment for his army.

Cutting ingots

Casting ingots

The hot slab is ready for rolling.

Roller

The ingot moves back and forth between the rollers.

The ingot has now cooled, ready for further rolling.

By the last rolling, the ingots have turned into foil.

Cardboard tubes

Roll of foil

Filling boxes

Finished roll

"Rats! Foiled again!"

NUCLEAR POWER

Splitting an atom releases vast amounts of energy. Just two tiny pellets of uranium fuel can generate one person's annual electricity supply.

1. Uranium dioxide fuel pellets are sealed inside cans, which are stacked in sleeves, which in turn are sealed inside cases. Eight cases make up each fuel rod.

2. When engineers pull out the graphite control rods, a nuclear chain reaction (see below) heats the reactor core. Gas flowing through the core carries heat away.

Hot gas

Graphite sleeve

Graphite control rod

Steel case

"Breakfast!"

Heat exchanger

Fuel pellet

Steel can

Water turns into steam

A pump recirculates the coolant gas around the reactor core.

Pressure vessel

Pump

The core is sheathed in concrete.

A neutron hits the uranium nucleus.

The nucleus splits and releases two more neutrons.

A domestic transformer reduces the voltage.

"Anything good on?"

Nuclear chain reaction
Atoms of certain materials such as uranium give off tiny particles called neutrons. This is called radioactive decay. The neutrons collide at high speed with the nuclei (centers) of nearby atoms. The collision causes these atoms to decay in turn, giving off more neutrons. Huge amounts of energy are released as heat. Reactors harvest this energy.

PAPER

Paper began replacing parchment (animal skins) in Europe 800 years ago. Most paper today is made from wood pulp.

1. The logs arrive at the factory, and a machine cuts them up into chips. The chips then pass through a digester, which reduces them to stock (fibers and water).

2. The stock spreads from a slot onto a wire belt, draining off excess water.

3. Then the paper begins a long drying process. It passes between heated drums, which drive off most of the surplus water as steam.

Debarking

Chipping

Digester uses steam and heat

Washer

Bleacher

Stock tank

The stock moves onto a wire belt.

Rollers draw paper over felt blankets.

Heated drum

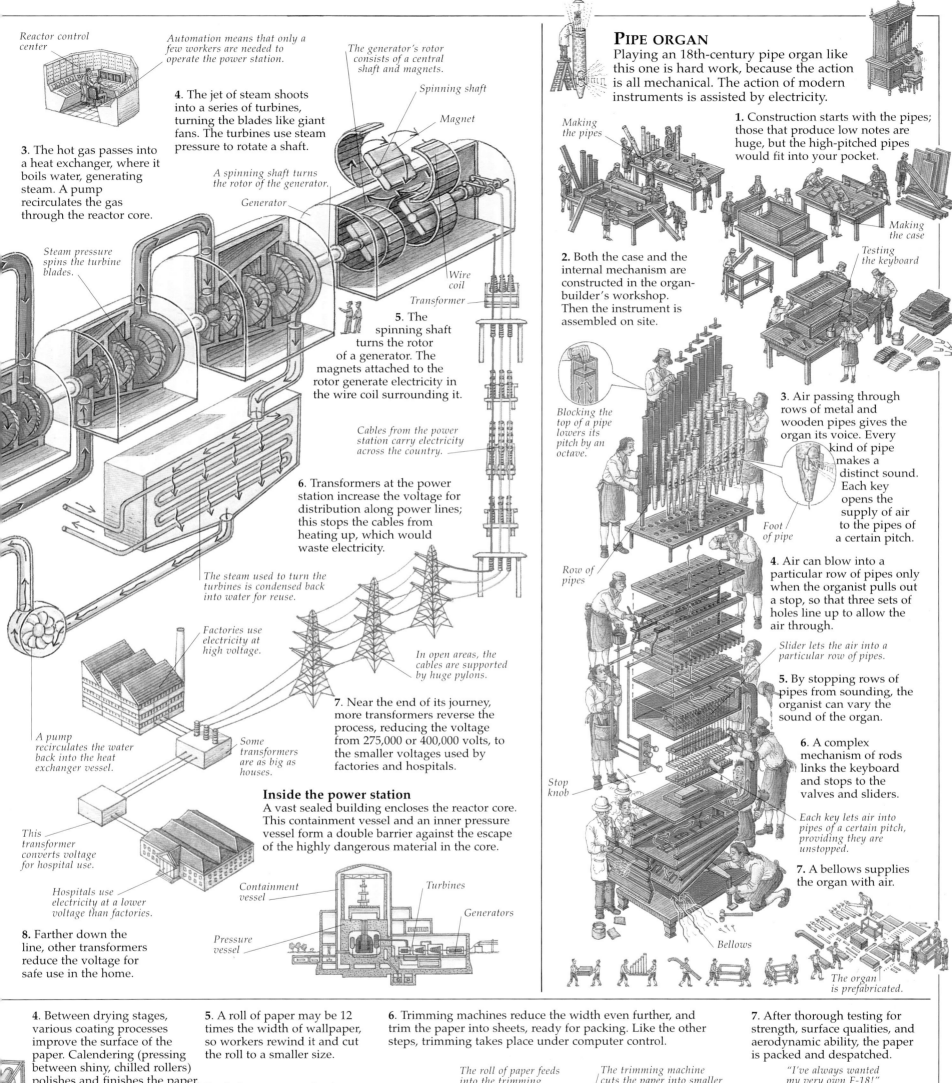

Reactor control center

Automation means that only a few workers are needed to operate the power station.

The generator's rotor consists of a central shaft and magnets.

Spinning shaft

Magnet

3. The hot gas passes into a heat exchanger, where it boils water, generating steam. A pump recirculates the gas through the reactor core.

4. The jet of steam shoots into a series of turbines, turning the blades like giant fans. The turbines use steam pressure to rotate a shaft.

A spinning shaft turns the rotor of the generator.

Generator

Steam pressure spins the turbine blades.

Wire coil

Transformer

5. The spinning shaft turns the rotor of a generator. The magnets attached to the rotor generate electricity in the wire coil surrounding it.

Cables from the power station carry electricity across the country.

6. Transformers at the power station increase the voltage for distribution along power lines; this stops the cables from heating up, which would waste electricity.

The steam used to turn the turbines is condensed back into water for reuse.

Factories use electricity at high voltage.

In open areas, the cables are supported by huge pylons.

A pump recirculates the water back into the heat exchanger vessel.

This transformer converts voltage for hospital use.

Some transformers are as big as houses.

7. Near the end of its journey, more transformers reverse the process, reducing the voltage from 275,000 or 400,000 volts, to the smaller voltages used by factories and hospitals.

Hospitals use electricity at a lower voltage than factories.

8. Farther down the line, other transformers reduce the voltage for safe use in the home.

Inside the power station
A vast sealed building encloses the reactor core. This containment vessel and an inner pressure vessel form a double barrier against the escape of the highly dangerous material in the core.

Containment vessel

Turbines

Generators

Pressure vessel

PIPE ORGAN
Playing an 18th-century pipe organ like this one is hard work, because the action is all mechanical. The action of modern instruments is assisted by electricity.

Making the pipes

1. Construction starts with the pipes; those that produce low notes are huge, but the high-pitched pipes would fit into your pocket.

Making the case

Testing the keyboard

2. Both the case and the internal mechanism are constructed in the organ-builder's workshop. Then the instrument is assembled on site.

Blocking the top of a pipe lowers its pitch by an octave.

3. Air passing through rows of metal and wooden pipes gives the organ its voice. Every kind of pipe makes a distinct sound. Each key opens the supply of air to the pipes of a certain pitch.

Foot of pipe

Row of pipes

4. Air can blow into a particular row of pipes only when the organist pulls out a stop, so that three sets of holes line up to allow the air through.

Slider lets the air into a particular row of pipes.

5. By stopping rows of pipes from sounding, the organist can vary the sound of the organ.

6. A complex mechanism of rods links the keyboard and stops to the valves and sliders.

Stop knob

Each key lets air into pipes of a certain pitch, providing they are unstopped.

7. A bellows supplies the organ with air.

Bellows

The organ is prefabricated.

4. Between drying stages, various coating processes improve the surface of the paper. Calendering (pressing between shiny, chilled rollers) polishes and finishes the paper.

Calendering

The finished roll is huge.

5. A roll of paper may be 12 times the width of wallpaper, so workers rewind it and cut the roll to a smaller size.

Rewinding

Cutting

6. Trimming machines reduce the width even further, and trim the paper into sheets, ready for packing. Like the other steps, trimming takes place under computer control.

"Phew! That's easier to manage!"

The roll of paper feeds into the trimming machine.

The trimming machine cuts the paper into smaller sheets, ready for packing.

7. After thorough testing for strength, surface qualities, and aerodynamic ability, the paper is packed and despatched.

"I've always wanted my very own F-18!"

59

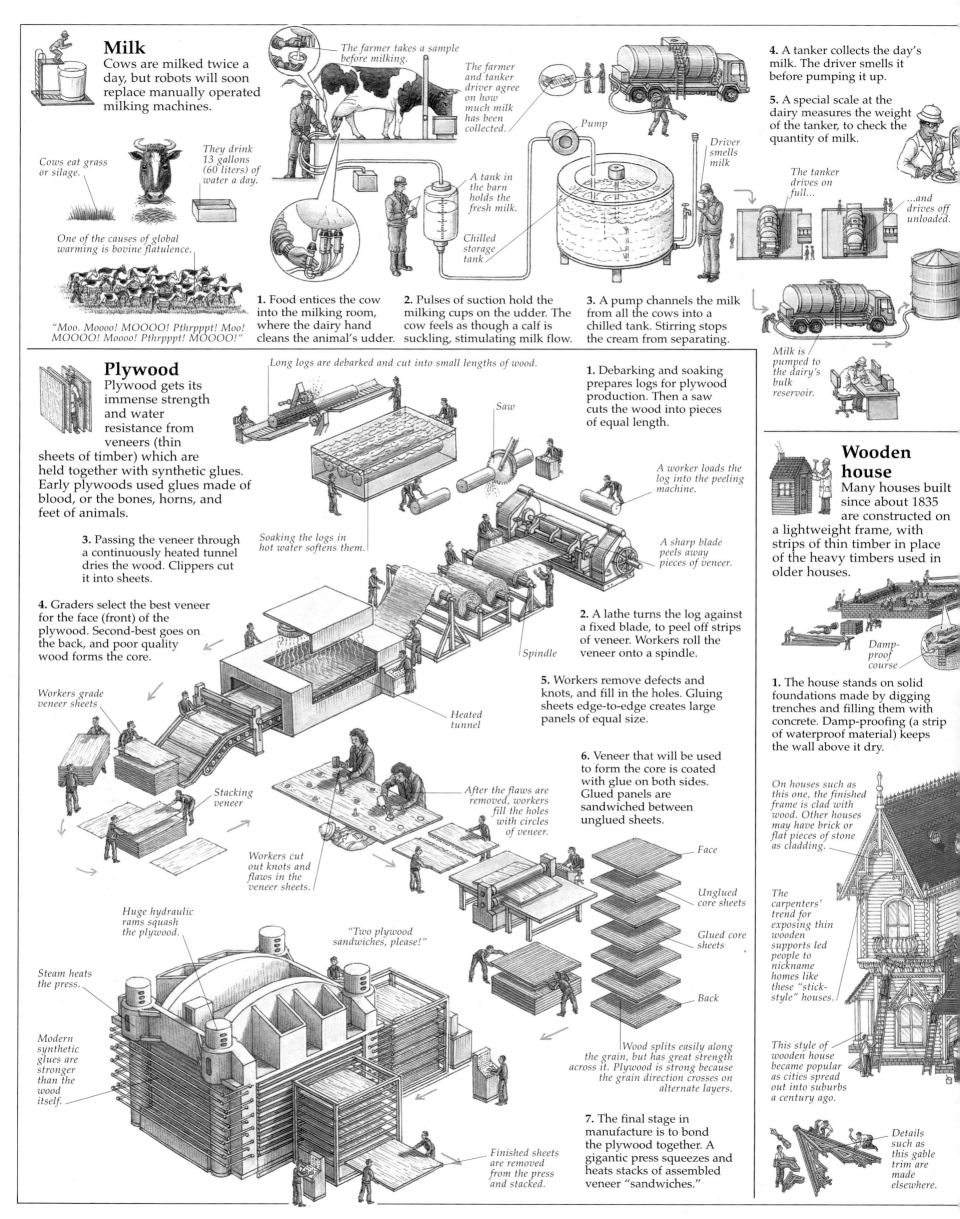

Milk

Cows are milked twice a day, but robots will soon replace manually operated milking machines.

The farmer takes a sample before milking.

The farmer and tanker driver agree on how much milk has been collected.

Pump

4. A tanker collects the day's milk. The driver smells it before pumping it up.

5. A special scale at the dairy measures the weight of the tanker, to check the quantity of milk.

Cows eat grass or silage.

They drink 13 gallons (60 liters) of water a day.

A tank in the barn holds the fresh milk.

Driver smells milk

Chilled storage tank

The tanker drives on full...

...and drives off unloaded.

One of the causes of global warming is bovine flatulence.

"Moo. Moooo! MOOOO! Pthrpppt! Moo! MOOOO! Moooo! Pthrpppt! MOOOO!"

1. Food entices the cow into the milking room, where the dairy hand cleans the animal's udder.

2. Pulses of suction hold the milking cups on the udder. The cow feels as though a calf is suckling, stimulating milk flow.

3. A pump channels the milk from all the cows into a chilled tank. Stirring stops the cream from separating.

Milk is pumped to the dairy's bulk reservoir.

Plywood

Plywood gets its immense strength and water resistance from veneers (thin sheets of timber) which are held together with synthetic glues. Early plywoods used glues made of blood, or the bones, horns, and feet of animals.

Long logs are debarked and cut into small lengths of wood.

Saw

1. Debarking and soaking prepares logs for plywood production. Then a saw cuts the wood into pieces of equal length.

A worker loads the log into the peeling machine.

3. Passing the veneer through a continuously heated tunnel dries the wood. Clippers cut it into sheets.

Soaking the logs in hot water softens them.

A sharp blade peels away pieces of veneer.

4. Graders select the best veneer for the face (front) of the plywood. Second-best goes on the back, and poor quality wood forms the core.

Spindle

2. A lathe turns the log against a fixed blade, to peel off strips of veneer. Workers roll the veneer onto a spindle.

Workers grade veneer sheets

Heated tunnel

5. Workers remove defects and knots, and fill in the holes. Gluing sheets edge-to-edge creates large panels of equal size.

Stacking veneer

After the flaws are removed, workers fill the holes with circles of veneer.

6. Veneer that will be used to form the core is coated with glue on both sides. Glued panels are sandwiched between unglued sheets.

Workers cut out knots and flaws in the veneer sheets.

Face

Huge hydraulic rams squash the plywood.

"Two plywood sandwiches, please!"

Unglued core sheets

Steam heats the press.

Glued core sheets

Modern synthetic glues are stronger than the wood itself.

Back

Wood splits easily along the grain, but has great strength across it. Plywood is strong because the grain direction crosses on alternate layers.

Finished sheets are removed from the press and stacked.

7. The final stage in manufacture is to bond the plywood together. A gigantic press squeezes and heats stacks of assembled veneer "sandwiches."

Wooden house

Many houses built since about 1835 are constructed on a lightweight frame, with strips of thin timber in place of the heavy timbers used in older houses.

Damp-proof course

1. The house stands on solid foundations made by digging trenches and filling them with concrete. Damp-proofing (a strip of waterproof material) keeps the wall above it dry.

On houses such as this one, the finished frame is clad with wood. Other houses may have brick or flat pieces of stone as cladding.

The carpenters' trend for exposing thin wooden supports led people to nickname homes like these "stick-style" houses.

This style of wooden house became popular as cities spread out into suburbs a century ago.

Details such as this gable trim are made elsewhere.

6. A dairy technician checks the milk before pumping it out of the tanker and into one of the bulk reservoirs.

Hot water pasteurizes milk

7. A separator skims off the lighter, fattier cream from the rest of the milk. The cream will make cheese or butter – or ice cream!

Sterilizing milk bottles

Storage tank

Filling bottles

Packing for shipment

8. Heating the milk to 162° F (72° C) for 15 seconds kills bacteria – a process called pasteurization.

The milk entering the plant cools the pasteurized milk leaving it, and is itself warmed up.

Cold water chills milk

Quality control is important.

9. The packing plant pours milk into cartons or bottles, and keeps it chilled until delivery. Milk stays fresh for a week at 40° F (4.5° C) or less.

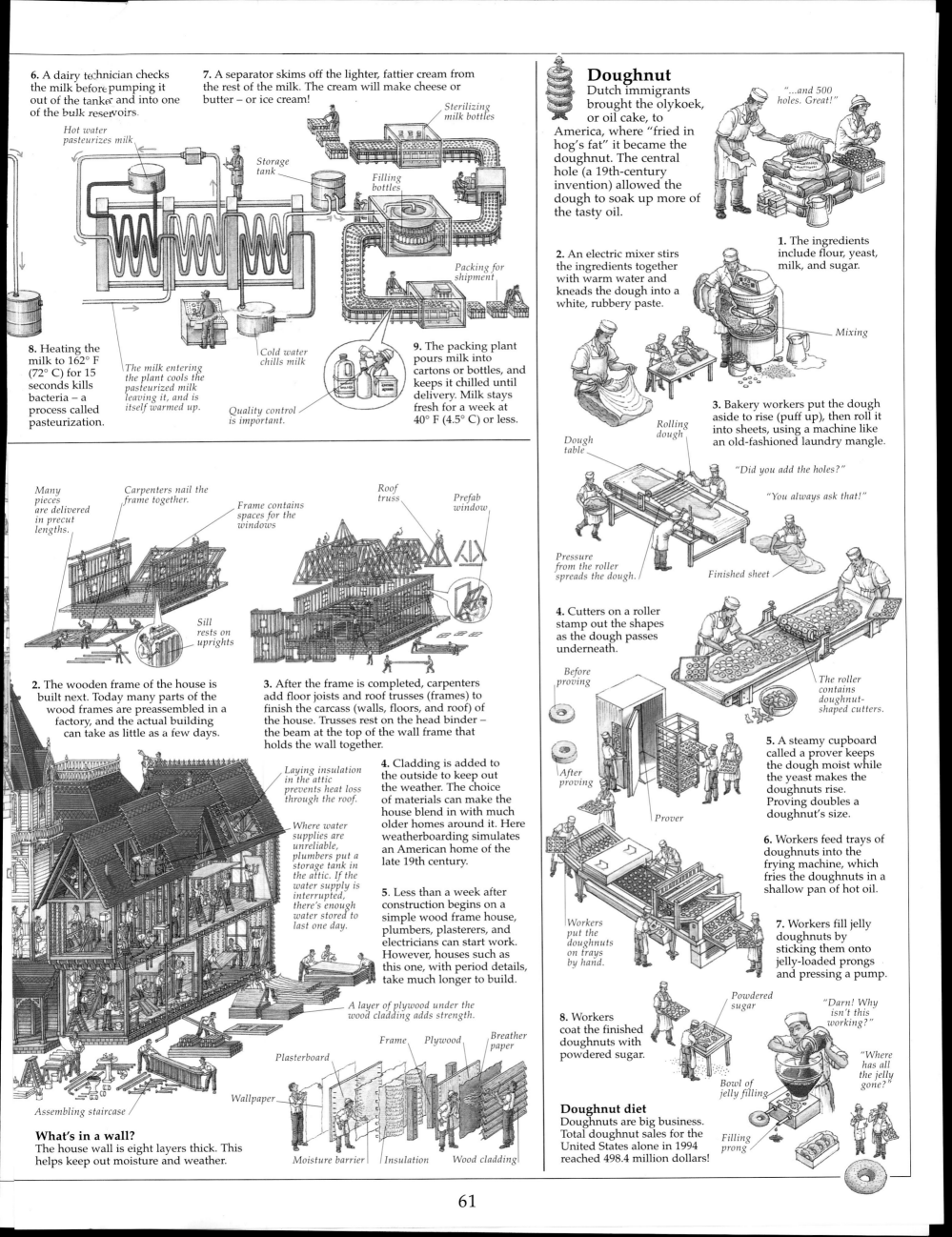

Doughnut

Dutch immigrants brought the olykoek, or oil cake, to America, where "fried in hog's fat" it became the doughnut. The central hole (a 19th-century invention) allowed the dough to soak up more of the tasty oil.

"...and 500 holes. Great!"

1. The ingredients include flour, yeast, milk, and sugar.

2. An electric mixer stirs the ingredients together with warm water and kneads the dough into a white, rubbery paste.

Mixing

Dough table

Rolling dough

3. Bakery workers put the dough aside to rise (puff up), then roll it into sheets, using a machine like an old-fashioned laundry mangle.

"Did you add the holes?"

"You always ask that!"

Pressure from the roller spreads the dough.

Finished sheet

4. Cutters on a roller stamp out the shapes as the dough passes underneath.

Before proving

After proving

The roller contains doughnut-shaped cutters.

5. A steamy cupboard called a prover keeps the dough moist while the yeast makes the doughnuts rise. Proving doubles a doughnut's size.

Prover

6. Workers feed trays of doughnuts into the frying machine, which fries the doughnuts in a shallow pan of hot oil.

Workers put the doughnuts on trays by hand.

7. Workers fill jelly doughnuts by sticking them onto jelly-loaded prongs and pressing a pump.

Powdered sugar

8. Workers coat the finished doughnuts with powdered sugar.

"Darn! Why isn't this working?"

"Where has all the jelly gone?"

Bowl of jelly filling

Filling prong

Doughnut diet
Doughnuts are big business. Total doughnut sales for the United States alone in 1994 reached 498.4 million dollars!

Many pieces are delivered in precut lengths.

Carpenters nail the frame together.

Frame contains spaces for the windows

Roof truss

Prefab window

Sill rests on uprights

2. The wooden frame of the house is built next. Today many parts of the wood frames are preassembled in a factory, and the actual building can take as little as a few days.

3. After the frame is completed, carpenters add floor joists and roof trusses (frames) to finish the carcass (walls, floors, and roof) of the house. Trusses rest on the head binder – the beam at the top of the wall frame that holds the wall together.

Laying insulation in the attic prevents heat loss through the roof.

Where water supplies are unreliable, plumbers put a storage tank in the attic. If the water supply is interrupted, there's enough water stored to last one day.

4. Cladding is added to the outside to keep out the weather. The choice of materials can make the house blend in with much older homes around it. Here weatherboarding simulates an American home of the late 19th century.

5. Less than a week after construction begins on a simple wood frame house, plumbers, plasterers, and electricians can start work. However, houses such as this one, with period details, take much longer to build.

A layer of plywood under the wood cladding adds strength.

Assembling staircase

What's in a wall?
The house wall is eight layers thick. This helps keep out moisture and weather.

Wallpaper

Plasterboard

Frame

Plywood

Breather paper

Moisture barrier

Insulation

Wood cladding

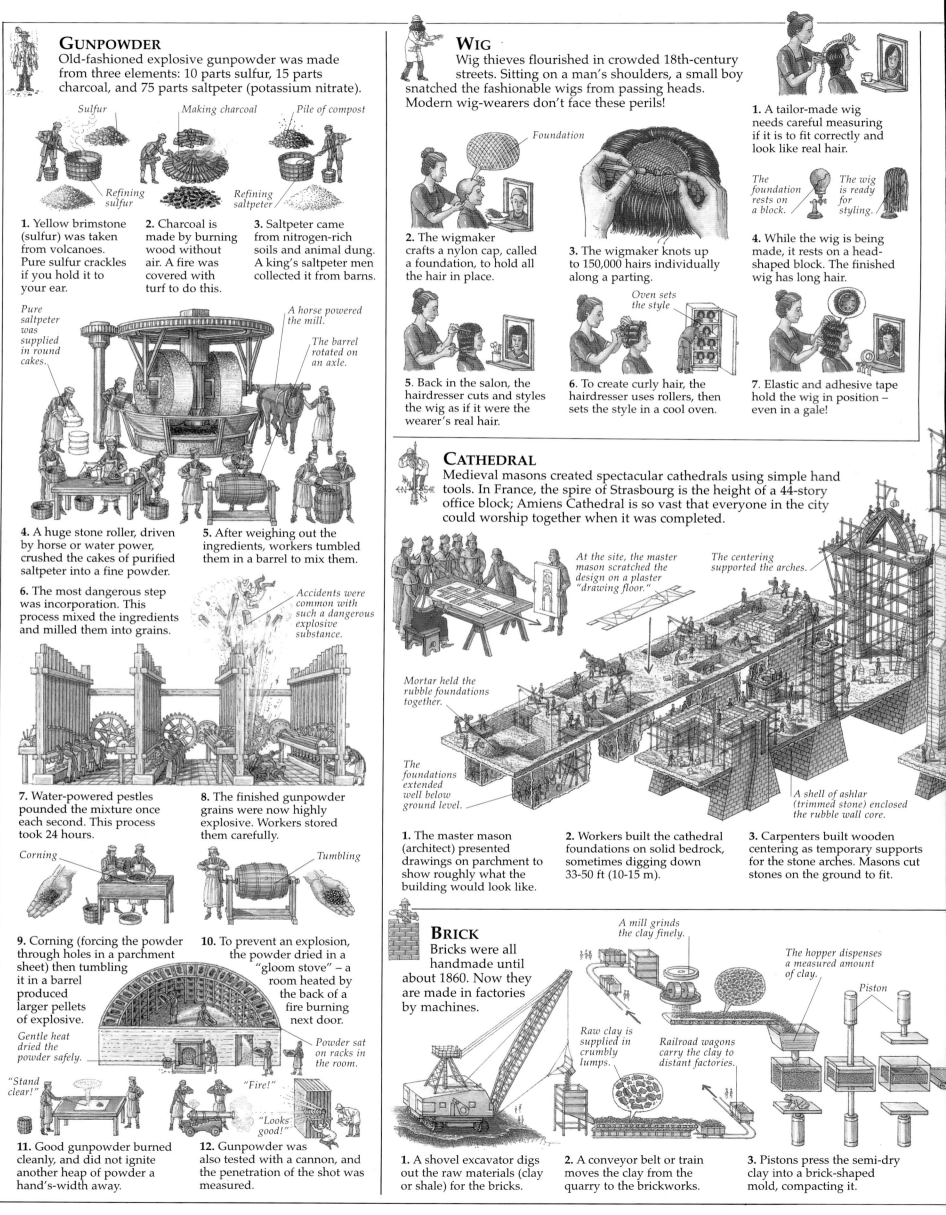

GUNPOWDER

Old-fashioned explosive gunpowder was made from three elements: 10 parts sulfur, 15 parts charcoal, and 75 parts saltpeter (potassium nitrate).

Sulfur   *Making charcoal*   *Pile of compost*

Refining sulfur   *Refining saltpeter*

1. Yellow brimstone (sulfur) was taken from volcanoes. Pure sulfur crackles if you hold it to your ear.

2. Charcoal is made by burning wood without air. A fire was covered with turf to do this.

3. Saltpeter came from nitrogen-rich soils and animal dung. A king's saltpeter men collected it from barns.

Pure saltpeter was supplied in round cakes.

A horse powered the mill.

The barrel rotated on an axle.

4. A huge stone roller, driven by horse or water power, crushed the cakes of purified saltpeter into a fine powder.

5. After weighing out the ingredients, workers tumbled them in a barrel to mix them.

6. The most dangerous step was incorporation. This process mixed the ingredients and milled them into grains.

Accidents were common with such a dangerous explosive substance.

7. Water-powered pestles pounded the mixture once each second. This process took 24 hours.

8. The finished gunpowder grains were now highly explosive. Workers stored them carefully.

Corning   *Tumbling*

9. Corning (forcing the powder through holes in a parchment sheet) then tumbling it in a barrel produced larger pellets of explosive.

10. To prevent an explosion, the powder dried in a "gloom stove" – a room heated by the back of a fire burning next door.

Gentle heat dried the powder safely.

Powder sat on racks in the room.

"Stand clear!"   *"Fire!"*   *"Looks good!"*

11. Good gunpowder burned cleanly, and did not ignite another heap of powder a hand's-width away.

12. Gunpowder was also tested with a cannon, and the penetration of the shot was measured.

WIG

Wig thieves flourished in crowded 18th-century streets. Sitting on a man's shoulders, a small boy snatched the fashionable wigs from passing heads. Modern wig-wearers don't face these perils!

Foundation

1. A tailor-made wig needs careful measuring if it is to fit correctly and look like real hair.

The foundation rests on a block.   *The wig is ready for styling.*

2. The wigmaker crafts a nylon cap, called a foundation, to hold all the hair in place.

3. The wigmaker knots up to 150,000 hairs individually along a parting.

4. While the wig is being made, it rests on a head-shaped block. The finished wig has long hair.

Oven sets the style

5. Back in the salon, the hairdresser cuts and styles the wig as if it were the wearer's real hair.

6. To create curly hair, the hairdresser uses rollers, then sets the style in a cool oven.

7. Elastic and adhesive tape hold the wig in position – even in a gale!

CATHEDRAL

Medieval masons created spectacular cathedrals using simple hand tools. In France, the spire of Strasbourg is the height of a 44-story office block; Amiens Cathedral is so vast that everyone in the city could worship together when it was completed.

At the site, the master mason scratched the design on a plaster "drawing floor."

The centering supported the arches.

Mortar held the rubble foundations together.

The foundations extended well below ground level.

A shell of ashlar (trimmed stone) enclosed the rubble wall core.

1. The master mason (architect) presented drawings on parchment to show roughly what the building would look like.

2. Workers built the cathedral foundations on solid bedrock, sometimes digging down 33-50 ft (10-15 m).

3. Carpenters built wooden centering as temporary supports for the stone arches. Masons cut stones on the ground to fit.

BRICK

Bricks were all handmade until about 1860. Now they are made in factories by machines.

A mill grinds the clay finely.

The hopper dispenses a measured amount of clay.

Piston

Raw clay is supplied in crumbly lumps.

Railroad wagons carry the clay to distant factories.

1. A shovel excavator digs out the raw materials (clay or shale) for the bricks.

2. A conveyor belt or train moves the clay from the quarry to the brickworks.

3. Pistons press the semi-dry clay into a brick-shaped mold, compacting it.

A lead weight
The lead covering the roof of the cathedral was often the most valuable part of the whole building. The amount of metal on a roof could be huge. During the Great Fire of London in 1666, the roof of Old St. Paul's Cathedral melted and sent a river of molten lead flowing through the streets.

"Hmm, this looks like it will hold for a few centuries!"

Masons used ladders and scaffolding to reach their work.

Lead sheeting protected the wooden roof against rain.

Buttresses prevented the walls from splaying out under the weight of the lead roof.

Wooden scaffolding

Slender columns allowed for big windows of colored glass.

Winch lifts stones

Layer of concrete

Vault rib

The mosaic floor maze was for worship: the faithful traced the winding path on their knees.

It's all your vault...
Vaults were the only way medieval masons could construct a large ceiling area. Only the thick stone ribs needed wooden supports during construction.

1. Masons built the ribs of the vault first.

2. Pieces of wood held up the stones while the mortar between them set.

3. Flat stones were added to create a lightweight ceiling.

4. Finally, a layer of concrete covered the entire vault to seal it.

ATHLETIC SHOE
Developing the design for a new athletic shoe takes many years. Only after extensive research and modifications will the shoe go on sale to the public.

"I think it needs a thicker sole."

1. The athletes who will use the shoe are consulted at the design stage.

Finished sample shoe *Trim* *Upper* *Cushion* *Sole* *Sole insert*

2. A sample shoe is built. Most athletic shoes have five main parts, but there may be many more.

"Phew! We need to work on the ventilation!" *"It runs by itself!"*

3. Field trials are carried out.

Cutting pieces of leather *Sewing machine*

4. The shoes are assembled mainly by hand. Workers stitch the uppers and trim, then glue the soles to the uppers.

"Glad we got that ventilation fixed!"

5. The quality of the finished shoes is carefully checked.

Building many identical bays extended the cathedral's length.

4. Masons completed work on one bay (the section between two main columns) before starting the next. Building work stopped in the winter, and thatch covered uncompleted walls to prevent damage by rain and frost.

5. Construction of the vaults (arched stone ceilings) was the trickiest part of the entire building job. Carpenters constructed a temporary roof, so that masons could then work on the first stage of the vaults protected from the weather.

6. Once the roof was covered with lead, the vaults could be finished, and the floor of the cathedral laid. Last of all, the interior was decorated.

7. Building a cathedral took so long that the architect was often dead by the time the cathedral opened. Some cathedrals took hundreds of years to complete.

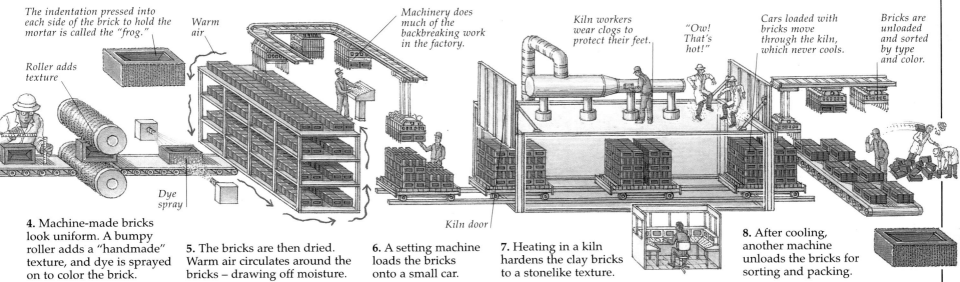

The indentation pressed into each side of the brick to hold the mortar is called the "frog."

Roller adds texture

Warm air

Machinery does much of the backbreaking work in the factory.

Kiln workers wear clogs to protect their feet.

"Ow! That's hot!"

Cars loaded with bricks move through the kiln, which never cools.

Bricks are unloaded and sorted by type and color.

Dye spray

Kiln door

4. Machine-made bricks look uniform. A bumpy roller adds a "handmade" texture, and dye is sprayed on to color the brick.

5. The bricks are then dried. Warm air circulates around the bricks – drawing off moisture.

6. A setting machine loads the bricks onto a small car.

7. Heating in a kiln hardens the clay bricks to a stonelike texture.

8. After cooling, another machine unloads the bricks for sorting and packing.

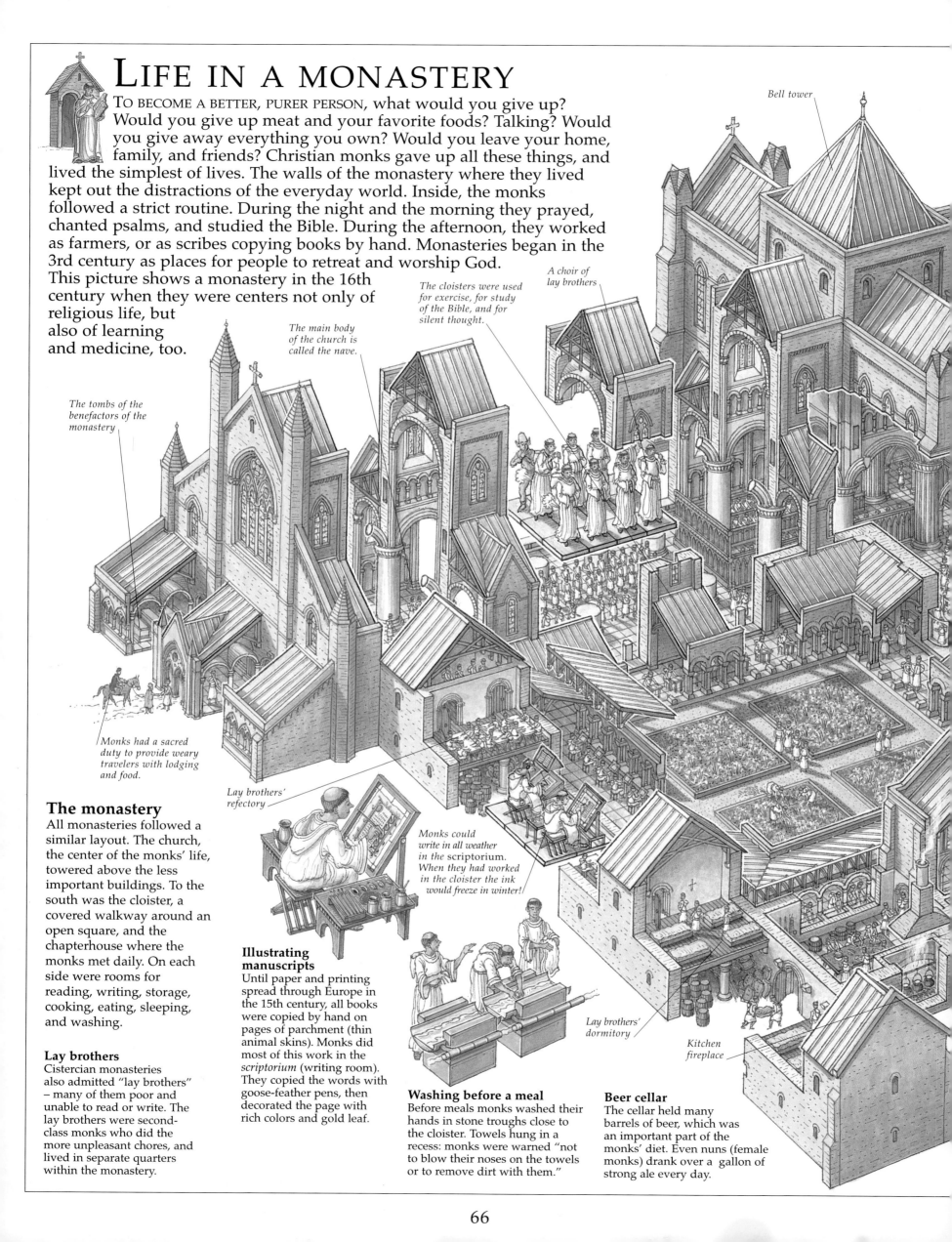

LIFE IN A MONASTERY

TO BECOME A BETTER, PURER PERSON, what would you give up? Would you give up meat and your favorite foods? Talking? Would you give away everything you own? Would you leave your home, family, and friends? Christian monks gave up all these things, and lived the simplest of lives. The walls of the monastery where they lived kept out the distractions of the everyday world. Inside, the monks followed a strict routine. During the night and the morning they prayed, chanted psalms, and studied the Bible. During the afternoon, they worked as farmers, or as scribes copying books by hand. Monasteries began in the 3rd century as places for people to retreat and worship God. This picture shows a monastery in the 16th century when they were centers not only of religious life, but also of learning and medicine, too.

Bell tower

A choir of lay brothers

The cloisters were used for exercise, for study of the Bible, and for silent thought.

The main body of the church is called the nave.

The tombs of the benefactors of the monastery

Monks had a sacred duty to provide weary travelers with lodging and food.

Lay brothers' refectory

Monks could write in all weather in the scriptorium. *When they had worked in the cloister the ink would freeze in winter!*

Lay brothers' dormitory

Kitchen fireplace

The monastery
All monasteries followed a similar layout. The church, the center of the monks' life, towered above the less important buildings. To the south was the cloister, a covered walkway around an open square, and the chapterhouse where the monks met daily. On each side were rooms for reading, writing, storage, cooking, eating, sleeping, and washing.

Lay brothers
Cistercian monasteries also admitted "lay brothers" – many of them poor and unable to read or write. The lay brothers were second-class monks who did the more unpleasant chores, and lived in separate quarters within the monastery.

Illustrating manuscripts
Until paper and printing spread through Europe in the 15th century, all books were copied by hand on pages of parchment (thin animal skins). Monks did most of this work in the *scriptorium* (writing room). They copied the words with goose-feather pens, then decorated the page with rich colors and gold leaf.

Washing before a meal
Before meals monks washed their hands in stone troughs close to the cloister. Towels hung in a recess: monks were warned "not to blow their noses on the towels or to remove dirt with them."

Beer cellar
The cellar held many barrels of beer, which was an important part of the monks' diet. Even nuns (female monks) drank over a gallon of strong ale every day.

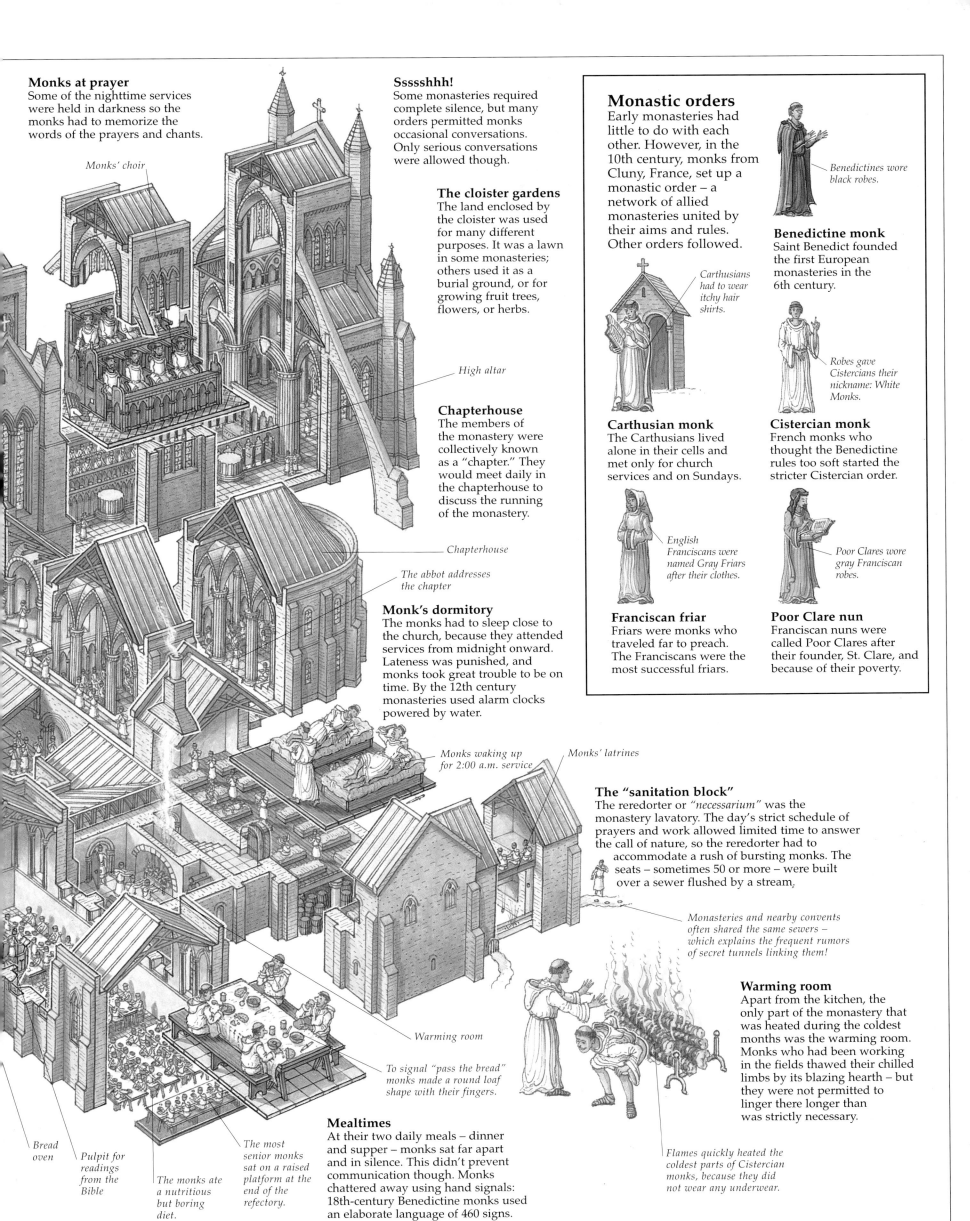

Monks at prayer
Some of the nighttime services were held in darkness so the monks had to memorize the words of the prayers and chants.

Monks' choir

Sssssshhh!
Some monasteries required complete silence, but many orders permitted monks occasional conversations. Only serious conversations were allowed though.

The cloister gardens
The land enclosed by the cloister was used for many different purposes. It was a lawn in some monasteries; others used it as a burial ground, or for growing fruit trees, flowers, or herbs.

High altar

Chapterhouse
The members of the monastery were collectively known as a "chapter." They would meet daily in the chapterhouse to discuss the running of the monastery.

Chapterhouse

The abbot addresses the chapter

Monk's dormitory
The monks had to sleep close to the church, because they attended services from midnight onward. Lateness was punished, and monks took great trouble to be on time. By the 12th century monasteries used alarm clocks powered by water.

Monks waking up for 2:00 a.m. service

Monks' latrines

The "sanitation block"
The reredorter or *"necessarium"* was the monastery lavatory. The day's strict schedule of prayers and work allowed limited time to answer the call of nature, so the reredorter had to accommodate a rush of bursting monks. The seats – sometimes 50 or more – were built over a sewer flushed by a stream.

Monasteries and nearby convents often shared the same sewers – which explains the frequent rumors of secret tunnels linking them!

Warming room
Apart from the kitchen, the only part of the monastery that was heated during the coldest months was the warming room. Monks who had been working in the fields thawed their chilled limbs by its blazing hearth – but they were not permitted to linger there longer than was strictly necessary.

Warming room

To signal "pass the bread" monks made a round loaf shape with their fingers.

Bread oven

Pulpit for readings from the Bible

The monks ate a nutritious but boring diet.

The most senior monks sat on a raised platform at the end of the refectory.

Mealtimes
At their two daily meals – dinner and supper – monks sat far apart and in silence. This didn't prevent communication though. Monks chattered away using hand signals: 18th-century Benedictine monks used an elaborate language of 460 signs.

Flames quickly heated the coldest parts of Cistercian monks, because they did not wear any underwear.

Monastic orders
Early monasteries had little to do with each other. However, in the 10th century, monks from Cluny, France, set up a monastic order – a network of allied monasteries united by their aims and rules. Other orders followed.

Benedictines wore black robes.

Benedictine monk
Saint Benedict founded the first European monasteries in the 6th century.

Carthusians had to wear itchy hair shirts.

Robes gave Cistercians their nickname: White Monks.

Carthusian monk
The Carthusians lived alone in their cells and met only for church services and on Sundays.

Cistercian monk
French monks who thought the Benedictine rules too soft started the stricter Cistercian order.

English Franciscans were named Gray Friars after their clothes.

Poor Clares wore gray Franciscan robes.

Franciscan friar
Friars were monks who traveled far to preach. The Franciscans were the most successful friars.

Poor Clare nun
Franciscan nuns were called Poor Clares after their founder, St. Clare, and because of their poverty.

Windmill

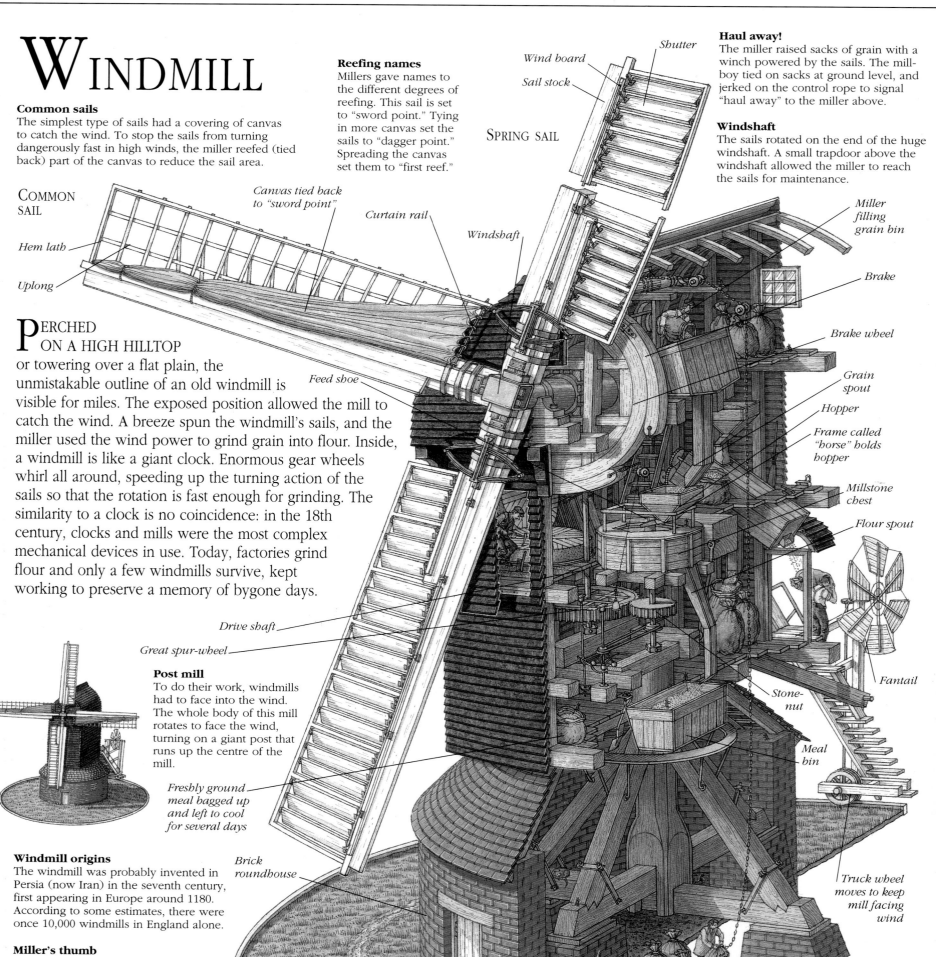

Common sails

The simplest type of sails had a covering of canvas to catch the wind. To stop the sails from turning dangerously fast in high winds, the miller reefed (tied back) part of the canvas to reduce the sail area.

COMMON SAIL

Hem lath

Uplong

Reefing names

Millers gave names to the different degrees of reefing. This sail is set to "sword point." Tying in more canvas set the sails to "dagger point." Spreading the canvas set them to "first reef."

Wind board

Sail stock

SPRING SAIL

Shutter

Haul away!

The miller raised sacks of grain with a winch powered by the sails. The mill-boy tied on sacks at ground level, and jerked on the control rope to signal "haul away" to the miller above.

Windshaft

The sails rotated on the end of the huge windshaft. A small trapdoor above the windshaft allowed the miller to reach the sails for maintenance.

Canvas tied back to "sword point"

Curtain rail

Windshaft

Miller filling grain bin

Brake

Brake wheel

Grain spout

Hopper

Frame called "horse" holds hopper

Millstone chest

Flour spout

PERCHED
ON A HIGH HILLTOP
or towering over a flat plain, the unmistakable outline of an old windmill is visible for miles. The exposed position allowed the mill to catch the wind. A breeze spun the windmill's sails, and the miller used the wind power to grind grain into flour. Inside, a windmill is like a giant clock. Enormous gear wheels whirl all around, speeding up the turning action of the sails so that the rotation is fast enough for grinding. The similarity to a clock is no coincidence: in the 18th century, clocks and mills were the most complex mechanical devices in use. Today, factories grind flour and only a few windmills survive, kept working to preserve a memory of bygone days.

Feed shoe

Drive shaft

Great spur-wheel

Fantail

Stone-nut

Meal bin

Post mill

To do their work, windmills had to face into the wind. The whole body of this mill rotates to face the wind, turning on a giant post that runs up the centre of the mill.

Freshly ground meal bagged up and left to cool for several days

Brick roundhouse

Truck wheel moves to keep mill facing wind

Windmill origins

The windmill was probably invented in Persia (now Iran) in the seventh century, first appearing in Europe around 1180. According to some estimates, there were once 10,000 windmills in England alone.

Miller's thumb

To test the quality of flour, millers rubbed it between their thumbs and index fingers. This habit flattened their thumbs, making the hands of a miller instantly recognizable. Millers charged their customers by keeping some of the flour for themselves. Some grew wealthy by keeping more than their fair share.

Dangerous mills

Windmills were cramped, dangerous places, and a careless miller could easily be crushed by the whirling wheels, each weighing as much as a small car. As well, millers with long hair risked catching it in the gears and being scalped.

Sacks of grain to be milled

Mill-boy ties chain to sacks to be hoisted to top floor

Path of the power

1. Wind pressure turns the sails.
2. The sails turn the windshaft.
3. The windshaft turns the huge brake wheel.
4. Cogs on the brake wheel drive around the smaller wallower.
5. A shaft from the wallower makes the great spur-wheel turn.
6. The great spur-wheel meshes with the two stone-nuts, turning them.
7. The stone-nuts turn the stones above.

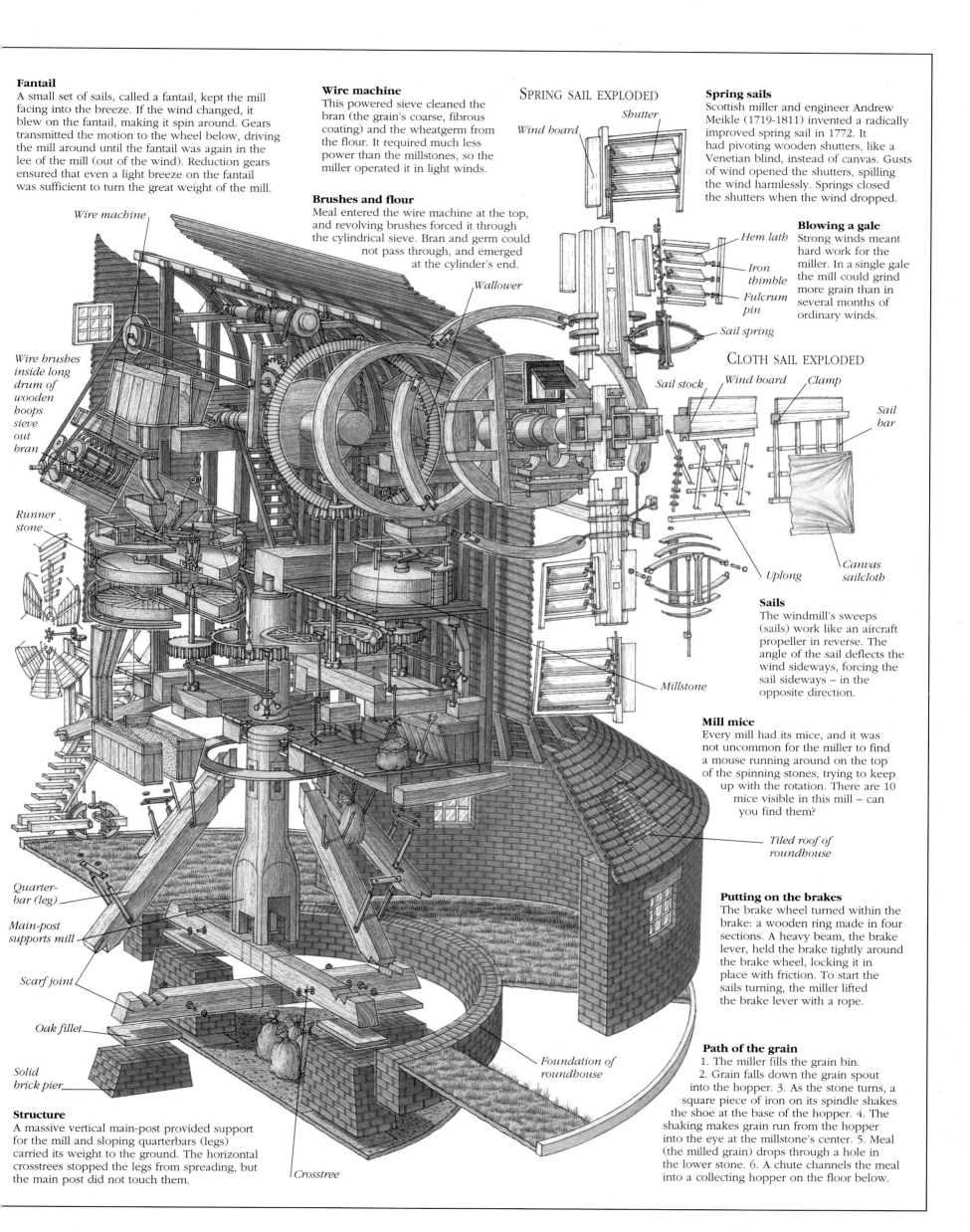

Fantail

A small set of sails, called a fantail, kept the mill facing into the breeze. If the wind changed, it blew on the fantail, making it spin around. Gears transmitted the motion to the wheel below, driving the mill around until the fantail was again in the lee of the mill (out of the wind). Reduction gears ensured that even a light breeze on the fantail was sufficient to turn the great weight of the mill.

Wire machine

Wire brushes inside long drum of wooden hoops sieve out bran

Runner stone

Quarter-bar (leg)

Main-post supports mill

Scarf joint

Oak fillet

Solid brick pier

Structure

A massive vertical main-post provided support for the mill and sloping quarterbars (legs) carried its weight to the ground. The horizontal crosstrees stopped the legs from spreading, but the main post did not touch them.

Crosstree

Wire machine

This powered sieve cleaned the bran (the grain's coarse, fibrous coating) and the wheatgerm from the flour. It required much less power than the millstones, so the miller operated it in light winds.

Brushes and flour

Meal entered the wire machine at the top, and revolving brushes forced it through the cylindrical sieve. Bran and germ could not pass through, and emerged at the cylinder's end.

Wallower

Millstone

Foundation of roundhouse

SPRING SAIL EXPLODED

Wind board

Shutter

Hem lath

Iron thimble

Fulcrum pin

Sail spring

CLOTH SAIL EXPLODED

Sail stock

Wind board

Clamp

Sail bar

Uplong

Canvas sailcloth

Spring sails

Scottish miller and engineer Andrew Meikle (1719-1811) invented a radically improved spring sail in 1772. It had pivoting wooden shutters, like a Venetian blind, instead of canvas. Gusts of wind opened the shutters, spilling the wind harmlessly. Springs closed the shutters when the wind dropped.

Blowing a gale

Strong winds meant hard work for the miller. In a single gale the mill could grind more grain than in several months of ordinary winds.

Sails

The windmill's sweeps (sails) work like an aircraft propeller in reverse. The angle of the sail deflects the wind sideways, forcing the sail sideways – in the opposite direction.

Mill mice

Every mill had its mice, and it was not uncommon for the miller to find a mouse running around on the top of the spinning stones, trying to keep up with the rotation. There are 10 mice visible in this mill – can you find them?

Tiled roof of roundhouse

Putting on the brakes

The brake wheel turned within the brake: a wooden ring made in four sections. A heavy beam, the brake lever, held the brake tightly around the brake wheel, locking it in place with friction. To start the sails turning, the miller lifted the brake lever with a rope.

Path of the grain

1. The miller fills the grain bin. 2. Grain falls down the grain spout into the hopper. 3. As the stone turns, a square piece of iron on its spindle shakes the shoe at the base of the hopper. 4. The shaking makes grain run from the hopper into the eye at the millstone's center. 5. Meal (the milled grain) drops through a hole in the lower stone. 6. A chute channels the meal into a collecting hopper on the floor below.

CROSS-SECTIONS
CASTLE

Travel back 600 years in time and join the inhabitants of a medieval castle as enemy armies advance upon it. Frightened villagers scurry into the castle for protection, the last stockpiles of food and supplies are brought in, and all over the castle soldiers shout orders as they prepare for battle. Finally, the portcullis is lowered, and the drawbridge is raised. The siege has begun!

SPY

MEMORANDUM
The 12th day of May in the 25th year of our good
kinge Edward III
THE LORD *of the castle doth proclaim*

A WARRANT
for the arrest of an enemy
SPY
name unknown

Seen skulking near the walls of this castle in the forenoon yesterday. Those who espied him hath sworn that his visage betrayed his intention to commit a FELONY against the person of THE LORD.

Should any person aid in the apprehension of the spy they shall receive a REWARD.

If he be a Villein said reward being a relief for a twelve-month of boon-work.

And if he be a knight then he shall be relieved for a twelve-month from the duties of knight service.

INTRODUCTION

Towering high above the landscape, European castles still look commanding. Imagine, then, how powerful a castle looked 600 years ago, when it was new. Bright flags flapped from the towers. Sunlight glinted from the armor of soldiers patrolling the walls. A castle was built to impress. It was the fortified home of a powerful warlord. From its safety he ruled the surrounding land.

The castle shown here dates from around 1350, but castle building began in the 10th century. The first castles replaced temporary wooden forts. Castles evolved and became stronger as methods of warfare changed. In the pages that follow, you'll see how warriors surrounded and attacked a castle, how the people in the castle prepared for war, how they defended themselves, and how they lived in peacetime.

THE ANATOMY OF A CASTLE

There was no standard shape and structure for a castle: the builders adapted their designs to suit the site, the budget, and the military dangers of the day. This castle is based on Chinon in France, and on Chepstow, which guards the border between England and Wales.

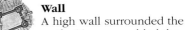

Moat
A water-filled ditch enclosed the castle on the two sides that were not protected by cliffs. Fish and fowl from the moat also provided food for the castle.

Wall
A high wall surrounded the castle. Towers enabled the defenders to see anyone approaching the castle and to fire at them with bows or siege engines.

Gatehouse
The first point of attack was usually the main entrance. A sturdy gatehouse protected the way in to the castle. Fiendishly clever traps awaited the intruder.

Bailey
The wall enclosed several courtyards, each called a bailey. In war, animals and villagers sheltered here; in peacetime, these areas housed workshops.

Wells
A water supply was vital, especially if the castle was surrounded. Wells, dug into the rock below the castle, provided water for drinking and washing.

Keep
The lord and his family lived at the heart of the castle – in the keep. If the castle was attacked, the defenders retreated to the keep and fought to the death.

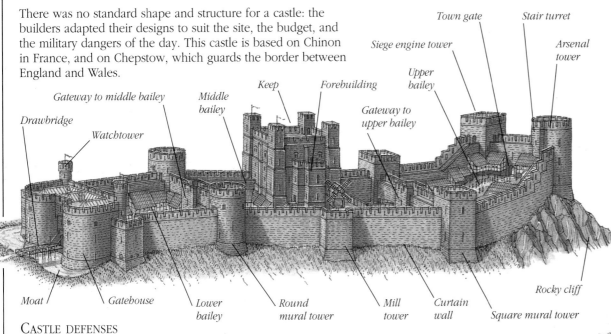

Town gate *Stair turret* *Siege engine tower* *Arsenal tower* *Upper bailey* *Keep* *Forebuilding* *Gateway to upper bailey* *Gateway to middle bailey* *Middle bailey* *Drawbridge* *Watchtower* *Moat* *Gatehouse* *Lower bailey* *Round mural tower* *Mill tower* *Curtain wall* *Square mural tower* *Rocky cliff*

CASTLE DEFENSES

High walls and solid towers were the castle's main defense. They kept out the attacking soldiers, and the parapets (the walls' jagged tops) provided the defenders with a safe view over the surrounding land. Every castle also made maximum use of the natural features of its site. By building the castle on a high point, the defenders had gravity on their side. Attacking warriors had to struggle up a slope to reach the stronghold while facing a devastating shower of arrows from the defenders on the walls.

Thick walls
The thickness of castle walls made them very strong. Most were more than 8 ft (2.5 m) thick, and the walls of castle towers were thicker still.

Rough limestone masonry
Rubble (rocks) mixed with mortar
Internal walls were plastered smooth

Preparing for the battle
Surprise attacks on castles were unusual. More often, the castle defenders had plenty of warning of an attack. While they waited for the enemy to arrive, they were busy preparing and strengthening the castle's defenses. The lord also summoned loyal knights for guard duty.

CASTLE PERSONALITIES

Noble family *Page* *Knight* *Priest* *Fool* *Gong farmer*

The noble family were at the center of castle life. Everyone else served or protected them. The page was a young servant. Like the knight who fought for the lord, he came from a noble family.

A humble priest led the family's worship and acted as secretary. The fool entertained them, and a host of other workers, such as the gong farmer, kept life in the castle comfortable – or at least bearable.

Fetching supplies
A castle under attack had to survive on its stockpiles of food and other supplies. Before the fighting started, the castle guard collected all they could. This often left the peasants in the countryside with nothing to eat.

Crenels

The gaps between the raised sections of stonework were called crenels. The crenels were often filled with hinged wooden shutters to give extra protection to the defenders.

You can't get the staff
Watchmen were among the worst-paid members of the garrison. They were paid about the same as farm laborers and received only one-fifth of the pay of skilled workers such as crossbow makers.

Hole for boarding timbers

Women and children first
Women and children took shelter in the castle when fighting began. But if food ran out, the defenders ejected anyone who couldn't fight. In the French town of Calais in 1346, the defenders threw out the sick and injured. The attackers would not let them pass, so many starved to death. The survivors ate anything they could find, including dogs and rats.

Hoardings
The most important preparation for battle was to build hoardings. These were wooden extensions to the wall walk which protected the defenders.

Watch turret
A high tower raised above the castle walls gave a fine view over the nearby countryside. Some castles, such as Urquhart in Scotland, were sited especially to provide the best possible view.

Roofing
Attacking armies often fired flaming arrows over the walls to set fire to thatched roofs inside, so castle roofs were constructed from fireproof materials whenever possible. Lead, tile, or slate were best.

Fine leather binding

Animal hides stretched over the hoarding's wooden roof provided some protection from flaming arrows.

Early recycling
Lead was too precious to waste. The roofers melted down old lead and made new sheets by pouring the molten metal onto a flat bed of sand.

Latrines
This part of the gatehouse tower contained some of the castle's toilets.

Drawbridge
In its normal position, the drawbridge or turning bridge spanned the water-filled moat. But when danger threatened, the castle guard raised the bridge.

Knight giving orders

When the drawbridge was raised, the way in was protected by the deep, water-filled moat.

Gateway guard

Portcullis
Lowering a strong oak grille called a portcullis protected the gate against attack. A layer of beaten iron covered the portcullis as a fire precaution.

DEFENSE AND SIEGE

IN PEACETIME, the castle could be an office, an administrative center, a home, a storehouse – even a market. But in wartime, the castle threw off these peaceful disguises. It became a fortress, in control of a wide area. When hostile armies surrounded the castle, soldiers raised the drawbridge and prepared for a furious fight. A siege had begun!

Inside, the castle garrison waited for reinforcements or hoped the attackers would just go away. The besieging army waited for the inhabitants to die of hunger or disease. The attacking soldiers spent the long hours of waiting trying to break into the castle. If they were successful, they swarmed inside. Often the attackers bribed someone inside the castle to open the gates. Sometimes the siege ended because attackers and defenders made a formal agreement, a lot like a modern peace treaty.

Bats in the belfry
The biggest siege engine was the belfry (bell tower). This huge wooden tower was tall enough to look over the castle walls.

On your marks . . .
The belfry could hold hundreds of men. At the 1266 siege of Kenilworth Castle, 200 archers and 11 catapults operated from a single tower.

Pull up the ladder
Only desperate or foolish soldiers tried to scale the walls on ladders, because they were defenseless as they climbed the swaying poles.

Lowering the drawbridge allowed attacking soldiers to swarm across into the castle

Hook to secure top of ladder

Soldiers operating drawbridge

Lowering ladder into position

Signaling a siege

A siege formally began only when the attacking forces fired their siege weapons against the castle walls. Until this signal, the commander could surrender his castle and its inhabitants without shame.

Trebuchet
The trebuchet was a large siege engine which hurled projectiles high in the air – over the castle walls – up to a distance of 980 ft (300 m). It was powered by a counterweight which swung the long end of the arm up and over to release the missile.

Mangonel
The mangonel threw projectiles on a low trajectory (they did not fly high in the sky). Rocks fired from the mangonel smashed against the castle, rather than flying over the wall into the bailey.

Murderous missiles
The trebuchet didn't fire just rocks: soldiers also loaded it with pots of lime, which burned the skin, or dead animals, hoping to introduce disease into the castle. For a really grisly attack, besiegers fired severed human heads.

Counterweight swings arm over

Fast and far
The range of the mangonel was about 1,300 ft (400 m), substantially more than the trebuchet.

Accuracy
A skilled bowman could put a crossbow quarrel (arrow) straight through an arrow loop, but even the best archer needed 5 or 6 attempts to be sure of hitting the target.

Archer preparing incendiary arrow

Archers firing incendiary arrows

Carrying materials to fill in moat

Pulley

Counterweight
The simplest trebuchets had no counterweight. Instead, troops just pulled down on the shorter end of the arm.

Mantlet

A portable barrier called a mantlet provided protection for archers or miners who were within range of the castle.

Pile of severed heads

Miner problems
If the castle resisted attack, soldiers called sappers tried to break in by mining – digging tunnels under the walls to make them collapse.

Pass the bacon
Once the sappers were under the walls, they lit a fire to destroy the wooden props supporting the tunnel and make the mine collapse. At one siege in 1215, the commander ordered "forty of the fattest pigs, of the sort least good for eating" to fuel the fire.

Cats, rats, and tortoises
Soldiers at the foot of the castle wall worked under a wheeled shelter. They moved it forward gradually, and the shelter got the nickname "tortoise" from its slow pace. It was also called a "cat" or a "rat" because of its creeping advance.

Rolling road
Soldiers in the cat tried to fill the moat with rocks and soil. Then they built a roadway of logs to form a bridge to the castle walls.

The moat made mining difficult

Roadway of split logs

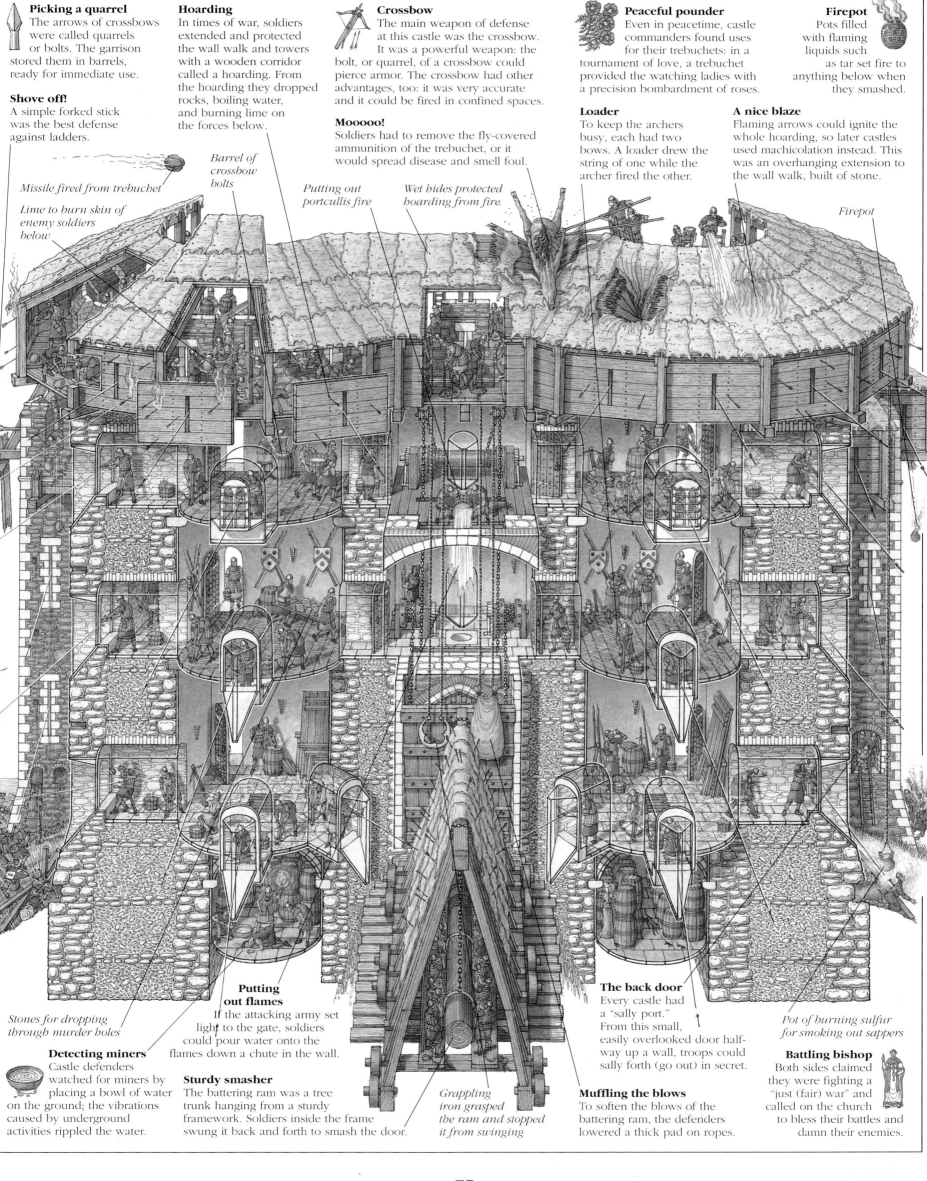

Picking a quarrel
The arrows of crossbows were called quarrels or bolts. The garrison stored them in barrels, ready for immediate use.

Shove off!
A simple forked stick was the best defense against ladders.

Missile fired from trebuchet

Lime to burn skin of enemy soldiers below

Hoarding
In times of war, soldiers extended and protected the wall walk and towers with a wooden corridor called a hoarding. From the hoarding they dropped rocks, boiling water, and burning lime on the forces below.

Barrel of crossbow bolts

Putting out portcullis fire

Crossbow
The main weapon of defense at this castle was the crossbow. It was a powerful weapon: the bolt, or quarrel, of a crossbow could pierce armor. The crossbow had other advantages, too: it was very accurate and it could be fired in confined spaces.

Mooooo!
Soldiers had to remove the fly-covered ammunition of the trebuchet, or it would spread disease and smell foul.

Wet hides protected hoarding from fire

Peaceful pounder
Even in peacetime, castle commanders found uses for their trebuchets: in a tournament of love, a trebuchet provided the watching ladies with a precision bombardment of roses.

Loader
To keep the archers busy, each had two bows. A loader drew the string of one while the archer fired the other.

A nice blaze
Flaming arrows could ignite the whole hoarding, so later castles used machicolation instead. This was an overhanging extension to the wall walk, built of stone.

Firepot
Pots filled with flaming liquids such as tar set fire to anything below when they smashed.

Firepot

Putting out flames
If the attacking army set light to the gate, soldiers could pour water onto the flames down a chute in the wall.

Stones for dropping through murder holes

Detecting miners
Castle defenders watched for miners by placing a bowl of water on the ground; the vibrations caused by underground activities rippled the water.

Sturdy smasher
The battering ram was a tree trunk hanging from a sturdy framework. Soldiers inside the frame swung it back and forth to smash the door.

Grappling iron grasped the ram and stopped it from swinging

The back door
Every castle had a "sally port." From this small, easily overlooked door halfway up a wall, troops could sally forth (go out) in secret.

Muffling the blows
To soften the blows of the battering ram, the defenders lowered a thick pad on ropes.

Pot of burning sulfur for smoking out sappers

Battling bishop
Both sides claimed they were fighting a "just (fair) war" and called on the church to bless their battles and damn their enemies.

GARRISON AND PRISONERS

THE GROUP OF SOLDIERS guarding the castle was called the garrison. The men of the garrison spent much of their time in the massive gatehouse that controlled the entrance. Within its sturdy walls there were ingenious gates and deadly traps. Only the most determined invasion force could enter the castle once the garrison had secured its stronghold.

The gatehouse was also the castle prison. The towers' massive construction meant that they kept prisoners in just as effectively as they kept invaders out. Noblemen captured in battle had luxurious quarters high up in one of the gatehouse towers. They were held until their families paid ransom (large fees). While they waited, ransom prisoners lived almost as well as the lord himself. Few prisoners were this lucky, though. Most shivered and starved in the dungeons – the basement prisons beneath the gatehouse floor.

FEUDAL SYSTEM

The lord of the castle (usually a wealthy knight or baron) did not own the land in the sense that we understand today. The lord earned the right to use the land and build his castle by swearing an oath of loyalty to a baron – a more important lord – or to the king himself. The lord also promised to do knight service (to fight on horseback) if the king needed his help in war. Under the lord's control were the many people who lived on the land. The lord protected them in exchange for fines or fees. This social structure was called feudalism.

THE VILLEIN OR PEASANT
The lord protected the people on his land in exchange for money, goods such as farm produce, or work. Most people were villeins: little better than slaves. They could not leave the lord's lands.

THE FREEMAN
A few of the people on the castle lands were not villeins but freemen. They had a higher status than villeins and were free to move from place to place.

Villeins
Freemen
Knights
Baron

THE KNIGHTS
Barons (very wealthy noblemen) could not control all their land without help, so they in turn divided it between rich knights. Each knight swore allegiance to a baron and owed him 40 days knight service a year.

THE KING
At the top of feudal society, the king ruled over everyone in the country. At least, that was what he thought. In fact, powerful barons in some feudal societies allowed the king to rule only as long as he agreed with them.

THE BARON
Barons were very wealthy noblemen who swore allegiance directly to the king. In exchange, he gave them huge areas of land. The barons were often in the presence of the king, and some had special duties.

BASTARD FEUDALISM

By the 14th century, when this castle was complete, feudalism had changed. Instead of knight service, the lord paid money to the king or baron, who used it to hire soldiers when he needed them. This system was called bastard feudalism.

Herbal remedies
Sweet-smelling herbs hanging in bundles on the wall perfumed the air. Herbs on the floor, called strew, gave out a pleasant aroma when crushed underfoot.

Guard duty
A wealthy man who farmed the lord's land paid rent by contributing to the castle guard. He had to provide soldiers, weapons, armor, and sometimes horses. These duties resulted from the act of homage, when the man put his hands between those of his lord and swore to "be his man." "Paying homage" still means performing duties for a more important person, or promising to.

Are you sitting comfortably?
The toilets were not nearly as primitive as you might imagine. They often had wooden seats, and some even had wash basins. There was no toilet paper, but a handful of hay did the job almost as well.

Yoo-hoo!
"Murder holes" in the gateway provided a handy way of shouting orders, but this was not their main function. If enemy soldiers got through the outer door, the garrison dropped the portcullis, and archers then picked off the enemy one by one.

Constable's quarters
The most luxurious room in the gatehouse was the constable's. This important man controlled the castle when the lord and his family were not at home. He was responsible for every aspect of day-to-day routine: for authorizing spending on building and repairs, for supplying provisions, and for the security of prisoners.

A slippery climb
Invaders desperate to get inside the castle even tried clambering up the latrine shaft, and this approach broke the siege of Château Gaillard, on the Seine River in France, in 1204. However, if the invaders got stuck and died in the attempt, the drains needed a good cleaning before the latrine could be used again.

Stone latrine seat

Retrieving the fallen
After a battle, each side collected their dead and took them away for burial.

Castle guards asleep
Constable's servants asleep

Mustn't grumble
The life of ransom prisoners was really quite good. They may even have had the freedom to roam around the castle. Their captor granted these privileges because the prisoner gave his word not to try and escape. Some prisoners also signed a document upon surrendering, in which they agreed to be obedient prisoners and to pay the ransom, and they recognized that breaking the terms would bring dishonor on them.

Lookout
Nicknamed "Jim Crow" because of his lofty perch, the lookout sounded a series of coded calls on his hunting horn to signal the approach of friends or enemies.

What a stink!
Windows in the latrine tower provided plenty of ventilation. Glass was a rare luxury.

Watch-turret

Latrine tower

Standards were decorated with the coat-of-arms of the lord

Winch room
The portcullis that protected the castle gateway was very heavy. The garrison used a winch so that two men could lift it between them. Lowering the portcullis was easy: knocking out a stop or brake let it drop quickly to trap intruders.

Draft excluder
Costly tapestry hangings over the doors kept out the howling castle drafts.

Lead sheeting

Portcullis

Slot for portcullis

Ransom prisoner

Chimney
Only later castles had chimneys. The hot air rising up the chimney created a draft that kept the fire below blazing, sucking smoke from the room. Some early castles simply had a hole in the roof, and the fire burned in a grate in the middle of the floor. Others had fireplaces which vented through openings in the wall.

Sleeping mattress stuffed with straw

Shut the gate
Metal studs on the thick oak gates blunted the axes of the soldiers who tried to break in.

Knife fight
Guarding the castle in a siege was boring yet often dangerous, and the stress made the mercenaries very jumpy.

Guard caught asleep on watch

Timber in storage

Gatekeeper's room

Murder hole

Metal studs

Treasure chest
The constable guarded the valuables of the castle and was probably quite wealthy himself. The job of constable was usually well-paid and provided many extra opportunities to get rich.

Peepholes
Loops in the entrance arch allowed guards in side passages to inspect visitors in safety.

Gates within gates
Even in peacetime the garrison shut the castle gates at night. Visitors entered through a wicket gate – a small door within the main gate.

Jailer takes a fee for accepting another prisoner

Prisoner in chains

Forget-me-not
Hidden at the back of the dungeon was a cramped cell-within-a-cell. This "oubliette" took its name from the French word *oublier*, to forget. Unwanted prisoners were pushed into the oubliette and forgotten.

A squint
A tiny peep-hole called a squint allowed the jailer to check on his charges.

Smelly job
Emptying the latrine pit was an unpleasant and unhealthy task. The unfortunate worker with the bucket and spade was called a "gong farmer."

BUILDING THE CASTLE

CASTLES WERE VERY EXPENSIVE to construct and repair. Only the most rich and powerful lords could afford to build them, and they picked castle locations with great care. They chose positions that they knew would be important to hold in a battle.

However, castle builders didn't think only about warfare. They planned for peacetime, too. The castle was a home, so there had to be ample supplies of food and fuel within easy reach. It was also a center of administration for the lord of the manor and usually had to be within a day's walk of his lands.

Finally, the site itself was important. The castle needed solid foundations to take the weight of the massive walls. Perhaps most important of all, within the castle walls there had to be a source of clean drinking water to supply the defenders and their livestock during a siege.

STONEMASONS

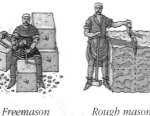

Master mason   *Freemason*   *Rough mason*

The master mason was highly paid, often a foreigner, and traveled from castle to castle to supervise construction. Under the master mason worked freemasons. They were skilled masons who could cut freestone into any shape required. The lowest grade of mason, the rough mason, rough cut and prepared stones for the more complex work of the freemason.

NAILS

An important part of the blacksmith's work was making nails (screws were not invented until the 16th century). The nails were not strong enough to hammer in directly; craftsmen first made a hole with a gimlet.

Wooden pegs held beams together

The blacksmith formed nails from hammered lengths of wire

In 1327, York Castle had a stock of 43,000 nails

SELECTION OF TOOLS

Tradesmen used to make many of their own tools or have them made locally by the blacksmith. Shapes of tools varied from place to place; there were no standard designs.

The gimlet made small holes in wood for nails

Brushes were simply bundles of hair tied to a handle

The carpenter's brace had a simple bit, rather than the spiral bits common today

The carpenter's adze was like an ax but with the blade turned to cross the handle

LICENSE TO CRENELLATE

Building a castle needed royal permission. This was called "license to crenellate," because it was the crenellations (battlements) that made a castle different from all other buildings. Adulterine castles (illegally fortified houses) could be seized by the king.

Awarding the license to crenellate to a lord

The king's scribe or secretary wrote out the license to crenellate on a sheet of parchment

Seals bore an image of the lord

Wax seal

The king made the document official with a seal (a wax token embossed with a special symbol). A parchment ribbon fixed the seal to the license.

ARROW LOOPS

Archers fired through narrow slits, called arrow loops, in the castle wall.

Longbows needed a tall loop

Adding a horizontal slit gave a wider field of fire

Circular oeillets may have been cut for larger crossbows

A few loops have several cross-slits

Arrow loops were splayed (spread out) on the inside, so that an archer could take careful aim without exposing himself to fire. Not all slits in the wall were for firing arrows. Many were in place of windows, letting in air and light.

Blacksmith

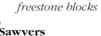

Anything made from metal was costly, because making iron required huge amounts of fuel. To make 55 lb (25 kg) of iron required one mature oak tree.

Limey cement

Lime – the equivalent of today's cement – was made by heating chalk or limestone in a simple furnace (oven) often built close to the castle site.

Simple tools

A carpenter made holes with an auger or awl. After every few turns he pulled it from the hole to remove the chippings. Drill bits, which have a spiral groove to remove wood chips continuously, did not appear until the 15th century.

Hewing stone

Not all stone was suitable for castle walls. Very hard stones such as granite were difficult to cut. Suitable stone for working was called freestone. The masons trimmed it into ashlar: regular, flat-surfaced blocks and the shapes needed for the arrow loops and arches.

Smelly walls

To make the walls waterproof, the workers plastered them with daub. This was a mixture of clay, animal dung, and horse hair. The hair reinforced the mixture and gave it strength.

Stone cart

Much of the stone for the castle had to come from a quarry nearby; transporting the stone even a short distance doubled its cost.

Hay loft

Scaffolding

Masons' lodge

Rough limestone

Concrete

Basket boys

Master mason

Mason carving freestone blocks

Master mason discussing progress

Sawyers

Some sawing went on at the site of the castle, but sawyers (workers who sawed wood) also worked in the forest. There they chopped down trees and cut them into lighter beams.

Making mortar

The "glue" that held the castle wall together was mortar: a mixture of lime, sand, and water.

Lifting gear
This simple crane was fixed, but more elaborate types, called slewing cranes, rotated to bring the load directly over the rising tower.

Treadmill
Two men walked around inside the wheel to turn it and wind up the load, much as a hamster runs in an exercise wheel.

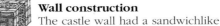

Wall construction
The castle wall had a sandwichlike structure. Neatly trimmed blocks of ashlar formed the outside and inside surfaces of the wall. Between these two layers there was a filling of rubble: stones of assorted size and quality, held together with mortar.

Scaffolding
So that they could work on the walls as they grew higher, the craftsmen built scaffolding. Holes in the walls, called putlog holes, supported the inner end of some of the timbers.

Making bate
Tannery workers softened animal skins by soaking them in bate. This was a combination of water and dog excrement from the castle kennels. After putting this mixture in a vat, a workman climbed in and trampled it to a pulp with his bare feet.

Blazing roof
Thatch was the cheapest roofing material, but it burned easily. Attacking forces fired burning barrels of tar from a trebuchet or shot flaming arrows to ignite the thatch.

Basket boys
Mortar and smaller stones went up the walls in baskets carried on laborers' shoulders.

Lead sheeting being laid on roof

Shingles
By splitting oak logs into thin, flat rectangles called shingles, woodsmen made a cheap, lightweight roofing material. A large shingle roof needed constant repair because the shingles rotted quickly and the nails holding them in place rusted.

Sharpening swords on a grindstone

Thatch roof on fire

Shingle roof

Blacksmith
Forge
Bellows

Twelve Jurymen

Taxes and tithes
When the people of the manor came to pay the lord what they owed, a lesser official checked the payments. A scribe noted down the payment in the castle records, which were written by hand on parchment.

I am the judge
The lord himself was the judge of serious crimes, but for lesser cases an official such as the steward might take his place. A jury of 12 men listened to evidence and decided guilt or innocence in serious cases.

Court documents

Prisoner

Judge

Scribe

Court archive
The castle cellar housed court documents. They were called the rolls, because the clerk recorded everything on sheets of parchment (hammered animal skins) that were rolled for storage.

Covering wattle with daub

Lime wash
A splash of lime helped to seal the surface of the wattle and daub walls and made them look nicer.

Thatcher at work
The cheapest roofing material was thatch. This was a thick covering of reeds, straw, heather, or even bracken.

Weaving wattle
To fill the gaps between the beams, builders wove wattle – panels of flexible hazel twigs.

Well well!
A reliable supply of water was essential if the castle was to survive a siege.

TRADES AND SKILLS

"YOU STUPID half-witted apprentice! Have you got ale froth for brains? Give me that hammer!" Every day, the high stone walls of the bailey rang with the shouts and curses of the busy craftworkers whose workshops clustered around the walls. When things went wrong (which was often) it was usually the youngest apprentice, or trainee worker, who got the blame.

Most manufacturing and processing took place in the castle or nearby. Billowing steam swirled around the wheelwrights as they fitted a metal rim to a cartwheel. Deafening hammering from the armorer almost drowned the gentler squeak of the potter's wheel and the whooshing of the wind in the mill sails. The malty smell of fresh-brewed ale mingled with the sizzling of melting fat from the candle makers.

THE ALE CONNER

Testing the purity of beer was the job of the ale conner. He poured a pool of ale onto a wooden bench and then sat in it. The ale passed the test if his leather britches were not stuck to the bench after half an hour. Poor-quality beer was sugary and would glue him to the seat. The punishment for producing low-quality beer was probably the pillory.

DRESSING A KNIGHT

Quilted with feathers, aketon overshirt softened blows

Long mail hauberk protected the body

Armpit and elbow protected by circular plates tied to mail

Helmet with mail coif

Knight wore normal hose on legs

Gauntlets had plates on the top to protect fingers

Mail leggings covered the hose

"Coat of plates" was actually many small plates

Surcoat laced up side with cords

Armor changed and evolved constantly. In the 14th century, knights wore three layers of body armor over their shirts and hose. The innermost layer, a quilted knee-length coat, or aketon, was all that poor foot soldiers could afford. On top of this, knights wore chain mail, then a "coat of plates," overlapping panels of metal fastened to a sturdy shirt. Finally, the surcoat kept the sun off the armor.

HOW MAIL WAS MADE

Nobody knows for sure how mail was manufactured, but the process was probably as follows:

1 The mail maker's apprentice wound wire around a rod, then cut the coil with a hammer and chisel to make loops.

2 Passing the loops through a tapering tube tightened the rings so their ends overlapped.

3 The apprentice then flattened the ends of the rings with this tool.

4 The rings were pierced at both ends with this tool.

5 The mail maker himself added the prepared link to the coat and riveted it tight.

SPINNING WHEEL

Yarn was wound onto a spindle

Basket of combed wool

This invention was the very first labor-saving machine to use continuous rotary (turning) motion and a belt drive. Until about 1300, women spun yarn by twisting it onto a distaff – a long pole. The wheel made spinning much faster.

Plumber

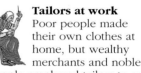

The plumber shaped and joined lead sheet and pipes. His trade took its name from the Latin word for lead, *plumbum.*

Watching paint dry

Painting the walls of the keep with limewash protected it against rain and made the castle gleam brilliant white in the sun.

Keep

When the castle was besieged, the keep was the last place of refuge (hiding), so it was designed to be easily defended. A drawbridge and a steep flight of stairs guarded the entrance in the forebuilding.

Tailors at work

Poor people made their own clothes at home, but wealthy merchants and noble people employed tailors to sew them fine robes. Crouched over their sewing in damp workshops, tailors often suffered from bad stomachs, curved spines, and lingering coughs.

Armor needed constant polishing to remove rust

Mail being made

Hermit's cell

Some religious people who did not agree with the teachings of the Church sometimes withdrew to cells (small rooms) in the castle. Educated people valued these hermits for their wisdom and holiness. However, their odd habits often made them a source of amusement and curiosity to the ignorant.

Make do and mend

A suit of armor was very expensive to make. It cost about the same as a car costs today. Also like a car, armor was never replaced after a minor accident. The armorer simply bashed out the dents.

Fits like a glove

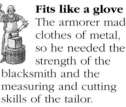

The armorer made clothes of metal, so he needed the strength of the blacksmith and the measuring and cutting skills of the tailor.

Bellows pumping air into the forge

Cutting brushwood

The willow saplings growing in the ditch didn't go to waste. Farm animals browsed on the leaves, and the hurdle maker then used the bare branches to make gates and fences.

Official checking on progress

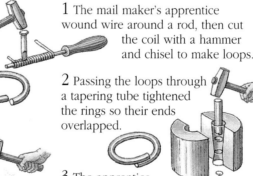

Clearing the ditch

Workers used baskets to carry the rich mud they dug out of the ditch. They fertilized the nearby fields with the mud.

Workers "kilted" their tunics up for muddy work

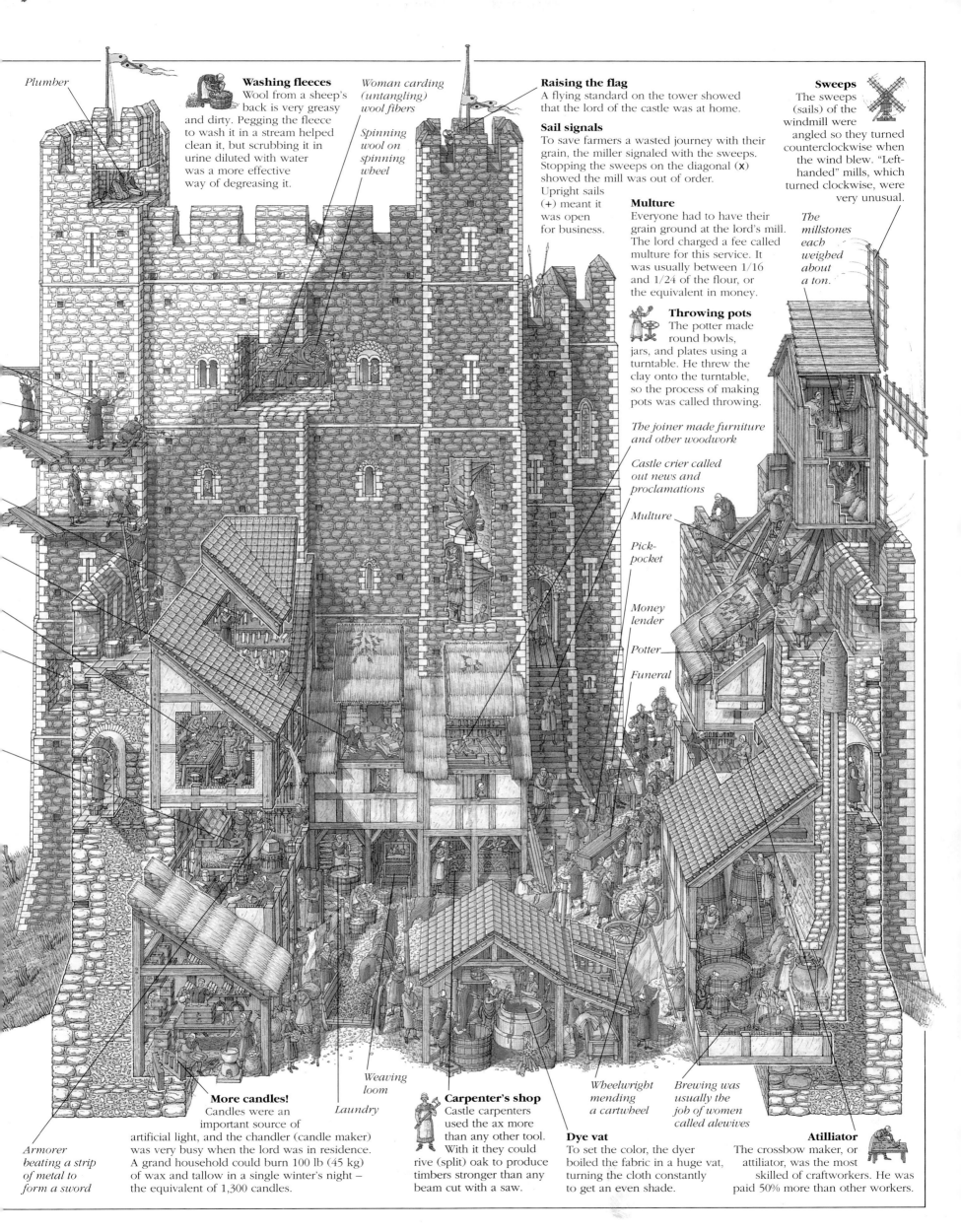

Plumber

Washing fleeces
Wool from a sheep's back is very greasy and dirty. Pegging the fleece to wash it in a stream helped clean it, but scrubbing it in urine diluted with water was a more effective way of degreasing it.

Woman carding (untangling) wool fibers

Spinning wool on spinning wheel

Raising the flag
A flying standard on the tower showed that the lord of the castle was at home.

Sail signals
To save farmers a wasted journey with their grain, the miller signaled with the sweeps. Stopping the sweeps on the diagonal (x) showed the mill was out of order. Upright sails (+) meant it was open for business.

Multure
Everyone had to have their grain ground at the lord's mill. The lord charged a fee called multure for this service. It was usually between 1/16 and 1/24 of the flour, or the equivalent in money.

Sweeps
The sweeps (sails) of the windmill were angled so they turned counterclockwise when the wind blew. "Left-handed" mills, which turned clockwise, were very unusual.

The millstones each weighed about a ton.

Throwing pots
The potter made round bowls, jars, and plates using a turntable. He threw the clay onto the turntable, so the process of making pots was called throwing.

The joiner made furniture and other woodwork

Castle crier called out news and proclamations

Multure

Pick-pocket

Money lender

Potter

Funeral

More candles!
Candles were an important source of artificial light, and the chandler (candle maker) was very busy when the lord was in residence. A grand household could burn 100 lb (45 kg) of wax and tallow in a single winter's night – the equivalent of 1,300 candles.

Armorer beating a strip of metal to form a sword

Weaving loom

Laundry

Carpenter's shop
Castle carpenters used the ax more than any other tool. With it they could rive (split) oak to produce timbers stronger than any beam cut with a saw.

Wheelwright mending a cartwheel

Brewing was usually the job of women called alewives

Dye vat
To set the color, the dyer boiled the fabric in a huge vat, turning the cloth constantly to get an even shade.

Atilliator
The crossbow maker, or attiliator, was the most skilled of craftworkers. He was paid 50% more than other workers.

LIVING LIKE A LORD

THE LORD OF THE CASTLE and his family lived in grand style. Their status in society depended on them spending money and appearing to enjoy life. And spend they did: on lavish food, on richly embroidered wall hangings, on beautiful clothes, on gold and silver plate, and on entertaining a host of friends and relations.

Their greatest luxury, though, was privacy. They had suites of rooms such as the solar, a kind of private apartment attached to the great hall where they could withdraw from their servants and guests and do as they pleased. For everyone else who worked and lived in the castle, privacy was impossible. All poor people lived their lives in full view of their neighbors, friends, and family. They lived in the same houses, ate together, slept together, washed together, and did almost everything else in public.

HERALDRY

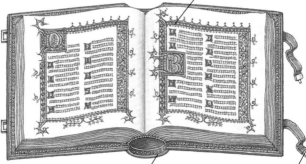

Even the horse wore the knight's emblems

The knight's shield was painted with his arms

Armor made everyone look the same, so to avoid being killed by their own men, knights decorated their outfits with distinctive patterns called arms. The patterns became very elaborate, and there were complex rules, called heraldry, for their creation.

Husband's arms

The background to the arms was called the "field"

The charge was the symbol itself

Wife's arms

When families married, they merged their arms by dividing the shield. When their children married, it was divided again – and so on. This was called quartering, and by the 14th century, only heralds could understand the complex system.

HERALDIC CHARGES

pale	*fess*	*bend*	*bend sinister*
lion rampant	*cross*	*dragon*	*chevron*

ILLUMINATED MANUSCRIPT

Until printing became widespread in Europe in the 15th century, scribes had to copy out all books in handwriting. This made books very valuable and rare possessions; many noble households owned only a Bible, and few people had more than a dozen books on their shelves.

Illuminated margin

Bibles used in the lord's chapel had richly jeweled bindings

Clasps held the book closed, protecting the pages

The monks and scribes who copied out the text worked in a special room called a *scriptorium*. They decorated the pages with beautiful illustrations. This was called illumination because it illuminated, or lit up, the page.

POSSESSIONS

Even rich people had few possessions in the sense that we now understand the word. In a typical duke's 14th-century household, the most expensive items were the robes and hangings for the chapel. Together with household tapestries, these made up half the value of the duke's goods. Beds, clothes, gold, and silver made up the rest.

The lord often commissioned jeweled chalices to donate to abbeys and churches

Money and other precious items were stored in the castle itself

One of the lord's most precious personal possessions was his sword, which was specially made for him

Dubbing
To make a young squire into a knight, the lord dubbed him. He struck a symbolic blow with the flat side of a sword or with his hand.

Relief!
Guards on duty on the castle wall couldn't always leave their posts.

Unblocking the gutters

Waterspout
Lead troughs carried the water through the wall, and a spout on the outside discharged it well away from the wall. Carvings of ugly faces, called gargoyles, often decorated the waterspouts.

Reading in the latrine

Banking
The locked chest at the foot of the bed contained a hoard of silver plate (tableware). This wasn't just for a showy display on the dinner table: buying plate was like saving money, because the silver could be melted down and sold when times were hard.

Gallery
In the thick wall of the tower, a gallery provided access to other rooms and staircases. Musicians also played from the gallery during feasts.

Charity
Giving alms (charitable gifts) to the poor and needy was an essential part of the medieval code of chivalry; the more a lord gave, the faster he would go to heaven when he died.

Lady of manor dictating letters

Doctor
Physicians were respected and wealthy, but medical treatment was crude and often did little to help the sick recover. Many doctors examined the patient's urine to determine the cause of the sickness. Cures were a combination of astrology, herbal preparations, change of diet, bloodletting (bleeding), and prayer.

Lord's almoner
The lord of the castle employed an almoner to distribute alms. The almoner also had the job of collecting left-over food after meals and handing this out to beggars.

Leper
Leprosy sufferers were outcasts even among beggars, and they carried bells or clappers to warn of their approach. Everyone was so afraid of infection that they would not touch a leper but threw food instead.

Throwing food to a leper

Quintain
This cunning target was good practice for the joust. Originally just a shield fixed to a post, it evolved into an elaborate, pivoted device with a counterweight that could knock the rider from his horse.

Sewage built up in moat

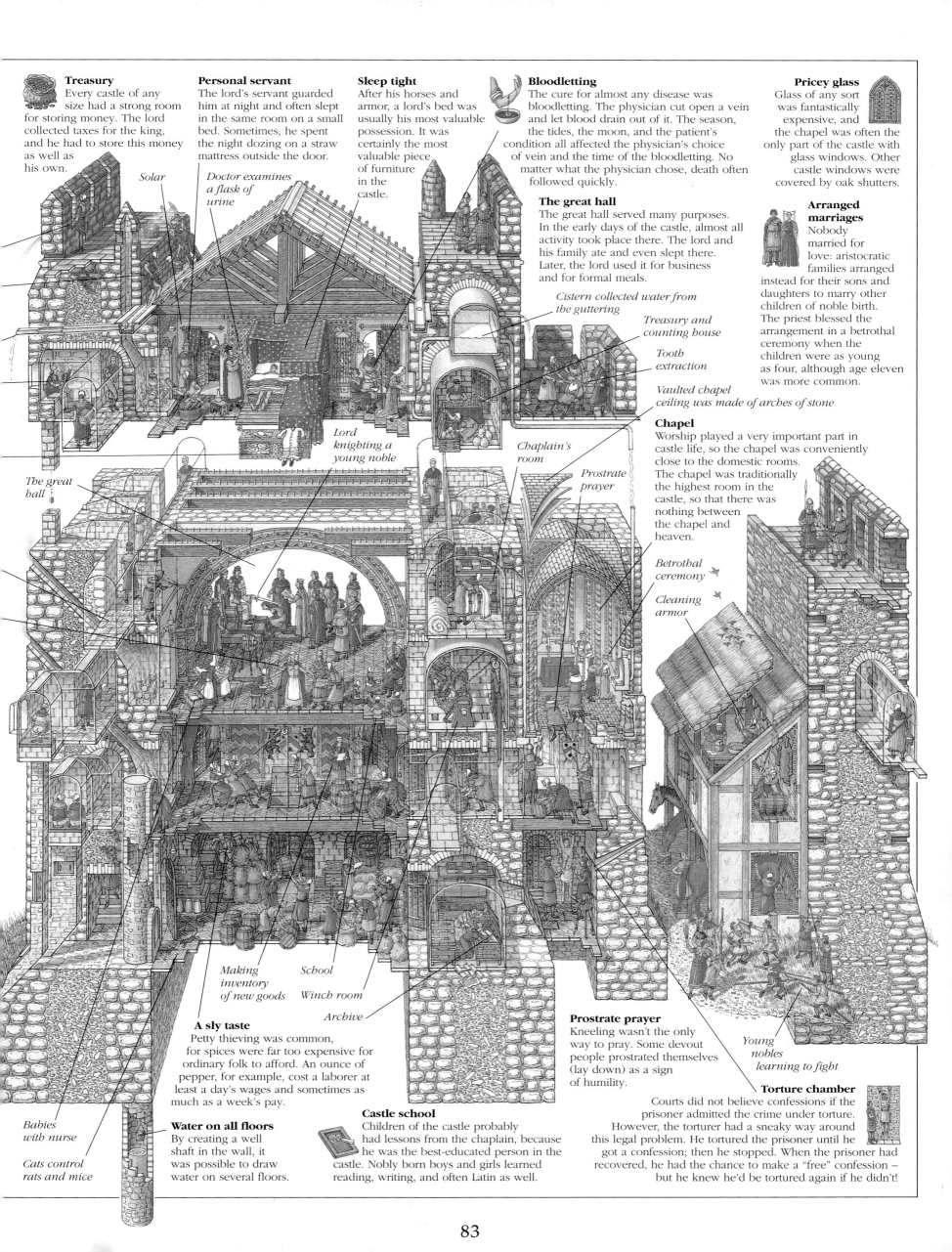

Treasury
Every castle of any size had a strong room for storing money. The lord collected taxes for the king, and he had to store this money as well as his own.

Solar

Personal servant
The lord's servant guarded him at night and often slept in the same room on a small bed. Sometimes, he spent the night dozing on a straw mattress outside the door.

Doctor examines a flask of urine

Sleep tight
After his horses and armor, a lord's bed was usually his most valuable possession. It was certainly the most valuable piece of furniture in the castle.

Bloodletting
The cure for almost any disease was bloodletting. The physician cut open a vein and let blood drain out of it. The season, the tides, the moon, and the patient's condition all affected the physician's choice of vein and the time of the bloodletting. No matter what the physician chose, death often followed quickly.

Pricey glass
Glass of any sort was fantastically expensive, and the chapel was often the only part of the castle with glass windows. Other castle windows were covered by oak shutters.

Arranged marriages
Nobody married for love: aristocratic families arranged instead for their sons and daughters to marry other children of noble birth. The priest blessed the arrangement in a betrothal ceremony when the children were as young as four, although age eleven was more common.

The great hall
The great hall served many purposes. In the early days of the castle, almost all activity took place there. The lord and his family ate and even slept there. Later, the lord used it for business and for formal meals.

Cistern collected water from the guttering

Treasury and counting house

Tooth extraction

Vaulted chapel ceiling was made of arches of stone

Chapel
Worship played a very important part in castle life, so the chapel was conveniently close to the domestic rooms. The chapel was traditionally the highest room in the castle, so that there was nothing between the chapel and heaven.

The great hall

Lord knighting a young noble

Chaplain's room

Prostrate prayer

Betrothal ceremony

Cleaning armor

Making inventory of new goods

School

Winch room

Archive

A sly taste
Petty thieving was common, for spices were far too expensive for ordinary folk to afford. An ounce of pepper, for example, cost a laborer at least a day's wages and sometimes as much as a week's pay.

Babies with nurse

Cats control rats and mice

Water on all floors
By creating a well shaft in the wall, it was possible to draw water on several floors.

Castle school
Children of the castle probably had lessons from the chaplain, because he was the best-educated person in the castle. Nobly born boys and girls learned reading, writing, and often Latin as well.

Prostrate prayer
Kneeling wasn't the only way to pray. Some devout people prostrated themselves (lay down) as a sign of humility.

Young nobles learning to fight

Torture chamber
Courts did not believe confessions if the prisoner admitted the crime under torture. However, the torturer had a sneaky way around this legal problem. He tortured the prisoner until he got a confession; then he stopped. When the prisoner had recovered, he had the chance to make a "free" confession – but he knew he'd be tortured again if he didn't!

FOOD AND FEASTING

AT FESTIVALS, or when the lord had noble guests, it was time for feasting in the castle. The kitchens worked day and night, and walls echoed with crackling fires and the songs of minstrels.

The menus for castle banquets seem odd today. Now, we serve different kinds of food – such as fish, meat, and dessert – in individual courses. But castle cooks mixed sweet and savory foods. In a single course, roast heron and a pig's head might share the table with fish and a sickly sweet pie made of cream, eggs, dates, and prunes.

Wealthy people enjoyed spicy food, but the cook didn't have to use spices to hide the taste of rotting ingredients. In fact, food was often very fresh. Meals were spicy because this was the fashionable way to cook. Spices were very costly, and spiced food was a sign of wealth and luxury.

WHAT'S ON THE MENU?

A LORD'S DIET

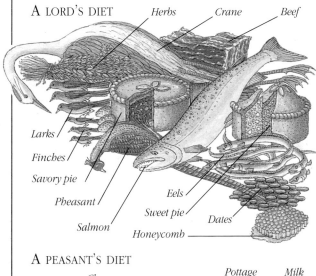

Herbs · Crane · Beef · Larks · Finches · Savory pie · Pheasant · Salmon · Eels · Sweet pie · Dates · Honeycomb

A PEASANT'S DIET

Cheese · Bacon · Pottage · Milk

Wealthy castle dwellers ate almost anything that moved – and much else as well. Besides all manner of fish, beef, pork, and lamb, a feast might feature birds of every size, from herons and cranes down to larks, thrushes, and even finches. These made their entrance in pies or simply roasted. Poor people, however, had a simple and boring diet. They ate mainly bread and pottage (thick vegetable soup) with a little bacon, milk, and cheese.

BELOW THE SALT

Castle cooks didn't use salt to season the food. Instead, lucky diners helped themselves from a boat-shaped saltcellar. This was placed in front of the lord, separating him and his family and guests from others at the table. The salt became a measure of social status, and so describing someone as "below the salt" came to mean that they were not respectable.

JESTER

The fool or jester was a specially privileged entertainer. Traditionally, his colorful outfit made fun of fashionable clothes. Wealthy and powerful people allowed the jester to tell funny stories or sing rude songs about them. However, there was a sinister side to their laughter. Nobody took the jester seriously because often he was mentally ill.

Rattle

SPICES AND HERBS

Buckwheat · Cloves · Ginger · Coriander · Cinnamon · Cumin · Aniseed · Licorice · Pepper

Kitchen spice cupboards bulged with exotic flavorings. The list above includes some that we would not call spices today.

TABLE MANNERS

Books of table manners gave detailed information about how to behave at the feast. Here are a few useful tips from a 15th-century manuscript:

- Do not spit upon or over the table.
- If you wash your mouth out while at table do not spit the water back into the bowl, but instead spit politely, onto the floor.
- If there is a man of God (such as a priest) at the table, take special care where you spit.
- Do not pick your teeth at the table with a knife, straw, or stick.
- Do not belch near anyone's face – if you have bad breath.

Trenchermen

Food was not served on plates. Instead, everyone had a trencher – a thick slice of stale bread – or shared one, as shown here. Servants placed food on the trencher. After the meal, a servant called a ewerer brought water for the lord to wash his fingers in.

Nobleman shaving by rubbing his chin with a pumice stone

Not so subtle

To end each course, servants brought in an elaborate dish called a subtlety. This was more like sculpture than food, and was crafted from sugar. Subtleties sometimes had religious themes, with worthy inscriptions. Often they represented natural scenes, such as a hunt.

Servants dressing nobleman

Musicians

In the grander castles, music might accompany the whole meal, but usually the musicians played only between courses.

Roast peacock

Castle stream

Castle moats were not just a defense against mining and a source of fish – they had many other uses, too. For instance, game birds bred on artificial islands in the ponds, and reeds and rushes growing on the banks provided thatching materials.

Sluice

The supply of fish was so important that some castles had an elaborate series of ponds separated by dikes and linked by ditches. Sluices (sliding shutters) controlled the flow of water between the different pools.

Leftover trenchers being handed out to the poor

Gone fishin'

Fish in the ponds were usually the lord's property, but the castle moat was often open to anyone with a pole and a hook. Sometimes certain villagers had fishing rights: in one manor, only pregnant women were allowed to fish.

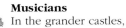

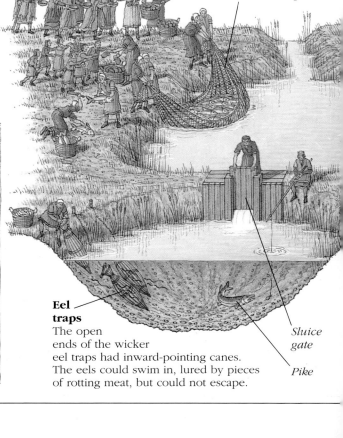

Large fish being moved to another pond

Eel traps

The open ends of the wicker eel traps had inward-pointing canes. The eels could swim in, lured by pieces of rotting meat, but could not escape.

Sluice gate

Pike

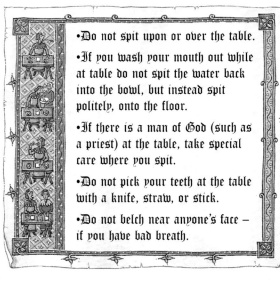

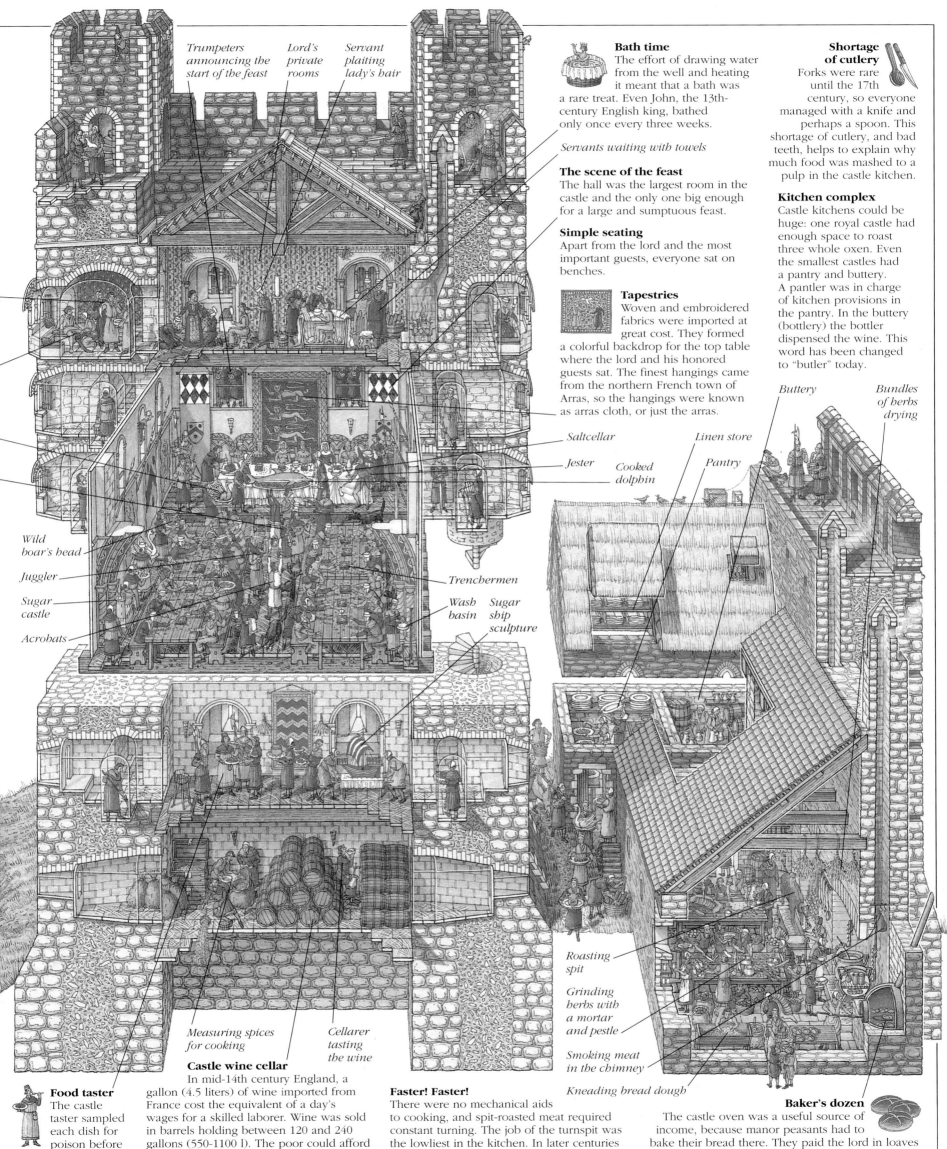

Trumpeters announcing the start of the feast

Lord's private rooms

Servant plaiting lady's hair

Bath time
The effort of drawing water from the well and heating it meant that a bath was a rare treat. Even John, the 13th-century English king, bathed only once every three weeks.

Servants waiting with towels

The scene of the feast
The hall was the largest room in the castle and the only one big enough for a large and sumptuous feast.

Simple seating
Apart from the lord and the most important guests, everyone sat on benches.

Tapestries
Woven and embroidered fabrics were imported at great cost. They formed a colorful backdrop for the top table where the lord and his honored guests sat. The finest hangings came from the northern French town of Arras, so the hangings were known as arras cloth, or just the arras.

Shortage of cutlery
Forks were rare until the 17th century, so everyone managed with a knife and perhaps a spoon. This shortage of cutlery, and bad teeth, helps to explain why much food was mashed to a pulp in the castle kitchen.

Kitchen complex
Castle kitchens could be huge: one royal castle had enough space to roast three whole oxen. Even the smallest castles had a pantry and buttery. A pantler was in charge of kitchen provisions in the pantry. In the buttery (bottlery) the bottler dispensed the wine. This word has been changed to "butler" today.

Saltcellar

Jester

Cooked dolphin

Buttery

Bundles of herbs drying

Linen store

Pantry

Wild boar's head

Juggler

Sugar castle

Acrobats

Trenchermen

Wash basin

Sugar ship sculpture

Measuring spices for cooking

Cellarer tasting the wine

Roasting spit

Grinding herbs with a mortar and pestle

Smoking meat in the chimney

Kneading bread dough

Food taster
The castle taster sampled each dish for poison before people of royal or noble families ate.

Castle wine cellar
In mid-14th century England, a gallon (4.5 liters) of wine imported from France cost the equivalent of a day's wages for a skilled laborer. Wine was sold in barrels holding between 120 and 240 gallons (550-1100 l). The poor could afford a pint of wine at a tavern occasionally, but they could never afford a whole barrel.

Faster! Faster!
There were no mechanical aids to cooking, and spit-roasted meat required constant turning. The job of the turnspit was the lowliest in the kitchen. In later centuries his work was done by a dog running in a wheel, much like a hamster's exercise wheel.

Baker's dozen
The castle oven was a useful source of income, because manor peasants had to bake their bread there. They paid the lord in loaves for the use of the oven and paid a fine if the reeve (village policeman) caught them baking at home.

ENTERTAINMENT

CASTLE LIFE WAS SOMETIMES COLD, often uncomfortable, but never boring. There was always some task to attend to, and when the day's work was done the lord and his family amused themselves with sports. Two favorite sports were hunting and jousting.

Hunting took many forms, and some still continue today. The most noble was hawking. The hunter sent tamed birds of prey, such as falcons, to swoop down and capture smaller birds. Hunting with dogs was popular, too. The hawks, dogs, and other hunt animals were highly prized and lived a better life than many poor people.

A jousting tournament was the most glamorous sport. It was an event in which knights charged at each other on horses. Lowering long lances as they drew closer, each aimed to knock the other off his horse.

Let battle commence
The tournament started as mock warfare, with rival knights fighting over a wide area. The battles destroyed crops and killed warriors, so many kings tried to ban them. Gradually, though, rules evolved to make the tournament safer. By the mid-14th century it had become a formal contest featuring armored knights charging at each other on horseback.

Hawking
Royal and wealthy castle dwellers considered hunting with a bird of prey the finest of sports. The trained birds themselves lived like kings: they perched on their owners' wrists and traveled everywhere with them – even to meals and to church.

Tournament armor
Not much is known about 14th-century tournament armor, because most existing pieces date from the 15th and 16th centuries. Early jousting helms may have been slightly thicker to withstand the impact of an opponent's lance, with a reinforcing plate below the eye slits. In addition, a long solid gauntlet (glove) called a *manifer* may have been worn.

Hunting dogs
Hunting was an important part of castle life, and hunting dogs were treated as well or better than many humans. They lived in heated kennels, and they had a special bread – brom bread – baked for their meals.

"It's behind you!"
Both adults and children enjoyed the puppet shows which traveling minstrels and players performed on a makeshift stage. The figures were glove puppets, and although the show resembled a Punch-and-Judy show, these characters did not appear until the 19th century.

Woman doing embroidery

Women playing a harp and a psaltery

Chivalry
Knights were all supposed to obey a code of good conduct – a set of rules for gentlemen. The code, called chivalry, demanded that the knight should be brave, truthful, godly, gentle, faithful, and fearless. Chivalry also meant behaving honorably toward women. However, the laws of chivalry only applied to noble-born Christian people. They did not protect "heathens" (non-Christians), villeins, and other peasants.

Ladies waving to knights

Herald
Wealthy barons and knights employed one or more heralds to help them at the joust. A herald had many duties, but the most important at the joust was to act as a representative for his master.

More lances
Lances could be elaborately decorated with bright colors. The sound of splintering lances delighted the audiences. When one heroic knight got through 300 decorated lances in a single day, he had to start on his unpainted ones.

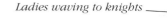

Swinging bait to recall hawks

Musicians

Knights jousting

Defeated knight giving up his armor to the victor

Successful knight's pile of winnings

Defeated knight held for ransom in victor's tent

Herb garden

Tents of competitors

Lances

Sally port (small door to outside)

Heralds announce arrivals of knights

Squires

Drive on the right
Knights in the joust always passed to their opponent's left, so the left-hand side of the suit of armor was much more heavily reinforced than the right.

Trumpeters announce start

Fatal fights
There were deaths at most tournaments, but some were worse than others. At a French tournament held in 1240, many knights suffocated from heat and dust.

Squires dressing knight for joust

Knight's helmet being removed

Squire carrying knight's helmet

Collecting the winnings
Joust rules varied, but often the defeated knight lost his valuable armor and horse and could even be taken prisoner and held for ransom. This meant that tournaments could be very profitable for skilled or cunning warriors.

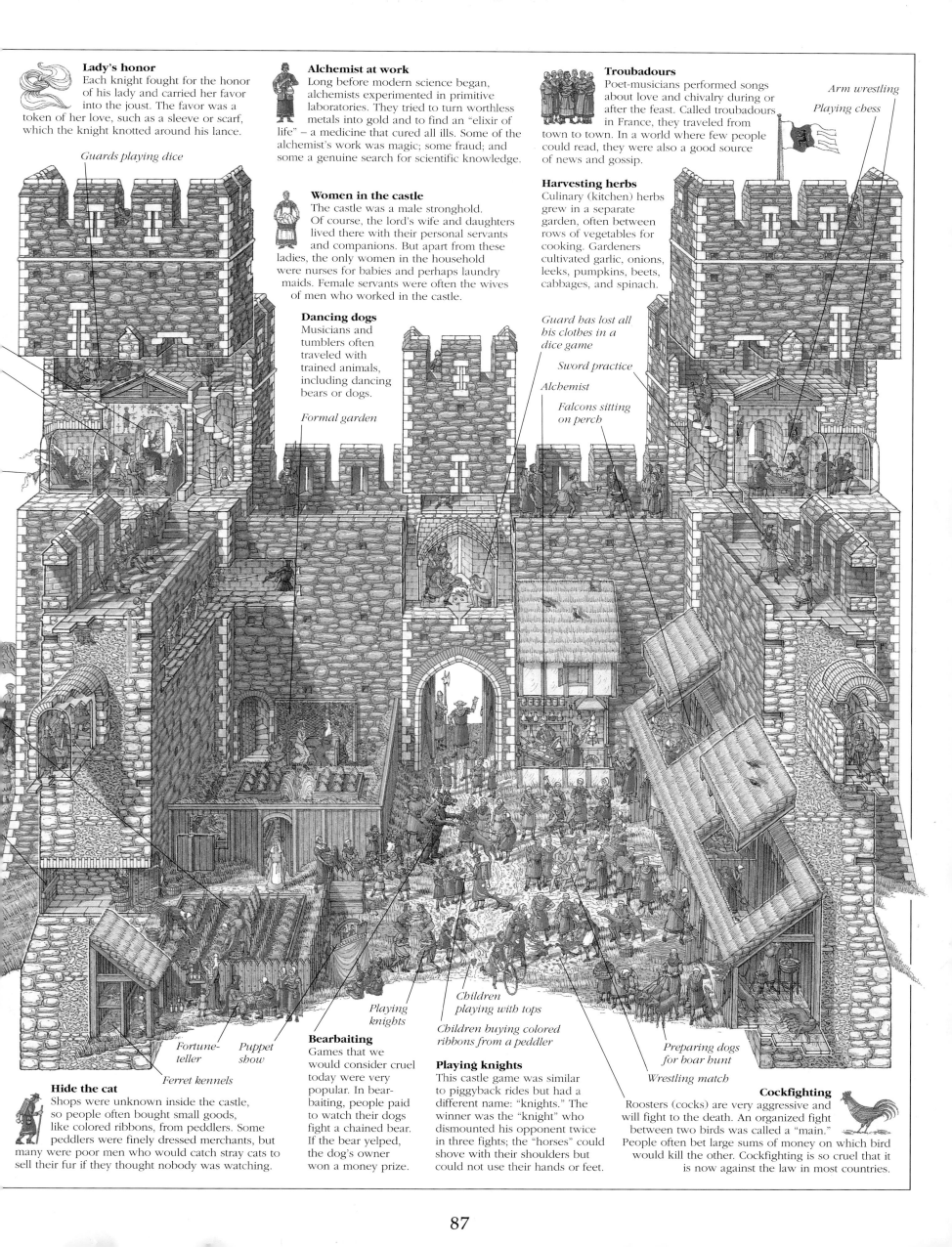

Lady's honor
Each knight fought for the honor of his lady and carried her favor into the joust. The favor was a token of her love, such as a sleeve or scarf, which the knight knotted around his lance.

Guards playing dice

Alchemist at work
Long before modern science began, alchemists experimented in primitive laboratories. They tried to turn worthless metals into gold and to find an "elixir of life" – a medicine that cured all ills. Some of the alchemist's work was magic; some fraud; and some a genuine search for scientific knowledge.

Women in the castle
The castle was a male stronghold. Of course, the lord's wife and daughters lived there with their personal servants and companions. But apart from these ladies, the only women in the household were nurses for babies and perhaps laundry maids. Female servants were often the wives of men who worked in the castle.

Dancing dogs
Musicians and tumblers often traveled with trained animals, including dancing bears or dogs.

Formal garden

Troubadours
Poet-musicians performed songs about love and chivalry during or after the feast. Called troubadours in France, they traveled from town to town. In a world where few people could read, they were also a good source of news and gossip.

Arm wrestling

Playing chess

Harvesting herbs
Culinary (kitchen) herbs grew in a separate garden, often between rows of vegetables for cooking. Gardeners cultivated garlic, onions, leeks, pumpkins, beets, cabbages, and spinach.

Guard has lost all his clothes in a dice game

Sword practice

Alchemist

Falcons sitting on perch

Children playing with tops

Children buying colored ribbons from a peddler

Playing knights

Fortune-teller

Puppet show

Ferret kennels

Preparing dogs for boar hunt

Wrestling match

Hide the cat
Shops were unknown inside the castle, so people often bought small goods, like colored ribbons, from peddlers. Some peddlers were finely dressed merchants, but many were poor men who would catch stray cats to sell their fur if they thought nobody was watching.

Bearbaiting
Games that we would consider cruel today were very popular. In bearbaiting, people paid to watch their dogs fight a chained bear. If the bear yelped, the dog's owner won a money prize.

Playing knights
This castle game was similar to piggyback rides but had a different name: "knights." The winner was the "knight" who dismounted his opponent twice in three fights; the "horses" could shove with their shoulders but could not use their hands or feet.

Cockfighting
Roosters (cocks) are very aggressive and will fight to the death. An organized fight between two birds was called a "main." People often bet large sums of money on which bird would kill the other. Cockfighting is so cruel that it is now against the law in most countries.

LIVESTOCK AND PRODUCE

SUPPLYING THE CASTLE with food was a major task. When the lord was at home, there were up to two hundred hungry people to feed. Much of the food came from the manor – the land under the control of the castle and its lord. The lord of the manor owned most of the land, but he allowed his subjects – the local people – to farm some of it. In exchange, they had to cultivate the lord's fields, called the demesne lands.

The changing seasons controlled everyone's diet. In summer and autumn there was plenty of fresh food. Food for animals was scarce in winter, so the villagers slaughtered many of their pigs, sheep, poultry, and cattle at the end of fall. To stop the meat from rotting, they preserved it in salt or by smoking. Other foods, such as beans, were preserved by drying. A few foodstuffs, such as apples, grew or could be stored until spring.

CARRIER PIGEON

Message secured to leg

Pigeons carried messages faster than the speediest horse. With a message tied to one leg, the birds could find their way back to the castle from hundreds of miles away. With a basket of pigeons a spy could send messages back to the castle about the enemy's strengths and weaknesses.

SHEEP

The sheep that grazed on and around the castle banks were valuable property. Their wool was sold to make cloth.

Modern breed

Metal shears

Medieval sheep

SHEARING

Medieval sheep produced only a sixth as much wool as today's sheep. Shearing (clipping) them produced matted fleeces of wool which fetched a high price abroad. The wool trade was important to England for hundreds of years.

Peasants cut the grain with sharp sickles

The reeve tells everyone what to do

TAX DEMAND

Most people living on the lord's manor had to pay a bewildering array of charges, fees, and taxes. Here are a few examples:

Wood-penny: *for the right to collect firewood on the lord's land*

Agistment: *for the right to graze animals in the forest*

Chiminage: *for the right to carry goods through the forest*

Bodel silver: *for the right to live in a house on the lord's land*

Foddercorn: *grain a villein had to provide to feed the lord's horses*

Heriot: *upon death, a family had to give the lord the dead man's best animal*

BOON DAY

At harvest time, the lord called a "boon day," and every able-bodied person had to help in cutting, turning, and stacking the hay. Cutting the hay and grain was very hard work, but it had its rewards: the villagers were given a large meal and often all the ale they could drink. At the day's end, there were amusing harvest traditions. A sheep was released into the stubble, and the villagers could keep it if it stayed in the field. If it strayed, the lord reclaimed the beast.

Stacking grain in stooks to dry

Loading grain on an ox-cart

Herbage

The grass that grew on the banks at the foot of the castle wall was not wasted. This pasture was called herbage. Villagers paid the lord a fee to graze their flocks there.

Cattle
During the winter, when grass grew slowly, cows had to eat hay from a stack. They had huge appetites, so most castles kept only enough cows for breeding in the spring. A few kept extra cattle for milking.

Acorn feast
Pigs cost almost nothing to keep, because they did not need feeding: they scratched for food in the forest. However, feeding hogs acorns fattened them up nicely, and roast boar was a favorite dish for the lord at Christmas.

Slaughtering pigs

Tools and carts
The castle blacksmith and carpenter made every tool and implement the castle needed. The tools and carts were together called "deadstock," to distinguish them from the animals – the livestock.

Dumping offal (animal guts) was illegal

More ale!
Ale did not keep well, so brewing went on all the time. The castle brewed some of its own ale but also bought barrels of ale in the market. To satisfy the thirsty occupants of the largest castles, the carter hauled wagonloads of ale through the castle gates.

Slaughterhouse

Firewood
Every castle needed fuel for cooking and heating. Villagers and servants collected firewood, taking care to take only dead or fallen timber: healthy wood was a valuable building material.

Ale being delivered

No dumping
Disposing of garbage was a problem in a castle. Much of the garbage was just tipped over the walls into a stinking heap in the castle ditch. Flies attracted to the dump caused health problems if the castle was near a town.

Sheep grazing on grassy bank

Beauty parlor
Everyone itched from the bites of fleas, lice, and other parasites. A fine-toothed comb helped remove them from hair, but the lice learned to hide in the seams of clothes, where they were almost impossible to get at.

Guards hurry to arrest man throwing offal over castle wall

Mucking out

Ox shed

Peacock

Pigsty

Slaughterhouse
A skilled castle butcher could kill a pig almost painlessly. He took great care to make sure that the beast was happy right up to the moment when he hit it on the head with a hammer. This was common sense, not kindness: if the pig was scared, its meat was much tougher.

Siege engine tower

Collecting eggs   *Town gate*

Pigeon pie tonight
Collecting pigeons for the pot was easiest at night. Once they had roosted (gone to sleep), the cook's assistants could lift them as easily as picking fruit from a tree.

Garlic store

Salt fish store

Geese

Bee skeps
Honey was the only common sweetener, and the castle bees lived in hives high on the walls. The hives, called skeps, were made of straw.

Butter making

Bee skeps

Clerk taking inventory

Salted meat stored in barrels

Salt store

Mucking out
Oxen produced almost as much in dung as they ate in food, and removing the muck was a full-time job.

Fleece store

Stores of apples and onions

Game birds (pheasant, partridge, woodcock)

Winter fuel store

Barley and rye

Grain

Pricey peacock
The wealthiest barons kept peacocks and swans to decorate their castle grounds and to eat. A favorite banquet dish was roast peacock.

Salting meat
The most common way of preserving pork and beef through the winter was to salt it. The salt worked by locking up the water in the meat. The microorganisms that rot meat need water to live, so salt protected the meat from spoiling.

Fat of the land
Animal fat made tallow candles, prevented armor from rusting, and greased the wooden axles of carts and wagons.

Salt fish store
The castle kept a supply of salted fish called stockfish. Fish was more popular than it is today and was on the castle menu as often as meat.

89

WEAPONS AND PUNISHMENT

CASTLES THAT PROTECTED TOWNS often had a second entrance, much like a back door to a house. This "town gate" was a convenient way in and out of the castle. Grisly sights greeted the traders and troops who passed through the town gate. Staring down from pikes high on the walls were the rotting heads of executed traitors. Below, in the ditch, stood the gallows and pillory. Like the severed heads above, they reminded townfolk of the severe punishments for breaking the law.

In the shadow of the town gate were the butts. These were targets where every able-bodied man had to practice his archery skills each week. There were preparations for warfare inside the castle walls, too. When they weren't rehearsing their fighting skills, the castle garrison was busy stockpiling supplies and ammunition or mending their weapons.

CROSSBOW

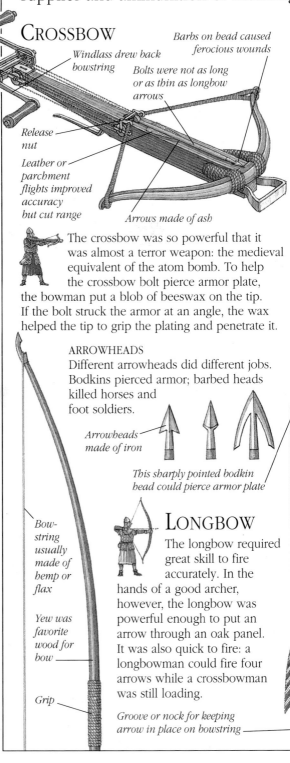

Windlass drew back bowstring

Barbs on head caused ferocious wounds

Bolts were not as long or as thin as longbow arrows

Release nut

Leather or parchment flights improved accuracy but cut range

Arrows made of ash

The crossbow was so powerful that it was almost a terror weapon: the medieval equivalent of the atom bomb. To help the crossbow bolt pierce armor plate, the bowman put a blob of beeswax on the tip. If the bolt struck the armor at an angle, the wax helped the tip to grip the plating and penetrate it.

ARROWHEADS
Different arrowheads did different jobs. Bodkins pierced armor; barbed heads killed horses and foot soldiers.

Arrowheads made of iron

This sharply pointed bodkin head could pierce armor plate

Bow-string usually made of hemp or flax

Yew was favorite wood for bow

Grip

LONGBOW

The longbow required great skill to fire accurately. In the hands of a good archer, however, the longbow was powerful enough to put an arrow through an oak panel. It was also quick to fire: a longbowman could fire four arrows while a crossbowman was still loading.

Groove or nock for keeping arrow in place on bowstring

BRANDING

Branding on the cheek meant all could see the mark

The underside of the thumb was a common place to be branded

Branding on the chest was easier to hide

Branding – burning marks on a criminal's body – was the punishment for some offenses. A criminal branded on the hand with "M" (for malefactor, or evildoer) could not hide his guilt. The sentence was carried out immediately by an official with a hot branding iron.

PRESSING

The torturer added more weights each day

The prisoner had just enough food to stay alive

The punishment for prisoners who refused to plead (either admit or deny their guilt) was to be crushed or pressed to death. It was a slow and agonizing death, and many begged visitors to jump on the boards so that they would die more quickly.

FINGER PILLORY

The prisoner was trapped by his fingertips

For the most trivial offenses, such as drunkenness and rowdiness, the prisoner might be confined in a finger pillory, which trapped just the fingertips. This punishment was also used for unruly schoolchildren.

Gallows
Execution was the penalty for serious crime; only very minor offenses had less-severe punishments. Executions were by hanging: strangulation with a slipknot. It was a slow death, and on the way to the gallows (the frame from which the rope hung) many victims begged their friends to hasten death by pulling on their legs.

Pillory
The penalty for minor crimes, such as selling underweight goods, was a spell in the pillory. This was a wooden structure with holes to grip the offender's head and hands. For more serious offenses, such as spreading false rumors, the prisoner's ears were nailed back to the boards.

Key to turn windlass on mangonel

Windlass to pull the mangonel arm down to the firing position

Practicing marksmanship
Training in archery started in boyhood, with a small bow and a nearby target. However, men had to stand more than 220 yards (200 m) from the target and used much more powerful bows.

Iron-framed yett

Drawing
The penalty for treason (plotting against the king) was to be "hung, drawn, and quartered." When the victim was half-dead, the hangman took him down and cut out his insides. The hangman then held up the person's heart and shouted, "Behold the heart of a traitor!"

Quartering
The final stage of a traitor's fate was to be quartered: chopped up into four pieces. The quarters, or sometimes just the head, were put on public display.

Pillory

Man being prepared for hanging

Entrails being pulled out of body

Victim being quartered

Duck!
Another punishment was ducking in the moat or village pond. The offender was seated in a "ducking stool" and lowered into the water.

Bagpipes are played to humiliate the offender

More ammunition
For accurate firing, the mangonel needed carefully cut stones. Weight was important, because a stone that was too light would travel beyond the target. Heavier stones fell short.

Mangonel
The only war engine which could be operated from the top of a castle tower was the mangonel. Using a trebuchet on a tower would shake it to pieces.

Storing bows
The garrison stored their longbows carefully, unstrung in racks. The yew bow staves were not as costly as crossbows, but they were still valuable. A good bow would cost an archer between three and six days' wages.

Hanging in chains
For particularly unfortunate criminals, punishment didn't end on the gallows. The blacksmith riveted the corpse into "chains" – an iron framework – and the body was displayed hanging from a gibbet (beam) to discourage others from doing wrong.

Nesting box
Wind and weather quickly reduced a gibbeted body to bleached bones, and occasionally birds nested in the skull.

Putting head on a pike

Heads on view to public

Practice arrows
Instead of the sharp, armor-piercing points used in warfare, practice arrows had blunt tips.

Winching up rocks
A simple windlass helped the garrison lift rocks to supply the mangonel. They were too heavy to carry up the winding stairs.

Arrow being checked

Crossbows hung up

Cross-bow bolts

Getting ahead
The heads of traitors decorated the castle battlements above the gates as a warning to others who plotted against the king. The heads looked out over other public places, too, such as the entrances to London Bridge over the Thames River. There they were lightly boiled before a dip in preservative tar.

Longbow being strung

Dovecot

Bowstrings

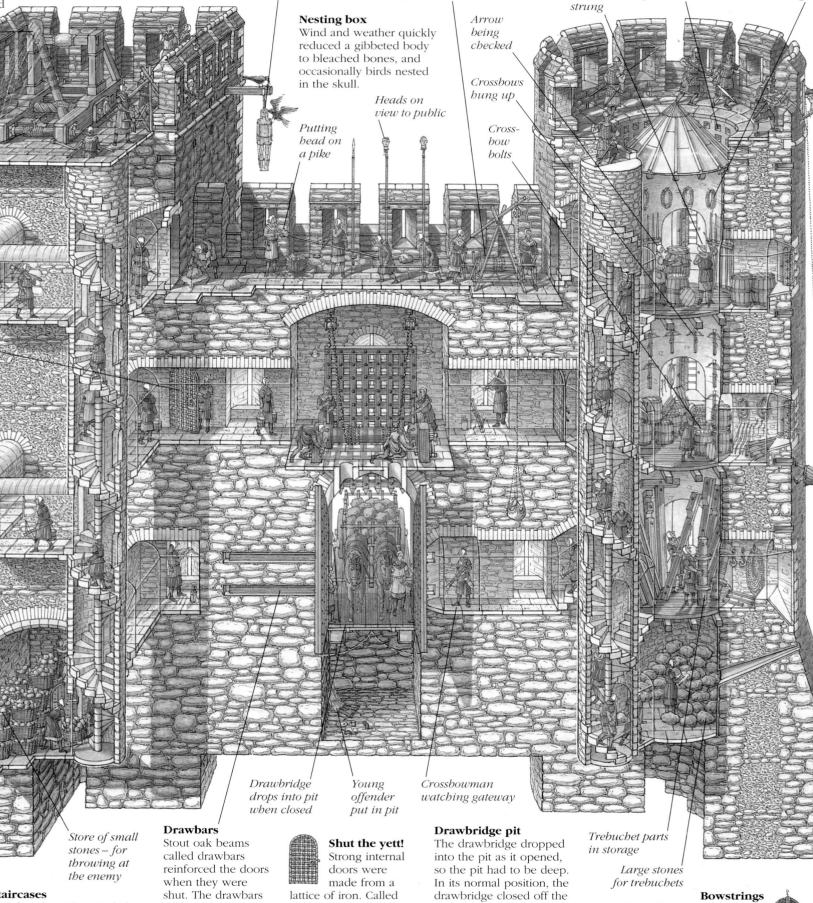

Drawbridge drops into pit when closed

Young offender put in pit

Crossbowman watching gateway

Trebuchet parts in storage

Large stones for trebuchets

Spiral staircases
In most castles, the stairs spiraled clockwise as they rose. This allowed a defender to retreat up the stairs while swinging his sword with his right hand, while an attacker had to lean around the corner to wield his sword.

Store of small stones – for throwing at the enemy

Drawbars
Stout oak beams called drawbars reinforced the doors when they were shut. The drawbars slid across behind the door, and when out of use they were stored in slots built into the gatehouse wall.

Shut the yett!
Strong internal doors were made from a lattice of iron. Called *yetts* in Scotland, the doors were often more like gates. In English castles, thick oak panels filled the gaps between the bars.

Drawbridge pit
The drawbridge dropped into the pit as it opened, so the pit had to be deep. In its normal position, the drawbridge closed off the pit, which made a useful extra punishment cell. A few drawbridges were booby trapped: releasing a trapdoor pitched unwanted visitors into the pit.

Bowstrings
When they weren't fighting, archers took the strings off their bows and kept them dry in a pouch or inside their shirts. In the castle, spare bowstrings were probably hung coiled on a dry wall.

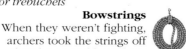

CROSS-SECTIONS
MAN-OF-WAR

WELCOME ABOARD an 18th-century warship! This 100-gun man-of-war, based on British Admiral Horatio Nelson's flagship, *HMS Victory*, is sailing into battle on the high seas. From the rat-infested bilges at the bottom of the ship, to high up in the mainmast, the crew is busy preparing for battle as the enemy ships advance. Soon the first shots will be fired, and everyone will be fighting for their lives!

"MAKE SAIL!"

This picture appears on each left-hand page. The white area tells you which cross-section of the ship you are looking at.

WITH THE ABOVE COMMAND, the captain of a wooden sailing warship, or "man-of-war", started a bustle of activity. In seconds, hundreds of sailors climbed high above the rolling deck. In minutes they unfurled huge sails to harness the power of the wind. On board, the ship carried everything the crew of about 800 needed for a voyage halfway around the world, with a deadly battle at the end. Sea battles decided which navy – a nation's warriors at sea – controlled the oceans. The seas were the main trade routes, so the country with the strongest navy ruled the world.

Life for the ordinary sailor on board a man-of-war was very hard. He faced death from battle, accidents, and disease, and his floating home was damp, dark, and crowded. This book will take you on a section-by-section tour through a man-of-war of Great Britain's Royal Navy in about the year 1800.

THE ANATOMY OF A MAN-OF-WAR

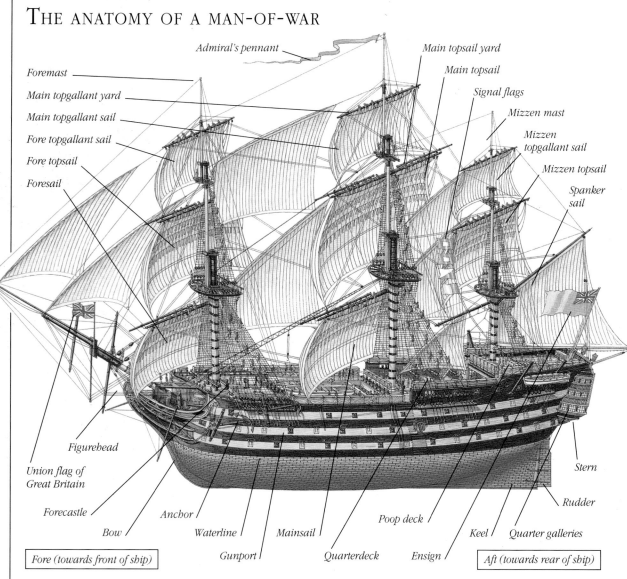

- Admiral's pennant
- Foremast
- Main topgallant yard
- Main topgallant sail
- Fore topgallant sail
- Fore topsail
- Foresail
- Main topsail yard
- Main topsail
- Signal flags
- Mizzen mast
- Mizzen topgallant sail
- Mizzen topsail
- Spanker sail
- Figurehead
- Union flag of Great Britain
- Forecastle
- Bow
- Anchor
- Waterline
- Gunport
- Mainsail
- Quarterdeck
- Poop deck
- Ensign
- Keel
- Quarter galleries
- Rudder
- Stern

Fore (towards front of ship)

Aft (towards rear of ship)

The picture above shows the main parts of an 18th-century wooden warship. Towering above the main body of the ship, the hull, rose three huge masts – fore, main, and mizzen. These supported the yards, large horizontal poles from which the sails hung. The hundreds of ropes controlled the sails and supported the masts, making the sailing warship, or "man-of-war", an incredibly complex piece of machinery.

A NOTE ON MEASUREMENTS
Measurements used in the Royal Navy belonged to the imperial system. Gun weights (for example 32-pounder) and food ration units (for example 1 lb of beef) were all measured this way. You can find metric equivalents in the text. In the imperial system, ounce is abbreviated as oz and pound as lb. In the metric system, centimetre is abbreviated as cm and metre as m.

Poop deck
The highest deck on the ship, the unarmed poop deck was used mainly by officers. From here, the signal lieutenant hauled up flags to signal to nearby vessels.

Quarter deck
At the stern of the ship, the quarter deck was also normally reserved for the officers. The captain slept in a cabin at the stern of this deck so he could be on hand quickly in an emergency. The quarter deck was armed with 12 cannons. They were called 12-pounders because they each fired an orange-sized cannonball weighing 12 lb (5.5 kg).

Forecastle
This raised deck covered the main deck at the bows. Gangways linked it to the quarter deck. Many of the ship's sails were controlled from here, and there were four guns as well. Two were carronades, or "smashers", a kind of short gun firing a heavy shot. They were most effective at short range. This man-of-war carried two huge 68-pounder (31 kg) carronades.

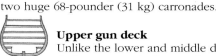

Upper gun deck
Unlike the lower and middle decks, this deck was open to the weather in the middle. Three of the man-of-war's small boats sat on cradles attached to the beams which crossed over the open space. It was armed with 24-pounder guns – 15 along each side. The admiral had his day cabin at the stern.

Rubbish
Most rubbish generated by the crew was simply thrown overboard.

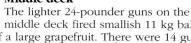

Middle deck
The lighter 24-pounder guns on the middle deck fired smallish 11 kg balls, the size of a large grapefruit. There were 14 guns on each side, and many of the crew slept and ate here. The galley, the ship's kitchen, was here, too. At the stern the officers had their cabins and wardroom (dining/living room).

Lower deck
This was the lowest gun deck. Down each side there were 15 32-pounder cannons, which fired 14 kg balls the size of coconuts. When the ship was not fighting in a battle, many of the seamen hung their hammocks between the beams of this deck.

Orlop deck
The orlop deck got its name from a Dutch word meaning "overlap", because the deck overlapped the hold. This deck was used for storage, and for the offices of some of the ship's crew who needed access to the hold, such as the purser and carpenter.

Hold
Located at the very bottom of the ship, the hold was like a giant warehouse. Here the crew stored provisions for the voyage – all the food and drink they needed, iron cannonballs, spare ropes and sails, and materials for repairing damage.

Heads
The ship's lavatories, called the heads, or "seats of ease", were just holes cut in the deck planking, with a seat built above. They weren't enclosed, so there was no privacy. There were six heads for the crew of 800.

Bows
The front of the ship was called the bows, or the head.

Buckler
To keep the sea out of ports (holes) in the ship's hull, the crew fitted a buckler – a kind of plug.

Roundhouse
Officers had many privileges – even on the lavatory. Junior officers had a small round cubicle, called a roundhouse, to provide privacy and keep out the wind, rain, and spray. The important officers had their own private lavatories in a more convenient position further aft (further back).

Safety nets
Strong winds and sea spray lashed the heads, and a big wave could wash anyone using them overboard.

Hawse-holes
Large ports, called hawse-holes, carried the anchor cable through the hull to the gun deck beyond.

Raising the anchor
Tackles (ropes and pulleys) made the job of lifting the anchor easier.

Fish tackle
Once the top of the anchor was made fast (fixed) to the cathead, the crew used a special tackle called a fish tackle to raise the other end.

Cathead
The crew stored the anchor lashed to the cathead – a thick, protruding beam which contained a "sheave block" or pulley.

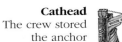

Splash!
Crew who couldn't reach the heads used a bucket. They took care to empty it on the side facing away from the wind or the contents would blow back in their faces.

Buckler

Figurehead

At the bows, every ship had a figurehead – a wooden carving, often of a human figure or an animal. This man-of-war was no exception. The figurehead was a shield bearing the coat-of-arms of Great Britain.

Keel
The spine of the ship was the keel. This was a giant length of teak – a very hard wood from a tropical tree. The keel was 46 m (150 ft) long and 50 cm (20 in) square.

Anchor cable
The weight of the huge anchor cable (rope) was what really stopped the ship from moving at anchor. The cable was so heavy that the whole crew had to fish haul it in.

Copper plating

Fluke of anchor

Anchor
When the crew wanted to stop the ship from drifting, they dropped the anchor. The two flukes (hooks) stuck in the seabed.

HEALTH AT SEA

LIFE ON BOARD A MAN-OF-WAR was full of health hazards. Sailors accepted some risks, such as enemy fire or falls from the rigging, as part of the job. But what they feared most was disease. Disease killed slowly, and was more deadly. For each seaman killed in action, as many as 40 died of diseases. Medical science was primitive, and even doctors did not fully understand why fevers spread so rapidly. They knew that crowding was part of the problem. Dirt and damp also didn't help. It was almost impossible for the men to wash themselves or their clothes properly. Soap was not issued to seamen until about 1825. To get their clothes clean, the crew soaked them in urine, then rinsed them in sea-water! Despite these health risks, sailors were probably sick no more often than their friends on land, who could not afford the regular meals or medical attention that sailors enjoyed.

SCURVY

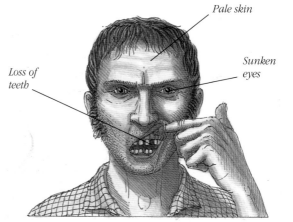

Pale skin

Sunken eyes

Loss of teeth

The symptoms of the disease called scurvy included gradual weakening, pale skin, sunken eyes, tender gums, muscular pain, loss of teeth, internal bleeding, and the opening of wounds such as sword cuts that had healed many years previously. Exhaustion, fainting, diarrhoea, and lung and kidney trouble followed. Eventually, the sailor "went to Davy Jones' locker" (naval slang for dying).

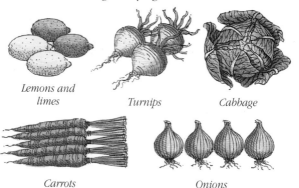

Lemons and limes

Turnips

Cabbage

Carrots

Onions

Scurvy was much rarer in 1800 than it had been 50 years previously, and the disease affected the crew only on long journeys. Doctors had not yet discovered the cause of scurvy (lack of vitamin C). However, in 1747, Commander George Anson had found that fresh fruit and vegetables fed to the sailors aboard his ship, HMS *Salisbury,* kept scurvy away. Fruit and vegetables contain vitamin C, so scurvy was beaten by giving the crew fresh vegetables, sauerkraut (pickled cabbage), or lemons and limes.

THE SURGEON AND HIS TOOLS

Ships' surgeons varied widely in ability. They were important in battles, when they had to amputate (cut off) smashed arms and legs. Speed was vital, because quick work reduced the risk of infection, which killed more men than the surgery itself.

RUM
The surgeon's patients were given rum to try and numb the pain, as amputations were done without anaesthetics. Brandy was also sometimes used.

GAG
Victims were given a gag made of rope or leather to bite on as another way of dulling the agonizing pain. Mercifully, the victim usually fainted.

KNIVES
Razor-sharp knives cut through skin, muscles, and ligaments to reach bones.

BONE SAW
Fine, sharp saws cut through leg and arm bones. They were standard tools in the surgeon's kit.

BOILING PITCH
After the amputation, the bloody arm or leg stump was dipped in boiling pitch (tar) to seal the wound and stop the bleeding.

PEG LEG
The amputee was given a wooden leg so he could walk again.

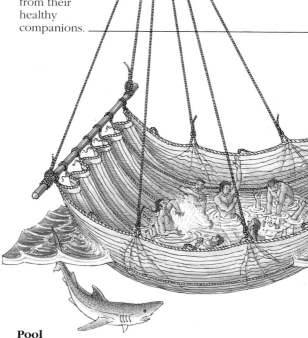

Washing hammocks
Washing hammocks was essential for health, but took up lots of room. The crew took turns scrubbing their hammocks whenever the weather was good enough to dry them.

The sick bay
Medical treatment for the sick was primitive. On many ships the only advantage of the sick bay was that it separated the sick men from their healthy companions.

Cathead
These beams were called catheads because the ends were originally carved into the shape of a cat's, or lion's, head.

Bible bashing
To scrub the decks, sailors used blocks of stone. They were the size and shape of big family bibles, so they were nicknamed "holystones".

Pool
In tropical waters, the crew rigged a sail over the side to form a shark-proof swimming pool.

Tropical diseases
The most unhealthy places to sail to were the tropical ports. The worst year was 1726: Admiral Hosier's expedition set out with 4,750 men, and 4,000 of them died of disease.

Scrubbing the decks
The ritual of cleaning the deck took place every morning. It was more like sandpapering than washing, because the holystones slid on a mixture of sand and water that the midshipmen sprinkled. After rinsing, the upper decks dried quickly, but the constant washing kept the lower decks permanently damp.

Overcrowding
The crew lived, worked, and slept in cramped, airless conditions. The lower decks were especially badly ventilated and smelled strongly of sweaty bodies.

"Ouch! my head!"
Low beams meant sailors had to stoop constantly. Some people thought that sailors went mad because they banged their heads so often.

Hammocks
Each seaman had two hammocks, so that he could sleep in one while the other was washed. Hammocks were stored rolled in nets on the upper deck.

Hammocks being washed

Dressing ulcers
Dirt and dampness caused infection of even small cuts and scratches. The ulcers that formed needed careful dressing.

Foremast
The foremast was the first of the man-of-war's three masts.

Washing clothes
Clothes rinsed in salt water never dried properly, so sailors tried to collect rainwater for rinsing laundry.

Sailor being forced to go to the sick bay

Extra rations
The very sick got extra rations, including "portable soup". This was made by boiling down broth to form a jelly which was easier to transport – more portable – than ordinary soup.

Canvas cover kept the hammocks dry

Vinegar being sprinkled in sick bay

Broken legs
Accidents were routine on board ship. Few men survived a fall from the rigging, but the ship's carpenter helped treat lesser fractures by making a splint to keep the broken limb still while it healed.

Portable stove
As ships' surgeons realized that damp was the cause of much disease (especially rheumatism), the crew tried to dry the decks with portable stoves.

Manger
The ship's manger held the livestock which provided fresh meat for those who were lucky enough to get it, mainly the officers. Pigs and cattle lived here.

Bucket of hot coals from stove

The ballast
Ballast kept the ship upright. It consisted of a layer of loose stones, called shingle, spread on top of flat blocks of iron called "pigs". Ballast was a health risk, because everything drained into it. On some French ships dead men were buried in the ballast.

Dispensary
The ship's drug supply was kept in the dispensary. Here seamen could obtain remedies for minor illnesses.

Fumigating
Replacing the ballast was the only sure way to make it healthy, but fumigation was used on many ships. Sailors sprinkled vinegar and brimstone (sulphur) over buckets of hot coals. The clouds of poisonous fumes were supposed to make the smells of the ballast less harmful.

Structures called gratings let in air and light

Fire buckets
In an all-wood ship, fire was a constant risk, particularly when stoves were in use.

Limeys
The surgeon prescribed lemon or lime juice for those suffering from scurvy. This earned British sailors the nickname "limeys".

Fresh air
Opening the gunport let in fresh air, but in bad weather it let in rain and sea-water, too!

Greening
The bottom of the ship was covered with thin copper plates to stop worms from boring holes in the hull. The copper soon turned green from the sea-water.

Sprinkling vinegar
The acid in vinegar was a simple disinfectant, so the surgeon's mates sprinkled it around the sick bay.

"I'm *not* sick"
Sick seamen had their grog (rum) ration stopped, so many pretended to be well rather than go to the sick bay.

Cooking and Eating

Read the ship's menu, and you'd never guess that the food was one of the attractions of joining the navy. Meals included: rotting, stinking meat; biscuits riddled with maggots; and cheese so tough that sailors carved it into buttons for their uniforms. The drink was just as bad. The "fresh" water soon turned to green slime, and the beer kept little better.

Meals tasted bad because it was very hard to keep food fresh. Voyages could last years, and there was no refrigeration. The ship usually carried live animals for food, but their meat, milk, and eggs were mostly reserved for the officers. Meat for the seamen was stored in salt, which made it dry and very tough. Bread went stale or mouldy so instead the navy issued hard biscuits made of flour and water. Despite all this, shipboard food was probably better than the food sailors enjoyed with their families at home.

Timekeeping
Most ships kept time using a half-hour sand-glass, like a big egg-timer. The quartermaster's mate rang the bell each time he turned the glass to measure the next half-hour.

The purser
Supplying food, clothing, and bedding was the purser's responsibility. He kept track of how much everyone used, and accounted for it at the end of the voyage. He also kept account of the crew's pay. The purser himself was paid very little, and had to sell food and other things at a profit. The purser was not popular: everyone suspected him of getting rich by stealing. Often they were right!

The steep tub
Meat had to soak in water before cooking to remove the salt that preserved it. Each piece was soaked, or steeped, in the steep tub.

What a mess!
Men ate in groups of 8 to 12, called a mess. They lowered a simple table between two guns, and sat around it to eat.

The à la carte menu

Daily	Sunday	Monday	Tuesday & Saturday	Wednesday & Friday	Thursday
Loaf of bread (in port) or biscuits (at sea)	Dried peas	Bowl of oatmeal	Salt beef	Bowl of oatmeal	Dried peas
	Salt pork	Butter		Butter	Salt pork
8 pints (4.5 litres) of beer		Piece of cheese		Piece of cheese	
				Dried peas	

Fresh food
Fresh food was brought aboard in the ship's boat whenever a new port was reached.

Disposing of waste

Greasy scarves
Sailors' neck scarves got very greasy, as they wiped their hands on them.

Pea soup and fresh veg
Dried peas were usually made into soup, and this was the one meal about which the sailors did not complain. The tedious routine of food varied a little when the ship was close to land. The purser then bought fresh vegetables, as this kept the scurvy away.

The cook

Each mess marked its meat with a metal tag

The ship's cook was often one-legged, as it was one of the few jobs a disabled seaman could do and remain in the navy. He was nicknamed "slushy" after the slush – the yellow grease that floated to the top of the pan in which the fatty salt meat cooked. The cook sold slush to the crew to spread on their biscuits, because the butter which the navy supplied was often rancid (stale) when it reached the ship.

Maggots in the biscuits

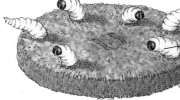

Maggots in a piece of biscuit

Crew members shared their biscuits with rats, maggots, and weevils. They called the maggots "bargemen", joking that the biscuit was the barge, and the maggot was sailing it. Rats were easy to identify, and you'd notice one if you bit into it. The other two were less noticeable. One sailor said, *"...black-headed maggots were fat and cold to the taste, but not bitter... like weevils"*.

Getting rid of maggots
1. Put a large dead fish onto the sack of biscuits, and the maggots crawl out to eat it.
2. When maggots cover the fish, throw fish in sea and replace with a fresh one.
3. Repeat steps **1** & **2** until no more maggots appear.

Mess-mates
Sailors messed together for the whole voyage, so mess-mates became close friends, almost like brothers. They took it in turns to be mess "cook". The cook drew the rations for the mess from the ship's stores, and prepared them for cooking. At meal time one of the mess turned his back and decided who got each plate. This ensured that everyone got a fair share, because he couldn't see how big the portions were.

Steward's room
The steward brought supplies of salt beef, dried peas, oatmeal, and biscuits up from the hold, and his mate measured them out from open casks for the waiting mess cooks.

Fuel store

The galley stove burned wood and coal. To keep the fuel dry the store was at the side of the hold, above the level of the bilges.

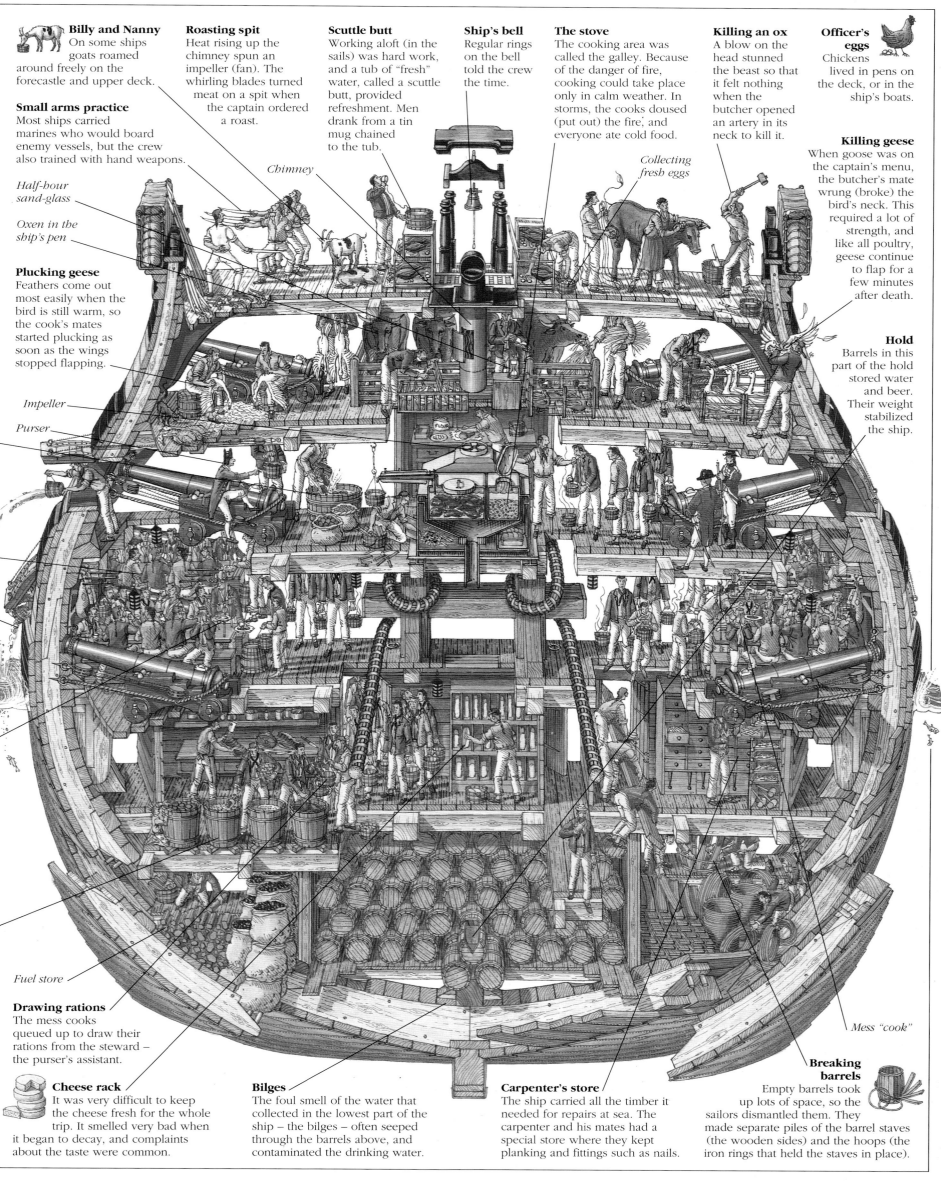

Billy and Nanny
On some ships goats roamed around freely on the forecastle and upper deck.

Small arms practice
Most ships carried marines who would board enemy vessels, but the crew also trained with hand weapons.

Half-hour sand-glass

Oxen in the ship's pen

Plucking geese
Feathers come out most easily when the bird is still warm, so the cook's mates started plucking as soon as the wings stopped flapping.

Impeller

Purser

Roasting spit
Heat rising up the chimney spun an impeller (fan). The whirling blades turned meat on a spit when the captain ordered a roast.

Chimney

Scuttle butt
Working aloft (in the sails) was hard work, and a tub of "fresh" water, called a scuttle butt, provided refreshment. Men drank from a tin mug chained to the tub.

Ship's bell
Regular rings on the bell told the crew the time.

The stove
The cooking area was called the galley. Because of the danger of fire, cooking could take place only in calm weather. In storms, the cooks doused (put out) the fire, and everyone ate cold food.

Collecting fresh eggs

Killing an ox
A blow on the head stunned the beast so that it felt nothing when the butcher opened an artery in its neck to kill it.

Officer's eggs
Chickens lived in pens on the deck, or in the ship's boats.

Killing geese
When goose was on the captain's menu, the butcher's mate wrung (broke) the bird's neck. This required a lot of strength, and like all poultry, geese continue to flap for a few minutes after death.

Hold
Barrels in this part of the hold stored water and beer. Their weight stabilized the ship.

Fuel store

Drawing rations
The mess cooks queued up to draw their rations from the steward – the purser's assistant.

Cheese rack
It was very difficult to keep the cheese fresh for the whole trip. It smelled very bad when it began to decay, and complaints about the taste were common.

Bilges
The foul smell of the water that collected in the lowest part of the ship – the bilges – often seeped through the barrels above, and contaminated the drinking water.

Carpenter's store
The ship carried all the timber it needed for repairs at sea. The carpenter and his mates had a special store where they kept planking and fittings such as nails.

Mess "cook"

Breaking barrels
Empty barrels took up lots of space, so the sailors dismantled them. They made separate piles of the barrel staves (the wooden sides) and the hoops (the iron rings that held the staves in place).

LEISURE AND SUPPLIES

EVERY SAILOR LOOKED FORWARD to a spell in port. It meant that the ship could take on fresh supplies. Fresh meat, bread, fruit, and vegetables made a change from the usual boring rations. But more importantly, being in port meant the chance of leave (holiday). Sailors spent months at a time obeying orders and living close together on crowded decks. They had little leisure time at sea. They longed for the opportunity to escape navy discipline and let themselves go. They dressed up in their best shore clothes, and drew their pay. Then most went ashore and spent it on getting drunk – preferably in the company of beautiful women. The sailors had a good time in port even if they didn't get shore leave. Traders came on board with local women and fresh food for sale. While the ship was in port, the lower decks resembled a wild party, with drinking, dancing, and antics day and night.

THE PRESS GANG

Getting recruits (new sailors) for the navy in wartime was always a problem, because not enough men volunteered. So in port, the ship sent out a press gang. This was a group of 8–12 men, who tried to persuade seamen they met on shore to join the navy. If the men didn't want to join, the press gang took them prisoner, and pressed (forced) them into the navy. The press gang was very unpopular, because once on board, there was no escape for the pressed man.

THE FLEET REGATTA

When the fleet anchored in safe waters, the crews of all the men-of-war used their leisure time to stage a regatta. This was a sea-going carnival day, with races and a nautical fancy-dress parade. The crews dressed up the ship's boats as exotic craft such as Chinese junks, and raced them, perhaps paddling with shovels. The sailors collected money from each ship, and the fastest team won it all.

TATTOOING

British sailors first saw tattoos decorating the bodies of Pacific Island people, and copied the custom themselves. They used needles to prick out patterns in the skin. Rubbing ink or even ash into the wound made a permanent mark. A good tattooist could use his skills to earn extra money from his ship-mates.

inks

needle

ink bottle

cloth

TOOLS OF THE TRADE
Tattoo tools included needles, coloured inks, and a cloth to wipe away the excess ink.

PATTERNS
Sailors liked nautical patterns for tattoos. Favourites included anchors, hearts-and-anchors, names of sweethearts, and more elaborately, ships. Some sailors eventually had their whole bodies tattooed.

Exotic pets
In foreign ports sailors bought unusual pets for their sweethearts, or to sell. Parrots were so popular that "bag, hammock, and bird-cage" was naval slang for a sailor's possessions.

A sailor ashore
It wasn't difficult to recognize a sailor ashore. His sunburn, tattoos, and strange language set the sailor on leave apart. But the fact that he was so drunk that he couldn't stand up was the surest guide!

Parbuckling
To haul casks on board ship, the crew sometimes used a parbuckle – they looped ropes around the barrel and rolled it up the ship's side.

Floating the barrels
Barrels and casks coming aboard ship were floated to the side of the ship where they could be hauled aboard.

Sailors waving to their sweethearts

Striking a bargain
Traders who boarded the ship knew what caught a sailor's eye. They packed colourful, gaudy fabric and ribbon, shiny shoe buckles, and cheap jewellery.

Gambling
Betting was illegal, but it still went on. A favourite game was "crown and anchor", played with a round board and three special dice. Fist-fights provided another opportunity for gambling. The crowd placed bets on who would win.

Paying off
The navy paid wages in full only when seamen left the navy, or transferred to another ship. Until then, sailors received part in cash, and part in "tickets" – vouchers that they could exchange for goods.

Sea chests
Some crew members kept their shore clothes in sea chests. Several mess-mates often shared a chest. Chests were stowed away most of the time, and the seamen had few personal possessions in daily use.

Purser at work
All the supplies that came on board had to be checked and recorded. This was the job of the purser. The rest of the crew mistrusted him, and his kindest nickname was the "sea-grocer".

Block and tackle
The heaviest loads were impossible to lift without cunning use of ropes. Making a loop or tackle by passing the rope through pulleys (called blocks) simplified any lift.

"Steady as she goes!"
Sailors shouted orders to each other. When the man obeying the order was out of earshot of the man giving it, sailors used a pass-it-on arrangement to get the message heard.

Rum ration
The senior hand from each mess collected the rum ration for his mess-mates. The master's mate mixed each measure of rum with three of water. This was called "grog".

Spitkid
The risk of fire meant that smoking was banned, so the men chewed tobacco, and spat into a bucket called a spitkid.

Searching for drink
Some women who came on board tried to smuggle gin to the sailors by storing it in a pig's bladder and hiding it under their petticoats. So officers searched them when they arrived.

Fishing
In good fishing waters even a poor fisherman could quickly improve his diet with a line and a baited hook.

Rats
Hungry rats gnawed through casks to get at the food inside. They even gnawed on the wood of the ship's hull!

Shore clothes
Sailors' shore clothes, or "tiddley suits", were much cleaner and neater than their work clothes. They also fitted properly – unlike the ship-board garments that they made themselves.

Iron pigs
Newer ships had removable iron pig ballast. When the ship was in dock, the ballast was removed and the bilges cleaned so that they did not smell so bad.

Securing barrels
Barrels in the hold were prevented from rolling around by the loose shingle of the ballast, which the barrels sank into. The crew also drove wedges under the edges of the stacks of barrels.

Cheeses

Oatmeal

Salt beef

Water

Reading and writing
Many sailors were illiterate – they could not read and write. Those who could, read books in their hammocks, or read and wrote letters for their illiterate mess-mates.

Working at Sea

A MAN-OF-WAR AT SEA needed constant attention. The helmsman at the wheel had to make sure he steered the ship on the correct course, but there were many other jobs, too. For example, just the right combination of sails had to be rigged. Too little sail, and the ship didn't move fast enough through the water. Too much sail, and a strong gust of wind could snap a mast. To trim (adjust) a sail, the crew had to climb to the yard (the horizontal bar that supported the sail), and either make sail (increase the area of sail that caught the wind) or furl (roll up) the sail. The smartest crews could put full sail on a man-of-war in just six minutes. Other work included the daily routine of cleaning, maintenance, and preparation for battle.

Going aloft
Even in harbour you had to be fit to climb the ratlines (rope ladders). But seamen also had to go aloft in gales, at night, and with ice coating every rope.

Sea shanties
Music lightened the heavy work. The crew sang sea shanties, work songs which had a very strong rhythm. On the beat, the men heaved. Everyone sang the chorus, and a shantyman made up the verses as he went along. Often the shantyman made fun of the officers in his songs, calling them rude names. The officers didn't mind as long as the shanties helped the men to heave harder on the capstan.

Capstan
All hands helped with heavy work. The most difficult task was hauling in the anchor cable. The crew used a capstan (a big winch) for this. They turned the capstan with heavy wooden capstan bars.

Caulking the decks
Cracks between deck planks could let in water, so they were stopped up by caulking. This meant hammering oakum (unravelled rope fibres) into the cracks and sealing them with pitch (tar).

Extra sails called "stunsails" were attached to these booms

Checking the gunlock
The firing mechanism of the gun (called a gunlock) was delicate, and needed special attention. When the gun was not in use, the crew protected the gunlock with a lead cover.

Man-handling
The huge anchor cable was made of hemp, and was very heavy, especially when wet. To prevent the cable from rotting, the crew stored it on a special slatted floor which allowed the water to drain off the cable, and air to circulate.

Sew-sew boys
Seamen made and mended their own clothes – this was usually a Saturday ritual. Members of the crew who were especially good with a needle were called "sew-sew boys", and mended officers' clothes for them.

Loosing sails
To make the ship go faster, the topmen (the men who worked aloft) unrolled the sails to catch more wind. On the command "let fall", they released a sail, taking care to unfurl it first at the yard-arm (the tips of the yard), and only then at the bunt (the middle). Loosing the bunt first allowed wind to fill the sail too soon, so that it rose above the yard. The full sail could easily knock the man at the yard-arm off his perch.

A fall from the rigging
Sailors worked aloft with no safety nets or other protection against falls. In the rush to loose sails, it was easy to make mistakes, with fatal results. Nobody ever suffered slight injuries from a fall. Either they plunged into the icy sea, or broke their bodies on the deck below. Despite the risks, many experienced sailors ran along the top of the yards to get into position, and then dropped onto the foot-ropes below!

Lubbers' hole
Most sailors clambered around the fighting top (platform) halfway up the mast. For those who felt insecure, however, there was a safe way up close to the mast called the "lubbers' hole". "Lubber" was slang for an inexperienced sailor.

Furling sails
When a sail was not in use, the topmen tied it up below the yard. They tried to furl the sail neatly, because everyone on the ship could see the furled sail high up in the rigging. However, in a strong wind it wasn't easy to gather the wet, flapping canvas and tie it in orderly folds.

Foot-ropes supported crew members working aloft

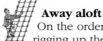

Away aloft
On the order "away aloft", the men scurried into the rigging up the ratlines. These were pieces of rope tied like rungs of a ladder between the shrouds – the ropes that supported the mast. Climbing all the way to the top-gallant (the highest yard) was exhausting, and often the last man to reach his post would be whipped for his slowness.

Sails were made from 60-cm (2-ft)-wide lengths of linen

Controlling the sails
The lines that controlled the "set" or position of the sails had to be carefully organized. The most often-used lines were tied around belaying pins which passed through holes in the rail behind the main mast. Belaying pins were simple quick-release mechanisms – pulling out the pin instantly released the line.

Airing sails

Mending sails
The big linen sails needed constant repair and patching, especially where they rubbed against ropes and spars. This was the job of the sailmaker and his mates.

Loose cannon
A loose, heavy object, such as a cannon, was as dangerous as enemy fire. As the ship rolled, the cannon rolled too, and would crush anything in its path.

Birds and boats
Canvas covers kept rain out of the boats on deck, and also sheltered the ship's poultry that lived inside them.

Lubbers
These inexperienced sailors are risking certain death. Seamen always went aloft on the windward side of the ship, so that the wind would press them onto the rigging.

Burying the dead
Dead men were "buried at sea" (thrown overboard). One of the sailmaker's least pleasant jobs was sewing up dead men in sailcloth. He put a cannonball at the head and foot to make the corpse sink.

Gunport closed and cannon secured for heavy weather

Airing sails
To prevent spare sets of sails and ropes from rotting, the crew took them out of their lockers and aired them whenever there was good weather.

Get knotted

Ropes that parted (broke) could not be replaced, so landsmen (new recruits) had to learn how to splice (join) together the broken ends.

Messenger cable
The anchor cable was too thick to wind directly round the capstan. So the crew tied the cable to a long loop of thinner rope called a messenger cable, and wrapped this round the capstan.

Checking sails
Like the anchor cable, the sails needed constant care and attention. Each one had a wooden tag sewn onto it, indicating which yard it was made for. The crew took care to store sails with all the tags showing, so they could find any sail quickly, without unfolding them all.

Mending planks
At sea the carpenters mended major timbers only after the ship had been badly damaged. But they were never short of work, because their whole world was made of wood, and there was always a bit wearing out.

Killing rats

Hungry rats could chew through planks to reach food. Killing and trapping them was a full-time job.

BATTLE STATIONS

GOING INTO BATTLE on a wooden warship was both an exciting and a terrifying experience. The cries of wounded comrades and the booms of cannon fire drowned out the sounds of creaking timbers and flapping canvas. The smell of blood and burning gunpowder hid the comforting smells of tar and the sea. But especially frightening was how close the enemy ships came before a single shot rang out. A man-of-war's guns had tremendous destructive power, but they were only accurate at short range. So, tension grew as the ships sailed closer and closer, holding their fire until they were sure it would be deadly. When the ships had sailed close enough for their fire to be effective, each would try to be the first to fire a broadside – a huge blast from all the guns on one side of a ship firing together. The massive power of a broadside could often cripple the enemy at the start of a battle.

BATTLE RAGES

When cannonballs holed the ship's hull, carpenters worked quickly to repair the damage. Few ships sank in battle. More often gunfire killed the crew, or destroyed the rigging, thus disabling the ship. If all else failed, the crew would attack by boarding the enemy ship. Hand guns took so long to reload that, after one shot, seamen would continue fighting with pikes, knives, and hatchets.

SIX-MAN GUN CREW

| One | Two | Three | Four | Five | Six |

Crew members were known by numbers to simplify orders. One – the gun captain – primed, aimed, and fired the gun. Two turned and raised the gun barrel. Three loaded the gun. Four damped down sparks before reloading. Five moved the gun barrel and passed ammunition. Six was the "powder monkey", who delivered fresh gunpowder. Powder monkeys were often the youngest members of the crew — some of them boys only 10 or 12 years old!

FIRING A CANNON

Gun crews worked very quickly. It took them only two to five minutes to clean, load, aim, and fire a cannon!

1 After firing, the crew cleaned the gun and damped down sparks to prevent an explosion during re-loading. They loaded the gun with shot and gunpowder and inserted a quill filled with powder as a fuse.

2 The crew used handspikes and ropes to lever the gun into position. Then they waited for the roll of the ship in the water to point the gun up, to shoot at the enemy's rigging, or down, to aim at its hull.

3 As the gun captain lit the fuse, the men jumped out of the way and covered their ears. The violent explosion blasted the cannon backwards into the ship. The crew immediately leaped forward to reload.

TYPES OF SHOT

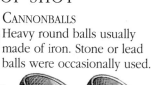

CANNONBALLS
Heavy round balls usually made of iron. Stone or lead balls were occasionally used.

CHAIN SHOT
Heavy balls joined by a chain. They tangled in the enemy ship's rigging and tore it down.

GRAPE SHOT
Iron balls, each the size of a tennis ball, bound in canvas bags.

CANISTER SHOT
Cylindrical cases containing pistol balls. They were used at close range to kill people.

Breastwork
In battle, the crew rolled up the ship's hammocks and stuffed them into the nets on the upper decks. This formed a wall called "breastwork" to provide some protection from enemy musket fire. However, cannon shot could go right through!

Firing chain shot
By elevating the guns, the crew aimed chain shot at the enemy ship's rigging.

Splinters
A direct hit on the gun deck created a shower of deadly flying splinters, scattering the terrified crew. Many would be killed instantly.

Double-shotting
To make holes in the enemy ship, crews loaded two balls in the cannon with plenty of powder. This was called "double-shotting".

Plugging holes
When the enemy scored a direct hit at the waterline, the carpenters got to work. They rushed along the carpenters' walk – a special corridor that provided easy access for repairs – with their tools, and quickly nailed timbers or sheets of lead over the hole. Surprisingly few ships were actually sunk by cannon fire.

Shot splash

Survivors clinging to wreckage

Job hazards
The crews loading, aiming, and firing the guns faced instant death or horrible injuries. They could be killed or have limbs severed by cannon shot, crushed by an out-of-control gun, or badly cut by flying splinters from a direct hit. Accounts of battle also tell of crew members being instantly cut in half or decapitated (heads cut off) by enemy shot.

Shot garlands
Rusty cannon balls were scraped, greased, and stored in special racks called shot garlands.

Keep your powder dry!
Powder monkeys rushed the dangerous cartridges of gunpowder from the handling chamber, along the narrow gangways and ladders, to the guns. They were helped in this dangerous task by anyone else who was not manning a gun – including any women on board.

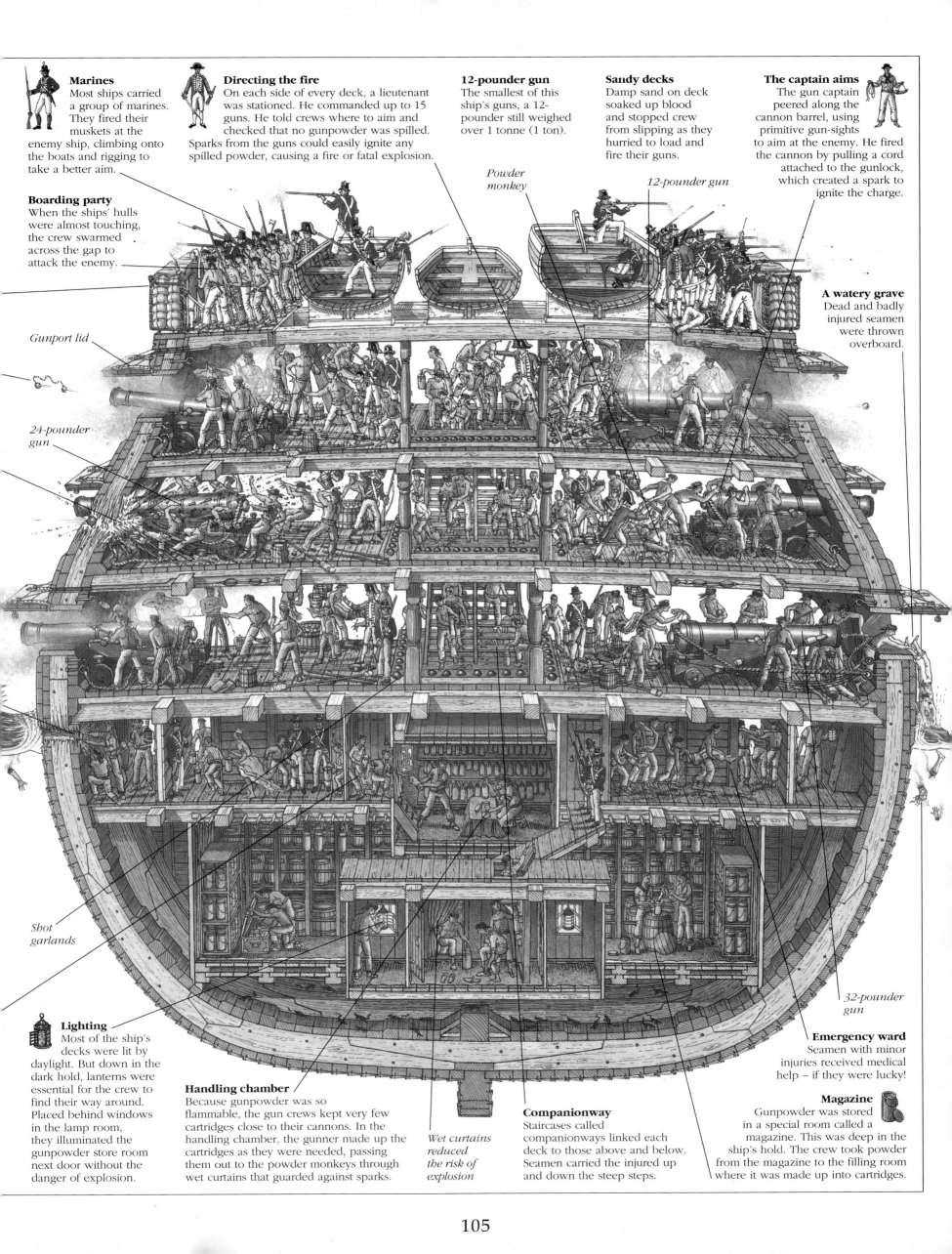

Marines
Most ships carried a group of marines. They fired their muskets at the enemy ship, climbing onto the boats and rigging to take a better aim.

Boarding party
When the ships' hulls were almost touching, the crew swarmed across the gap to attack the enemy.

Gunport lid

24-pounder gun

Shot garlands

Lighting
Most of the ship's decks were lit by daylight. But down in the dark hold, lanterns were essential for the crew to find their way around. Placed behind windows in the lamp room, they illuminated the gunpowder store room next door without the danger of explosion.

Directing the fire
On each side of every deck, a lieutenant was stationed. He commanded up to 15 guns. He told crews where to aim and checked that no gunpowder was spilled. Sparks from the guns could easily ignite any spilled powder, causing a fire or fatal explosion.

12-pounder gun
The smallest of this ship's guns, a 12-pounder still weighed over 1 tonne (1 ton).

Powder monkey

Sandy decks
Damp sand on deck soaked up blood and stopped crew from slipping as they hurried to load and fire their guns.

12-pounder gun

The captain aims
The gun captain peered along the cannon barrel, using primitive gun-sights to aim at the enemy. He fired the cannon by pulling a cord attached to the gunlock, which created a spark to ignite the charge.

A watery grave
Dead and badly injured seamen were thrown overboard.

32-pounder gun

Handling chamber
Because gunpowder was so flammable, the gun crews kept very few cartridges close to their cannons. In the handling chamber, the gunner made up the cartridges as they were needed, passing them out to the powder monkeys through wet curtains that guarded against sparks.

Wet curtains reduced the risk of explosion

Companionway
Staircases called companionways linked each deck to those above and below. Seamen carried the injured up and down the steep steps.

Emergency ward
Seamen with minor injuries received medical help – if they were lucky!

Magazine
Gunpowder was stored in a special room called a magazine. This was deep in the ship's hold. The crew took powder from the magazine to the filling room where it was made up into cartridges.

SLEEPING

AT NIGHT, shipboard life slowed down. Sailors had to be in their hammocks by the start of first watch (8 o'clock). This was bedtime for only half the crew, though. The other half stood watch until midnight, when the master of the glass rang eight bells. The bells signaled the start of the second watch, and the two teams changed over. This system meant that most sailors got no more than four hours sleep at a time. However, it had advantages. Navy rules limited hammocks to 14 in (37 cm) in width. But with half the crew on watch, those in their hammocks had double the sleeping space. Things got very crowded, however, in port. There, only a few sailors stood watch, and the mass of sleeping bodies made the lower decks very stuffy. In the morning, the air was so foul that waking sailors felt like they had slept with mouths full of copper coins. They called this feeling "fat head."

THE ART OF THE HAMMOCK

Unroll hammock and hang it between two beams.

Add blankets and swing right leg up, balancing with left hand.

With a jump and a twist, spring into hammock – but don't fall out the other side!

Getting into a hammock looked difficult, but it was an art that every seaman learned quickly. Getting out was more difficult, especially if the occupant was asleep when the boatswain's mate came to wake him. "Out or down!" he'd cry. "Out or down" was a threat to cut down the hammocks of the last sailors to get up – a painful drop down onto the hard deck below!

ROLL THOSE HAMMOCKS!
When not in use, hammocks were rolled up. Sailors then had to pass their hammocks through an iron ring to make sure that they were rolled tightly enough.

DRUMMING DAYBREAK

Gun fires to signal sunrise

When the ship was at anchor with the rest of the fleet, there was a careful ritual to follow every morning. At first light, a drummer on board each ship began to beat his drum; this continued until it was light enough "to see a gray goose at a mile." Then the flagship fired a gun. When the sun rose, each ship hauled up its colors (flags).

THE NIGHT WATCH

A lighted box called a binnacle enclosed the ship's two compasses.

A special night telescope was used – but the image it showed was upside down!

Seeing clearly in the dark at sea was difficult. However, on the open sea when there were no other ships nearby, it was possible to sail safely at night without fear of collision or grounding on rocks. Lanterns lit the ship's two compasses so that the quartermaster could see in which direction the ship was headed. At night, the watch used a special telescope, called a "night glass," for a brighter image than with a "day glass."

Taking prisoners
Taking prisoners in battle was inconvenient: they had to be fed just like the crew – and guarded too. However, there was often a bounty (prize money) for prisoners. This could add up to quite a large sum, so capturing prisoners was worthwhile. During long wars, the two sides sometimes exchanged prisoners. This was another reason to keep enemy sailors alive.

A scrub in the tub
Prisoners were often in a filthy state when they were captured. They got a bath not just because they smelled, but because they were a health risk for the crew.

Short back and sides
Lice could easily introduce disease to the ship. The barber shaved the heads of the prisoners to reduce this risk.

New clothes
The purser's mate issued prisoners with clothes up to the value of the bounty they were worth.

Asleep on biscuits
Small hammock mattresses were called biscuits because they resembled ship's biscuits in shape and color.

Blanket Bay
Seamen had many nicknames for their hammocks and for sleeping. "Blanket Bay" is one nickname with obvious origins.

Sold before the mast
If a seaman died, his messmates "sold his possessions before the mast" – they auctioned off his belongings. The proceeds went to the man's family, so out of generosity everybody paid far more than the goods were really worth.

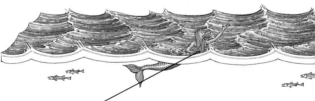

Mermaids
Sailors who had been at sea too long dreamed about seeing beautiful half-women, half-fish creatures called mermaids in the waves alongside the ship.

Midshipman's mess
Only the purser and surgeon were supposed to sleep on the orlop deck, but it was a popular place to sling a hammock. Though there was no natural light and little air, the orlop deck was spacious and quiet compared with the gun decks above.

Chain pump
Leather washers fixed to a ring-shaped chain formed an efficient pump. Pulling on the chain sucked water out of the bilges and sent it flowing down the "pump dale" – a gulley that crossed the gun deck. However, if a cannonball holed the ship below the waterline, the sea leaked in as quickly as it could be pumped out. Then the crew had to man the pumps day and night, until the carpenters could make a repair.

Smallest servants
The youngest "officer's servants" were no more than eight years old and so small that they had to be lifted into their hammocks to sleep.

Swab the decks
Before battle, the gun crews threw sand on the decks. This prevented them from slipping in pools of blood. After the battle, they washed away the sand, and any blood with it.

After the battle
Cannonballs didn't just smash the ship's side; they were sometimes red hot and could start fires. So during and after a battle, the gun crew threw water over any burnt timbers.

Bucket line
Water for firefighting came from the ship's pumps; the crew formed a chain, passing the leather buckets of water from hand to hand, and trying not to spill any.

Elm tree pump
Trunks of elm trees formed the body of some of the ship's pumps. Bored hollow, they brought seawater up from near the keel.

Chaplain
Nicknamed "Holy Joe" or "The Bish" (bishop) by the crew, the chaplain's job was not clearly defined. How much spiritual guidance he gave the crew was usually a decision the captain made. The chaplain sometimes held Divine Service after a battle, to thank God for the ship's successes, or to pray for better luck during the next engagement. There was also a service every Sunday.

Hammocks in storage

Refilling shot racks
After a battle, one of the first tasks was to make sure the ship was ready to fight again as soon as possible. The crew were quick to refill the shot racks with a fresh supply of cannonballs.

Swabbing the decks

Dead seaman's possessions being sold

Prisoners

Prisoner being washed

Pump dale

Legs and wings
Seamen jokingly called amputated limbs "legs and wings," as if the surgeon were carving a chicken at the dinner table.

Operating theater
The surgeon operated at the aft of the orlop deck because it was below the waterline, and less in danger of enemy fire than higher decks.

Cleaning shot
Cannonballs rusted in storage, and the crew had to clean them before taking them up to the guns. A layer of grease or paint protected the clean shot.

Shot locker
The store for the heavy iron shot was close to the keel. Higher up, the weight of the cannonballs would have made the ship unstable.

Limber passage
This was where drainage collected.

Seamen waiting for treatment

Bottom of pump shaft was open to the sea

Amputation
The only worthwhile surgery was amputating (cutting off) arms and legs. Operating on internal injuries usually caused infections that were more deadly than the injuries themselves.

NAVIGATION AND DISCIPLINE

PUNISHING DISOBEDIENT SAILORS and guiding the ship's course were among the captain's most difficult duties – but for very different reasons. To keep the ship running smoothly, the captain had to punish those who did not obey orders, often by flogging (whipping). Navy rules gave captains a lot of latitude in choosing the amount of punishment for an offender. If a captain ordered too few lashes, the crew would think he was weak. A captain who ordered too many lashes was equally unpopular.

Navigation was tricky because charts (sea maps) were often inaccurate, and instruments primitive. Officers could accurately estimate how far the ship had traveled north or south, but reckoning how far the ship had sailed east or west was harder. An error of just a few miles at the end of a long ocean journey could wreck a ship on jagged rocks.

OFFENDER IN LEG IRONS

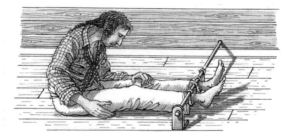

Flogging was a very formal punishment that disrupted the ship's routine, so for minor offenses, a seaman might spend some time in irons. These were metal rings that locked around the sailor's legs, so that he was unable to move. The irons were on an exposed deck, so everyone saw the offender, and he was scorched by the sun and soaked by rain and spray.

SHOT ROLLING

Ships on the verge of mutiny were known in the navy as "shot-rolling ships." This was because discontented crew members tried to knock unwary officers off their feet by sending cannonballs rolling along the deck. Shot-rolling ships usually became that way because the captain ordered too many punishments.

LOGBOOK

The ship's logbook was a sort of daily diary kept by the captain of the ship. In it he wrote the ship's position in degrees of latitude (distance north or south) and longitude (distance east or west). He also recorded the weather conditions and barometric pressure, as well as daily events such as floggings, what ports the ship visited, changes to the ship's course, and any actions the ship took part in.

NAVIGATION EQUIPMENT

All ships carried basic navigation equipment, including a compass, sextant, set of charts, and a log line. The first three helped the captain work out the ship's position and course, although charts were often wrong. The log line measured the speed at which the ship was sailing.

SHIP'S COMPASS
The compass was the principal instrument for navigation. The printed card covered a magnetized needle that pointed north, helping the captain and crew find their way.

LOG LINE
A device called a log line measured the ship's speed. It was towed in the water behind the ship on a knotted rope, and the speed at which the knots were paid out was noted. This is the origin of the nautical measurement of speed: "knots."

SEXTANT

The sextant was a navigational instrument developed from an earlier, similar-looking device called an octant. Sextants measured the sun's height at noon. Using this measurement, sailors could calculate how far north or south the ship was.

CHARTS
Charts showed islands, rocks and reefs, coastlines, and landmarks such as lighthouses. In 1800, many charts were still wildly inaccurate, showing, for example, islands where none existed.

Fire buckets

Even in peacetime, an accidental fire could destroy a ship, so fire buckets were always handy. Buckets of sand alternated with buckets of water.

Running the gauntlet
Thieves were unpopular, and the whole crew punished them. Everyone found a piece of rope and formed two lines. The thief walked between the lines as his shipmates whipped him. To stop the thief from going too fast, the master at arms walked in front with his cutlass (short sword) touching the man's belly. A marine walked behind with his bayonet on the man's back, to stop him from going too slowly. Running the gauntlet was abolished in 1806.

Gun drill
The crew trained regularly so that they could load and fire the guns rapidly. Officers timed them – the fastest gun crews took ninety seconds a shot.

Fighting
Fights often broke out when seamen had drunk too much rum. The boatswain's mates broke up the fights with their rattans (small cane whips).

Left hand down a bit
Steering the ship was the job of the quartermaster. The wheel turned a wooden drum, and ropes wrapped around the drum moved the tiller as the quartermaster turned the wheel.

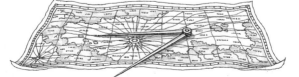

Getting a checked shirt
Flogging made a diamond pattern of deep bloody cuts across the victim's back. The seamen's lighthearted nickname for the scars – "a checked shirt" – helped them forget the pain of the flogging.

Flogging around the fleet
The worst punishment of all was "flogging around the fleet." The offender was tied to capstan bars in the ship's largest boat and rowed around every ship of the fleet. Boatswain's mates from each ship whipped the man about 24 times, so that, in all, he received as many as 300 lashes. A doctor stood by to check that the flogging did not kill the man immediately. If he fainted, the rest of the punishment was delayed until he recovered. Most victims later died.

Spitting on deck
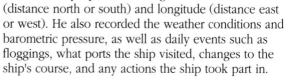
Smoking was a fire hazard, so seamen chewed tobacco instead, spitting it out into a small tub called a spitkid. Seamen who spat on deck were tied up with the spitkid round their necks. Then their messmates played target practice!

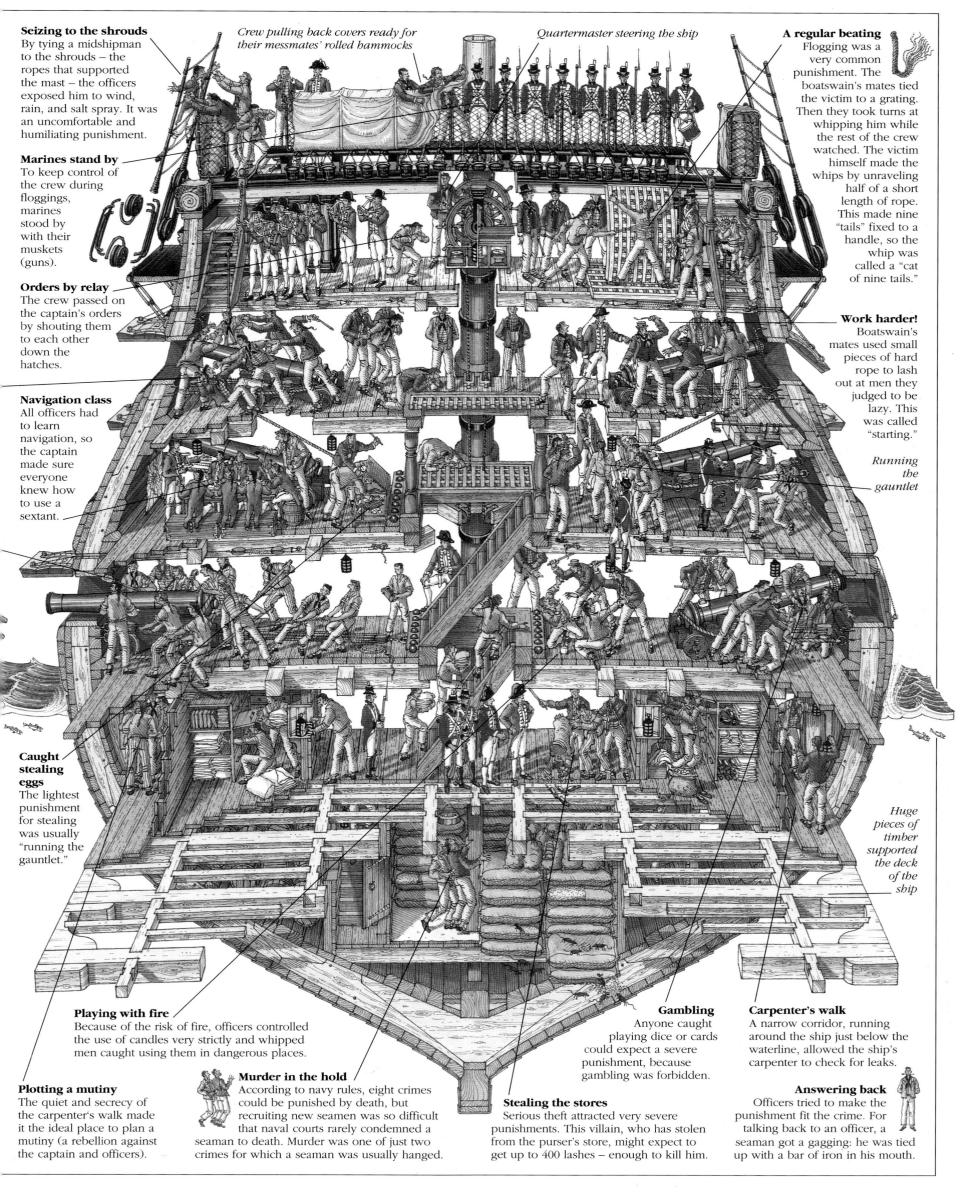

Seizing to the shrouds
By tying a midshipman to the shrouds – the ropes that supported the mast – the officers exposed him to wind, rain, and salt spray. It was an uncomfortable and humiliating punishment.

Marines stand by
To keep control of the crew during floggings, marines stood by with their muskets (guns).

Orders by relay
The crew passed on the captain's orders by shouting them to each other down the hatches.

Navigation class
All officers had to learn navigation, so the captain made sure everyone knew how to use a sextant.

Caught stealing eggs
The lightest punishment for stealing was usually "running the gauntlet."

Crew pulling back covers ready for their messmates' rolled hammocks

Quartermaster steering the ship

A regular beating
Flogging was a very common punishment. The boatswain's mates tied the victim to a grating. Then they took turns at whipping him while the rest of the crew watched. The victim himself made the whips by unraveling half of a short length of rope. This made nine "tails" fixed to a handle, so the whip was called a "cat of nine tails."

Work harder!
Boatswain's mates used small pieces of hard rope to lash out at men they judged to be lazy. This was called "starting."

Running the gauntlet

Huge pieces of timber supported the deck of the ship

Playing with fire
Because of the risk of fire, officers controlled the use of candles very strictly and whipped men caught using them in dangerous places.

Plotting a mutiny
The quiet and secrecy of the carpenter's walk made it the ideal place to plan a mutiny (a rebellion against the captain and officers).

Murder in the hold
According to navy rules, eight crimes could be punished by death, but recruiting new seamen was so difficult that naval courts rarely condemned a seaman to death. Murder was one of just two crimes for which a seaman was usually hanged.

Stealing the stores
Serious theft attracted very severe punishments. This villain, who has stolen from the purser's store, might expect to get up to 400 lashes – enough to kill him.

Gambling
Anyone caught playing dice or cards could expect a severe punishment, because gambling was forbidden.

Carpenter's walk
A narrow corridor, running around the ship just below the waterline, allowed the ship's carpenter to check for leaks.

Answering back
Officers tried to make the punishment fit the crime. For talking back to an officer, a seaman got a gagging: he was tied up with a bar of iron in his mouth.

THE OFFICERS

A MAN-OF-WAR was like a small city floating in a wooden box. On board there were many kinds of people, ranging from wealthy gentlemen down to laborers. Ruling over the whole ship was the captain (or the admiral on a flagship). He was powerful, but he did not command the ship alone. He had officers to help him. The most important were the lieutenants. Below the lieutenants was a large range of warrant officers. The lowest, such as sailmaker, was hardly higher in rank than a rating (an ordinary sailor).

When the captain issued an order, such as "follow that ship!," each officer interpreted that order. The first lieutenant might shout "steer to port" to the quartermaster; the quartermaster then looked at the compass and shouted "five points to port" to his mate who turned the wheel. This was called the ship's chain of command. Disobedient sailors were severely punished.

WHO WAS WHO ON BOARD

MARINES-There were 131 privates of marines (soldiers who fought at sea).

CAPTAIN   LIEUTENANTS   SERGEANTS   CORPORALS   DRUMMERS

SEAMEN
There were 569 ratings, or ordinary seamen, on board. They were organized into two "watches."

PETTY OFFICERS
Steward, Captain's Clerk, 4 Yeoman of the sheets *kept the sails in order*, Trumpeter, 6 Quartermasters' mates, 6 Quartermasters *responsible for steering the ship and keeping lookout* , 6 Master mates, 4 Boatswain's mates, 4 Gunner's mates, 2 Carpenter's mates, 24 Midshipmen *trainee officers*, 25 Quarter Gunners *each in charge of four guns*, Sailmaker's mate, 2 Corporals *assistants to the master-at-arms*, Coxwain *looked after the ship's boats and steered them.*

WARRANT SEA OFFICERS
Master *navigated the ship and piloted (guided) it close to the coast and on rivers*, Boatswain *storesman and administrator; responsible for the rigging and sails*, Gunner *in charge of all the cannons*, Carpenter, Surgeon, Purser *in charge of supplies.*

IDLERS
Steward's mate, Carpenter's crew, Sailmaker's crew *made and mended the sails.*

INFERIOR WARRANT OFFICERS
Chaplain, Cook, Schoolmaster, 5 Surgeon's mates, Armorer *repaired and maintained not only weapons, but all the ship's metalwork.* Master-at-arms *instructed the crew in the use of small arms (hand guns and muskets)*, Sailmaker *repaired the sails.*

LIEUTENANTS
Assisted the captain in carrying out orders and directing gunfire in battle.

1ˢᵀ LIEUTENANT
The captain's assistant, commanding the ship in his absence or if he was killed.

CAPTAIN
Commanded the ship. Responsible for sailing, discipline, and battle command.

ADMIRAL
Commanded the fleet and worked out battle plans.

Hanging cot
The captain slept in a boxlike cot that hung from the deckhead (ceiling). It's no coincidence that the cot looks like a coffin: it was made to fit the sleeper, and if he died, he was nailed into it with some shot. The crew heaved the cot-coffin over the side, complete with cannonballs and captain, and it sank like a stone.

"Heave to"
There were only two ways to communicate with other ships and boats: by shouting ("heave to" meant "stop immediately") or by using flags (see next page).

Dinner for one
The captain's life was a lonely one. A captain was expected to be firm with his men, not friendly. Captains who tried to be popular quickly lost the respect of their crew. The captain dined alone, unless he was eating with the ship's officers in the wardroom or entertaining them in his own dining room. However, only a wealthy captain could afford to do this often.

Admiral's dining cabin
The admiral entertained in style. He had a grander dining room than even the captain. The paneling and furniture were folded neatly away in the preparation for battle.

Boat fall

The ship's boats were used to ferry the captain and other officers to shore

Washstand
The captain's handy washstand had a chamber pot in a drawer hidden in the base for his convenience at night. A servant emptied it over the side in the morning.

Officer's cabin
Commissioned (senior) officers had a little space of their own between the guns on the middle deck. How much room they had varied greatly from ship to ship.

Paneled partitions
The captain's accommodation was paneled like a fine country house of the time. However, the guns in the "dining room" were a reminder that this was a fighting ship. Before a battle, the crew removed all the paneling. They either stowed it in the hold or, in an emergency, threw the panels overboard. This turned the captain's suite of rooms into an extension of the gun deck.

Gunroom
The stern end of the lower deck was called the gun room. It was used as a store for hand weapons such as cutlasses and pistols.

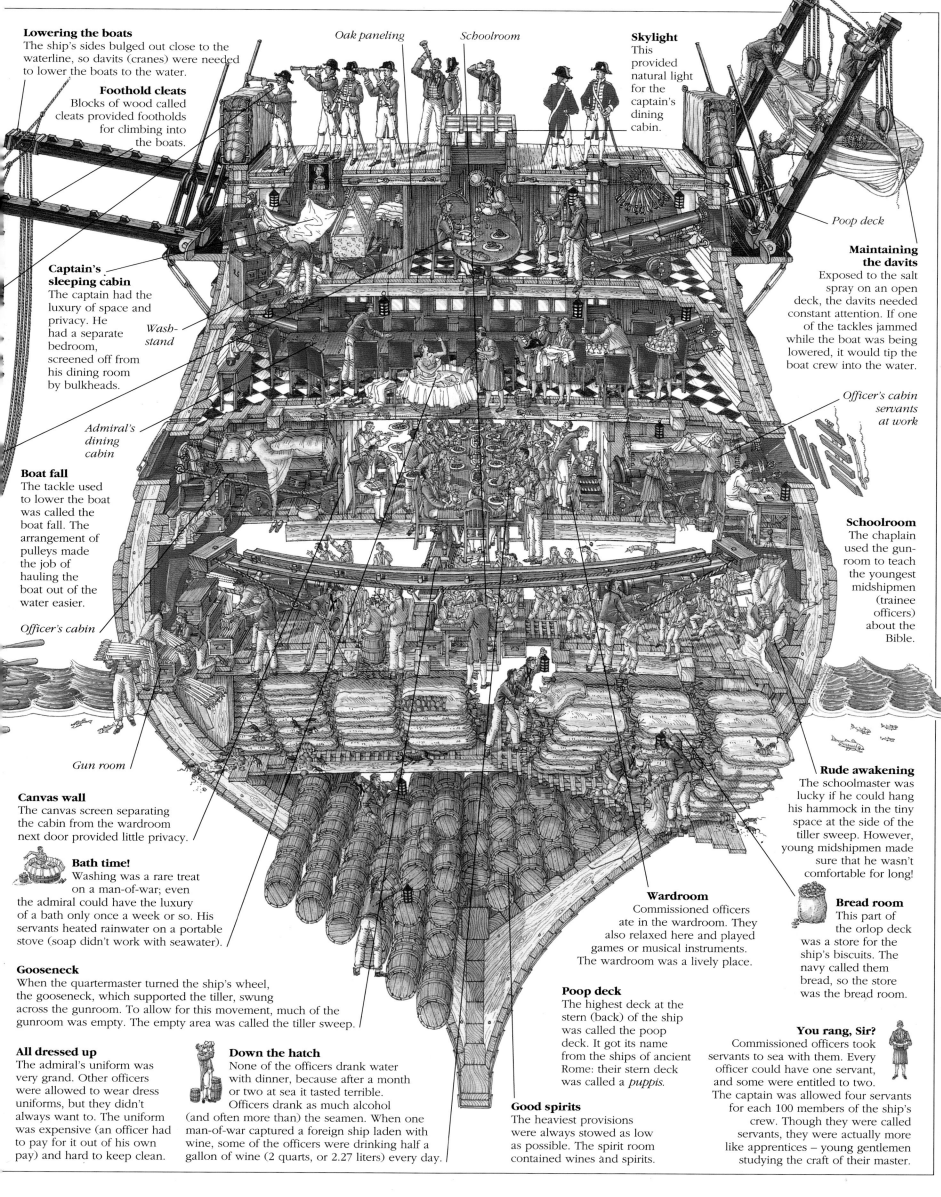

Lowering the boats
The ship's sides bulged out close to the waterline, so davits (cranes) were needed to lower the boats to the water.

Foothold cleats
Blocks of wood called cleats provided footholds for climbing into the boats.

Oak paneling

Schoolroom

Skylight
This provided natural light for the captain's dining cabin.

Captain's sleeping cabin
The captain had the luxury of space and privacy. He had a separate bedroom, screened off from his dining room by bulkheads.

Wash-stand

Admiral's dining cabin

Boat fall
The tackle used to lower the boat was called the boat fall. The arrangement of pulleys made the job of hauling the boat out of the water easier.

Officer's cabin

Gun room

Canvas wall
The canvas screen separating the cabin from the wardroom next door provided little privacy.

Bath time!
Washing was a rare treat on a man-of-war; even the admiral could have the luxury of a bath only once a week or so. His servants heated rainwater on a portable stove (soap didn't work with seawater).

Gooseneck
When the quartermaster turned the ship's wheel, the gooseneck, which supported the tiller, swung across the gunroom. To allow for this movement, much of the gunroom was empty. The empty area was called the tiller sweep.

All dressed up
The admiral's uniform was very grand. Other officers were allowed to wear dress uniforms, but they didn't always want to. The uniform was expensive (an officer had to pay for it out of his own pay) and hard to keep clean.

Down the hatch
None of the officers drank water with dinner, because after a month or two at sea it tasted terrible. Officers drank as much alcohol (and often more than) the seamen. When one man-of-war captured a foreign ship laden with wine, some of the officers were drinking half a gallon of wine (2 quarts, or 2.27 liters) every day.

Poop deck

Maintaining the davits
Exposed to the salt spray on an open deck, the davits needed constant attention. If one of the tackles jammed while the boat was being lowered, it would tip the boat crew into the water.

Officer's cabin servants at work

Schoolroom
The chaplain used the gun-room to teach the youngest midshipmen (trainee officers) about the Bible.

Rude awakening
The schoolmaster was lucky if he could hang his hammock in the tiny space at the side of the tiller sweep. However, young midshipmen made sure that he wasn't comfortable for long!

Bread room
This part of the orlop deck was a store for the ship's biscuits. The navy called them bread, so the store was the bread room.

Wardroom
Commissioned officers ate in the wardroom. They also relaxed here and played games or musical instruments. The wardroom was a lively place.

Poop deck
The highest deck at the stern (back) of the ship was called the poop deck. It got its name from the ships of ancient Rome: their stern deck was called a *puppis*.

Good spirits
The heaviest provisions were always stowed as low as possible. The spirit room contained wines and spirits.

You rang, Sir?
Commissioned officers took servants to sea with them. Every officer could have one servant, and some were entitled to two. The captain was allowed four servants for each 100 members of the ship's crew. Though they were called servants, they were actually more like apprentices – young gentlemen studying the craft of their master.

THE ADMIRAL

A MAN-OF-WAR rarely sailed on its own. Usually, it cruised with a group of similar and smaller ships. Together they sailed as a fleet, with an admiral in command. Admirals were chosen from among the best captains. The post of admiral was the highest in the navy, and it was a very responsible job. When there was a victory, the admiral took much of the credit. In defeat, he took the blame. If the admiral made the wrong decision, he would be in trouble when the fleet returned to port. But while at sea, there was no quick way to get messages back to the Admiralty (the government department in charge of the navy). In return for all this responsibility, the admiral was richly rewarded. He lived well in the ship, with his own cook and as many as 20 servants. When the fleet captured an enemy ship, the admiral got a one-eighth share of the prize.

THE NAVAL SALUTE

Tar-covered palm

Every sailor greeted a senior officer with a salute, but the admiral got a particularly enthusiastic salute. The naval salute was unusual: the sailor held his palm turned in toward his face. This concealed his palm, which was blackened by tar from the ropes.

PRIZE MONEY

The admiral got a big share of all the prize money from the entire fleet.

Ordinary seamen (ratings) only got a small fraction of their ship's prize money.

After a victorious battle, the government awarded prizes equal to the value of the enemy ships captured. One-quarter of the prize was divided between all the seamen on the ship that made the capture. On a 100-gun ship, each rating thus got less than one two-thousandth of the prize. The admiral won one-eighth and the captain one-quarter. However, the captain received prize money only for vessels his ship captured, while the admiral got one-eighth of the prizes from *every* capture in the fleet. Admirals could get very rich this way.

FLAG SIGNALS

Admiral's masthead pennant

The admiral's ship was called the flagship because it flew his flag. From the quarterdeck of the flagship, the admiral used colored flags to send signals to the rest of the fleet, even if they were out of shouting distance. To reduce the number of flags needed, the admiral sent signals in number codes. Letters of the alphabet were numbered, so that 1 meant "A," 2, "B," and 10, "J," 11, "K," and so on until 26. Common words and commands had a 3-figure code. 253, for example, meant "England."

NELSON'S SIGNAL

England	Expects	That	Every
Man	Will	Do	His
D	U	T	Y

Just before the Battle of Trafalgar in 1805, England's famous admiral, Horatio Nelson, sent a flag signal to cheer up his fleet. Nelson wanted to signal "England confides that every man will do his duty." However, his signal lieutenant, Mr. Pasco, suggested that "confides" was a difficult word. There was no number code for the word, so it would have had to be spelled out letter by letter. He suggested substituting "expects" – code 269 – so Nelson's signal appeared as above.

Signal flag locker

Each flag had a separate pigeonhole, so that the flags weren't confused when they were hoisted rapidly. Flags were stored carefully rolled in their compartments.

Cleaning duty

There was no water to flush the officers' lavatory in the quarter gallery, so cleaning it was not a popular job among the servants.

Fair or foul

The captain had to go on deck in all kinds of weather, so he kept an oilskin cape and boots handy.

Captain's day cabin

Like the captain's berth, his day cabin was at the stern of the ship. It was close to the wheel, so he could rush to take command in an emergency.

"Pieces of eight"

Some admirals owned caged parrots as souvenirs of trips across distant seas. The young midshipmen often taught the parrot to swear, call the admiral names, and say other rude things.

Admiral's barge

This was a long, light, narrow boat rowed by 10 or more oars. It was usually reserved for the personal use of the admiral.

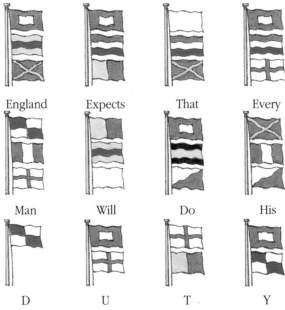

Sailor listening for orders

The admiral's barge flew his ensign (flag)

Quarter gallery

One of the quarter galleries at the far stern of the ship was the captain's lavatory. There were separate lavatories in the quarter galleries on lower decks for the other officers' use. The quarter galleries were decorated with colorful paint and carvings.

Admiral's day cabin

The admiral had an even more spacious day cabin than the captain. The "tiled" floor was actually a covering of stretched canvas painted with squares.

Furnishings

Captains could furnish their cabins as they pleased. Some lived in considerable luxury, fitting out their floating home just like a house on land. One captain turned his cabin into a library, so that it looked "more like a bookseller's shop than the captain's apartment in a man-of-war."

Lanterns
The ship showed lights on the poop deck to avoid collision when under way at night. Burning whale oil provided the flame.

Sorting out the flags
A junior officer or rating got out the flags needed for the signal.

Captain's day cabin

Servant cleaning lavatory

Stern windows
The stern of the ship rarely came under fire, so the captain's cabin had windows to give a good view and to let in lots of light.

Bench seats
The cushioned bench seats lining the windows lifted up. Underneath was storage space.

Signal lieutenant
The code book listed all the signals, but common ones were short enough to remember. For example, to signal one of Admiral Nelson's favorites, "Engage the enemy more closely" (move in more closely and fight) required just two flags: 1 and 6.

Captain's quarter gallery

Captain's desk
This is where the captain wrote letters and the ship's log.

A weather eye
The window of the quarter gallery provided a convenient view of the sails.

Wardroom quarter gallery

Master's cabin

First lieutenant's cabin
After the captain, the first lieutenant was the most senior officer. He had his own cabin with a desk and a hanging cot. A door led to a private lavatory in the quarter gallery.

Wardroom quarter gallery
Use of the wardroom quarter gallery was restricted to "gentlemen." The captain thought that some junior officers were not respectable enough to deserve the privilege. The unlucky ones had to share the heads in the open air with the ratings.

Cleaning small arms
The ship carried a variety of small weapons such as muskets, pistols, and swords. The sea air quickly rusted the ironwork, so cleaning and scouring was a never-ending task.

Gunner's berth
A canvas screen gave the gunner a little privacy at night. During the day the screen was removed to make more space.

Fencing practice

Rudder head cover
The large table in the officers' wardroom hid the rudder head, which stuck up through a hole in the floor.

Tiller
The tiller was a huge wooden beam that turned the rudder to steer the ship.

Master's cabin
The more junior the officer, the less luxurious the cabin. The ship's master had his own cabin on the quarter deck because he needed to be near the wheel. However, he had no private quarter gallery.

Rudder head

On the fiddle
When they didn't have duties to attend to, a few officers passed the time with music and fencing (sword) practice.

Plotting a battle
In a flagship, the admiral gave most of the orders; often, the captain was young and inexperienced. The captain and senior officers helped the admiral make important decisions.

Lady's hole
The stern of the hold was the safest place on the ship. It was called the lady's hole because it was a possible hiding place for women and children.

Studying for exams

12-pounder gun
Just like other cabins used by the officers, the captain's day cabin was armed with a 12-pounder gun.

Stern chasers
Almost all of the ship's guns pointed sideways, but the two cannons at the stern of the gunroom were exceptions. Called "stern chasers," they were useful for firing at enemy vessels following behind.

Chairs overboard!
Before a battle, the order "clear for action" was given. The admiral's fine furniture was either stowed in the hold or in some cases simply thrown overboard.

Studying to pass
To advance to a higher rank, all officers had to take examinations. A lot of studying for the exams was practical, but some book study was also involved, even to reach the post of gunner.

INCREDIBLE
BODY

SEE THE HUMAN BODY from the inside by following two tiny
explorers as they make their way through the labyrinth of
arteries, veins, bones, and organs that make up Stephen Biesty's
body. Using special equipment carried in their backpacks, the
intrepid voyagers investigate every nook and cranny of Stephen's
body to find out how it works.

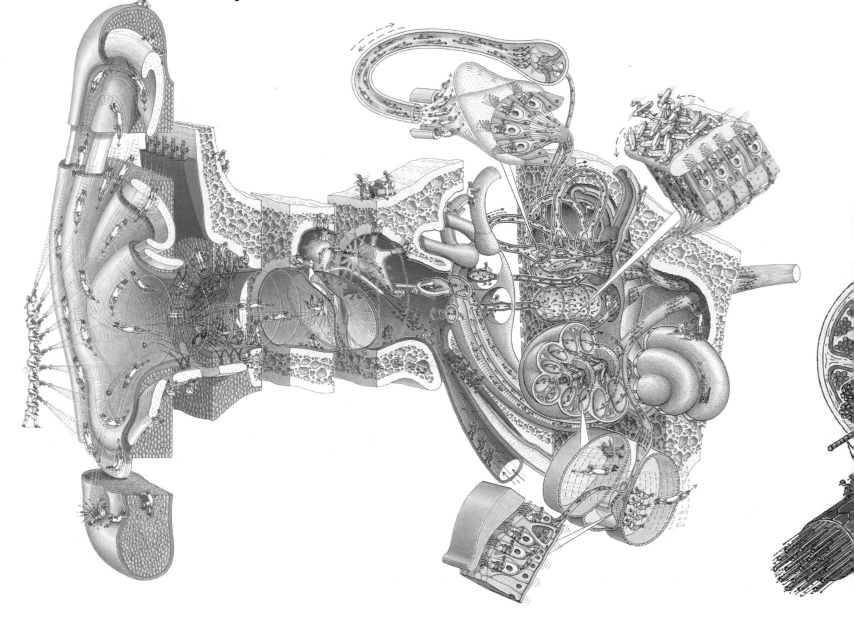

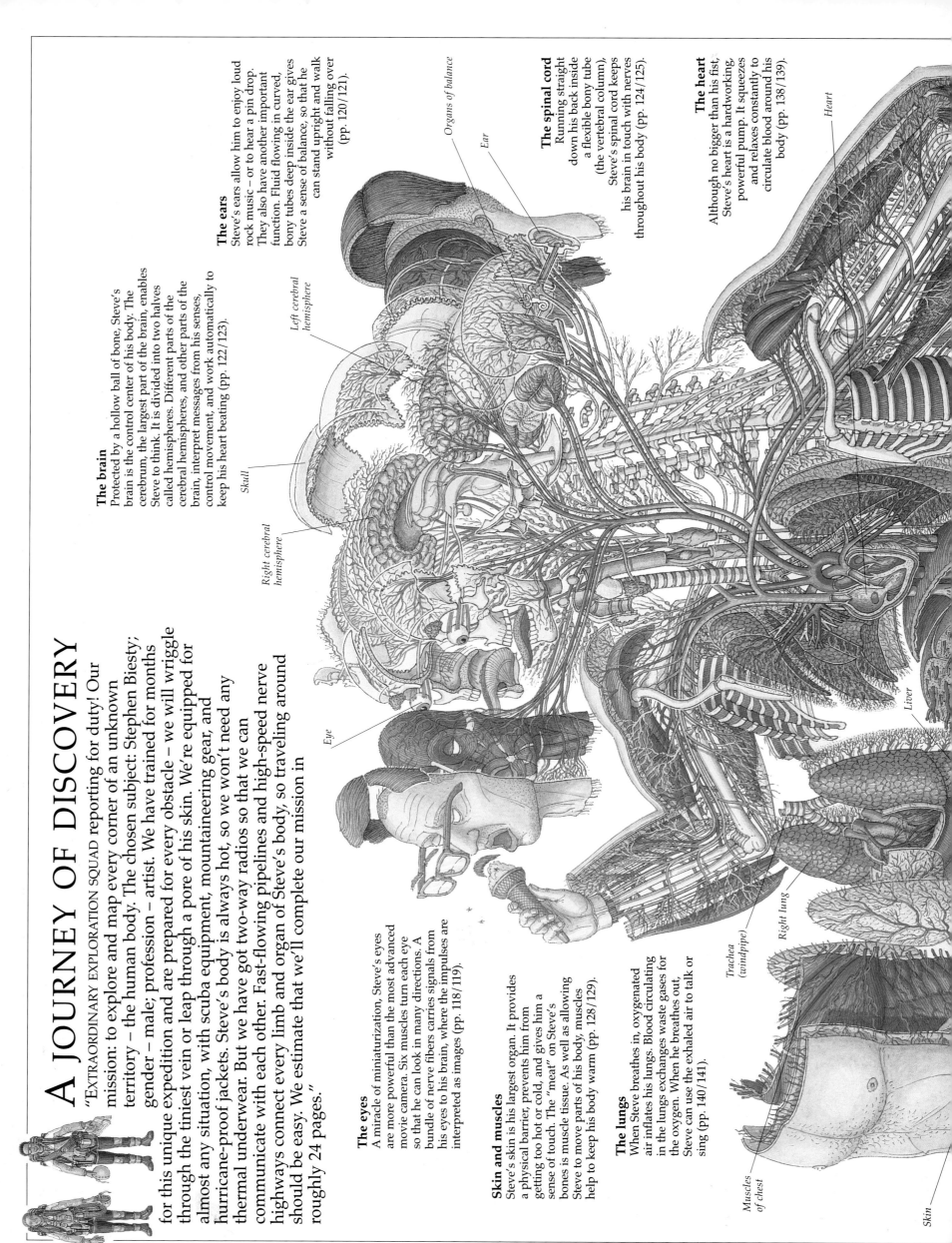

A JOURNEY OF DISCOVERY

"EXTRAORDINARY EXPLORATION SQUAD reporting for duty! Our mission: to explore and map every corner of an unknown territory – the human body. The chosen subject: Stephen Biesty; gender – male; profession – artist. We have trained for months for this unique expedition and are prepared for every obstacle – we will wriggle through the tiniest vein or leap through a pore of his skin. We're equipped for almost any situation, with scuba equipment, mountaineering gear, and hurricane-proof jackets. Steve's body is always hot, so we won't need any thermal underwear. But we have got two-way radios so that we can communicate with each other. Fast-flowing pipelines and high-speed nerve highways connect every limb and organ of Steve's body, so traveling around should be easy. We estimate that we'll complete our mission in roughly 24 pages."

The eyes
A miracle of miniaturization, Steve's eyes are more powerful than the most advanced movie camera. Six muscles turn each eye so that he can look in many directions. A bundle of nerve fibers carries signals from his eyes to his brain, where the impulses are interpreted as images (pp. 118/119).

Skin and muscles
Steve's skin is his largest organ. It provides a physical barrier, prevents him from getting too hot or cold, and gives him a sense of touch. The "meat" on Steve's bones is muscle tissue. As well as allowing Steve to move parts of his body, muscles help to keep his body warm (pp. 128/129).

The lungs
When Steve breathes in, oxygenated air inflates his lungs. Blood circulating in the lungs exchanges waste gases for the oxygen. When he breathes out, Steve can use the exhaled air to talk or sing (pp. 140/141).

The brain
Protected by a hollow ball of bone, Steve's brain is the control center of his body. The cerebrum, the largest part of the brain, enables Steve to think. It is divided into two halves called hemispheres. Different parts of the cerebral hemispheres, and other parts of the brain, interpret messages from his senses, control movement, and work automatically to keep his heart beating (pp. 122/123).

The ears
Steve's ears allow him to enjoy loud rock music – or to hear a pin drop. They also have another important function. Fluid flowing in curved, bony tubes deep inside the ear gives Steve a sense of balance, so that he can stand upright and walk without falling over (pp. 120/121).

The spinal cord
Running straight down his back inside a flexible bony tube (the vertebral column), Steve's spinal cord keeps his brain in touch with nerves throughout his body (pp. 124/125).

The heart
Although no bigger than his fist, Steve's heart is a hardworking, powerful pump. It squeezes and relaxes constantly to circulate blood around his body (pp. 138/139).

Organs of balance

Ear

Left cerebral hemisphere

Skull

Right cerebral hemisphere

Eye

Heart

Liver

Trachea (windpipe)

Right lung

Muscles of chest

Skin

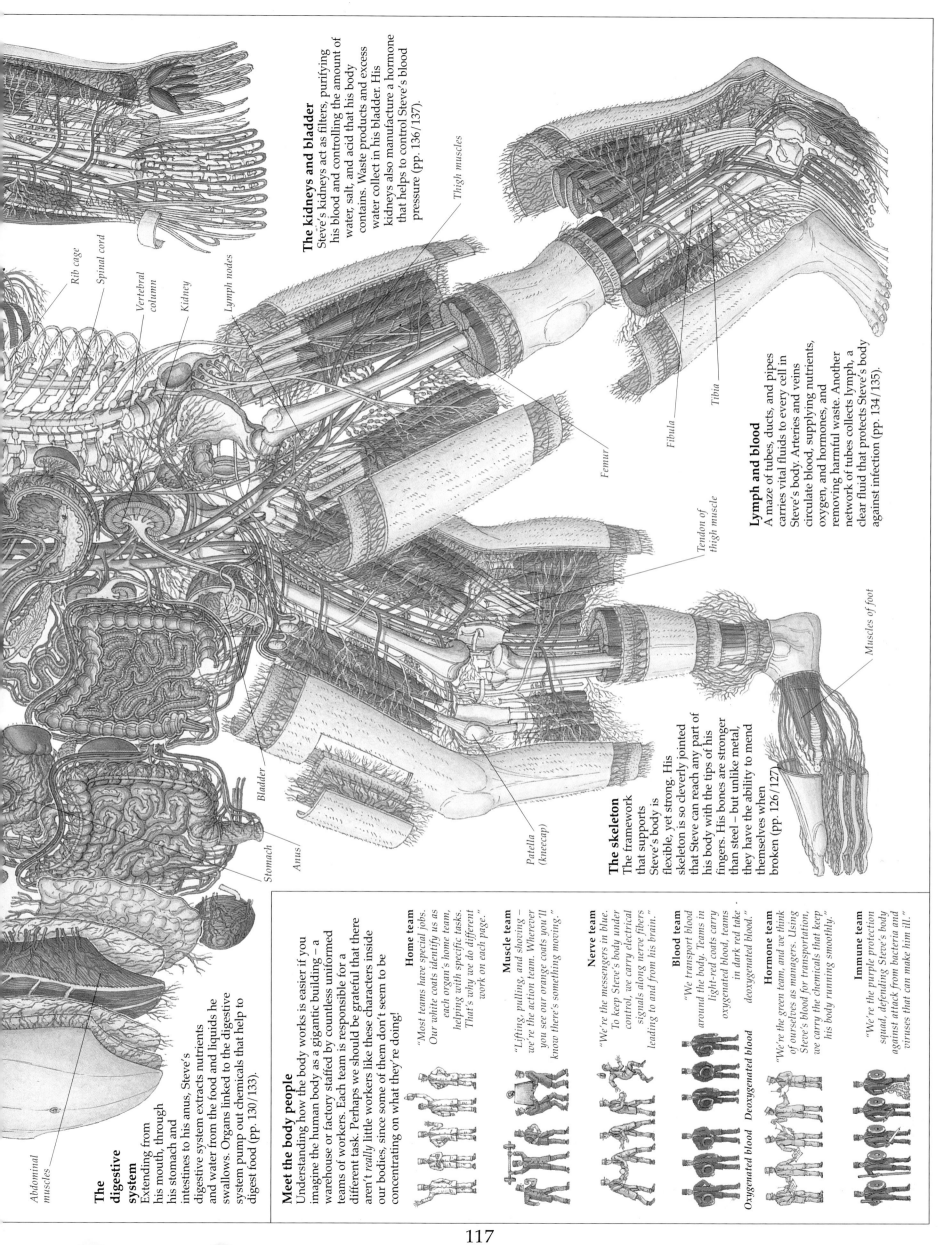

The kidneys and bladder
Steve's kidneys act as filters, purifying his blood and controlling the amount of water, salt, and acid that his body contains. Waste products and excess water collect in his bladder. His kidneys also manufacture a hormone that helps to control Steve's blood pressure (pp. 136/137).

Thigh muscles

Rib cage

Spinal cord

Vertebral column

Kidney

Lymph nodes

Femur

Fibula

Tibia

Lymph and blood
A maze of tubes, ducts, and pipes carries vital fluids to every cell in Steve's body. Arteries and veins circulate blood, supplying nutrients, oxygen, and hormones, and removing harmful waste. Another network of tubes collects lymph, a clear fluid that protects Steve's body against infection (pp. 134/135).

Tendon of thigh muscle

Muscles of foot

The skeleton
The framework that supports Steve's body is flexible, yet strong. His skeleton is so cleverly jointed that Steve can reach any part of his body with the tips of his fingers. His bones are stronger than steel – but unlike metal, they have the ability to mend themselves when broken (pp. 126/127).

Patella (kneecap)

Bladder

Stomach

Anus

Abdominal muscles

The digestive system
Extending from his mouth, through his stomach and intestines to his anus, Steve's digestive system extracts nutrients and water from the food and liquids he swallows. Organs linked to the digestive system pump out chemicals that help to digest food (pp. 130/133).

Meet the body people
Understanding how the body works is easier if you imagine the human body as a gigantic building – a warehouse or factory staffed by countless uniformed teams of workers. Each team is responsible for a different task. Perhaps we should be grateful that there aren't *really* little workers like these characters inside our bodies, since some of them don't seem to be concentrating on what they're doing!

Home team
"Most teams have special jobs. Our white coats identify us as each organ's home team, helping with specific tasks. That's why we do different work on each page."

Muscle team
"Lifting, pulling, and shoving – we're the action team. Wherever you see our orange coats you'll know there's something moving."

Nerve team
"We're the messengers in blue. To keep Steve's body under control, we carry electrical signals along nerve fibers leading to and from his brain."

Blood team
"We transport blood around the body. Teams in light-red coats carry oxygenated blood, teams in dark red take deoxygenated blood."

Oxygenated blood *Deoxygenated blood*

Hormone team
"We're the green team, and we think of ourselves as managers. Using Steve's blood for transportation, we carry the chemicals that keep his body running smoothly."

Immune team
"We're the purple protection squad, defending Steve's body against attack from bacteria and viruses that can make him ill."

THE EYE

STARTING OUR JOURNEY seemed easy: we planned to climb into Steve's mouth. But as we scaled his face, a hurricane-force wind plucked us into the air and sucked us up his nose. The sneeze that followed blasted us down a dark, narrow corridor, knocking us both unconscious. When we came around we thought at first we were in a movie theater. The domed ceiling and floor were vivid red. Behind us a giant lens projected a moving picture onto the wall, but the image was upside down! Then it dawned on us – we had reached an eye through Steve's tear duct. Struggling out the same way, we saw cleaners at work. As we watched them, one gave us a message. "Take this impulse up the optic nerve to Steve's brain," he said, "and watch out for those follicle mites. They can give you a nasty bite."

Egyptian eyewash
Ancient Egyptians used urine for eyewash. Other eye treatments included the droppings of flies, pelicans, lizards, or crocodiles.

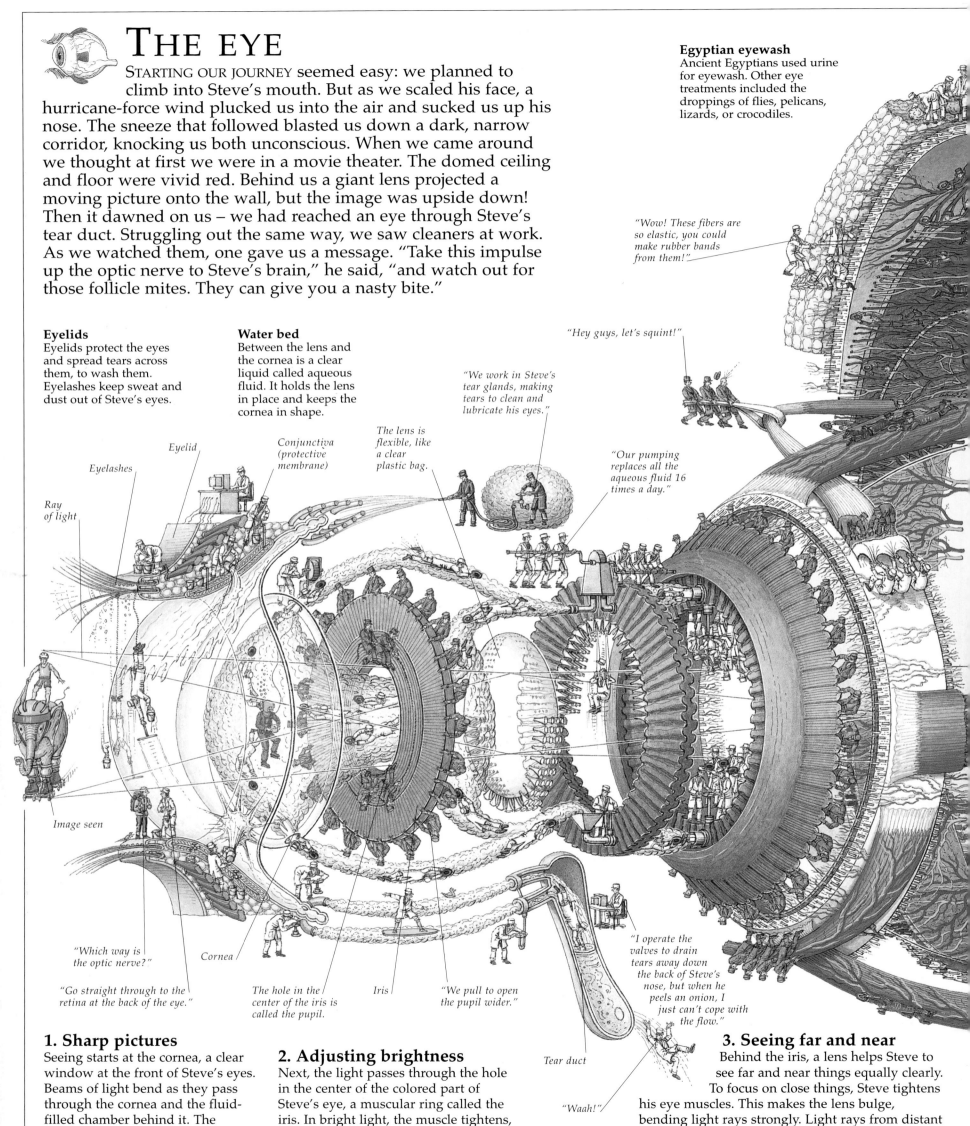

"Wow! These fibers are so elastic, you could make rubber bands from them!"

"Hey guys, let's squint!"

Eyelids
Eyelids protect the eyes and spread tears across them, to wash them. Eyelashes keep sweat and dust out of Steve's eyes.

Water bed
Between the lens and the cornea is a clear liquid called aqueous fluid. It holds the lens in place and keeps the cornea in shape.

We work in Steve's tear glands, making tears to clean and lubricate his eyes."

The lens is flexible, like a clear plastic bag.

"Our pumping replaces all the aqueous fluid 16 times a day."

Conjunctiva (protective membrane)

Eyelid

Eyelashes

Ray of light

Image seen

"Which way is the optic nerve?"

Cornea

"Go straight through to the retina at the back of the eye."

The hole in the center of the iris is called the pupil.

Iris

"We pull to open the pupil wider."

"I operate the valves to drain tears away down the back of Steve's nose, but when he peels an onion, I just can't cope with the flow."

Tear duct

"Waah!"

1. Sharp pictures
Seeing starts at the cornea, a clear window at the front of Steve's eyes. Beams of light bend as they pass through the cornea and the fluid-filled chamber behind it. The bending focuses the light, gathering the rays so that they form a clear picture on the eye's inner surface.

2. Adjusting brightness
Next, the light passes through the hole in the center of the colored part of Steve's eye, a muscular ring called the iris. In bright light, the muscle tightens, narrowing the hole in the middle. This reduces the amount of light entering the eye, so Steve isn't dazzled.

3. Seeing far and near
Behind the iris, a lens helps Steve to see far and near things equally clearly. To focus on close things, Steve tightens his eye muscles. This makes the lens bulge, bending light rays strongly. Light rays from distant objects need less bending. So Steve relaxes his eye muscles, allowing the rubbery fibers to stretch the lens into a flatter shape that bends light less.

Sight problems

Far-sighted people have eyeballs that are too short and need glasses to see nearby objects. Near-sighted people have egg-shaped eyeballs and can't see distant objects without glasses. Steve doesn't need glasses, but a quarter of all children wear them, as do most grandparents.

Eagle eyes

Steve's eyes are sharp enough to pick out a golf ball at a distance of 1,500 yards (1.4 km), but he's not unusual. Most of us can see this well, although we may need glasses to make the most of our remarkable vision.

"This spongy layer of fat provides soft, protective padding for Steve's eyeball."

"This squishy jelly gives the eye its circular shape and holds the retina in place. Light passes straight through it."

Rod cells

One hundred and twenty million rod-shaped cells enable Steve to see shapes and movement. They work even in the dimmest starlight.

Cone cells

The six million cone-shaped cells work in bright light only. They detect colors and give Steve a clearer picture of objects he studies closely.

5. Seeing cells

Light falling on the retina activates special cells shaped like rods and cones. The cells send tiny impulses down nerve fibers linking the eye and brain. Steve's brain (pp. 122/123) processes the nerve signals, turning them into a picture that Steve can understand.

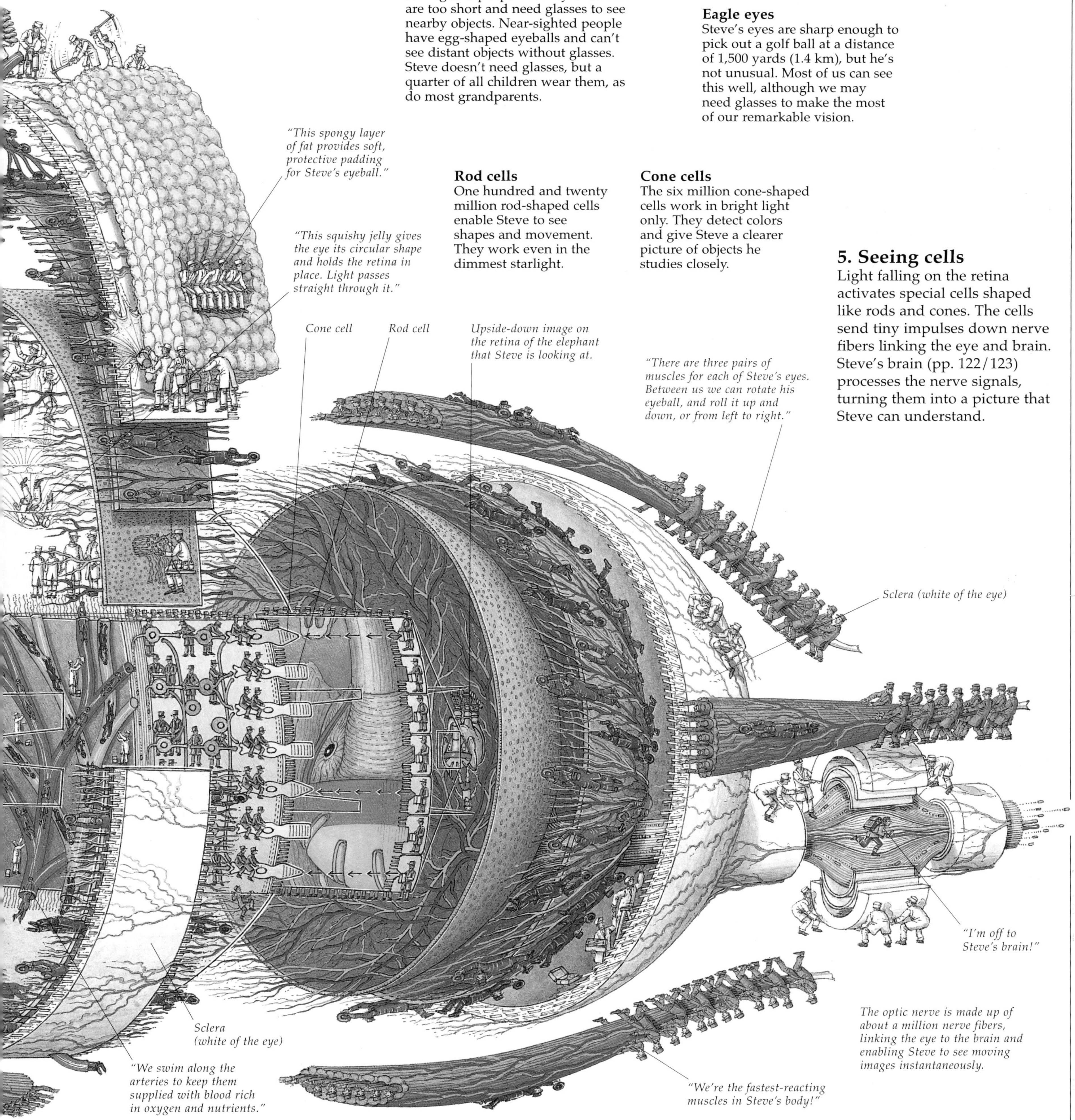

Cone cell   Rod cell

Upside-down image on the retina of the elephant that Steve is looking at.

"There are three pairs of muscles for each of Steve's eyes. Between us we can rotate his eyeball, and roll it up and down, or from left to right."

Sclera (white of the eye)

"I'm off to Steve's brain!"

The optic nerve is made up of about a million nerve fibers, linking the eye to the brain and enabling Steve to see moving images instantaneously.

Sclera (white of the eye)

"We swim along the arteries to keep them supplied with blood rich in oxygen and nutrients."

"We're the fastest-reacting muscles in Steve's body!"

4. Projecting the picture

The inside of the eye works like a camera. The lens projects a sharp image onto the back surface of the eye. There a layer of light-sensitive cells called the retina works like photographic film. The image on the retina is upside down, but Steve's brain (pp. 122/123) will turn it the right side up.

The blind spot

Everyone's retina has a "blind spot" where there are no nerve cells for seeing. The blind spot is the point where nerve fibers from all over the retina gather together to form the optic nerve.

THE EAR

FEELING OUR WAY along a shiny bundle of nerve fibers, we squeezed through a small, circular hole where the fibers branched. Should we take the left or the right fork? We tossed a coin and chose the left. It led to a narrow tunnel, like the inside of a seashell. Baffled, we consulted our map. Only one part of Steve's body looked like this: the inner ear. The spiraling liquid-filled tube changes sound waves into nerve impulses. The air-filled middle ear contains tiny bones that conduct sound. These delicate mechanisms are hidden away deep inside Steve's head. The crumpled flaps of cartilage on the sides of his head that we call ears do not do the hearing. They funnel sound down a short tube that leads to the middle ear.

Positive identification

Steve's outer ear is unique: nobody else's looks quite the same. Its shape began to form before Steve was born, but has not changed since his first birthday. In fact, forensic scientists have suggested using ear shape to identify criminals who wear masks that cover only the front of their heads.

"Hey! Can you hear me? The pinna (outer ear) is shaped to collect and guide sound into Steve's external auditory canal."

"We're riding on the sound waves traveling into Steve's ear."

1. What's noise?

Noise produces vibrations that travel through the air as sound waves. When sound waves reach Steve's ears, they are gathered by the pinna (outer ear), which directs them into the auditory canal.

Sound waves coming from the right reach the right ear a split second before they reach the left ear. This is why Steve can tell which direction the sound is coming from.

Fast growers

Steve's ears get bigger by about 0.08 in (2 mm) every nine years, which is ¼ in (6.35 mm) every 30 years. If Methuselah really had lived to be 969 years old (as the Bible reports), his ears would have been bigger than his head, and he could have used his earlobes as a hat!

"Hey, watch where you're throwing that ear wax!"

Helix (Outer rim)

Antihelix (Inner rim)

External auditory canal

Lobule (Earlobe)

"It's going to take me forever to clean Steve's ears. They seem to get bigger every day!"

The temporalis muscle runs in front of the ear to the jaw.

A thick layer of skull bone protects the inner ear.

Earwax is manufactured by the ceruminous glands.

"I move the hairs in Steve's auditory canal by operating the erector muscles."

Sound waves hit the eardrum, making it vibrate.

Malleus (hammer)

"BUZZ OFF you nasty thing!"

"This earwax comes in handy for pelting insects."

"I'm going around the bend here."

"Wow, the echo in here is fantastic. These walls reflect sound excellently."

"Phew! I hope Steve's earlobes don't grow any longer."

Earlobe is made up of fat and connective tissue.

Hairy filters

The hairs in the external auditory canal help keep out dirt and unwanted visitors such as wasps. By the way, don't believe what you hear about earwigs. People used to believe that they could crawl into your ears while you were asleep and burrow into your brain – but it's not true.

2. Banging the drum

The outer ear ends at the eardrum, a flattened layer of stretched skin that separates the auditory canal and the middle ear, providing an airtight seal. When the waves hit the eardrum, it begins to vibrate.

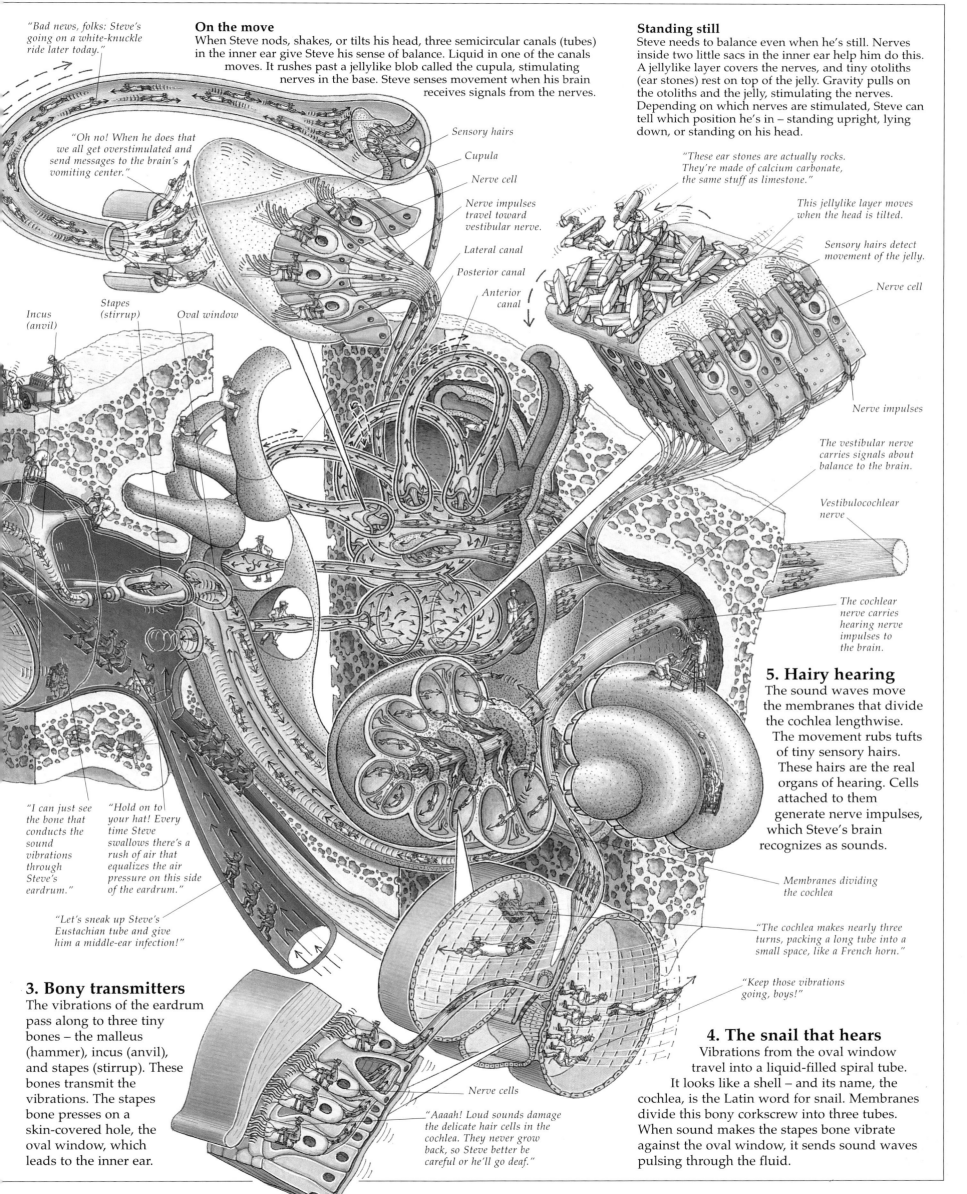

On the move

When Steve nods, shakes, or tilts his head, three semicircular canals (tubes) in the inner ear give Steve his sense of balance. Liquid in one of the canals moves. It rushes past a jellylike blob called the cupula, stimulating nerves in the base. Steve senses movement when his brain receives signals from the nerves.

"Bad news, folks: Steve's going on a white-knuckle ride later today."

"Oh no! When he does that we all get overstimulated and send messages to the brain's vomiting center."

Standing still

Steve needs to balance even when he's still. Nerves inside two little sacs in the inner ear help him do this. A jellylike layer covers the nerves, and tiny otoliths (ear stones) rest on top of the jelly. Gravity pulls on the otoliths and the jelly, stimulating the nerves. Depending on which nerves are stimulated, Steve can tell which position he's in – standing upright, lying down, or standing on his head.

"These ear stones are actually rocks. They're made of calcium carbonate, the same stuff as limestone."

Sensory hairs

Cupula

Nerve cell

Nerve impulses travel toward vestibular nerve.

Lateral canal

Posterior canal

Anterior canal

Incus (anvil)

Stapes (stirrup)

Oval window

This jellylike layer moves when the head is tilted.

Sensory hairs detect movement of the jelly.

Nerve cell

Nerve impulses

The vestibular nerve carries signals about balance to the brain.

Vestibulocochlear nerve

The cochlear nerve carries hearing nerve impulses to the brain.

5. Hairy hearing

The sound waves move the membranes that divide the cochlea lengthwise. The movement rubs tufts of tiny sensory hairs. These hairs are the real organs of hearing. Cells attached to them generate nerve impulses, which Steve's brain recognizes as sounds.

Membranes dividing the cochlea

"The cochlea makes nearly three turns, packing a long tube into a small space, like a French horn."

"Keep those vibrations going, boys!"

"I can just see the bone that conducts the sound vibrations through Steve's eardrum."

"Hold on to your hat! Every time Steve swallows there's a rush of air that equalizes the air pressure on this side of the eardrum."

"Let's sneak up Steve's Eustachian tube and give him a middle-ear infection!"

3. Bony transmitters

The vibrations of the eardrum pass along to three tiny bones – the malleus (hammer), incus (anvil), and stapes (stirrup). These bones transmit the vibrations. The stapes bone presses on a skin-covered hole, the oval window, which leads to the inner ear.

Nerve cells

"Aaaah! Loud sounds damage the delicate hair cells in the cochlea. They never grow back, so Steve better be careful or he'll go deaf."

4. The snail that hears

Vibrations from the oval window travel into a liquid-filled spiral tube. It looks like a shell – and its name, the cochlea, is the Latin word for snail. Membranes divide this bony corkscrew into three tubes. When sound makes the stapes bone vibrate against the oval window, it sends sound waves pulsing through the fluid.

THE BRAIN

WE LEFT THE EAR AS WE HAD ENTERED: along a bundle of nerves. We chased a nervous impulse as it swooped inside Steve's skull and dived into his brainstem, but then lost it in the cerebellum. Searching would have been pointless: there are 100 billion nerve cells in a brain. Each is connected to thousands of neighbors, making the brain more complex than any computer. It needs to be. Steve's brain must carry out many tasks just to keep him alive. The brainstem keeps his heart beating and lungs breathing. The cerebrum, which makes up nine-tenths of the brain, enables him to think, and helps store memories. It also interprets nervous impulses from his senses and enables him to control his muscles. The brain is one of Steve's largest organs; it weighs around 3 lb (1.4 kg).

Cerebrum
The wrinkled cerebrum is divided into two halves, which are joined by a "bridge" called the corpus callosum. The cerebrum is responsible for what we call intelligence: it integrates Steve's ability to speak, read, write, to understand and remember things, to plan ahead, and to have original thoughts.

The brain's "skin"
Three "skins," together called the meninges, enclose and protect the brain. Cerebrospinal (brain and spine) fluid is absorbed into the blood in tiny outgrowths from the middle cobweblike layer.

"Just testing the cushioning effect of the meninges."

Outer layer   *Middle layer*   *Inner layer*

Left and right brain
The two sides of the cerebrum look very similar, and share much of the work of thinking. However, each side has special tasks. The left side enables Steve to figure out problems logically, to speak and write, and to understand science and numbers. The right side is his creative side. He gets his vivid imagination and artistic ability from here, as well as his appreciation of music.

The brain's inner room
Nerves carrying Steve's sensations converge on a region called the thalamus (inner chamber). The thalamus relays nervous impulses to the cerebrum, but can interpret sensation on its own: it helps Steve realize he is in pain, but other areas of the brain tell him where it hurts. The hypothalamus keeps Steve's autonomic nervous system working: it helps him to control the movements of his heart, digestive system, and bladder; makes him hungry and thirsty; makes him feel angry or aggressive; and stops him from falling asleep during the day.

"We operate Steve's muscles; when we send out commands, different parts of the body obey. Each one of us controls different muscles."

"Hello! What's it like over there? Here in the motor cortex they never seem to rest. There's always some muscle that needs moving."

Nerve impulses

"Our job is thought elaboration. Without us, Steve would feel, but he couldn't think."

Corpus callosum

Ventricles

Frontal lobe (area) of the cerebrum

Gray matter

"We enable Steve to recognize basic sound qualities, such as the beat of music, and to distinguish between low and high notes."

Meninges

"Ick! It smells just like that chicken farm where Steve worked as a boy. We're the sniffers: our close link with Steve's "emotional brain" (see top right) explains why smells bring back such vivid memories."

Thinking takes place only in the gray cells at the surface of the cerebrum. The creases give Steve's brain a large surface area. If it were a smooth ball, his head would need to be nearly twice as big for him to have the same intelligence.

"If we'd been working overtime when Steve was younger, we could have made him grow into a 8-ft (2.5-m) giant."

Growth control
Like some other glands, the pituitary manufactures hormones – control chemicals distributed in the bloodstream. One of the functions of the pituitary gland is to control growth.

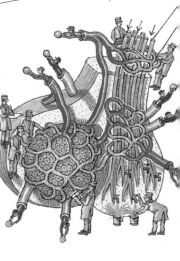

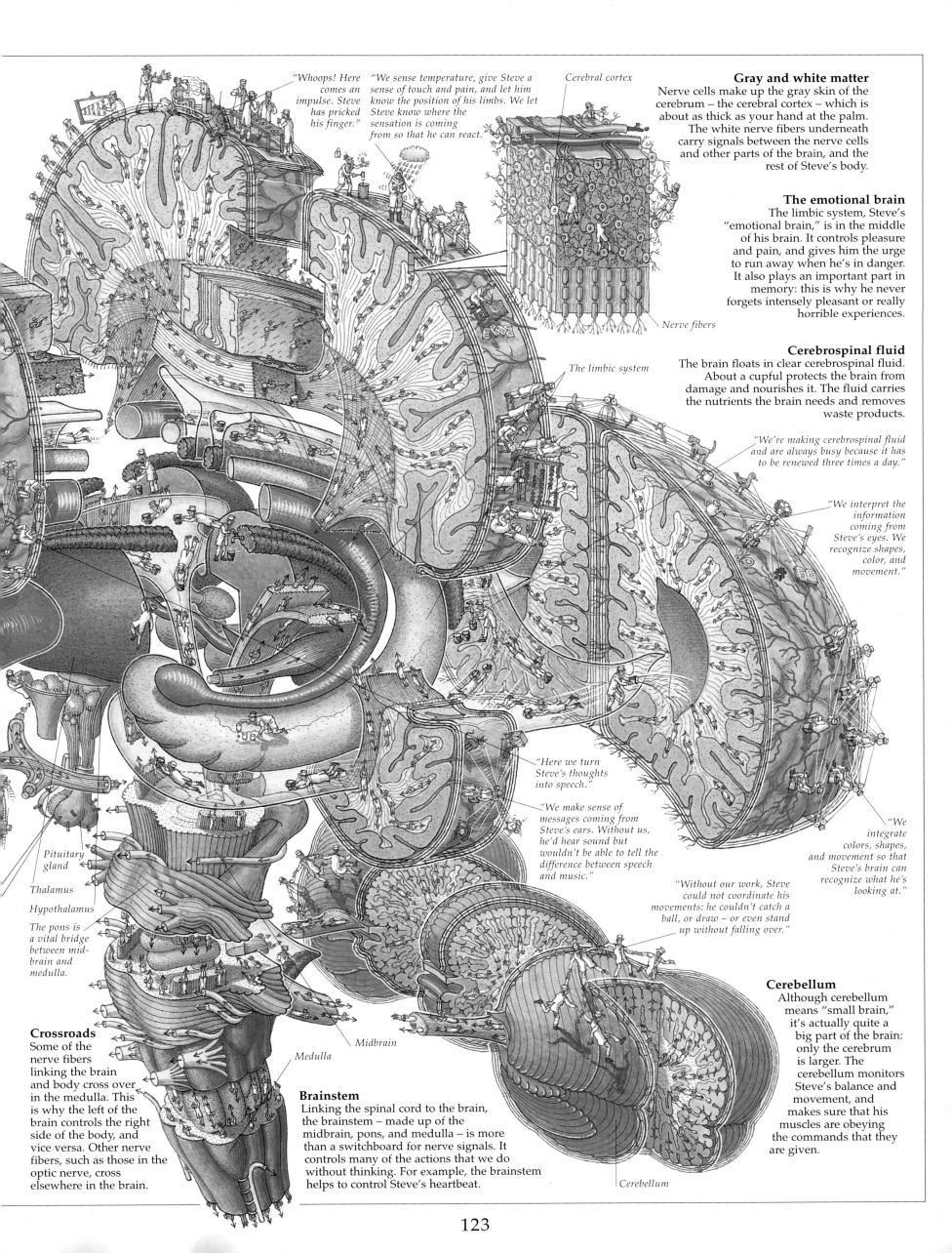

Gray and white matter
Nerve cells make up the gray skin of the cerebrum – the cerebral cortex – which is about as thick as your hand at the palm. The white nerve fibers underneath carry signals between the nerve cells and other parts of the brain, and the rest of Steve's body.

The emotional brain
The limbic system, Steve's "emotional brain," is in the middle of his brain. It controls pleasure and pain, and gives him the urge to run away when he's in danger. It also plays an important part in memory: this is why he never forgets intensely pleasant or really horrible experiences.

Cerebrospinal fluid
The brain floats in clear cerebrospinal fluid. About a cupful protects the brain from damage and nourishes it. The fluid carries the nutrients the brain needs and removes waste products.

"We're making cerebrospinal fluid and are always busy because it has to be renewed three times a day."

"We interpret the information coming from Steve's eyes. We recognize shapes, color, and movement."

Cerebral cortex

Nerve fibers

The limbic system

"Whoops! Here comes an impulse. Steve has pricked his finger."

"We sense temperature, give Steve a sense of touch and pain, and let him know the position of his limbs. We let Steve know where the sensation is coming from so that he can react."

"Here we turn Steve's thoughts into speech."

"We make sense of messages coming from Steve's ears. Without us, he'd hear sound but wouldn't be able to tell the difference between speech and music."

"Without our work, Steve could not coordinate his movements: he couldn't catch a ball, or draw – or even stand up without falling over."

"We integrate colors, shapes, and movement so that Steve's brain can recognize what he's looking at."

Pituitary gland

Thalamus

Hypothalamus

The pons is a vital bridge between midbrain and medulla.

Crossroads
Some of the nerve fibers linking the brain and body cross over in the medulla. This is why the left of the brain controls the right side of the body, and vice versa. Other nerve fibers, such as those in the optic nerve, cross elsewhere in the brain.

Midbrain

Medulla

Brainstem
Linking the spinal cord to the brain, the brainstem – made up of the midbrain, pons, and medulla – is more than a switchboard for nerve signals. It controls many of the actions that we do without thinking. For example, the brainstem helps to control Steve's heartbeat.

Cerebellum
Although cerebellum means "small brain," it's actually quite a big part of the brain: only the cerebrum is larger. The cerebellum monitors Steve's balance and movement, and makes sure that his muscles are obeying the commands that they are given.

Cerebellum

123

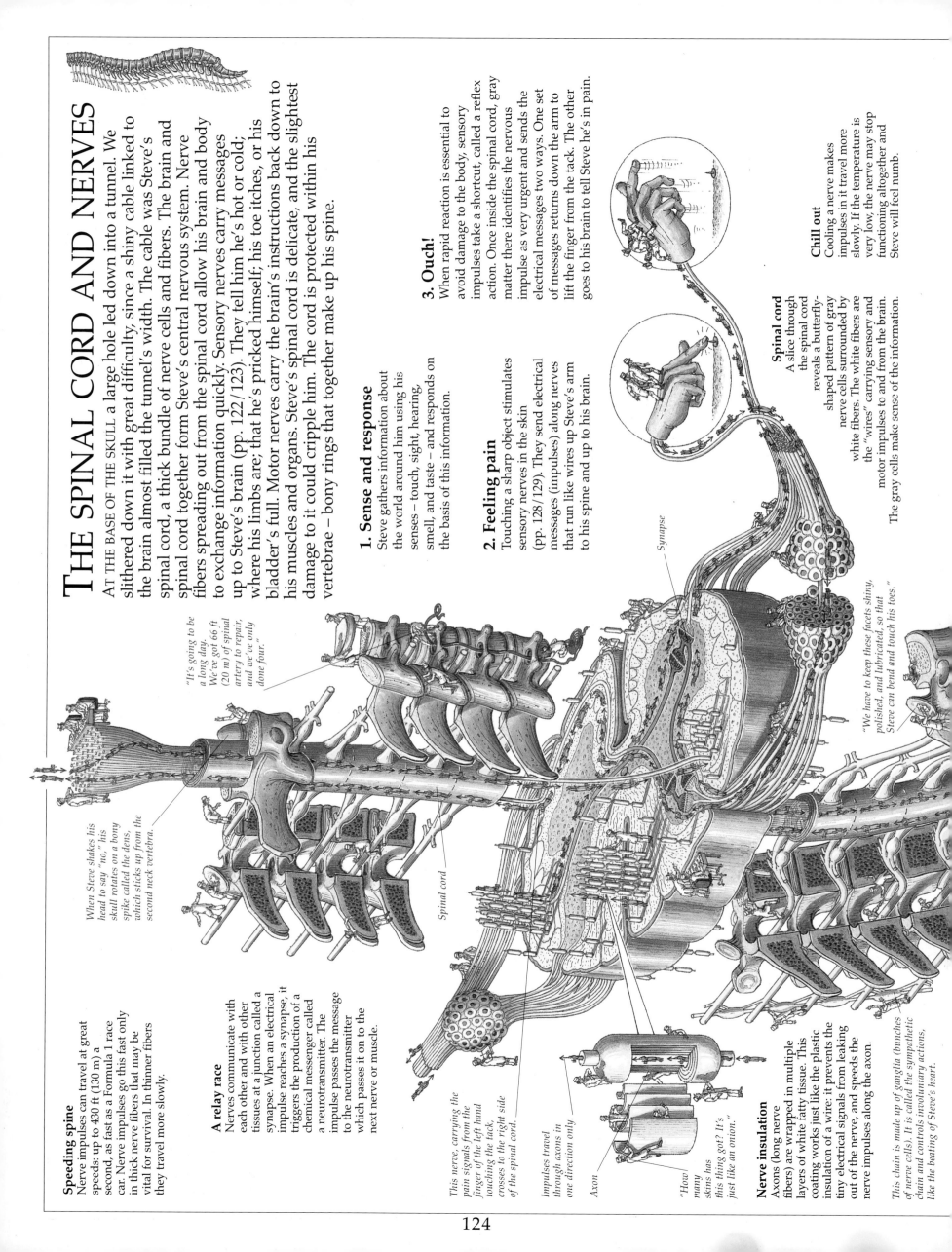

THE SPINAL CORD AND NERVES

AT THE BASE OF THE SKULL a large hole led down into a tunnel. We slithered down it with great difficulty, since a shiny cable linked to the brain almost filled the tunnel's width. The cable was Steve's spinal cord, a thick bundle of nerve cells and fibers. The brain and spinal cord together form Steve's central nervous system. Nerve fibers spreading out from the spinal cord allow his brain and body to exchange information quickly. Sensory nerves carry messages up to Steve's brain (pp. 122/123). They tell him he's hot or cold; where his limbs are; that he's pricked himself; his toe itches, or his bladder's full. Motor nerves carry the brain's instructions back down to his muscles and organs. Steve's spinal cord is delicate, and the slightest damage to it could cripple him. The cord is protected within his vertebrae – bony rings that together make up his spine.

Speeding spine
Nerve impulses can travel at great speeds: up to 430 ft (130 m) a second, as fast as a Formula 1 race car. Nerve impulses go this fast only in thick nerve fibers that may be vital for survival. In thinner fibers they travel more slowly.

A relay race
Nerves communicate with each other and with other tissues at a junction called a synapse. When an electrical impulse reaches a synapse, it triggers the production of a chemical messenger called a neurotransmitter. The impulse passes the message to the neurotransmitter which passes it on to the next nerve or muscle.

Nerve insulation
Axons (long nerve fibers) are wrapped in multiple layers of white fatty tissue. This coating works just like the plastic insulation of a wire: it prevents the tiny electrical signals from leaking out of the nerve, and speeds the nerve impulses along the axon.

1. Sense and response
Steve gathers information about the world around him using his senses – touch, sight, hearing, smell, and taste – and responds on the basis of this information.

2. Feeling pain
Touching a sharp object stimulates sensory nerves in the skin (pp. 128/129). They send electrical messages (impulses) along nerves that run like wires up Steve's spine and up to his brain.

3. Ouch!
When rapid reaction is essential to avoid damage to the body, sensory impulses take a shortcut, called a reflex action. Once inside the spinal cord, gray matter there identifies the nervous impulse as very urgent and sends the electrical messages two ways. One set of messages returns down the arm to lift the finger from the tack. The other goes to his brain to tell Steve he's in pain.

Chill out
Cooling a nerve makes impulses in it travel more slowly. If the temperature is very low, the nerve may stop functioning altogether and Steve will feel numb.

Spinal cord
A slice through the spinal cord reveals a butterfly-shaped pattern of gray nerve cells surrounded by white fibers. The white fibers are the "wires" carrying sensory and motor impulses to and from the brain. The gray cells make sense of the information.

"It's going to be a long day. We've got 66 ft (20 m) of spinal artery to repair, and we've only done four."

When Steve shakes his head to say "no," his skull rotates on a bony spike called the dens, which sticks up from the second neck vertebra.

Synapse

Spinal cord

"We have to keep these facets shiny, polished, and lubricated, so that Steve can bend and touch his toes."

This nerve, carrying the pain signals from the finger of the left hand touching the tack, crosses to the right side of the spinal cord.

Impulses travel through axons in one direction only.

Axon

"How many skins has this thing got? It's just like an onion."

This chain is made up of ganglia (bunches of nerve cells). It is called the sympathetic chain and controls involuntary actions, like the beating of Steve's heart.

124

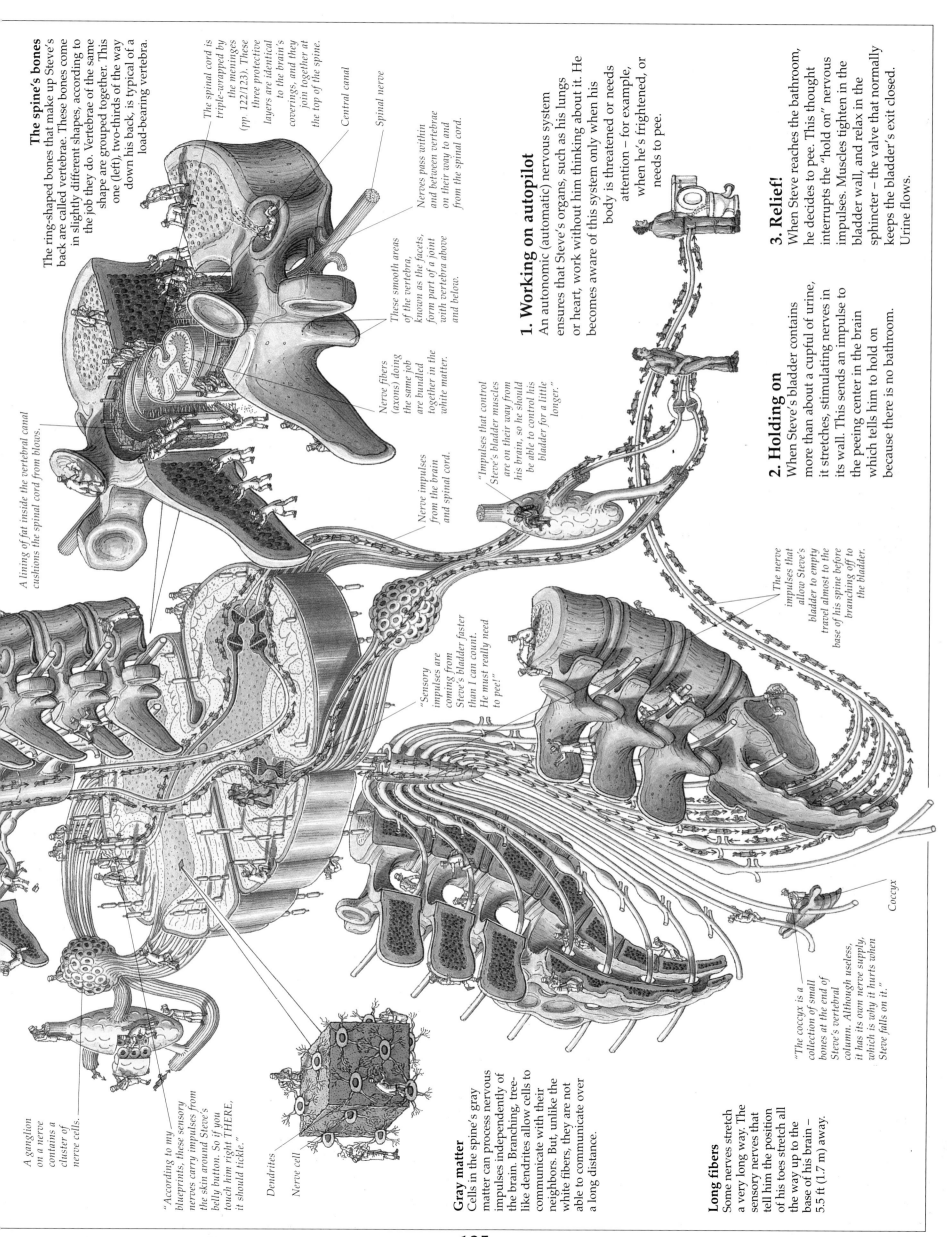

The spine's bones

The ring-shaped bones that make up Steve's back are called vertebrae. These bones come in slightly different shapes, according to the job they do. Vertebrae of the same shape are grouped together. This one (left), two-thirds of the way down his back, is typical of a load-bearing vertebra.

The spinal cord is triple-wrapped by the meninges (pp. 122/123). These three protective layers are identical to the brain's coverings, and they join together at the top of the spine.

Central canal

Spinal nerve

Nerves pass within and between vertebrae on their way to and from the spinal cord.

These smooth areas of the vertebra, known as the facets, form part of a joint with vertebra above and below.

Nerve fibers (axons) doing the same job are bundled together in the white matter.

Nerve impulses from the brain and spinal cord.

A lining of fat inside the vertebral canal cushions the spinal cord from blows.

1. Working on autopilot

An autonomic (automatic) nervous system ensures that Steve's organs, such as his lungs or heart, work without him thinking about it. He becomes aware of this system only when his body is threatened or needs attention – for example, when he's frightened, or needs to pee.

2. Holding on

When Steve's bladder contains more than about a cupful of urine, it stretches, stimulating nerves in its wall. This sends an impulse to the peeing center in the brain which tells him to hold on because there is no bathroom.

3. Relief!

When Steve reaches the bathroom, he decides to pee. This thought interrupts the "hold on" nervous impulses. Muscles tighten in the bladder wall, and relax in the sphincter – the valve that normally keeps the bladder's exit closed. Urine flows.

"Impulses that control Steve's bladder muscles are on their way from his brain, so he should be able to control his bladder for a little longer."

The nerve impulses that allow Steve's bladder to empty travel almost to the base of his spine before branching off to the bladder.

"Sensory impulses are coming from Steve's bladder faster than I can count. He must really need to pee!"

"The coccyx is a collection of small bones at the end of Steve's vertebral column. Although useless, it has its own nerve supply, which is why it hurts when Steve falls on it."

Coccyx

Gray matter

Cells in the spine's gray matter can process nervous impulses independently of the brain. Branching, tree-like dendrites allow cells to communicate with their neighbors. But, unlike the white fibers, they are not able to communicate over a long distance.

"According to my blueprints, these sensory nerves carry impulses from the skin around Steve's belly button. So if you touch him right THERE, it should tickle."

A ganglion on a nerve contains a cluster of nerve cells.

Dendrites

Nerve cell.

Long fibers

Some nerves stretch a very long way. The sensory nerves that tell him the position of his toes stretch all the way up to the base of his brain – 5.5 ft (1.7 m) away.

THE SKELETON

ROPED TOGETHER FOR SAFETY, we climbed down from Steve's neck vertebrae into his rib cage. There we set up a base camp from which to investigate the rest of his bones. We were surprised by how fiendishly clever the skeleton is. You might think that the 206 bones of Steve's skeleton would weigh a lot, but the unique honeycomb structure of bone keeps it very light. Nevertheless bone is strong enough to support the weight of Steve's flesh and organs, and to protect vulnerable areas such as the brain. Bones are also a warehouse of vital minerals, and the bone marrow inside them produces Steve's blood cells. Different sorts of joints allow the skeleton to twist and bend freely in the most vigorous of activities. When we had finished our study, we hitched a ride on a red blood cell, clinging on tightly as it whirled away, carrying oxygen around Steve's body.

The skull
The 22 bones of Steve's skull help to give his face its unmistakable shape, and protect his brain from damage.

"These ear bones are the tiniest in Steve's body. But without them, Steve wouldn't hear a thing (pp. 150/151)."

Tough teeth
Steve's teeth are made of dentine – a material similar to bone. The shiny coating of enamel on the visible part of his teeth is the hardest material in the human body, and the only one that is not exchanged or replaced as Steve gets older.

A ball-and-socket joint is the most flexible kind of joint in the body.

Ball-and-socket joint
This kind of joint allows for the greatest range of movement. A bony ball at the end of one bone fits inside a cup-shaped socket of another bone. In the shoulder joint, the rounded end of the humerus (upper arm) bone fits inside a socket in the scapula (shoulder blade), allowing Steve's arm to turn in many directions.

"Wheel The bones of Steve's arms and legs are the longest in his body."

Humerus (upper arm bone)

Scapula (shoulder blade)

Hinge joint
Steve's arm bends in the middle at the elbow. This joint is a hinge – like a door hinge, it opens and closes in one direction only.

Teeth remain intact long after the rest of the body has decomposed.

"These hollows in Steve's facial bones not only make his skull lighter, they also make his voice echo, giving it a distinctive sound."

"Steve's jaw bone is the only moving part of his skull – and the muscles that move it are some of the strongest in his body."

Atlas

Axis

Pivot joint
A rotating joint at the top of Steve's spine allows him to turn his head left and right. A projection from the axis bone turns within a socket in the atlas bone.

Sternum (breastbone)

"Steve gets shorter every day – and taller every night! Pressure from being upright squashes these rubbery discs while he's awake, making him lose almost half an inch or so in height between morning and evening. The discs expand again when he lies down."

"Look: Steve broke his collarbone here when he was younger."

Clavicle (collarbone)

"It didn't break completely so it's called a greenstick fracture."

"It's healed up, because bone tissue is constantly renewed all over Steve's body."

Ribs
Narrow, curving bones called ribs support Steve's chest and protect the vital organs inside. Muscles attached to them help Steve to breathe by expanding and contracting his chest cavity (pp. 140/141). Steve has 12 pairs of ribs. All but the bottom two pairs are attached to the backbone and, via strips of flexible cartilage, to the sternum. The bottom two pairs of "floating ribs" are attached only to the spine at the back.

The ribs are attached to the sternum by cartilage, allowing the rib cage to expand and contract.

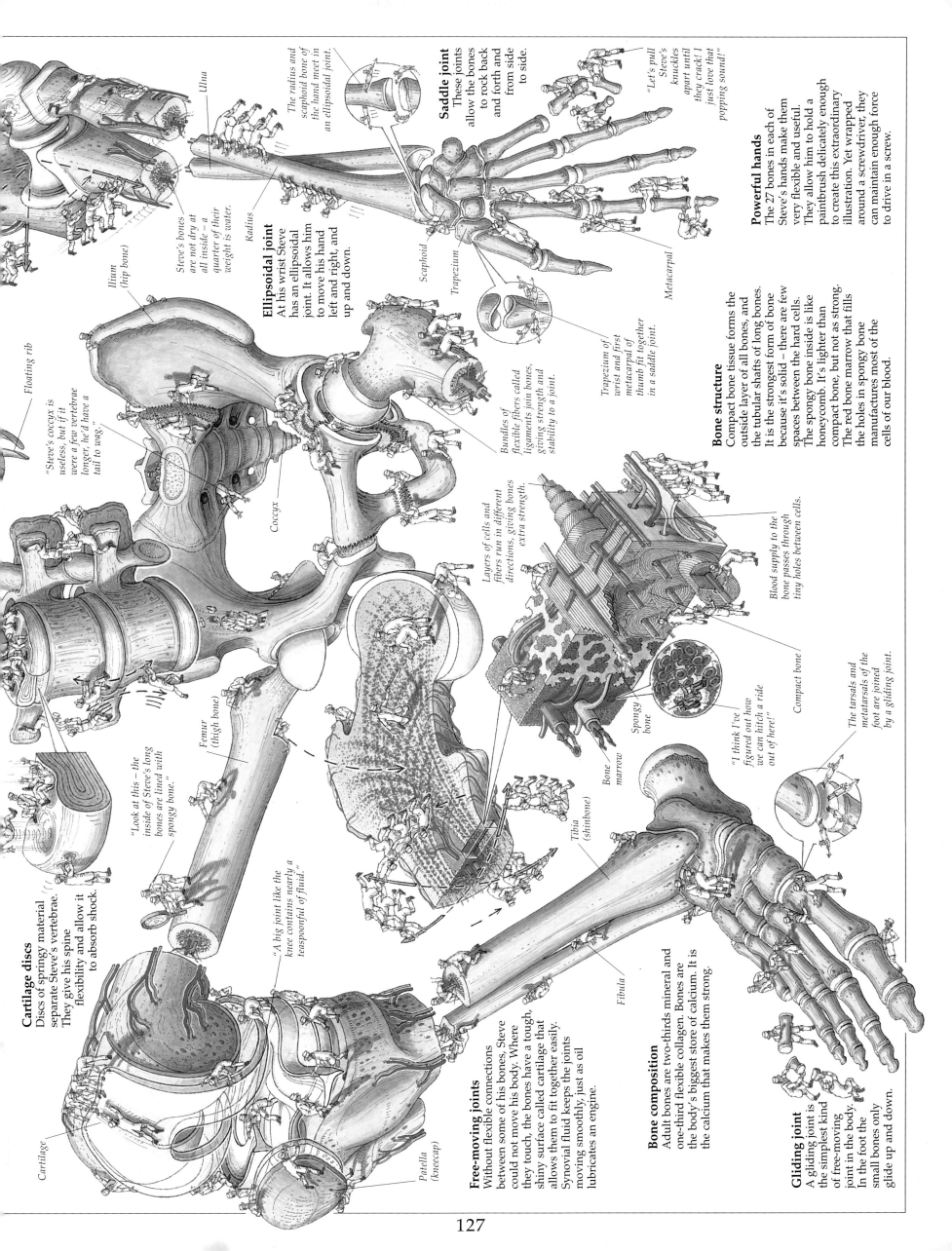

Saddle joint
These joints allow the bones to rock back and forth and from side to side.

The radius and scaphoid bone of the hand meet in an ellipsoidal joint.

Ulna

Radius

Steve's bones are not dry at all inside – a quarter of their weight is water.

Ilium (hip bone)

"Let's pull Steve's knuckles apart until they crack! I just love that popping sound!"

Powerful hands
The 27 bones in each of Steve's hands make them very flexible and useful. They allow him to hold a paintbrush delicately enough to create this extraordinary illustration. Yet wrapped around a screwdriver, they can maintain enough force to drive in a screw.

Ellipsoidal joint
At his wrist Steve has an ellipsoidal joint. It allows him to move his hand left and right, and up and down.

Scaphoid

Trapezium

Metacarpal

Bundles of flexible fibers called ligaments join bones, giving strength and stability to a joint.

Trapezium of wrist and first metacarpal of thumb fit together in a saddle joint.

Bone structure
Compact bone tissue forms the outside layer of all bones, and the tubular shafts of long bones. It is the strongest form of bone because it's solid – there are few spaces between the hard cells. The spongy bone inside is like honeycomb. It's lighter than compact bone, but not as strong. The red bone marrow that fills the holes in spongy bone manufactures most of the cells of our blood.

Floating rib

"Steve's coccyx is useless, but if it were a few vertebrae longer, he'd have a tail to wag."

Coccyx

Layers of cells and fibers run in different directions, giving bones extra strength.

Blood supply to the bone passes through tiny holes between cells.

Compact bone

Spongy bone

Bone marrow

The tarsals and metatarsals of the foot are joined by a gliding joint.

"I think I've figured out how we can hitch a ride out of here!"

Cartilage discs
Discs of springy material separate Steve's vertebrae. They give his spine flexibility and allow it to absorb shock.

"Look at this – the inside of Steve's long bones are lined with spongy bone."

Femur (thigh bone)

"A big joint like the knee contains nearly a teaspoonful of fluid."

Tibia (shinbone)

Fibula

Free-moving joints
Without flexible connections between some of his bones, Steve could not move his body. Where they touch, the bones have a tough, shiny surface called cartilage that allows them to fit together easily. Synovial fluid keeps the joints moving smoothly, just as oil lubricates an engine.

Cartilage

Bone composition
Adult bones are two-thirds mineral and one-third flexible collagen. Bones are the body's biggest store of calcium. It is the calcium that makes them strong.

Patella (kneecap)

Gliding joint
A gliding joint is the simplest kind of free-moving joint in the body. In the foot the small bones only glide up and down.

127

SKIN AND MUSCLES

WHEN THE RED BLOOD cell we were riding slowed down we jumped off, landing under the skin of Steve's chin. Besides protecting his body, this supple leathery layer keeps him cool, gives him a sense of touch, and even makes vitamins! But after a close shave with a razor blade we decided to retreat to somewhere safer. We snuggled down into a facial muscle, planning to rest, but it was hopeless. It turned out that the muscle was fixed to the corners of Steve's mouth, and he was laughing at his own jokes! Giving up hope of sleep, we split up and explored other parts of Steve's skin and muscles.

Muscles and movement
To move his body, Steve uses muscles – bundles of fleshy tissue attached to his bones. Each muscle is made of small fibers that contract (get shorter) or relax (lengthen) when a nerve signal reaches them. By shortening or lengthening, the muscles may cause bones to move or lips to smile.

Muscle tone
When Steve lies down to rest, his muscles relax and his body goes limp. But even at rest, muscles never relax completely; a few fibers are always contracting, giving muscles a firmness called tone.

Fingerprints
The patterns of ridges and furrows on the skin of Steve's hands are unique – nobody else leaves fingerprints that are quite the same as his.

Frowning muscles
Steve may use nine muscles when he frowns – to furrow his brow, narrow his eyes, widen his nostrils, and pull down the corners of his mouth.

Furrowing the brow

Narrowing the eye

Flaring the nostrils

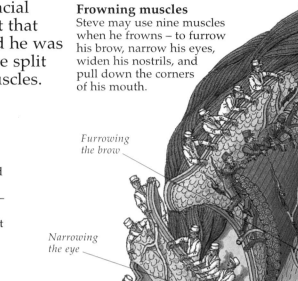

Pricking the skin and injecting dye beneath it makes a permanent mark called a tattoo.

Biceps

The muscles running outside the rib cage help Steve to breathe.

"Come and look at these tendons – his hand's like a rope factory."

"There she blows! This disgusting pus is caused by oil blocking a hair follicle, making it infected. We call it a zit."

If Steve tried all the muscles out in different combinations, he could make 7,000 different faces.

Nail

Nail structure
The nails on Steve's fingers and toes are made of cells rich in a tough protein called keratin. Nails grow from special cells hidden under the cuticle.

Cuticle

The sartorius muscle that crosses the thigh is the longest muscle in Steve's body.

Muscle structure
Muscles are made like bundles of bundles of bundles. Look closely at one and you'll see it's made of many tiny fibers, all aligned the same way. With a microscope, you could see that each fiber is also a bundle of even smaller threads. These threads are themselves bundles of even smaller threads called fibrils.

Ligaments are flexible enough to allow free movement, yet tough enough to stand up to powerful pulling forces.

Ligaments
Actions such as running put great stress on Steve's joints. Ligaments stop his bones from flying apart. These bands of rubbery tissue are attached to the bones close to where they meet at each joint (pp. 126/127).

Muscle filaments
The smallest fibrils are so tiny that if a human hair were a tube, 150 million fibrils would fit inside. They give the muscle its pulling ability. When a nervous impulse from the brain reaches them (pp. 122/123), filaments inside the fibrils slide past each other, making the muscle contract.

Fiber

Fibrils

The largest muscle fibers are as thick as a human hair, and the smallest are a tenth as thick.

Pulling down the corners of the mouth.

Smiling muscles
A big, hearty grin may use eight muscles – to pull up the brow, to widen the eyes, to raise the upper lip, and to pull up the corners of the mouth.

Pulling up the brow

Head hair
Steve's scalp is similar to skin elsewhere on his body. The main difference is that the hairs on his head grow longer, coarser, and faster than the fine hairs that cover the skin on the rest of his body.

"Looking after these hairs is a piece of cake. My last job was on a sheep, and its fleece grew three times as fast."

Tiny hard scales cover a softer, flexible core.

Hair
The hair that's visible above Steve's scalp is completely dead. It's mostly made of keratin. Hairs are alive only at the root, where growth takes place.

Muscles at work
During activity, Steve contracts (shortens) some of his muscles and relaxes others. To ensure that every part of Steve's body can move back as well as forward, each muscle has another one opposing (working against) it. For example, the biceps bend the arm at the elbow. The triceps straighten it.

Skin contains pigment to protect it from the damaging effects of sunlight. Sunlight speeds up pigment production, which is why skin tans.

Widening the eyes

The skin of Steve's eyelids is thinner than anywhere else.

Pulling the mouth up

Raising the upper lip

Lifting the corner of the mouth

Triceps

Deltoid

Bacteria multiply on the skin in the warm, sweaty conditions of the armpit and create a smell.

Protective skin
All that separates Steve from the world around him is 22 square feet (2 m²) of skin. Besides keeping his body in, skin also keeps water, dirt, and microbes out, and helps to regulate his body temperature.

When Steve plays squash for seven minutes, his muscles produce enough heat to boil water for four cups of coffee.

Epidermis

Oil glands produce a waxy goo that helps waterproof the skin.

Steve's skin flakes off constantly and is continually replaced.

"No, YOU come HERE! I'm busy with the plumbing in Steve's skin."

Tendons are so tough and elastic that those of animals were once used to strengthen archery bows.

Dermis

Achilles tendon

Muscles in his tongue contract when he sticks it out

Many different kinds of nerves lie just beneath the skin's surface. They allow Steve to detect heat, cold, pressure, touch, vibration, tickle, and pain (pp. 14/15).

Dermis
Beneath the epidermis is a tough, flexible layer containing blood vessels, nerves, and hair follicles. This layer is thin over Steve's joints where it has to be especially flexible, and is thickest on his palms and soles. New skin cells are manufactured here and migrate through the epidermis, where they are eventually shed.

Epidermis
The outer layer of Steve's skin is about as thick as a piece of good-quality writing paper. Nine-tenths of its cells manufacture keratin. Keratin collects on the skin's surface, making it waterproof, and protecting the layers below. Most of the remaining cells produce pigment or help protect Steve from infection.

Tendons
Muscles aren't always attached directly to the bones they move. Sometimes a tough tissue called a tendon links the bone to a distant muscle. The tendon acts like a rope: muscular contractions pull the tendon, and the tendon in turn pulls the bone.

THE DIGESTIVE SYSTEM

AFTER STRUGGLING through the muscles that surround Steve's salivary glands, we emerged through a gumboil. We had hardly gotten our bearings straight before we were knocked over by a gigantic french fry, then chewed and churned in a terrifying way. Thus began our journey through Steve's digestive system. This long tube begins at Steve's mouth and ends at his anus. When he eats, food is digested as it travels slowly through the digestive system. Digestion is the process of breaking down food into smaller parts so that the nutrients can be processed and absorbed. Parts of the digestive system do special jobs. The stomach, for instance, mixes food and breaks it up. The small intestine absorbs nutrients. Other organs, such as the liver and pancreas, aid digestion by supplying hormones and enzymes to dissolve and absorb food. And one organ, the appendix, is completely useless. It does nothing but cause trouble!

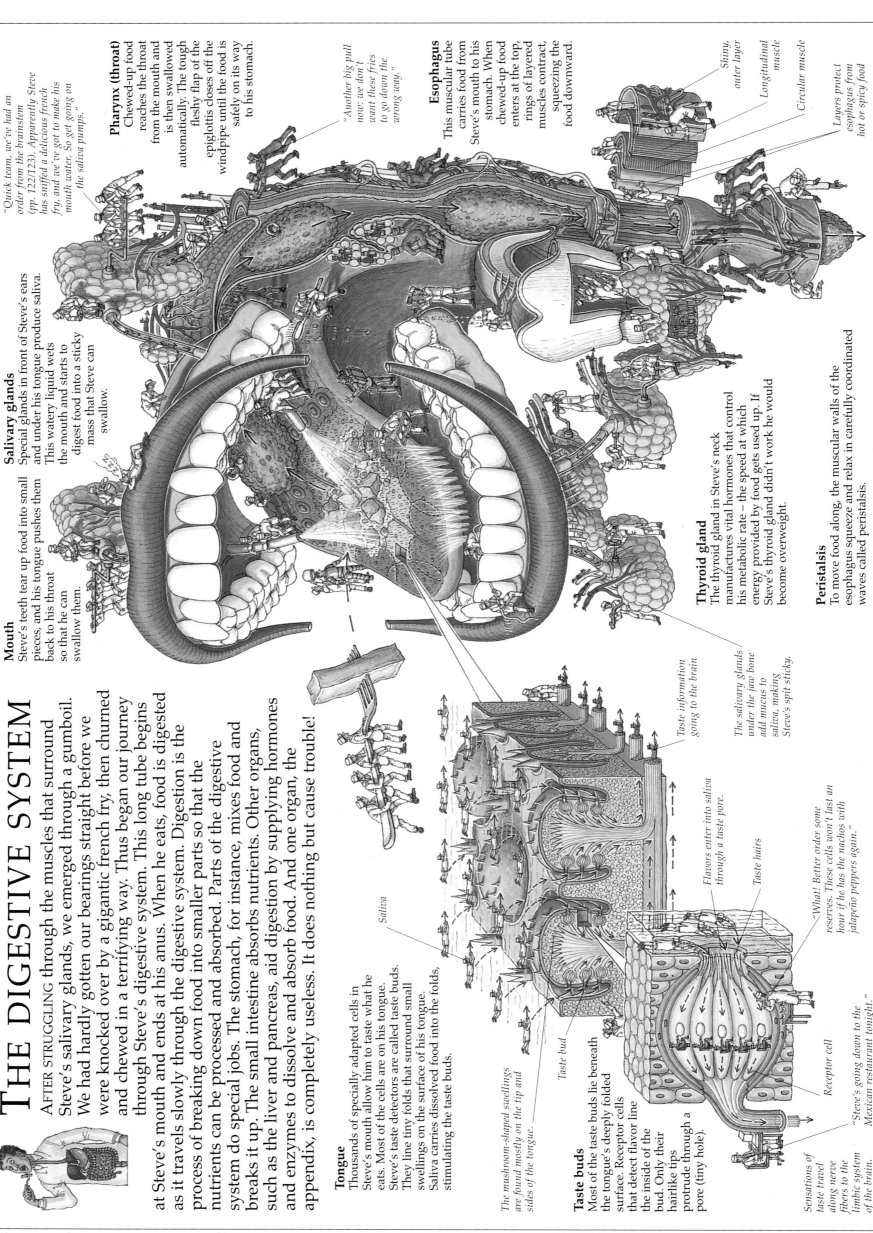

"Quick team, we've had an order from the brainstem (pp. 122/123). Apparently Steve has sniffed a delicious french fry, and we've got to make his mouth water. So get going on the saliva pumps."

Pharynx (throat)
Chewed-up food reaches the throat from the mouth and is then swallowed automatically. The tough fleshy flap of the epiglottis closes off the windpipe until the food is safely on its way to his stomach.

"Another big pull now: we don't want these fries to go down the wrong way."

Esophagus
This muscular tube carries food from Steve's mouth to his stomach. When chewed-up food enters at the top, rings of layered muscles contract, squeezing the food downward.

Shiny, outer layer

Longitudinal muscle

Circular muscle

Layers protect esophagus from hot or spicy food

Mouth
Steve's teeth tear up food into small pieces, and his tongue pushes them back to his throat so that he can swallow them.

Salivary glands
Special glands in front of Steve's ears and under his tongue produce saliva. This watery liquid wets the mouth and starts to digest food into a sticky mass so that Steve can swallow.

Thyroid gland
The thyroid gland in Steve's neck manufactures vital hormones that control his metabolic rate – the speed at which energy provided by food gets used up. If Steve's thyroid gland didn't work he would become overweight.

Peristalsis
To move food along, the muscular walls of the esophagus squeeze and relax in carefully coordinated waves called peristalsis.

Tongue
Thousands of specially adapted cells in Steve's mouth allow him to taste what he eats. Most of the cells are on his tongue. Steve's taste detectors are called taste buds. They line tiny folds that surround small swellings on the surface of his tongue.

Taste information going to the brain

The salivary glands under the jaw bone add mucus to saliva, making Steve's spit sticky.

The mushroom-shaped swellings are found mostly on the tip and sides of the tongue.

Saliva

Flavors enter into saliva through a taste pore.

Taste hairs

"What! Better order some reserves. These cells won't last an hour if he has the nachos with jalapeño peppers again."

Taste buds
Most of the taste buds lie beneath the tongue's deeply folded surface. Receptor cells that detect flavor line the inside of the bud. Only their hairlike tips protrude through a pore (tiny hole).

Taste bud

Receptor cell

"Steve's going down to the Mexican restaurant tonight."

Sensations of taste travel along nerve fibers to the limbic system of the brain.

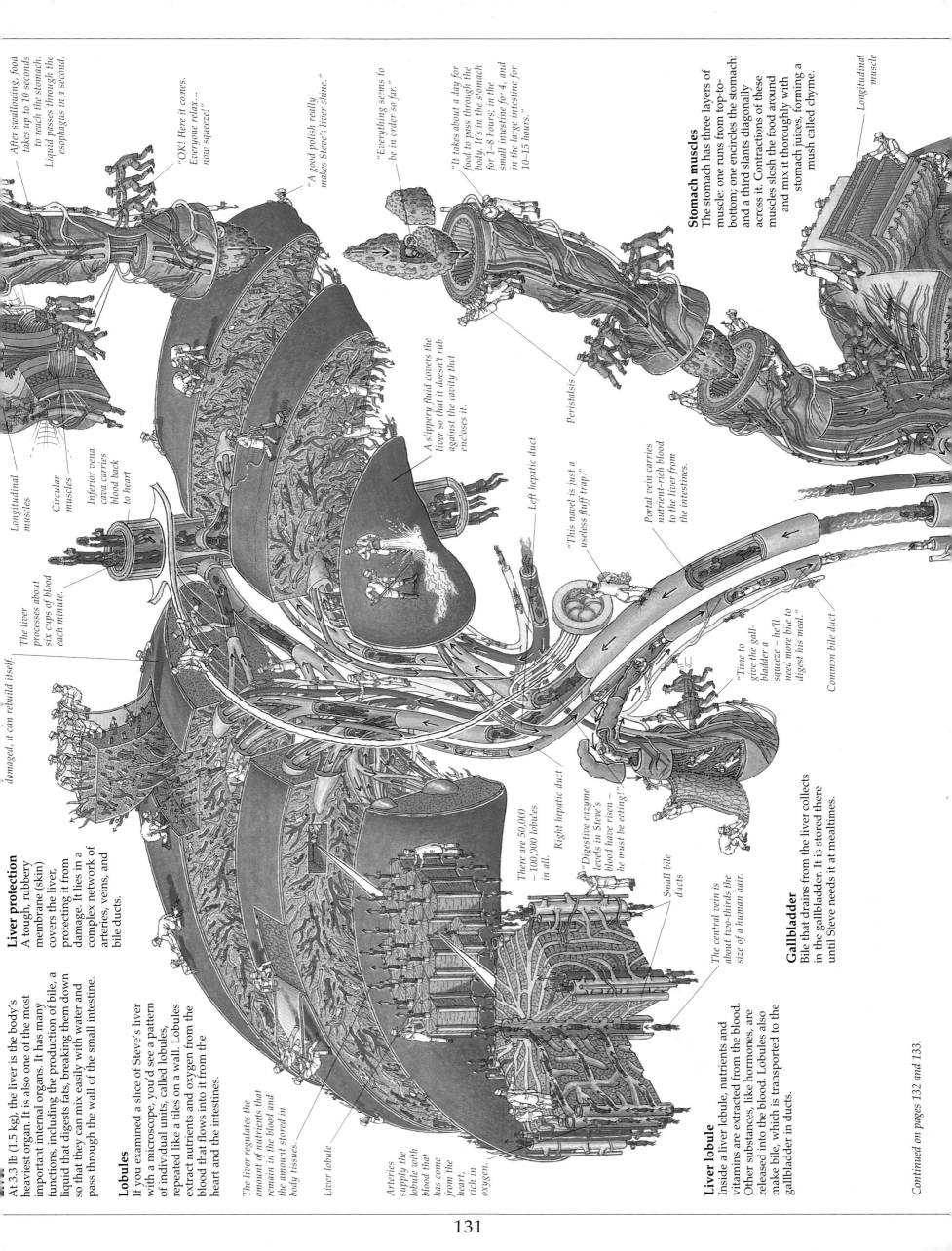

After swallowing, food takes up to 10 seconds to reach the stomach. Liquid passes through the esophagus in a second.

"OK! Here it comes. Everyone relax... now squeeze!"

"A good polish really makes Steve's liver shine."

"Everything seems to be in order so far."

"It takes about a day for food to pass through the body. It's in the stomach for 1–8 hours; in the small intestine for 4, and in the large intestine for 10–15 hours."

Stomach muscles
The stomach has three layers of muscle: one runs from top-to-bottom; one encircles the stomach; and a third slants diagonally across it. Contractions of these muscles slosh the food around and mix it thoroughly with stomach juices, forming a mush called chyme.

Longitudinal muscle

A slippery fluid covers the liver so that it doesn't rub against the cavity that encloses it.

Left hepatic duct

"This navel is just a useless fluff trap."

Portal vein carries nutrient-rich blood to the liver from the intestines.

Peristalsis

Longitudinal muscles

Circular muscles

Inferior vena cava carries blood back to heart

The liver processes about six cups of blood each minute.

"Digestive enzyme levels in Steve's blood have risen – he must be eating!"

There are 50,000 – 100,000 lobules in all.

Right hepatic duct

"Time to give the gallbladder a squeeze – he'll need more bile to digest this meal."

Common bile duct

Small bile ducts

The central vein is about two-thirds the size of a human hair.

Gallbladder
Bile that drains from the liver collects in the gallbladder. It is stored there until Steve needs it at mealtimes.

Liver lobule
Inside a liver lobule, nutrients and vitamins are extracted from the blood. Other substances, like hormones, are released into the blood. Lobules also make bile, which is transported to the gallbladder in ducts.

Arteries supply the lobule with blood that has come from the heart, rich in oxygen.

The liver regulates the amount of nutrients that remain in the blood and the amount stored in body tissues.

Liver lobule

Lobules
If you examined a slice of Steve's liver with a microscope, you'd see a pattern of individual units, called lobules, repeated like tiles on a wall. Lobules extract nutrients and oxygen from the blood that flows into it from the heart and the intestines.

Liver protection
A tough, rubbery membrane (skin) covers the liver, protecting it from damage. It lies in a complex network of arteries, veins, and bile ducts.

...damaged, it can rebuild itself.

At 3.3 lb (1.5 kg), the liver is the body's heaviest organ. It is also one of the most important internal organs. It has many functions, including the production of bile, a liquid that digests fats, breaking them down so that they can mix easily with water and pass through the wall of the small intestine.

Continued on pages 132 and 133.

Continued from pages 130 and 131.

Pyloric sphincter

A "gatekeeper" valve normally keeps the outlet of the stomach closed. But when the stomach has done its work the valve opens, allowing two or three teaspoonfuls of chyme (partly digested food) to squirt into the small intestine. This continues until the stomach is empty.

"Time to open the valve: Steve's stomach is full, and it's getting very acidic in there."

Small intestine

From the stomach, food passes into the small intestine, where the process of digestion continues. The pancreas and gallbladder pour digestive juices and bile into the small intestine to break down nutrients further so that they can be absorbed through the intestinal wall into the bloodstream.

Squirt of chyme

Intestinal wall

The first section of the small intestine has to withstand the strongly acidic chyme flowing from the stomach. Special cells in the intestine lining pump out mucus that both protects the intestinal wall and neutralizes the acid.

"I'm watching chyme, bile, and pancreatic juices being mixed together in the small intestine."

Pancreas

The sock-shaped pancreas produces enzymes – speed-up chemicals – that aid in the digestion of starch, proteins, and fats. The pancreas also produces important hormones, the body's control chemicals, and sodium bicarbonate (baking soda) which makes the contents of the intestine less acidic.

"I'm singing in the slime! Just singing in the slime......"

Many of the cells in the pancreas produce pancreatic juice, which flows down ducts into the intestine.

Circular muscle

Oblique muscle

Stomach

Shaped like the letter "J," the stomach is a flexible bag. When empty it is not much bigger than a salami, yet the stomach can expand to hold about 2.5 pints (1.5 liters). Powerful chemicals in the stomach juices digest the food, and the stomach's muscular walls squeeze and churn it into a liquid mess.

Circular muscles

Longitudinal muscles

Stomach wall

In between folds in the stomach wall are special pits with an important role in digestion. The pits are tiny – 11,000 would fit on the head of a pin – but at the bottom of each pit lie gastric (stomach) glands. These glands produce gastric juice. This highly acidic liquid breaks food into simpler particles, which the intestines can absorb more easily.

Gastric glands

Inside the gastric glands are cells that manufacture hydrochloric acid. This kills germs and helps digest food. The acid is very strong; it would burn the skin on your hand. Special mucus cells produce sticky slime that coats the stomach walls. The slime helps

Pancreatic juice flows into the intestines through a duct in the intestinal wall. Some people have a spare in case the first duct gets blocked. If both get blocked, the pancreas may digest itself.

Peristalsis churning chyme inside the small intestine

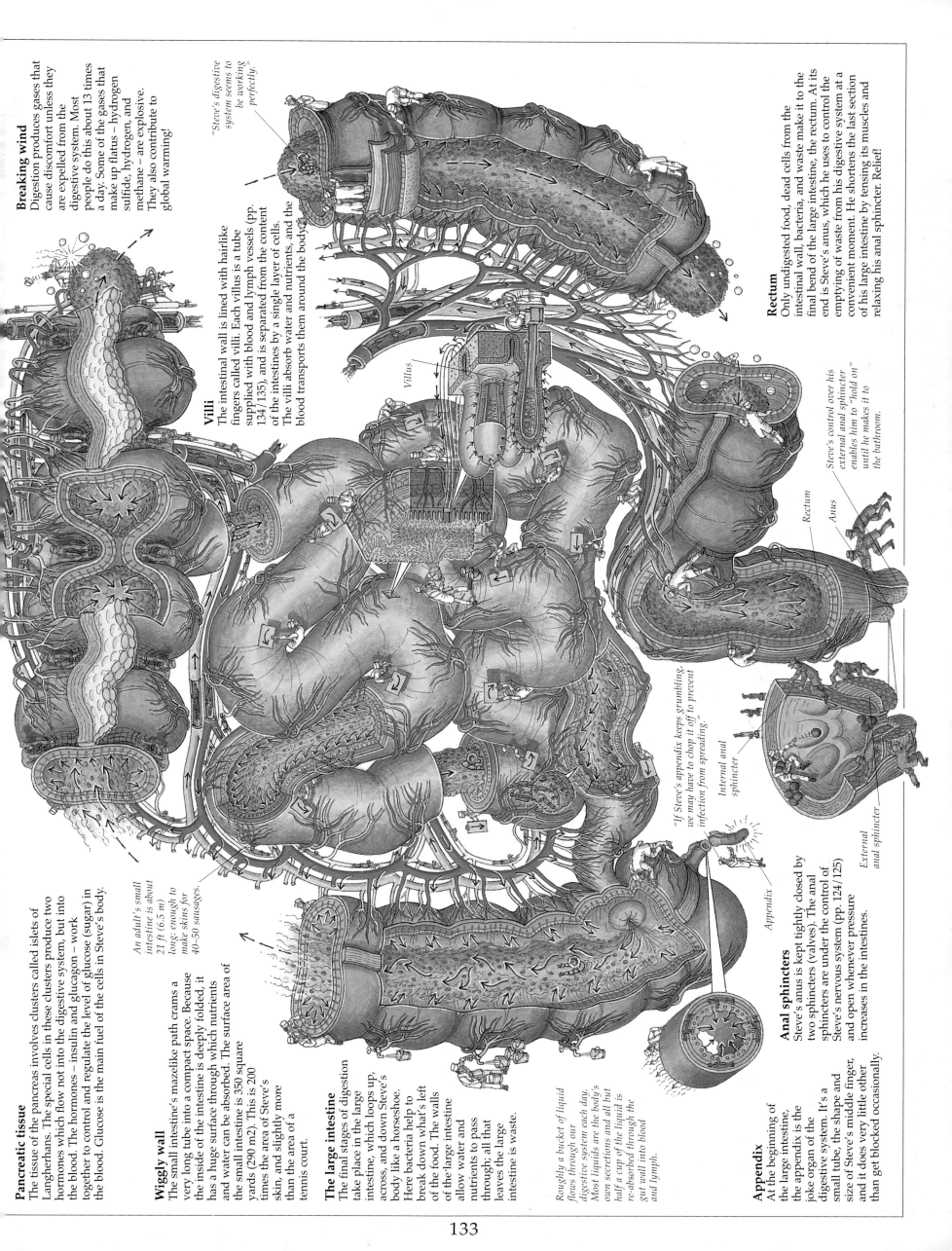

Breaking wind

Digestion produces gases that cause discomfort unless they are expelled from the digestive system. Most people do this about 13 times a day. Some of the gases that make up flatus – hydrogen sulfide, hydrogen, and methane – are explosive. They also contribute to global warming!

"Steve's digestive system seems to be working perfectly."

Pancreatic tissue

The tissue of the pancreas involves clusters called islets of Langerhans. The special cells in these clusters produce two hormones which flow not into the digestive system, but into the blood. The hormones – insulin and glucagon – work together to control and regulate the level of glucose (sugar) in the blood. Glucose is the main fuel of the cells in Steve's body.

Wiggly wall

The small intestine's mazelike path crams a very long tube into a compact space. Because the inside of the intestine is deeply folded, it has a huge surface through which nutrients and water can be absorbed. The surface area of the small intestine is 350 square yards (290 m2). This is 200 times the area of Steve's skin, and slightly more than the area of a tennis court.

The large intestine

The final stages of digestion take place in the large intestine, which loops up, across, and down Steve's body like a horseshoe. Here bacteria help to break down what's left of the food. The walls of the large intestine allow water and nutrients to pass through; all that leaves the large intestine is waste.

Appendix

At the beginning of the large intestine, the appendix is the joke organ of the digestive system. It's a small tube, about the shape and size of Steve's middle finger, and it does very little other than get blocked occasionally.

An adult's small intestine is about 21 ft (6.5 m) long: enough to make skins for 40–50 sausages.

Roughly a bucket of liquid flows through our digestive system each day. Most liquids are the body's own secretions and all but half a cup of the liquid is re-absorbed through the gut wall into blood and lymph.

Villi

The intestinal wall is lined with hairlike fingers called villi. Each villus is a tube supplied with blood and lymph vessels (pp. 134/135), and is separated from the content of the intestines by a single layer of cells. The villi absorb water and nutrients, and the blood transports them around the body.

Villus

Anal sphincters

Steve's anus is kept tightly closed by two sphincters (valves). The anal sphincters are under the control of Steve's nervous system (pp. 124/125) and open whenever pressure increases in the intestines.

"If Steve's appendix keeps grumbling, we may have to chop it off to prevent infection from spreading."

Appendix

Rectum

Only undigested food, dead cells from the intestinal wall, bacteria, and waste make it to the final bend of the large intestine, the rectum. At its end is Steve's anus, which he uses to control the emptying of waste from his digestive system at a convenient moment. He shortens the last section of his large intestine by tensing its muscles and relaxing his anal sphincter. Relief!

Steve's control over his external anal sphincter enables him to "hold on" until he makes it to the bathroom.

Rectum

Anus

Internal anal sphincter

External anal sphincter

LYMPH AND BLOOD

I THOUGHT WE'D EXPLORED EVERY TUBE in Steve's body, but I was wrong. We hitched a ride on a sugar molecule in Steve's blood. As it took us through a particularly narrow channel, we were swept into a completely new network of tubes. They were filled with a clear liquid called lymph. An army of white cells swarmed around us. They protect Steve against infection (germ attack). Blood carries them around the body. It moves the white cells from their own special network of lymph tissue to where germs threaten. Germs attack through wounds and through Steve's mouth and nose. White cells remember every germ they fight and its weaknesses. (This way they can fight a germ more quickly if it makes a second attack.) To understand how effective they are, think of a piece of meat left out on a hot day – it decays rapidly. Steve's whole body would rot just as quickly if it weren't for the work of his white cells.

Spleen
The biggest collection of lymphatic tissue in Steve's body is the spleen, which nestles just behind Steve's stomach. Unlike lymph nodes, the spleen does not filter the lymph that flows through it. Instead, cells in the white pulp there eat up bacteria.

Red pulp
Spongy red tissue in the spleen filters large amounts of blood. If an injury cuts through one of Steve's arteries, the spleen can make extra red blood cells to make up for the blood Steve loses through the wound.

"Get a move on boys. We've got to sweep up two million dead red blood cells each SECOND!"

"Come and look at Steve's spleen: it's just like a sponge. At any one time nearly a fifth of his blood is being filtered in here."

Germ warfare
Steve would be very ill if germs spread around his body, so he has many ways to prevent infection. Some are general defenses that give him resistance against all germs. Others target one germ only. Both types leap into action if Steve cuts his knee.

Thymus gland
Sandwiched between Steve's windpipe and his chest wall is the thymus gland. This is where T-cells mature.

The thymus gland is named after its shape – it resembles the leaf of a thyme plant.

"GULP! Yum, I just can't get enough of these dead red blood cells!"

Adenoids
To protect himself against germs he breathes in, Steve has a big cluster of lymph tissue at the back of his nose.

"Everyone calls them adenoids, but they're actually more tonsils."

"Throw out these T-cells – they've been here a week, so they've grown up enough to go and fight germs by now."

Powerful plumbing
Steve's bloodstream transports white cells wherever they are needed. Arteries, a network of pipes, carry blood from Steve's heart (pp. 138/139) to his tissues. Blood flows back to the heart along pipes called veins. Tiny tubes called capillaries connect the veins and arteries. All these pipes and tubes are called blood vessels.

Tonsils
Right at the back of Steve's mouth, this large cluster of lymph tissue guards Steve against germs he eats or drinks. If germs infect Steve's tonsils, they swell and turn red.

"We do a vital job guarding against germs. The mouth and nose are their main route into Steve's body."

Lymph
This clear fluid moves white blood cells within the lymph tubes. Lymph also collects proteins from the tissues and adjusts the flow of the tissue fluid that bathes Steve's cells. In fact, lymph and tissue fluid are the same liquid. Tissue fluid is called lymph as soon as it enters a lymph tube.

Lymph tubes
A network of tiny tubes keeps lymph on the move. There's no central pump, like the heart, to squirt lymph along. Instead lymph flows when Steve's muscles contract, squeezing the tubes that carry it. Valves make sure the lymph moves one way only.

Lymph nodes
Spaced at intervals along the tubes, lymph nodes filter the lymph. As lymph flows through a node, the white blood cells in it identify and destroy anything that could harm Steve's body. There are several kinds of white blood cells: scavenger cells eat germs, T-cells and B-cells identify and kill germs.

"We will splash into a bigger lymph tube soon."

Fluid in the surrounding tissues seeps into the lymph tube through holes in the tube's walls.

Oxygenated blood from lungs

"Pump faster! We need to send lots of white blood cells to defend Steve's knee."

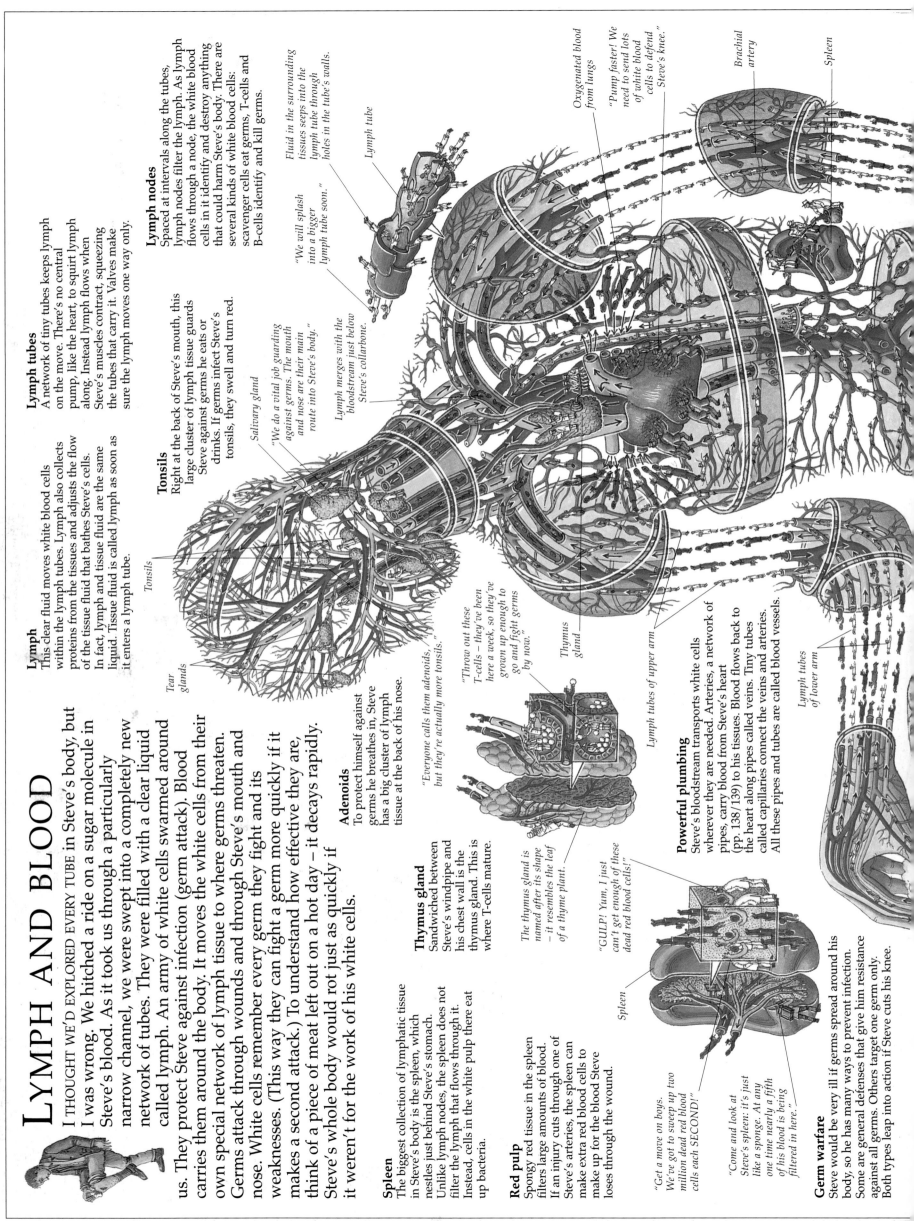

Brachial artery

Spleen

Lymph tube

Salivary gland

Tonsils

Tear glands

Lymph merges with the bloodstream just below Steve's collarbone.

Thymus gland

Lymph tubes of upper arm

Lymph tubes of lower arm

Spleen

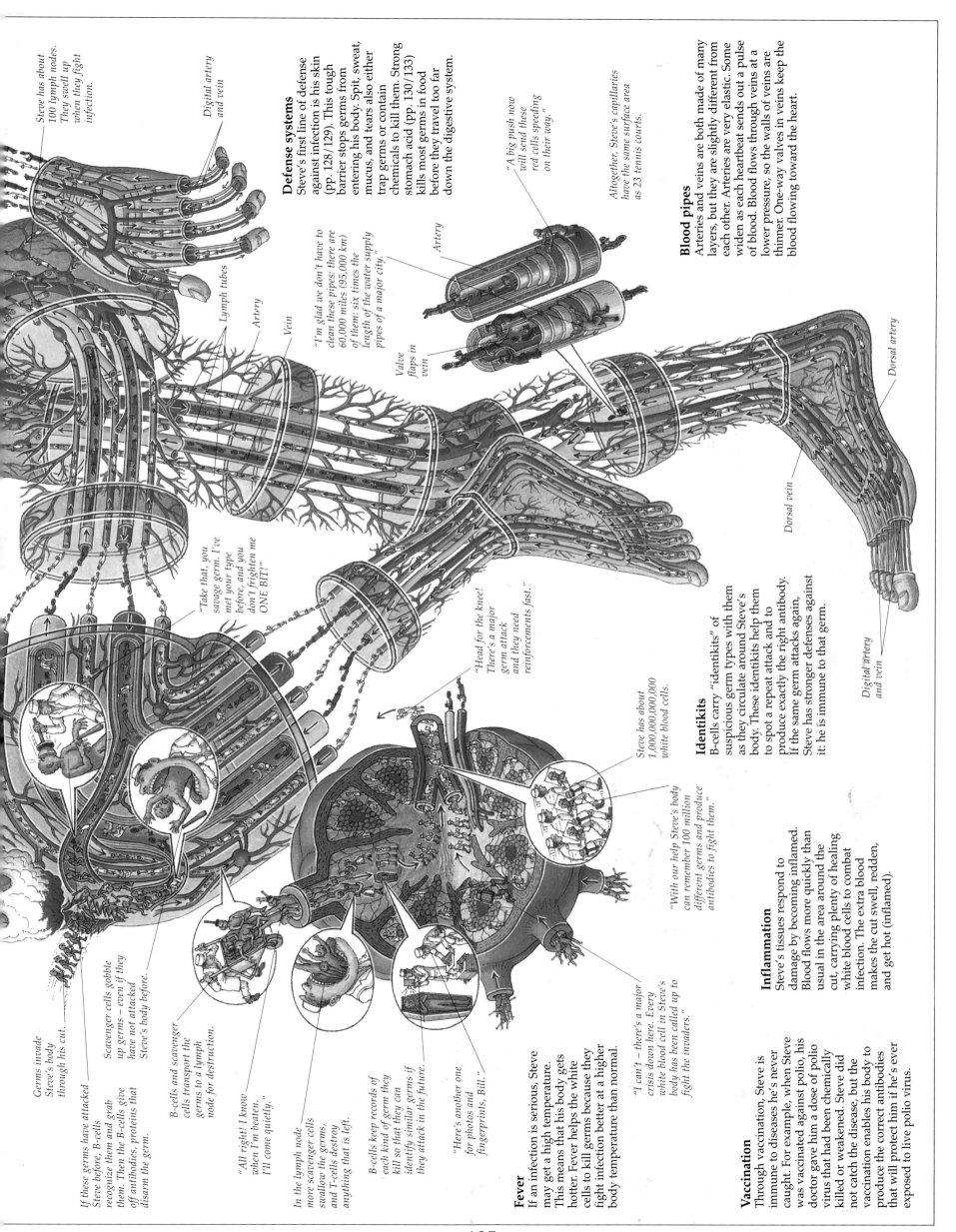

Steve has about 100 lymph nodes. They swell up when they fight infection.

Digital artery and vein

Defense systems

Steve's first line of defense against infection is his skin (pp. 128/129). This tough barrier stops germs from entering his body. Spit, sweat, mucus, and tears also either trap germs or contain chemicals to kill them. Strong stomach acid (pp. 130/133) kills most germs in food before they travel too far down the digestive system.

"A big push now will send these red cells speeding on their way."

Altogether, Steve's capillaries have the same surface area as 23 tennis courts.

Artery

Blood pipes

Arteries and veins are both made of many layers, but they are slightly different from each other. Arteries are very elastic. Some widen as each heartbeat sends out a pulse of blood. Blood flows through veins at a lower pressure, so the walls of veins are thinner. One-way valves in veins keep the blood flowing toward the heart.

Lymph tubes

Artery

Vein

"I'm glad we don't have to clean these pipes: there are 60,000 miles (95,000 km) of them: six times the length of the water supply pipes of a major city."

Valve flaps in vein

Dorsal artery

Dorsal vein

Dorsal vein

Digital artery and vein

"Take that, you savage germ. I've met your type before, and you don't frighten me ONE BIT!"

"Head for the knee! There's a major germ attack and they need reinforcements fast."

Steve has about 1,000,000,000 white blood cells.

Identikits

B-cells carry "identikits" of suspicious germ types with them as they circulate around Steve's body. These identikits help them to spot a repeat attack and to produce exactly the right antibody. If the same germ attacks again, Steve has stronger defenses against it: he is immune to that germ.

"With our help Steve's body can remember 100 million different germs and produce antibodies to fight them."

"I can't – there's a major crisis down here. Every white blood cell in Steve's body has been called up to fight the invaders."

Inflammation

Steve's tissues respond to damage by becoming inflamed. Blood flows more quickly than usual in the area around the cut, carrying plenty of healing white blood cells to combat infection. The extra blood makes the cut swell, redden, and get hot (inflamed).

Germs invade Steve's body through his cut.

If these germs have attacked Steve before, B-cells recognize them and grab them. Then the B-cells give off antibodies, proteins that disarm the germ.

Scavenger cells gobble up germs – even if they have not attacked Steve's body before.

B-cells and scavenger cells transport the germs to a lymph node for destruction.

"All right! I know when I'm beaten. I'll come quietly."

In the lymph node more scavenger cells swallow the germs, and T-cells destroy anything that is left.

B-cells keep records of each kind of germ they kill so that they can identify similar germs if they attack in the future.

"Here's another one for photos and fingerprints, Bill."

Fever

If an infection is serious, Steve may get a high temperature. This means that his body gets hotter. Fever helps the white cells to kill germs because they fight infection better at a higher body temperature than normal.

Vaccination

Through vaccination, Steve is immune to diseases he's never caught. For example, when Steve was vaccinated against polio, his doctor gave him a dose of polio virus that had been chemically killed or weakened. Steve did not catch the disease, but the vaccination enables his body to produce the correct antibodies that will protect him if he's ever exposed to live polio virus.

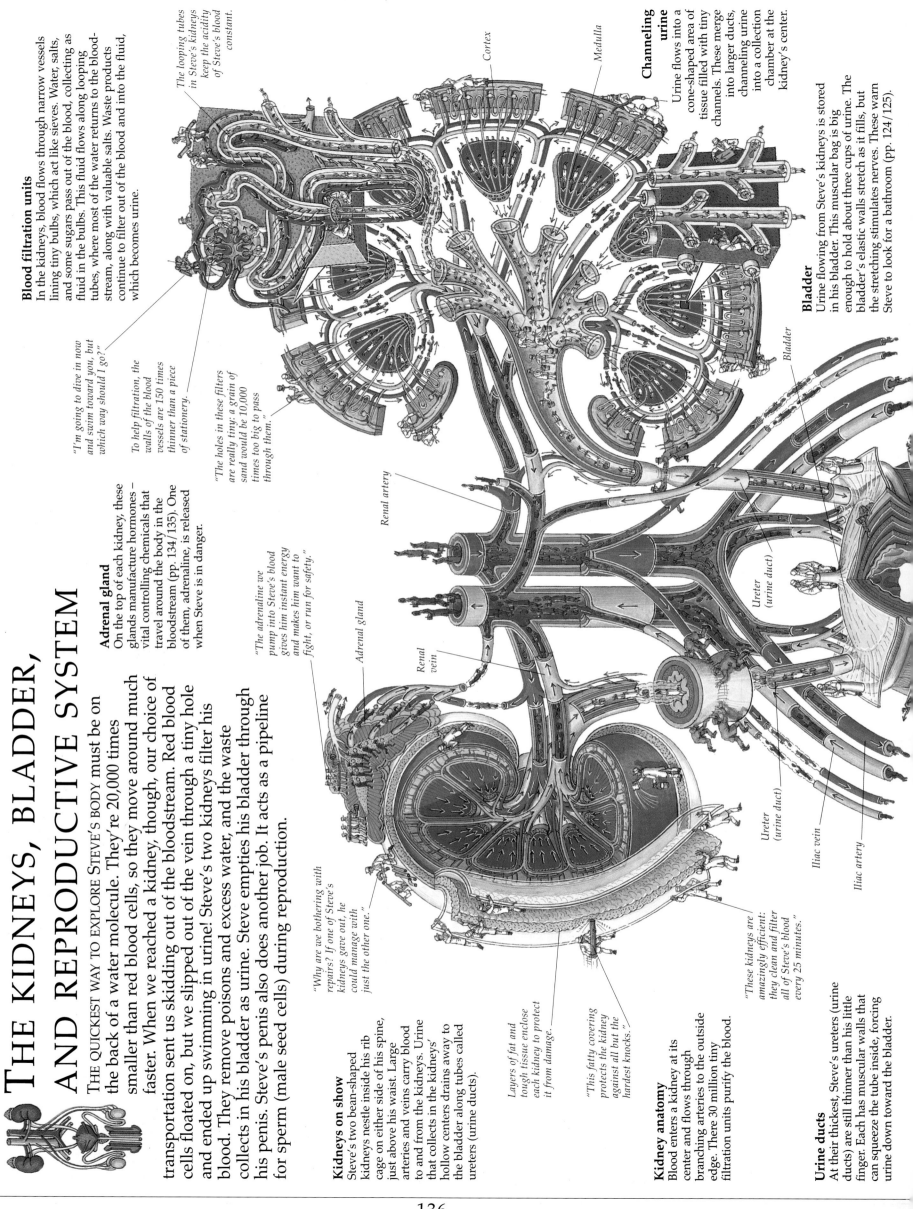

THE KIDNEYS, BLADDER, AND REPRODUCTIVE SYSTEM

THE QUICKEST WAY TO EXPLORE STEVE'S BODY must be on the back of a water molecule. They're 20,000 times smaller than red blood cells, so they move around much faster. When we reached a kidney, though, our choice of transportation sent us skidding out of the bloodstream. Red blood cells floated on, but we slipped out of the vein through a tiny hole and ended up swimming in urine! Steve's two kidneys filter his blood. They remove poisons and excess water, and the waste collects in his bladder as urine. Steve empties his bladder through his penis. Steve's penis also does another job. It acts as a pipeline for sperm (male seed cells) during reproduction.

Kidneys on show
Steve's two bean-shaped kidneys nestle inside his rib cage on either side of his spine, just above his waist. Large arteries and veins carry blood to and from the kidneys. Urine that collects in the kidneys' hollow centers drains away to the bladder along tubes called ureters (urine ducts).

Kidney anatomy
Blood enters a kidney at its center and flows through branching arteries to the outside edge. There 30 million tiny filtration units purify the blood.

"Layers of fat and tough tissue enclose each kidney to protect it from damage."

"This fatty covering protects the kidney against all but the hardest knocks."

"Why are we bothering with repairs? If one of Steve's kidneys gave out, he could manage with just the other one."

"These kidneys are amazingly efficient: they clean and filter all of Steve's blood every 25 minutes."

Urine ducts
At their thickest, Steve's ureters (urine ducts) are still thinner than his little finger. Each has muscular walls that can squeeze the tube inside, forcing urine down toward the bladder.

Blood filtration units
In the kidneys, blood flows through narrow vessels lining tiny bulbs, which act like sieves. Water, salts, and some sugars pass out of the blood, collecting as fluid in the bulbs. This fluid flows along looping tubes, where most of the water returns to the bloodstream, along with valuable salts. Waste products continue to filter out of the blood and into the fluid, which becomes urine.

The looping tubes in Steve's kidneys keep the acidity of Steve's blood constant.

"I'm going to dive in now and swim toward you, but which way should I go?"

To help filtration, the walls of the blood vessels are 150 times thinner than a piece of stationery.

"The holes in these filters are really tiny: a grain of sand would be 10,000 times too big to pass through them."

Adrenal gland
On the top of each kidney, these glands manufacture hormones – vital controlling chemicals that travel around the body in the bloodstream (pp. 134/135). One of them, adrenaline, is released when Steve is in danger.

"The adrenaline we pump into Steve's blood gives him instant energy and makes him want to fight, or run for safety."

Channeling urine
Urine flows into a cone-shaped area of tissue filled with tiny channels. These merge into larger ducts, channeling urine into a collection chamber at the kidney's center.

Bladder
Urine flowing from Steve's kidneys is stored in his bladder. This muscular bag is big enough to hold about three cups of urine. The bladder's elastic walls stretch as it fills, but the stretching stimulates nerves. These warn Steve to look for a bathroom (pp. 124/125).

Cortex

Medulla

Renal artery

Renal vein

Adrenal gland

Bladder

Ureter (urine duct)

Ureter (urine duct)

Iliac vein

Iliac artery

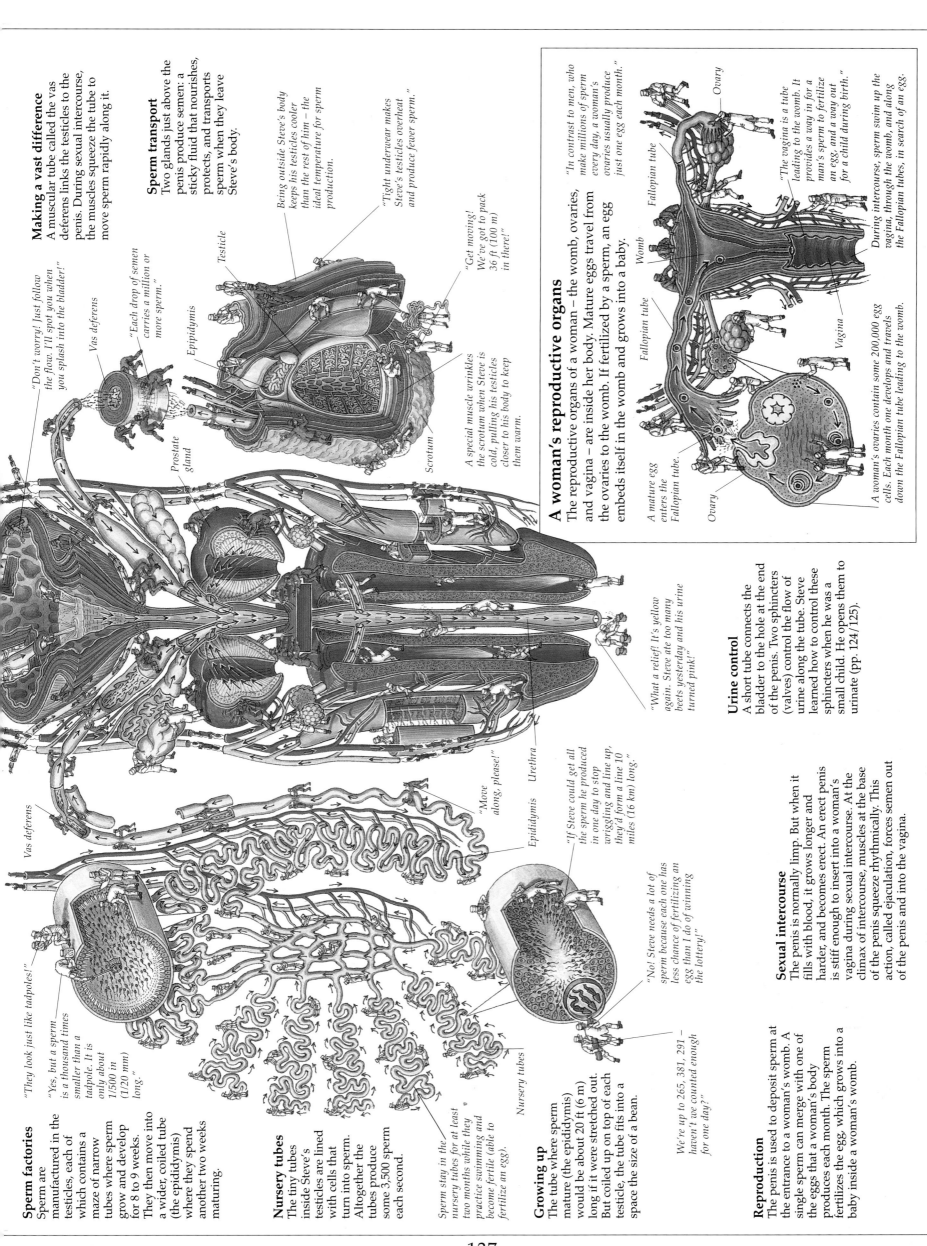

Making a vast difference

A muscular tube called the vas deferens links the testicles to the penis. During sexual intercourse, the muscles squeeze the tube to move sperm rapidly along it.

Sperm transport

Two glands just above the penis produce semen: a sticky fluid that nourishes, protects, and transports sperm when they leave Steve's body.

Being outside Steve's body keeps his testicles cooler than the rest of him – the ideal temperature for sperm production.

"Tight underwear makes Steve's testicles overheat and produce fewer sperm."

"Get moving! We've got to pack 36 ft (100 m) in there!"

"Don't worry! Just follow the flow. I'll spot you when you splash into the bladder!"

"Each drop of semen carries a million or more sperm."

Vas deferens

Testicle

Epididymis

Prostate gland

Scrotum

A special muscle wrinkles the scrotum when Steve is cold, pulling his testicles closer to his body to keep them warm.

A woman's reproductive organs

The reproductive organs of a woman – the womb, ovaries, and vagina – are inside her body. Mature eggs travel from the ovaries to the womb. If fertilized by a sperm, an egg embeds itself in the womb and grows into a baby.

"In contrast to men, who make millions of sperm every day, a woman's ovaries usually produce just one egg each month."

Ovary

Fallopian tube

Womb

"The vagina is a tube leading to the womb. It provides a way in for a man's sperm to fertilize an egg, and a way out for a child during birth."

Vagina

During intercourse, sperm swim up the vagina, through the womb, and along the Fallopian tubes, in search of an egg.

Fallopian tube

A mature egg enters the Fallopian tube.

Ovary

A woman's ovaries contain some 200,000 egg cells. Each month one develops and travels down the Fallopian tube leading to the womb.

"What a relief! It's yellow again. Steve ate too many beets yesterday and his urine turned pink!"

Urine control

A short tube connects the bladder to the hole at the end of the penis. Two sphincters (valves) control the flow of urine along the tube. Steve learned how to control these sphincters when he was a small child. He opens them to urinate (pp. 124/125).

"Move along, please!"

Epididymis

Urethra

"If Steve could get all the sperm he produced in one day to stop wriggling and line up, they'd form a line 10 miles (16 km) long."

"No! Steve needs a lot of sperm because each one has less chance of fertilizing an egg than I do of winning the lottery!"

Vas deferens

"They look just like tadpoles!"

"Yes, but a sperm is a thousand times smaller than a tadpole. It is only about 1/500 in (1/20 mm) long."

Sperm factories

Sperm are manufactured in the testicles, each of which contains a maze of narrow tubes where they grow and develop for 8 to 9 weeks. They then move into a wider, coiled tube (the epididymis) where they spend another two weeks maturing.

Nursery tubes

The tiny tubes inside Steve's testicles are lined with cells that turn into sperm. Altogether the tubes produce some 3,500 sperm each second.

Sperm stay in the nursery tubes for at least two months while they practice swimming and become fertile (able to fertilize an egg).

We're up to 265, 381, 291 – haven't 'ave counted enough for one day?"

Nursery tubes

Growing up

The tube where sperm mature (the epididymis) would be about 20 ft (6 m) long if it were stretched out. But coiled up on top of each testicle, the tube fits into a space the size of a bean.

Reproduction

The penis is used to deposit sperm at the entrance to a woman's womb. A single sperm can merge with one of the eggs that a woman's body produces each month. The sperm fertilizes the egg, which grows into a baby inside a woman's womb.

Sexual intercourse

The penis is normally limp. But when it fills with blood, it grows longer and harder, and becomes erect. An erect penis is stiff enough to insert into a woman's vagina during sexual intercourse. At the climax of intercourse, muscles at the base of the penis squeeze rhythmically. This action, called ejaculation, forces semen out of the penis and into the vagina.

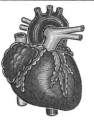

THE HEART

CLINGING TO A GLUCOSE MOLECULE, we surfed along Steve's veins. Eventually the blood splashed into a rounded room. No sooner was it full of blood than a drain opened in the floor, and the walls closed in, forcing the blood out. We were in Steve's heart! It was no bigger than his fist, but powerful enough to squeeze 75 times each minute. It works like a pair of pumps. Each has two chambers. The lower chambers, called ventricles, do most of the pumping. Above each one is an atrium, which works as a temporary blood warehouse. One-way valves at the exit from each atrium and ventricle stop blood from flowing backward. As the atria contract, followed quickly by the ventricles, the exit valves close making the relentless "lubb-dupp" beat.

Left or right?
Perhaps you are wondering why the right side of the heart is on the left-hand side of the page? Think about it. When Steve is facing you, on which side do you see his right hand?

1. At ease
At the start of every cycle of the heartbeat, the muscles relax momentarily. Blood pours into the right atrium. As the atrium contracts a three-pointed valve opens, and blood surges into the right ventricle.

"We're the timing team. The electrical impulses we create travel down conducting fibers to keep the heart beating in perfect rhythm."

The aorta is the biggest blood vessel in the body.

Conducting fibers in atrium

Superior vena cava

Right atrium

Sinoatrial node

Right pulmonary veins

Outer fibrous pericardium

The three-pointed valve is open to allow blood to flow from the right atrium to the right ventricle.

Pericardial fluid

Inner serous pericardium

Epicardium

"There's just enough liquid to scuba dive in."

Right ventricle

Papillary muscles

Cuff of three-pointed valve

This major vein leads into the right atrium, bringing back blood from the kidneys and other parts of the body to the heart.

Pulmonary valve

Thick, fibrous tissue acts like a skeleton to which the muscles and valves are attached.

Bags of protection
The heart is covered and protected by a multilayered sac, the pericardium, which also prevents it from bursting! In between the inner layers there is a slippery pericardial fluid – just 0.5–1.7 fl oz (15–50 ml) is all that's needed.

What blood does
The blood flowing around Steve's body supplies his tissues with the oxygen and nutrients they need to live, and carries away waste products. It also contains substances that influence the temperature of his body and contains cells that fight infection.

In full flow
At each beat, Steve's heart pumps about 3 fl oz (90 ml) of blood. That's about a soup-bowl full every three beats. Blood vessels channel the blood around. There are two types. Arteries carry blood out from the heart. It returns to the heart along another set of tubes called veins.

2. Squeeze!
Next, the three-pointed valve closes and the right ventricle contracts. This pushes blood out through the pulmonary valve into the arteries leading to the lungs. The lungs remove carbon dioxide from the blood and replenish the oxygen supply.

Blood gushes out of the arch of the aorta through three arteries to travel to the head and body.

"We're delivering red blood cells. When they come back from the lungs charged with oxygen, the cells are bright scarlet. On their tour of the body the cells give up the oxygen and change color. They return to the heart a duller color."

The pulmonary arteries are the only arteries in Steve's body to carry deoxygenated blood, rather than oxygenated blood.

Aortic valve

Left atrium

Mitral valve

The heart muscle has its own blood supply. It flows along the coronary arteries, which branch off the aorta just where it joins the heart.

Descending aorta

3. Back from the lungs

It takes about six heartbeats for the blood to go all around the lungs and return to the heart. When the heart muscles relax, blood, rich in oxygen from the lungs, whooshes into the left atrium. Blood gushes down from the atrium through the mitral valve into the left ventricle.

4. Squeeze again

The right atrium squeezes a fraction before its partner on the left. When both atria squeeze, they force blood down into both ventricles.

5. Squeeze harder!

Finally, the mitral valve shuts and the left ventricle contracts. This forces blood up and out through the aortic valve into the aorta. From there, the blood flows on to supply the rest of the body.

Powerful pumper

Steve's heart is fantastically strong and reliable. Each day it pumps enough blood to fill 70 bathtubs. When Steve is around 75 years old, his heart will have pumped four billion times.

Left pulmonary veins

Deoxygenated blood from the heart muscle returns along the great cardiac vein.

"Careful, the pericardium is slipperyyyeee!"

Left ventricle

"We pull on these fibers to stop the mitral valve from turning inside out."

Fibrous skeleton

Nucleus

Fibrous tendons

"That crowd on the right is a lazy bunch. They only have to pump blood around the lungs. Here on the left we have to pump blood around the whole body. That's why the muscles on the left of the heart are much thicker than those on the right."

Independent muscle

The muscle wall of the heart is called the myocardium. It's unlike any other muscle in the body. If it were left to beat on its own, without input from the brain, it would beat at about 100 beats a minute. However, nerve impulses usually slow it down to about 75 beats a minute, and can slow it down or speed it up as necessary.

"This big valve is called the mitral valve because it looks like a miter – the type of hat that bishops wear."

"We carry the electrical timing impulses along this special conduction system. But don't worry, we aren't in any danger of getting an electric shock, it would take a quarter of a million hearts to power a flashlight."

THE NOSE AND LUNGS

CLINGING TO A CARBON DIOXIDE MOLECULE, we rode the frothing red tide right through Steve's pulsing heart and beyond, into a wide pipe. The pipe divided into two narrower tubes, then forked again, and again, until the tube was almost too narrow to squeeze through. The noise of rushing air was almost deafening: we were in Steve's lungs. These two spongy bags almost fill his chest. His windpipe supplies them with air from his mouth and nose. Each branch of the airway ends in a tiny air sac, surrounded by blood vessels. Here, deep in the lungs, Steve's blood exchanges poisonous carbon dioxide gas for life-giving oxygen. Steve's respiration (breathing) ensures a regular supply of fresh air. Inhaling (breathing in) fills the lungs with fresh, oxygen-rich air. Exhaling (breathing out) discharges the stale air and allows Steve to talk, sing, shout, and tell terrible jokes. It was after one of these jokes that Steve suddenly sneezed and we found ourselves flying out through his nose. Our journey was over!

This stamp-sized area in the roof of Steve's nose cavity gives him a sense of smell.

Warm, slimy maze
Behind Steve's nose is a cavity that acts as an "air-conditioner" when he breathes in. Its surfaces are warmed by blood and covered in mucus (snot). The air that flows over them is made ready to enter the lungs – it gets warmer and damper, and the mucus traps any dust.

Voice box
When Steve breathes out, air passes through his voice box. To talk or sing, Steve tightens muscles to stretch his vocal chords (flaps of skin) in the path of the air. The chords vibrate, making a sound. The tightness of the chords changes Steve's pitch of speech.

Steve's voice box is visible on his throat – it's known as his Adam's apple!

Vocal chord

Windpipe

Breathing muscles
Narrow strips of muscle link Steve's ribs. By tightening them, Steve lifts his chest and makes it bigger. This helps to lower the air pressure in the lungs, drawing fresh air in through his nose and mouth. Normally, Steve only needs to relax the muscles to breathe out. However, when blowing up balloons he takes an extra-deep breath and forces the air out, making the muscles work harder.

"The muscle team makes Steve's breathing amazingly versatile. If he goes for a run, we work 25 times harder than when he's having a nap."

Muscles connecting ribs

Chest muscles

Windpipe
A broad windpipe channels air from Steve's mouth and nose into his lungs. It divides into two tubes, the right and left bronchi, giving each lung a separate air supply.

Clavicle (collar bone)

Rib

Lightweight organs
The word lung comes from a Greek word meaning "light." Because of the air they contain, the lungs are the only organs of the body that are light enough to float in water.

Pulmonary veins

Pulmonary artery

Blood supply
The right side of Steve's heart pumps blood to the lungs along a wide artery. This divides into smaller and smaller branches to form a network of tiny blood vessels that carry blood to each air sac.

Veins
Tiny veins carry oxygen-enriched blood away from the air sacs. They merge to form bigger blood vessels, piping the blood back to the left side of the heart, which pumps it on to the rest of the body.

Olfactory bulbs

"Without us, Steve wouldn't enjoy his food!"

The nose

Steve's nose is the first line of protection for his delicate lungs. Coarse nostril hair filters out insects and large particles of dust that might harm the lungs if he breathed them in.

Tiny hairs inside Steve's nose sweep snot back ¼ in (6 mm) every minute. This just isn't fast enough when Steve catches a cold, so he gets a runny nose.

In his lifetime, Steve will breathe out enough hot air to inflate 250 two-person hot-air balloons.

"I hate this job, but someone's got to clean the boogers out of Steve's nose."

"Cells in the wall of Steve's nose constantly replenish the layer of snot. If Steve catches a cold, these cells produce masses of snot to try and flush away the infection."

A huge spread

To ensure that enough oxygen reaches the blood, the surface area of the lungs is vast – 84 square yards (70 m²). Spread out flat, the lungs would provide enough parking space for seven cars!

Swapping gases

The airways of the lungs end in minute air sacs. Blood vessels supply each one. The walls of the air sacs are thin enough to allow oxygen and carbon dioxide gases to pass through, but thick enough to keep back the blood. Waste carbon dioxide in the blood passes into the air sac to be exhaled. Oxygen from fresh air Steve has breathed in passes the other way into the blood.

Oxygen mover

Oxygen in the lungs combines with saucer-shaped red blood cells. The cells carry the oxygen around the body and release it where it is needed.

Branching air ducts

The airways that lead from Steve's windpipe branch again and again, until they resemble an upside-down tree. They have far more endings than a tree, however. A large oak tree has about a quarter of a million leaves, but a human lung divides into millions of tiny air sacs.

Alveoli (air sacs)

"These blood vessels are only half the width of a red blood cell. How does blood flow through them?"

"Simple. The red blood cells are flexible. They change shape and squeeze through in single file!"

"Red" blood cells look purple when they reach the lungs. They turn crimson when they have been recharged with oxygen.

Bronchial tree

"Every drop of blood in Steve's body must flow through his lungs once a minute to be replenished with oxygen."

The walls of the respiratory membrane are incredibly thin. Stacked up together, 240 of them would only be as thick as a piece of paper.

Alveoli (air sacs)

Pleural cavity

"Whoa! Careful, it's really slippery here!"

Bronchiole (airway)

Powerful dome

Stretched across the bottom of Steve's chest is his diaphragm: a thick dome of powerful muscle. To breathe in, Steve tightens his diaphragm, making it flatter. This lowers air pressure in the lungs, sucking air in. Relaxing his diaphragm makes Steve breathe out.

Diaphragm

"Steve's diaphragm does most of the work when he breathes."

Surface of the lungs

Pleural tissue

Pleura

A double layer of slippery skin lines the lungs and chest cavity to stop them from rubbing against each other as Steve breathes. A slithery fluid "oils" the space in between them.

INDEX

A

adenoids, 134
admiral, 110, 112, 113
Admiralty, 112
adrenal gland, 136
adrenaline, 136
advertising, 42
air conditioning, 23
air traffic control, 24, 25
airliner, 22-23
airport, 24-25
    bays, 23
alchemist, 87
ale, 88
ale conner, 80
Allosaurus, 34
alms, 82
aluminum
    foil, 13, 58
    airliner fuselage skin, 22
ammunition
    war engine, 91
amphibians, 35
amputation, 96, 107
Amundsen, Roald, 52
Amundsen-Scott South Pole
    Station, 52-53
Anasazi people, 55
anchor, 95
animals, desert, 56
animatronics, 40
Antarctic base, 52-53
antibodies, 135
anus, 133
anvil (bone), 121
aorta, 139
Apatosaurus, 34
Apollo spacecraft, 26
appendix, 133
apron (airport), 25
APU (auxiliary power
    unit), 23
aqueous fluid, 118
aquifer, 56, 57
Arabian Desert, 56
archaeologists, 32
archers, 74, 75, 90
armor
    knights, 12, 80, 82
    tournament, 86
armorer, 18, 80, 110
arrowheads, 90
arrow loops, 78
arrows
    crossbow, 75, 90
    longbow, 90
    practice, 91
arteries, 134, 135,
    138, 140
ashlar, 78, 79
astronomers, 52, 53
Atacama Desert, 56

Athena, 62, 63
Athens, 62-63
athletic shoe, 13, 65
atrium, 138-139
auditory canal, 120
automatic sprinkler, 38
autonomic nervous system,
    122, 125
axons, 124

B

bailey, 72
baked beans, 13
balance, 121
ballast, 97, 101
baron, 76, 86
barrels, 99, 100, 101
bascule, 50, 51
bate, 79
baths, 85
battering ram, 75
battles, 104-5, 112
battlements, 78
Beaker people, 34
bear baiting, 87
Bedouin peoples,
    56, 57
beer, 66, 80, 98
Benedictine monks, 67
Big Bang, 35
bile, 131
bilges, 99, 101, 106
binnacle, 106
bird-strike test, 22
biscuits, ship's, 98, 111
blacksmith, 78, 88
bladder, 117, 125,
    135, 136
blind spot, 119
blood, 117, 134-135,
    138-139
    filtration, 136
blood cells, 126, 127
    red, 141
    white, 134
bloodletting, 83
blood vessels, 134, 135,
    138
boarding party, 105
boatswain/mate, 106,
    109, 110
body (human), 114-141
bodywork (car), 18-19,
    20
Boeing 747, 25
Boeing 777, 13, 22
boilers
    steam traction engine,
    14, 15
    Tower Bridge, 51
bolts, 23
bombs, 32, 51
bone marrow, 126, 127
bones, 126-127
boon day, 88
bottle (plastic), 13, 19
Boudicca, Queen, 34

bounty, 106
bow, *see* crossbow; longbow
bows (of ship), 95
bowstrings, 91
brain, 116, 119, 121,
    122-123
brainstem, 123
brake wheel (windmill),
    68, 69
brakes, 15, 21
branding, 90
breathing, 126, 140-141
brick, 12, 64-65
Bridge of Sighs, 47
bridges
    bascule, 50-51
    suspension, 13, 48-49, 50
    Venetian, 47
broadside, 104
bronchi, 140
bucket line, 107
buckler, 95
buildings
    airport, 24-25
    Antarctic base, 52-53
    castle, 70-91
    cathedral 64-65
    fire hazards of, 38-39
    high-rise, 32
    monastery, 66-67
    movie studio, 40-41
    Parthenon, 62-63
    skyscraper, 44-45
    Tower Bridge, 50-51
    windmill, 68-69
    wooden house, 60-61
bunks, 22
burial at sea, 103, 105
butcher, 89
butts, 90

C

cabins
    man-of-war, 94, 110,
    111, 112, 113
cables
    anchor, 95, 102, 103
    bridge, 48
caissons, 48
Cambrian period, 35
camel, 56
camera crew, 41
Campanile (Venice), 46
canals, 33
    Venetian, 46, 47
candles, 81, 89
candy, 13
canister shot, 104
cannonballs, 94, 104,
    107
cannons, 12, 94, 103,
    104, 105
capillaries, 134
capstan, 102, 103
captain, 94, 107,
    108, 110
car, 13

factory, 18-19
    race car, 20-21
carbon dioxide, 141
carbon-fiber-reinforced
    plastic, 23
carpenter, 64
    castle, 81, 88
    ship's, 97, 99, 103,
    104, 110
carpenter's walk, 104, 109
carrier pigeon, 88
Carthusian monks, 67
cartilage, 127
carvings, 63
casino, virtual, 23
castle, 70-91
    building, 78-79
    defenses, 72, 74-5
cathead, 95, 96
cathedral, 13, 64-65
cat-of-nine-tails, 109
cattle, 88
    dairy cows, 60
caulking, 102
central nervous system, 124
cerebellum, 123
cerebral cortex, 123
cerebrospinal fluid, 122, 123
cerebrum, 122, 123
chain mail, 80
chain shot, 104
chandler, 81
chapel, 83
chaplain, 107, 111
chapterhouse, 67
charcoal, 64
charts, 108
check-in (airport), 24
chivalry, 82, 86
chlorine, 19
chocolate bar, 12, 13, 44
church (monastery), 66-67
Cistercian monks, 67
cities, 32-35
    in desert, 57
clay, 64
climatic zones (Grand
    Canyon), 54-55
cloisters, 66, 67
clothes
    desert, 56
    racing driver's, 21
    seaman's, 101, 102
    space suit, 26-27
    uniforms, 111
    washing, 96, 97
coal mine, 33
coccyx, 125
cochlea, 121
cockfighting, 87
cockpit, 22
cocoa beans, 44
coin, 13, 18-19
coldest temperature, 53
Colorado River, 54, 55, 57
color printing, 42
colors (ship's), 106
columns, 62
command module, 26
compact disc, 16-17
    player, 13
companionways, 105

WYZ

ACKNOWLEDGEMENTS

Dorling Kindersley would like to thank the following individuals and organizations for their help with this book:

Incredible Cross-sections
Jane Abbott, Boeing International Corporation, BP Exploration UK Limited, British Coal Corporation, British Interplanetary Society, Cunard Line Limited, Robin Kerrod, London Underground Limited, Dr Anne Millard, The Science Museum, Andrew Smith, Martin Taylor, Westland Group plc. Lynn Bresler for the index.

Incredible Explosions
B.A.A. plc, Heathrow, Jack Fryer and the Cranbrook Windmill Association, Kent Fire Safety Division, Shelter (The National Campaign for Homeless People), Shepperton Studios for access to soundstages and workshops. Special thanks to: Lt. Katherine A. McNitt, Station Chief, National Oceanographic and Atmospheric Administration, Amundsen-Scott

South Pole Station.
Constance Novis for editorial support, Bohdan Paraschak for research, and Lynn Bresler for the index.

Incredible Everything
Brian Sims at News International Newspapers Ltd, Man Roland Druckmaschinen, London Brick Company, Peter Middleton at Peter Middleton Associates, Kay Grinter at Kennedy Space Center, Neil Marshall at the Humber Bridge Board, Dunkin' Donuts, National Dairy Council, Dara McDonough at Disctronics Europe Ltd, De Beers, Jack Ogden at the National Association of Goldsmiths, Kevin Crowley at Rexam Foil and Paper Ltd, Gordon Grieve at Wig Creations, Alistair Watkins, Federation International de l'Automobile, and Hugh Robertson at the London Transport Museum. Joanna Earl and Ann Cannings for design assistance, Francesca Baines, Shirin Patel, Miranda Smith, Angela Koo, Nancy Jones and Nigel Ritchie for editorial assistance, and Chris Bernstein for the index.

Cross-sections Man-of-War
The Commanding Officer of *HMS Victory* for assistance with research and background information, Sheila Hanly for editorial assistance, and Lynn Bresler for the index.

Cross-sections Castle
Constance Novis for editorial assistance, James Hunter for design assistance, and Lynn Bresler for the index.

Incredible Body
Angela Wilkes and Anna Scobie for editorial assistance, Joanna Pocock for design assistance, and Chris Bernstein for the index.

Absolutely Best Cross-Sections Book Ever
London Transport and Keith Lye. Chris Bernstein for the index.

Coolest Cross-Sections Ever
Kate Bradshaw for the index, and Andrew O'Brien for design assistance.